THE
BEST
OF
Gourmet

THE
BEST
OF

Gourmet

1986 EDITION

ALL OF THE BEAUTIFULLY
ILLUSTRATED MENUS FROM 1985
PLUS OVER 500 SELECTED RECIPES

FROM THE EDITORS OF GOURMET

CONDÉ NAST BOOKS
RANDOM HOUSE
NEW YORK

LIBRARY OF CONGRESS CATALOGING-IN-PUBLICATION DATA
Main entry under title:
The Best of Gourmet: 1986 Edition.
        Includes indexes.
        1. Cookery, International. I. Gourmet
TX725.A1B4827   1986   641.5   85-24458
ISBN 0-394-55258-X (v. 1)

Most of the recipes and menus in this work were previously published in *Gourmet* magazine.

Manufactured in the United States of America

98765432   24689753   23456789

First Edition

Grateful acknowledgment is made to the following for permission to reprint recipes previously published in *Gourmet* magazine:

Faye Levy: "Couscous Carbonara" (p. 187); "Couscous with Chanterelles and Parmesan" (p. 188); "Couscous with Red Pepper, Walnuts, and Basil" (p. 188); "Fried Couscous with Scallions and Ginger" (p. 188); "Omelet Strips" (p. 189); "Couscous Salad with Tomatoes, Pine Nuts, and Mint" (p. 227). Copyright © 1985 by Faye Levy. Reprinted by permission of the author.

Richard Sax: "Corn Muffins" (p. 104); "Corn Chowder with Thyme" (p. 114); "Beef Pie with Corn Custard" (p. 141); "Chicken in Succotash" (p. 161); "Layered Corn, Cheese, and Jalapeño Custard" (p. 199); "Corn Oysters" (p. 199). Copyright © 1985 by Richard Sax. Reprinted by permission of the author.

PROJECT STAFF

For Condé Nast Books
Jill Cohen, Director
Jonathan E. Newhouse, Special Consultant
Jim Fiorello, Director of Pre-Press Production
Diane Pesce, Composition Production Manager
Serafino J. Cambareri, Quality Control Manager

For *Gourmet* magazine
Jane Montant, Editor-in-Chief
Evie Righter, Project Editor
Romulo Yanes, Staff Photographer
Irwin Glusker, Designer

Produced in association with Media Projects Incorporated
Carter Smith, Executive Editor
Jeffrey Woldt, Project Manager
Ellen Coffey, Senior Editor
Julie Graham, Art/Production Director
Frank L. Kurtz, Indexer

The editors would like to thank the following people for valuable services rendered for *The Best of Gourmet—1986 Edition:* Georgia Chan Downard, for her helpful and creative assistance in compiling "A Gourmet Addendum," and Karen Tonningsen.

The text of this book was set in Times Roman by the Composition Department of Condé Nast Publications, Inc. The four-color separations were done by The Color Company, Seiple Lithographers, and Kordet Graphics. The book was printed and bound by R. R. Donnelly & Sons. Text paper is 80-pound Mountie Gloss. Manufacturing supervision by the Production Department of Random House, Inc.

CONTENTS

INTRODUCTION

*T*he *Best of Gourmet* is a first. Never before in the history of the magazine has a collection of material from the previous year been compiled. And what a collection *The Best of Gourmet* is! We have included all the 1985 menus with their dazzling four-color photography. There are more than five hundred recipes culled not only from the columns Gourmet's Menus and Cuisine Courante but also from Gastronomie sans Argent, In Short Order, and Last Touch. And there are three indexes: a recipe-title index, an index by subject, and an index of those recipes that can be accomplished in forty-five minutes or less. If you are in a hurry for dinner, we can't make it for you, but we can help you decide quickly on the dishes, then assist you in making them delicious.

The Best of Gourmet is divided into two parts. Part One, The Menu Collection, is lush with color and includes each 1985 *Gourmet* menu, arranged by season, followed by its Cuisine Courante counterpart. You'll turn nimbly back and forth and back again from the more elaborate menu to the less complicated one.

The variety is astonishing. There are formal menus, such as the romantic New Year's Eve dinners for two that open Part One. Zinfandel-sauced squab star, followed by caramel-topped ice cream in chocolate cups. A wonderful way for us to ring in any year. Or consider watching the clock strike twelve over lobster stew *sous croûte* and mocha meringues in cappuccino custard.

There are less formal menus, as well: soufflé suppers, tray meals, a summer cookout, and the like. And this book could hardly be called "the best of" without *Gourmet*'s holiday menus. You'll find a choice of brunch menus for Easter and two menus each for Thanksgiving and Christmas. And on July Fourth you can almost hear the fireworks pop as we celebrate alfresco with fried chicken, corn on the cob, and fresh peach pie. That's American fare at its finest.

Even entertaining becomes easy with *The Best of Gourmet*. Why not create an occasion around one of our ethnic menus? There is a formal, subtly orchestrated

Chinese dinner; an elegant, cool Japanese dinner; and an intriguing array of *tapas* dishes, those predinner delights that the Spanish have been savoring, and rightfully, for so long. Cocktail dining has rarely seemed as varied and as much fun. In sum, you have your choice, and then some.

Part Two contains the recipes, organized into chapters by category. Following the recipes, we encounter something altogether new. The final chapter is entitled A Gourmet Addendum: Provisions and Provisos and groups six basic recipes called for elsewhere in the text. These recipes include *pâte brisée* (basic pastry dough), cream puff pastry, and the preparation of pistachios and hazelnuts for baking. Such ingredients can be considered provisions of a sort, those kinds of items you either have on hand or not, depending on how well stocked your freezer or pantry is.

Here is where we break new ground. To enable you to use those basic recipes more frequently than is called for in the text, we have developed additional combinations for them. Some are savory, some sweet. Provided you have pastry dough on hand, you can proceed, with our guidance, to make flaky cheese straws, crumbly vanilla-sugar wafers, or fruit-filled turnovers, to name a few. Addendum recipes range from velvety béarnaise, provided you have clarified butter, to Italian meringue predicated on simple sugar syrup. It's remarkable, and one of the pleasures of the Addendum, to see how very basic recipes combine to such enjoyable ends.

This brings us to the end of *The Best of Gourmet*. What remains is for you to enjoy its beauty and the excellence of its menus and marvelous recipes. Let that enjoyment be long-lasting. In fact, we'd ask you to hold on to those feelings for a while, to the start of the next new year. That will be just long enough for us to prepare the 1987 edition of *The Best of Gourmet*.

This is the first, but hardly the last. A tradition has begun.

Jane Montant
Editor-in-Chief

PART ONE

THE MENU COLLECTION

In this section of *The Best of Gourmet* we have collected, for the first time, an entire calendar year of Gourmet's Menus and Cuisine Courante from those much-admired columns in the magazine. All menus are magnificently illustrated with full-color photographs, seasonally arranged, and suitable for a variety of occasions, from a gala rehearsal dinner for forty to the intimate excellence of a New Year's Eve dinner for two. Here you will find other holiday menus as well, ethnic menus, and wonderful menus for everyday. There are breakfasts, brunches, lunches, teas; a cocktail gathering, a cookout—imaginative, creative menus for virtually any occasion.

If it is winter, let us plan a ski weekend for you, starting with Friday's dinner straight through to Sunday's brunch. If it is spring, let us help you celebrate Easter with a choice of exceptional brunches, one featuring brioches stuffed with brandied chicken livers, the other asparagus custards served with Canadian bacon and an orange-flavored, silky hollandaise sauce. Or let us assist with your holiday festivities: A country Thanksgiving for eight stars roast turkey with smoked sausage and rosemary stuffing, while the menu for a smaller gathering, still very much traditional fare, fea-

tures turkey scaloppine with an unusual, tart and tangy cassis cranberry sauce. Last but not least, should you have a longing for a menu from a foreign shore, choose from a Japanese dinner, a Spanish *tapas* party, and an innovative multi-course Chinese dinner.

In each instance you will find the more formal and elaborate Gourmet's menu followed by the Cuisine Courante menu—a useful tip to remember should you be in search of a *carte* that can be done, as it were, on the run. Cuisine Courante menus are by definition shorter and simpler than the Gourmet's Menus and have been devised with the needs of a busy life-style in mind. The recipes for all these menus appear in their respective chapters in Part Two, A Recipe Compendium, and can be most readily located by referring to page 285, the Guide to Recipes in the Menu Collection.

And there is yet another way to enjoy these menus. Use the ideas you find in the following pages to make your own menus. Mix and match, as it were: Borrow here; insert one recipe for another there.

Whether you are re-creating these menus to a tee or creating ones of your own, there is one combination that remains incontestable: good food and good company and the pleasure to be derived therefrom. With the menus that follow, you are well on your way.

Smoked Salmon Biscuits with Salmon Roe

NEW YEAR'S EVE DINNERS FOR TWO

Perrier-Jouët '78   *Smoked Salmon Biscuits with Salmon Roe*

Château Mouton-Rothschild '76   *Broiled Squabs with Grapes and Zinfandel Sauce*

Butternut Squash Purée

Sautéed Kale with Red Bell Peppers

Ice Cream in Chocolate Cups with Caramel Cages

Domaine Chandon Napa Valley   *Prosciutto and Avocado*
Blanc de Noirs

Chalk Hill Winery Sonoma County   *Lobster Stew Sous Croûte*
Sauvignon Blanc '83

Endive and Walnut Salad

Mocha Meringues in Cappuccino Custard

Broiled Squabs with Grapes and Zinfandel Sauce, Butternut Squash Purée, Sautéed Kale
with Red Bell Peppers

Lobster Stew Sous Croûte, Endive and Walnut Salad

Parmesan Scallion Soufflés

SOUFFLÉ SUPPERS

Vega Sicilia '76

*Eggplant Soufflé with Red Pepper,
Tomato, and Coriander Sauce*

Shredded Romaine with Garlic Vinaigrette

Pita Bread

Sautéed Pears with Walnuts

*Bianco Vergine della
Valdichiana '83*

Parmesan Scallion Soufflés

Carrot Salad with Lemon Dill Dressing

French Bread

Cinnamon Apple Rings

Eggplant Soufflé with Red Pepper, Tomato, and Coriander Sauce,
Shredded Romaine with Garlic Vinaigrette

Apple-Filled Rolled Spice Cake

A SKI WEEKEND

Friday Dinner

Antipasto

*Torgiano
Bianco*

Fusilli and Broccoli
with Gorgonzola Sauce

Boston Lettuce with Sun-Dried
Tomato Vinaigrette

Orange Pecan Thins

Saturday Breakfast

Cinnamon Oatmeal with Maple Cream

Soft-Boiled Eggs

Buttered Toast

Saturday Lunch

Winter Vegetable Soup

Country Pâté

*Beaujolais-
Villages
Nouveau*

Layered Cream Cheese and
Smoked Salmon with Dill

Goat Cheese in Cracked Peppers

Assorted Breads

Red and Green Grapes

Saturday Dinner

Anchovy and Olive Spread

*Robert Mondavi
Red '82*

Moroccan Beef and Vegetable
Stew with Couscous

Orange, Radish, and Scallion Salad

Cucumber and Green Pepper
Salad with Lime

Apple-Filled Rolled Spice Cake

Sunday Brunch

Apricot Coffeecake

Bacon and Potato Frittata

Fresh Fruit with Raspberry Sauce

Winter Vegetable Soup, Country Pâté, Layered Cream Cheese and Smoked Salmon with Dill,
Goat Cheese in Cracked Peppers

Moroccan Beef and Vegetable Stew with Couscous

Chocolate Butterscotch Pudding Parfaits

CUISINE COURANTE

SAVORY PIE SUPPERS

Chappellet Vineyard
Napa Valley
Chenin Blanc '82

Chicken Pies with Biscuit Crust

Green Salad with
Creamy Mustard Vinaigrette

Chocolate Butterscotch
Pudding Parfaits

Torres Gran Coronas
White Label '78

Middle Eastern Lamb Pie

Pepper Cabbage Slaw

Sliced Oranges with
Almond Custard Sauce

Chicken Pies with Biscuit Crust,
Green Salad with Creamy Mustard Vinaigrette

TRAY MEALS

Breakfast

Rich Hot Chocolate

Pink Grapefruit and Orange Sections

Parmesan Coddled Eggs

Waffles

Oven Bacon

Tea

Potato Biscuits

Sardine Anchovy Butter

Cream Cheese and Olive Ribbon Sandwiches

Radish Hearts

Tangerine Buttermilk Pound Cake

Chocolate Hazelnut Macaroons

Coffee and Dessert

Chocolate Mousse Tart

Lime Cheesecake

Raspberry Sauce

Rich Hot Chocolate, Pink Grapefruit and Orange Sections,
Parmesan Coddled Eggs, Waffles, Oven Bacon

Sardine Anchovy Butter, Potato Biscuits, Cream Cheese and Olive Ribbon Sandwiches, Radish Hearts, Tangerine Buttermilk Pound Cake, Chocolate Hazelnut Macaroons

Artichokes Gribiche

A FIRESIDE DINNER

Rosso di Montalcino '81

Artichokes Gribiche

Eggplant Rollatini with Three Cheeses

Rugola Salad

Prosciutto Bread

Ginger Poached Pears

Eggplant Rollatini with Three Cheeses, Prosciutto Bread

Snow Pudding ''Eggs'' with Raspberry Sauce

EASTER BRUNCHES

Strawberries

Asparagus Custards with Canadian Bacon and Maltaise Sauce

Scallion Drop Biscuits

Rum-Marinated Mango Crêpes

Mimosas

Brioches Stuffed with Brandied Chicken Livers

Minted Peas and Onions

Snow Pudding "Eggs" with Raspberry Sauce

Asparagus Custards with Canadian Bacon and Maltaise Sauce, Mimosas, Scallion Drop Biscuits

Brioches Stuffed with Brandied Chicken Livers, Minted Peas and Onions

Strawberry Rhubarb Pie

A SPRING DINNER

Brauneberger Juffer
Riesling Kabinett '83

Salmon Steaks au Poivre
with Lime Butter

Lacy Potato Pancakes

Buttered Peas in Tomato Cups

Strawberry Rhubarb Pie

Salmon Steaks au Poivre with Lime Butter,
Lacy Potato Pancakes, Buttered Peas in Tomato Cups

Herb-Marinated Mozzarella

AN INFORMAL BUFFET

Sausage in Pastry with Honey Mustard

Herb-Marinated Mozzarella

Braised Veal Roast with Vegetables Provençale

Blanc de Laudun '84
and
Côtes du Rhône Rouge '83

Steamed Rice

French Bread

Boston Lettuce and Radicchio Salad
with Orange Vinaigrette

Cream Puffs with Vanilla Ice Cream
and Cherry Sauce

Boston Lettuce and Radicchio Salad
with Orange Vinaigrette, French Bread

Braised Veal Roast with Vegetables Provençale

Cream Puffs with Vanilla Ice Cream and Cherry Sauce

Rum Zabaglione with Strawberries and Amaretti

ELEGANT BUT EASY

Preston Vineyards
Dry Creek Sauvignon Blanc '83

Franciscan Vineyards
Napa Valley Zinfandel '80

Jalapeño Scallop Mousses with Shrimp

Deviled Roast Rock Cornish Game Hens

French Fried Sweet Potatoes

Green Beans Vinaigrette with
Red Onion and Coriander

Rum Zabaglione with
Strawberries and Amaretti

Deviled Roast Rock Cornish Game Hens, French Fried Sweet Potatoes,
Green Beans Vinaigrette with Red Onion and Coriander

Avocado Mousse with Salmon Roe, Melba Toast Hearts

A REHEARSAL DINNER

Inglenook Napa Valley
Sauvignon Blanc '83

Avocado Mousse with Salmon Roe
Melba Toast Hearts

Summer Squash Soup with Coriander Swirl

Vosne-Romanée
Les Suchots '78

Pistachioed Turkey Ballottine with
Madeira Sauce

Buttered Sugar Snap Peas and Carrots

Bulgur and Wild Rice Pilaf

Cold Raspberry Soufflé with Hazelnut Praline
Frangelico Chocolate Sauce

Apricot Jam Hearts
with
John Culbertson Champagne de Frontignan

Summer Squash Soup with Coriander Swirl

Pistachioed Turkey Ballottine with Madeira Sauce, Buttered Sugar Snap Peas and Carrots

Cold Raspberry Soufflé with Hazelnut Praline, Frangelico Chocolate Sauce, Apricot Jam Hearts

Anchovy and Mozzarella Pastry Fish

AN EARLY SUMMER COCKTAIL PARTY

Mandarin Champagne

Pineapple Daiquiris

Rugola Horseradish Dipping Sauce with Crudités

Riesling d'Alsace '83   *Tuna Escabeche*

Miniature Corn Muffins with Deviled Corn

Anchovy and Mozzarella Pastry Fish

Indonesian Crab-Meat Canapés

Gazpacho-Stuffed Cherry Tomatoes

Mandarin Champagne, Pineapple Daiquiri, Rugola Horseradish Dipping Sauce with Crudités, Tuna Escabeche, Miniature Corn Muffins with Deviled Corn

JULY FOURTH ALFRESCO

*Roasted Potato Skins
with Scallion Dip*

Beer-Batter Fried Chicken

Fireworks Coleslaw

Bacon and Potato Salad

*Corn on the Cob
with Basil Butter*

Sliced Tomatoes and Red Onions

Bread-and-Butter Pickles

Butter Fan Rolls

Lattice-Crust Peach Pie Watermelon

American Beers

Limeade Lemonade

Beer-Batter Fried Chicken, Sliced Tomatoes
and Red Onions, Bread-and-Butter Pickles,
Butter Fan Rolls, Fireworks Coleslaw, Bacon and Potato
Salad, Corn on the Cob with Basil Butter

Independence Day Ice-Cream Cake

A SUMMER COOKOUT

Robert Keenan Winery
　Napa Valley Chardonnay '82

Louis M. Martini Winery
　North Coast Zinfandel '81

Rosemary Shrimp

Lamb Chops Stuffed with Feta

Mint-Marinated Grilled Red Onions

Lemon Rice Salad

Independence Day Ice-Cream Cake

Lamb Chops Stuffed with Feta, Mint-Marinated
Grilled Red Onions, Lemon Rice Salad

Rosemary New Potato Salad with Roquefort,
Spicy Okra Ratatouille

PICNICS

At the Beach

Watermelon Screwdrivers

Fresh Tortilla Chips

Tropical Chicken Salad

Korean Beef Salad

Martin Bros.
Pasa Robles Chenin Blanc '82

Lobster Horseradish Salad

Pita Pockets

Chocolate Shell Cakes

Assorted Grapes

On a Fishing Trip

Cold Confetti Vegetable Soup

Pan-Fried Brook Trout with Bacon

Grave del Friuli Pinot Grigio
or Cold Beer

Rosemary New Potato Salad with Roquefort

Spicy Okra Ratatouille

Blueberry Cupcakes

Lobster Horseradish Salad,
Korean Beef Salad, Tropical
Chicken Salad, Pita Pockets

Watermelon Screwdrivers, Fresh Tortilla Chips

Chocolate Shell Cakes, Assorted Grapes

Cantaloupe Melon Mold

DINNER FROM A COOL KITCHEN

Sashimi

Oriental Noodles with Peanut Sauce

Sake

Spicy Carrot, Daikon, and Napa Cabbage Salad

Cantaloupe Melon Molds

Sashimi, Oriental Noodles with Peanut Sauce,
Spicy Carrot, Daikon, and Napa Cabbage Salad, Sake

Kahlúa Mocha Mousse with Chocolate Leaves

AUTUMN CHICKEN DINNERS

Sorrel Soup with Salmon Quenelles

Domaine de Chevalier
Graves Blanc '83
         Rolled Stuffed Chicken Breast with Hot Pepper Sauce

Saffron Rice Timbales

Warm Lima Bean Salad

Kahlúa Mocha Mousse with Chocolate Leaves

Vegetable "Pasta" with Tomato Concassé

Bonnezeaux '82
         Stuffed Chicken Normandy

Sweet Potatoes Duchesse

Sweet-and-Sour Braised Red Cabbage

Brandy Snaps with Strawberries

Rolled Stuffed Chicken Breast with Hot Pepper Sauce, Saffron Rice Timbales, Warm Lima
Bean Salad

Stuffed Chicken Normandy, Sweet Potatoes Duchesse, Sweet-and-Sour Braised Red Cabbage

Toasted Hazelnuts, Marinated Black and Green Olives, Toasted Blanched Almonds

A TAPAS PARTY

Fino Sherry

Toasted Hazelnuts

Marinated Black and Green Olives

Toasted Blanched Almonds

Chick-Pea and Chorizo Salad

Pork and Ham Meatballs
in Sherry Pepper Sauce

Squid and Celery Salad

Garlic Shrimp

Mussels with
Ham, Peppers, and Tomatoes

Octopus Salad

Chorizo-Stuffed Mushrooms

Steamed Clams with Peppers and Ham

From the top: Pork and Ham Meatballs in Sherry Pepper Sauce,
Chick-Pea and Chorizo Salad, Squid and Celery Salad, Garlic Shrimp

Stir-Fried Shrimp and Snow Peas in Bird's Nest

A CHINESE DINNER

Garlic Peanuts

Braised Black Mushrooms

Szechwan Pickled Cucumbers

*Bean Curd Noodles with Celery
and Carrot*

*Jekel Vineyard
Arroyo Seco
Chardonnay '82*

Steamed Stuffed Fish Rolls

*Stir-Fried Shrimp and Snow Peas
in Bird's Nest*

Sancerre Rouge '83

Spicy Pork and Peppers

Steamed Lotus Buns

Stir-Fried Watercress

*Clear Chicken Soup with Chicken Balls,
Watercress, and Mushrooms*

Lemon Sherbet with Starfruit

Coconut Almond Wafers

Garlic Peanuts, Braised
Black Mushrooms, Szechwan
Pickled Cucumbers, Bean Curd
Noodles with Celery and Carrot

Spicy Pork and Peppers, Steamed Lotus Buns

Clear Chicken Soup with Chicken Balls, Watercress, and Mushrooms

Lemon Sherbet with Starfruit, Coconut Almond Wafers

Seafood Sausage with Lemon Herb Sauce

SIMPLY STYLISH

Seafood Sausage with Lemon Herb Sauce

Château Grand-Puy-Lacoste '80   *Filets Mignons Persillés*

Oven-Fried Potatoes

Turnip and Carrot Julienne

Oranges in Caramel Syrup

Filets Mignons Persillés, Oven-Fried Potatoes,
Turnip and Carrot Julienne

Fried Oysters with Tartar Sauce

A COUNTRY THANKSGIVING

Pickled Carrot Sticks

Pickled Cauliflower

Celery Sticks   Olives

*Silverado Vineyards
Chardonnay '83*

Fried Oysters with Tartar Sauce

*Roast Turkey with Smoked Sausage
and Rosemary Stuffing*

Corn Sticks

Onion Raisin Cranberry Confit

Riced Sweet Potatoes   Riced Mashed Potatoes

Caraway Cabbage

Cranberry Maple Pear Pie

Pecan Pumpkin Pie

Onion Raisin Cranberry Confit

Caraway Cabbage

Roast Turkey with Smoked Sausage and Rosemary Stuffing, Corn Sticks

Purée of Fennel Soup

THANKSGIVING
FOR A SMALL GATHERING

Purée of Fennel Soup

Caymus Vineyards
Napa Valley
Zinfandel '81

Turkey Scaloppine with Cassis Cranberry Sauce

Savory Bread Pudding

Crisp-Baked Acorn Squash Rings

Sautéed Brussels Sprouts with Bacon

Brandied Pear Crisp

Turkey Scaloppine with Cassis Cranberry Sauce,
Savory Bread Pudding, Crisp-Baked Acorn Squash Rings

Mushroom Charlotte with Port and Currant Sauce

CHRISTMAS DINNER

Château La Lagune '80   *Mushroom Charlottes with Port and Currant Sauce*

Château Figeac '70   *Roast Prime Ribs of Beef with Cracked Pepper Crust*

Potato "Brioches"

Green Beans and Lima Beans with Herb Butter

Endive, Watercress, and Beet Salad
with Orange Caraway Vinaigrette

Apple Rosemary Sorbet

Chocolate Raspberry Dobostorte

Fonseca Vintage Port '63

Roast Prime Ribs of Beef with Cracked Pepper Crust, Potato "Brioches,"
Green Beans and Lima Beans with Herb Butter

Apple Rosemary Sorbet, Chocolate Raspberry Dobostorte

Fruitcake Parfaits

POST-CHRISTMAS BRUNCH

Two-Bean and Bacon Soup

Parmesan Toasts

Concannon Vineyards
Livermore Valley
Cabernet Sauvignon '82

Shepherd's Pie Crêpes   *Winter Tomato Sauce*

Honey-Glazed Carrots

Spinach Romaine Salad with Creamy Horseradish Dressing

Fruitcake Parfaits

Two-Bean and Bacon Soup, Parmesan Toasts,
Shepherd's Pie Crêpes, Honey-Glazed Carrots

PART TWO

A RECIPE COMPENDIUM

*P*art Two of *The Best of Gourmet* consists of more than five hundred recipes collected from the magazine's feature columns: Gourmet's Menus, Cuisine Courante, Gastronomie sans Argent, In Short Order, and Last Touch. The variety of recipes is remarkable. Some, like pistachioed turkey ballottine with Madeira sauce, are exotic and ideally suited for entertaining. Others—zucchini moussaka with feta, for example—are purposefully economical and were developed with seasonal considerations in mind.

Still others are gloriously efficient: They serve two, and can be completed in forty-five minutes or less. Sliced sirloin steak with chili sauce fits that bill just fine. And of course some, like Parmesan scallion soufflés, are integral to a menu, featured in Part One of the book. The choices go on and on and deliciously on.

To enable you to use this cookbook to the best possible advantage, we have divided the recipes into thirteen chapters. For easy reference in each chapter the recipes are arranged alphabetically by subject: soups, for instance, from A to Z. Where we could categorize recipes in even greater detail, we did: sauces, for example, as savory or sweet; breads, as yeast or "quick." You will notice that none of the recipes in the text carries a time symbol, indicating length of completion, as the recipes do in the magazine. An entire index, however, listing *only* those recipes that can be accomplished in forty-five minutes or less begins on page 3 9. So, if time is of the essence, turn to this index firs.. You will be delighted and astonished at the number of choices there to tempt you. Similarly, if you are curious as to whether or not a specific recipe is part of a menu, simply check page 285, which lists only menu recipes with their page numbers. You'll have a menu sooner than you think—and beautiful photographs of that menu as well.

In this volume there is no endless turning of pages in search of an accompaniment. Wherever possible when one recipe calls for another intrinsic to the completion of the master, that recipe follows the master one directly. A good example of this is steamed stuffed fish rolls, a Chinese dish, where we appended two auxiliary recipes.

Finally—and of this we are particularly proud—there is new material herein. In the chapter entitled "A Gourmet Addendum: Provisions and Provisos," which follows the chapter on beverages, we have collected six basic recipes that are called for only once or twice in other places in the text: basic pastry dough, for example, or how to blanch and oven-dry pistachio nuts. Knowing that you might well end up with leftover dough, or with more nuts than you need, we've developed brand-new recipes to provide additional uses for these. And we have tried wherever possible to combine two basic preparations into an exemplary finished dish: case in point, a sensational pistachio apple tart on flaky *pâte brisée* crust. Other wonderful recipes in the Addendum derive from a basic one for cream puff pastry—miniature hors d'oeuvres puffs with assorted savory fillings. Consider, as well, the splendid "extras" from a simple recipe for toasting and skinning hazelnuts: hazelnut-coated chicken scallops or hazelnut snow ball cookies. In short, don't stop reading at the end of the chapter on beverages, for numerous new discoveries await you in the Addendum.

Start sampling *The Best of Gourmet* now. There is a whole year ahead of you.

Top to bottom: Fried Mozzarella with Anchovy Butter (recipe page 178), Swiss Cheese Salad (recipe page 178), Parmesan Puffs (recipe page 178)

HORS D'OEUVRES, CANAPÉS, AND SPREADS

Toasted Blanched Almonds

½ pound natural almonds (with skins)
3 tablespoons olive oil
kosher salt to taste if desired

In a saucepan of boiling water blanch the almonds for 15 seconds and drain them. While the almonds are still warm press the large end of each almond to pop the almond from its skin and pat the almonds dry. In a large heavy skillet heat the oil over moderately high heat until it is hot and in it sauté the almonds, stirring constantly, for 3 to 5 minutes, or until they are golden. Transfer the almonds with a slotted spoon to paper towels to drain, sprinkle them with the salt if desired, and let them cool completely before serving. *Although best served the day they are made, the almonds may be prepared up to 1 week in advance and stored in an airtight container, chilled.* Serve the almonds at room temperature. Makes about 1½ cups.

Anchovy and Mozzarella Pastry Fish

1 recipe *pâte brisée* (page 274), substituting fresh lemon juice for the water
a 2-ounce can flat anchovy fillets, drained and halved lengthwise and crosswise
2 ounces whole-milk mozzarella, grated coarse (about ¼ cup)
an egg wash made by beating 1 large egg yolk with 1 teaspoon water
lemon slices and fresh parsley sprigs for garnish

Cut out a template from cardboard in the shape of a fish about 1½ inches long and ½ inch wide. Halve the *pâte brisée*, chill one half, wrapped in plastic wrap, and roll out the remaining half ⅛ inch thick on a floured surface. Using the template as a tracer, cut out about 40 fish shapes with a sharp paring knife and in the center of 20 of them arrange 1 of the anchovy pieces and ¼ teaspoon of the mozzarella. Moisten the edges of the topped cutouts with cold water and press one of the remaining fish-shaped cutouts over each, pinching the edges together gently to seal them. Transfer the pastries to a baking sheet and chill them, covered, for at least 30 minutes. Roll, cut, fill, and seal the remaining pastry in the same manner, transferring the pastries to a baking sheet and chilling them, covered, for at least 30 minutes. Brush the tops of the pastries with the egg wash and bake the pastries in a preheated 425° F. oven for 10 minutes, or until they are golden. Arrange the pastries on a serving tray and garnish the tray with the lemon slices and parsley. Makes about 40 hors d'oeuvres.

Anchovy and Olive Spread

a 5¾-ounce can pitted black olives, drained well
a 2-ounce can anchovy fillets, rinsed and patted dry
1 garlic clove, or to taste
3 tablespoons fresh lemon juice
3 tablespoons olive oil
¼ cup minced fresh parsley leaves
crusty bread as an accompaniment

In a blender purée the olives, the anchovies, and the garlic with the lemon juice, the oil, and the parsley, season the spread with pepper, and serve it with the bread. *The spread may be prepared up to 3 days in advance and kept covered and chilled.* Makes about 1 cup.

Antipasto

½ pound sliced *mortadella,* rolled
½ pound sliced *soppressata* or other Italian
    salami, rolled
6 stalks of celery, cut into sticks
½ cup black olives
½ cup pimiento-stuffed olives

Arrange the *mortadella* and the *soppressata* on a platter decoratively with the celery and garnish the dish with the olives. Serves 6.

Artichoke and Parmesan Phyllo Pastries

three 6-ounce jars marinated artichoke hearts
1 small garlic clove, minced
¾ cup freshly grated Parmesan
twelve 16- by 12-inch sheets of *phyllo,*
    stacked between 2 sheets of wax paper and
    covered with a dampened dish towel

Drain the artichoke hearts in a sieve set over a bowl and reserve the marinade. In a food processor blend the artichoke hearts, the garlic, and ½ cup of the Parmesan, pulsing the motor several times, until the artichokes are chopped fine and transfer the mixture to a bowl. Lay 1 sheet of the *phyllo* with a long side facing you on a work surface, brush it lightly with some of the reserved marinade, and sprinkle it with 2 teaspoons of the remaining Parmesan. Lay another sheet of *phyllo* over the first sheet and brush it lightly with some of the reserved marinade. With a sharp knife halve the sheets lengthwise and cut each length crosswise into thirds to make 6 pastry sections each approximately 6- by 5-inches. Put a rounded teaspoon of the artichoke filling in the center of each *phyllo* section and, working with 1 section at a time, gather the corners of the *phyllo* over the filling and twist the pastry closed. Transfer the pastries to oiled baking sheets and make pastries with the remaining *phyllo* and filling in the same manner. Bake the pastries in a preheated 375° F. oven for 15 minutes, or until they are golden. Makes 36 pastries.

Artichoke Heart Canapés

¼ cup minced onion
1½ teaspoons unsalted butter
4½ ounces frozen artichoke hearts, cooked
    according to the package instructions,
    drained, and chopped
¼ cup sour cream
3 slices of homemade-type white bread, crusts
    discarded, toasted lightly, and halved
    diagonally

In a small skillet cook the onion in the butter over moderately low heat, stirring occasionally, until it is softened and stir in the artichokes, the sour cream, and salt and pepper to taste. Divide the mixture among the toasts, mounding it, and broil the toasts on the rack of a broiler pan about 4 inches from the heat until they are browned lightly. Makes 6 canapés, serving 2.

Cheddar and Dried Apple Spread

¼ pound grated sharp Cheddar (about 1 cup)
¾ cup finely chopped dried apples
2 teaspoons bottled chutney, minced
1 tablespoon mayonnaise
3 tablespoons plain yogurt
2 teaspoons snipped fresh chives

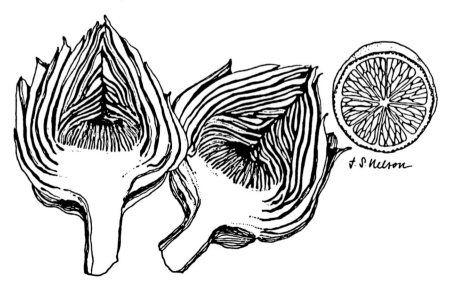

In a bowl combine the Cheddar and the dried apples. In a small bowl combine the chutney, the mayonnaise, the yogurt, and the chives and stir the mixture into the Cheddar mixture. Use the spread as a filling for celery, a topping for sliced apples, or with black bread and crackers. Makes about 1¼ cups.

Grilled Cheddar Hors d'Oeuvres

1½ ounces (about 3 tablespoons) softened
  cream cheese
1 ounce sharp Cheddar, grated (about ¼ cup)
1½ tablespoons minced dill pickle
¼ teaspoon fresh lemon juice
6 slices of thin-sliced bread, crusts discarded
1 garlic clove, crushed
2 tablespoons unsalted butter

In a small bowl combine well the cream cheese, the Cheddar, the pickle, and the lemon juice, spread the mixture on 3 slices of the bread, and top it with the remaining 3 bread slices. In a heavy skillet cook the garlic in the butter over moderately low heat, stirring, for 5 minutes, discard it, and brush both sides of each sandwich with the butter. Cook the sandwiches in the butter remaining in the skillet over moderate heat, turning them once, for 1 to 2 minutes, or until they are golden, transfer them to a cutting board, and cut each sandwich into 3 strips. Serve the hors d'oeuvres warm. Serves 2.

Cherry Tomatoes Stuffed with Smoked Oyster and Avocado Purée

30 cherry tomatoes
a 3¾-ounce can smoked oysters, drained
1 ripe California avocado, peeled, pitted, and
  cubed
5 teaspoons fresh lime juice
4 ounces cream cheese, softened
a pinch of cayenne

Cut off the tops of the tomatoes and with a small melon-ball cutter scoop out and discard the pulp and seeds. Sprinkle the tomato shells with salt and let them drain inverted on paper towels. In a food processor purée the oysters, the avocado, the lime juice, the cream cheese, the cayenne, and salt to taste until the mixture is smooth. Transfer the purée to a pastry bag fitted with a decorative tip and pipe it into the tomatoes. Chill the to-

matoes on a platter, covered loosely, for 1 hour. Makes about 30 hors d'oeuvres.

Gazpacho-Stuffed Cherry Tomatoes

½ cup peeled, seeded, and minced cucumber
⅛ teaspoon salt
¼ cup minced red bell pepper
¼ cup minced green bell pepper
½ small garlic clove, minced
1 tablespoon minced red onion
1 pint (about 20) cherry tomatoes, halved
  crosswise and seeded, reserving 4 whole
  tomatoes
2 teaspoons fresh lime juice
1 tablespoon olive oil
1 tablespoon minced fresh mint leaves

In a small bowl toss the cucumber with the salt, let it stand at room temperature for 15 minutes, and drain it. In a bowl combine well the cucumber, the bell peppers, the garlic, the onion, the 4 reserved tomatoes, seeded and chopped fine, the lime juice, the oil, the mint, and salt and pepper to taste and let the mixture stand, covered, for at least 30 minutes or overnight. Fill each cherry tomato half with a rounded teaspoon of the gazpacho mixture and arrange the tomatoes on a serving tray. Makes about 32 hors d'oeuvres.

Chicken Chutney Canapés

¼ cup drained chutney, minced
1 stick (½ cup) unsalted butter, softened
3 tablespoons minced scallion
1 tablespoon Dijon-style mustard
8 slices of thin-sliced dense whole-grain
  bread, crusts removed
6 ounces cooked boneless chicken breast,
  sliced thin
32 fresh coriander leaves
16 seedless green grapes, halved

In a bowl combine the chutney, the butter, the scallion, and the mustard until the mixture is smooth. Spread the bread with three fourths of the chutney mixture and cut each slice into quarters. Trim the chicken into squares to fit the bread and top the bread with it. Put a dot of the remaining chutney mixture on each canapé and afix a coriander leaf and a grape half to the chutney mixture on each canapé. Makes 32 canapés.

Chick-Pea and Chorizo Salad

2 cups dried chick-peas, picked over
1 bay leaf
1 teaspoon salt
½ pound *chorizo** (cured spicy pork sausage)
    or pepperoni, cut into ¼-inch slices
⅓ cup Sherry vinegar* or wine vinegar
⅔ cup olive oil
1 tablespoon Dijon-style mustard
1 teaspoon ground cumin
6 scallions, sliced thin

*available at Hispanic markets and
    specialty foods shops

In a large saucepan combine the chick-peas and 6 cups water, bring the water to a boil, and boil the chick-peas for 2 minutes. Remove the pan from the heat and let the mixture stand for 1 hour. Drain the chick-peas, return them to the pan, and add 6 cups fresh water and the bay leaf. Bring the water to a boil and simmer the chick-peas, covered, for 1 hour and 30 minutes to 2 hours, or until they are tender. Add the salt and simmer the chick-peas for 5 minutes more. Drain the chick-peas and in a large bowl combine them with the *chorizo*. Drizzle the mixture with 2 tablespoons of the vinegar and ¼ cup of the oil, toss the mixture well, and let it cool to room temperature.

In a small bowl whisk together the remaining vinegar, the mustard, the cumin, and salt and pepper to taste, add the remaining oil in a stream, whisking, and whisk the dressing until it is emulsified. Drizzle the dressing over the salad, add the scallions and salt and pepper to taste, and toss the mixture well. *The salad may be made up to 1 day in advance and kept covered and chilled.* Makes about 6 cups.

Bite-Size Chiles Rellenos

1 cup all-purpose flour
1 teaspoon salt
1 cup beer (not dark)
two 4-ounce cans whole mild green chilies,
    drained and cut lengthwise into ¾-inch
    strips
¼ pound jack cheese, cut into ¾- by ½- by
    ½-inch pieces
vegetable oil for deep-frying

In a bowl whisk together the flour and the salt, add the beer, and whisk the batter until it is smooth. Let the batter stand, covered, at room temperature for at least 1 hour or up to 3 hours. Wrap a strip of the chili around each piece of the cheese, secure the chili and the cheese with a wooden pick, and chill the cheese morsels on a plate for 1 hour.

In a deep large saucepan heat 1 inch of the oil to 400° F. Stir the batter, in batches coat the cheese morsels with it, letting any excess drip off, and fry them in the oil, turning them, for 15 seconds, or until they are golden and crisp. Transfer the *chiles rellenos* with a slotted spoon as they are fried to paper towels to drain and discard the wooden picks. Makes about 20 hors d'oeuvres.

Chinese Scallion Pancakes

2 cups all-purpose flour
2 teaspoons salt
1 bunch of scallions, trimmed and minced
¼ cup lard at room temperature
3 tablespoons Oriental sesame oil (available at
    Oriental markets and some supermarkets)
peanut or vegetable oil for frying

In a bowl combine the flour and 1 teaspoon of the salt, stir in 1 cup boiling water, and form the dough into a ball. Knead the dough on a floured surface until it is smooth and let it stand, covered with an inverted bowl, for 30 minutes.

In a small bowl stir together the scallions, the lard, and the remaining 1 teaspoon salt. Form the dough into a 12-inch log, cut it into 1-inch pieces, and cover the pieces with the inverted bowl. Flatten 1 piece of the dough, cut side down, on a floured surface and roll it into a 5-inch oval ¼ inch thick. Brush the top of the oval lightly with some of the sesame oil and spread it with 1½ teaspoons of the scallion mixture. Fold the oval lengthwise in thirds to enclose the filling, pinch the open ends closed, and, beginning with an end, roll the strip around itself, forming a coil. Flatten the coil slightly and roll it gently into a 5-inch round, being careful not to tear it. Make pancakes with the remaining dough, sesame oil, and scallion mixture in the same manner.

In a large heavy skillet at least 7 inches wide across the bottom heat ⅓ inch of the peanut oil over moderately high heat until it is very hot but not smoking and in it fry the pancakes, 1 at a time, turning them once, for 30 to 40 seconds, or until they are golden and bubbly, transferring them with a slotted spatula as they are fried to paper towels to drain. Arrange the pancakes, quartered if desired, on a platter. Serves 6 to 12 as an hors d'oeuvre.

Steamed Clams with Peppers and Ham

1 onion, chopped fine
1 green bell pepper, chopped fine
¼ pound thickly sliced smoked ham, chopped
    fine
3 tablespoons olive oil
2 garlic cloves, minced
⅓ cup medium-dry Sherry
2 dozen small hard-shelled clams, scrubbed
Italian or French bread as an accompaniment

In a kettle cook the onion, the bell pepper, and the ham in the oil over moderate heat, stirring, until the vegetables are softened. Add the garlic and cook the mixture, stirring, for 1 minute. Add the Sherry and the clams, bring the mixture to a boil, covered, and boil it, covered, for 4 to 6 minutes, or until the clams have opened. Discard any unopened clams and transfer the mixture to a heated serving bowl. Serve the clams with the Italian bread. Makes 24 clams.

Miniature Corn Muffins with Deviled Corn

For the muffins
1 cup yellow cornmeal
1 cup all-purpose flour
2 teaspoons double-acting baking powder
½ teaspoon baking soda
1¼ teaspoons salt
1 tablespoon plus 1 teaspoon sugar
2 large eggs, beaten lightly
½ stick (¼ cup) unsalted butter, melted and
    cooled, plus additional butter for brushing
    the tins
1 cup buttermilk
For the filling
½ cup cooked fresh corn kernels or thawed
    frozen corn
¼ cup minced boiled or smoked ham
¼ cup minced celery
⅓ cup mayonnaise
1 tablespoon Dijon-style mustard
a pinch of cayenne
1 teaspoon fresh lemon juice

fresh dill sprigs for garnish

Make the muffins: In a bowl combine well the cornmeal, the flour, the baking powder, the baking soda, the salt, and the sugar, add the eggs, the butter, and the buttermilk, and stir the batter until it is just combined.

Spoon rounded tablespoons of the batter into buttered ⅛-cup gem tins and bake the muffins in a preheated 425° F. oven for 10 minutes, or until a tester comes out clean. Let the muffins cool on a rack while making the filling.

Make the filling: In a bowl stir together the corn, the ham, the celery, the mayonnaise, the mustard, the cayenne, and the lemon juice and add salt and pepper to taste.

Cut off the tops of the muffins, reserving them, and hollow out the centers of the muffins with a small melon-ball cutter. Fill each muffin with a heaping teaspoon of the filling and bake the muffins on a baking sheet in the preheated 425° F. oven for 10 minutes. Garnish the filling in each muffin with a dill sprig, replace the tops of the muffins, and arrange the muffins on a serving tray. Makes about 30 muffins.

Country Pâté

2 small onions, quartered
1 garlic clove
⅓ cup packed fresh parsley leaves
1 pound sliced bacon
¼ cup dry white wine
1 tablespoon Cognac
1 teaspoon fines herbes
2 teaspoons salt
½ teaspoon coarsely ground pepper
1 pound ground veal
1½ pounds ground pork
cornichons, mustard, and assorted breads as
    accompaniments

In a food processor mince fine the onions, the garlic, and the parsley, add ½ pound of the bacon, and blend the mixture until it is smooth. Add the wine, the Cognac, the fines herbes, the salt, and the pepper and blend the mixture well. Transfer the mixture to a large bowl and knead in the veal and the pork. Line a 9- by 5-inch loaf pan with the remaining ½ pound bacon, letting it hang over the edges, pack the pâté mixture into the pan firmly, and fold any overhanging bacon up over the top. Bake the pâté, covered with a double layer of foil and set in a pan of hot water, in a preheated 375° F. oven for 1 hour and 45 minutes, or until the juices run clear. Discard the pan of water, let the pâté cool, topped with a 2-pound weight, and pour off the fat in the pan. *The pâté keeps, covered and chilled, for up to 1 week.* Discard the outer layer of bacon if desired and serve the pâté, sliced thin, with the *cornichons*, mustard, and breads. Serves 6 to 8.

Indonesian Crab-Meat Canapés

3 tablespoons fresh lemon juice
1 garlic clove, minced
¼ cup roasted unsalted peanuts
1 tablespoon vegetable oil
¼ teaspoon cayenne, or to taste
½ pound lump crab meat, picked over
½ cup mayonnaise (page 232)
3 tablespoons minced scallion
6 slices of homemade-type white bread, crusts
    discarded, toasted, and quartered
2 tablespoons minced fresh parsley leaves

In a food processor blend the lemon juice, the garlic, the peanuts, the oil, and the cayenne, scraping down the sides several times with a rubber spatula, until the peanuts are chopped fine but not puréed, and in a bowl combine the mixture with the crab meat, the mayonnaise, the scallion, and salt and pepper to taste. Spread 1 tablespoon of the mixture on each toast, bake the toasts on a baking sheet in a preheated 450° F. oven for 10 minutes, or until they are browned lightly on top, and arrange them on a serving tray. Garnish the toasts with the parsley. Makes 24 canapés.

Layered Cream Cheese and Smoked Salmon with Dill

¼ pound thinly sliced smoked salmon
2 well chilled 8-ounce packages cream cheese,
    halved horizontally
3 tablespoons snipped fresh dill
assorted breads as an accompaniment

Sandwich the salmon between the cream cheese layers, beginning and ending with cream cheese, and sprinkle the layered mixture all over with the dill, patting it gently onto the cream cheese to make it adhere. *The layered cream cheese and salmon may be prepared up to 2 days in advance and kept wrapped in plastic wrap and chilled.* Serve the cream cheese and salmon at room temperature with the breads. Serves 6 to 8.

Cucumber Canapés with Herbed Cheese

2 ounces creamy herbed cheese
3 tablespoons finely chopped radish plus thin
    radish slices for garnish
freshly ground pepper to taste
eight ¼-inch-thick slices of cucumber

In a bowl combine well the cheese, the chopped radish, and the pepper, pat the cucumber slices dry, and spread 4 of the slices with the cheese mixture. Top the cheese mixture with the remaining 4 cucumber slices, quarter the canapés, and arrange the radish slices on the tops. Serves 2 as an hors d'oeuvre.

Feta and Red Pepper Spread

6 ounces Feta, crumbled
⅓ cup coarsely chopped red bell pepper
2 tablespoons olive oil

In a food processor blend the Feta with the bell pepper, scraping down the sides, until the mixture is smooth. With the motor running add the oil and blend the mixture until it is smooth. Use the spread as a filling for cherry tomatoes and celery, a topping for sliced cucumbers, or with black bread and crackers. Makes about 1 cup.

Guacamole Canapés with Bacon

1 California avocado, peeled
3 tablespoons minced scallion
1 tablespoon minced fresh coriander leaves
1 tablespoon fresh lemon juice, or to taste
8 slices of lean bacon, cut crosswise into
    thirds
12 slices of thin-sliced dense pumpernickel,
    buttered lightly and crusts removed

In a bowl mash the avocado coarse, reserving the pit, and stir in the scallion, the coriander, the lemon juice, and salt to taste. Put the pit in the *guacamole* to prevent the mixture from darkening and chill the *guacamole*, covered, for 1 hour. Bake the bacon on a jelly-roll pan in a preheated 400° F. oven for 15 minutes, or until it is crisp, and drain it on paper towels. Spread the *guacamole* on the buttered bread, halve each slice, and top each canapé with a piece of bacon. Makes 24 canapés.

Toasted Hazelnuts

½ pound hazelnuts
3 tablespoons olive oil
kosher salt to taste if desired

Toast the hazelnuts in a jelly-roll pan in a preheated 350° F. oven for 10 to 15 minutes, or until the skins begin to separate from the nuts and the nuts are barely golden. Wrap the hazelnuts in a dish towel, let them steam for 5 minutes, and rub them in the towel to remove the skins. (With certain types of hazelnuts, not all the skin will rub off.) In a large heavy skillet heat the oil

over moderately high heat until it is hot and in it sauté the hazelnuts, stirring constantly, for 1 to 2 minutes, or until they are golden. Transfer the hazelnuts with a slotted spoon to paper towels to drain, sprinkle them with the salt if desired, and let them cool completely before serving. *Although best served the day they are made, the hazelnuts may be prepared up to 1 week in advance and stored in an airtight container, chilled.* Serve the hazelnuts at room temperature. Makes about 1¾ cups.

Middle Eastern Spiced Meatballs with Coriander Yogurt Dipping Sauce

For the dipping sauce
¼ cup minced fresh coriander
⅔ cup plain yogurt
For the meatballs
¼ cup golden raisins, soaked in hot water for
    15 minutes, drained, and chopped
2 tablespoons minced scallion
⅓ cup pine nuts, toasted lightly
½ teaspoon ground allspice
½ teaspoon cinnamon
¾ teaspoon salt
1 garlic clove, minced and mashed
½ pound ground lamb

3 tablespoons olive oil

Make the dipping sauce: In a small bowl stir the coriander into the yogurt with salt to taste and chill the sauce, covered, while the meatballs are being made.

Make the meatballs: In a bowl combine the raisins, the scallion, the pine nuts, the allspice, the cinnamon, the salt, the garlic, and the lamb, knead the mixture until it is combined well, and form it into 25 balls. In a large heavy skillet heat the oil over moderately high heat until it is hot but not smoking, in it sauté the meatballs, turning them, for 4 minutes, and transfer them to paper towels to drain. Serve the meatballs with the dipping sauce. Makes 25 hors d'oeuvres.

Mushrooms Stuffed with Monterey Jack and Jalapeño Chilies

six 2-inch mushrooms (about 6 ounces), stems
    removed and chopped fine
1 tablespoon olive oil
1 small garlic clove, minced
a 3-inch pickled *jalapeño* chili, chopped fine
    (wear rubber gloves)
5 tablespoons grated Monterey Jack

In a large heavy skillet cook the mushroom caps in the oil over moderately low heat, turning them, for 11 minutes and transfer them stemmed sides down to paper towels to drain. In the oil remaining in the skillet cook the chopped stems, the garlic, and the *jalapeño*, stirring, for 8 minutes, or until the stems are softened, transfer the mixture to a small bowl, and toss it with ¼ cup of the Monterey Jack. Divide the filling among the caps and top it with the remaining 1 tablespoon Monterey Jack. Broil the mushrooms in a flameproof pan under a preheated broiler about 4 inches from the heat for 1 to 2 minutes, or until the Monterey Jack is melted and bubbling. Serves 2 as an hors d'oeuvre.

Chorizo-Stuffed Mushrooms

1 tablespoon olive oil plus additional for
   brushing the mushroom caps
1 *chorizo* (cured spicy pork sausage, available
   at Hispanic markets and some specialty
   foods shops), skinned and chopped fine, or
   ⅓ cup finely chopped pepperoni
⅓ cup minced onion
1 garlic clove, minced
1 pound (about 14) large mushrooms, stems
   removed carefully and chopped fine
2 tablespoons medium-dry Sherry
½ cup coarse fresh bread crumbs, toasted
   lightly
1 large egg yolk, beaten lightly
2 tablespoons minced fresh parsley leaves

In a skillet heat 1 tablespoon of the oil over moderate heat until it is hot and in it sauté the *chorizo* for 1 minute. Add the onion and cook the mixture, stirring, until the onion is softened. Add the garlic and cook the mixture, stirring, for 1 minute. Add the mushroom stems and salt and pepper to taste and cook the mixture, stirring, until the liquid the mushrooms give off is evaporated. Add the Sherry and boil it until it is evaporated. Remove the skillet from the heat and stir in the bread crumbs. Let the mixture cool and blend in the egg yolk, the parsley, and salt and pepper to taste.

Brush the outside of each mushroom cap with some of the oil. Divide the filling among the caps, mounding it, arrange the stuffed mushrooms in a lightly oiled baking dish just large enough to hold them in one layer, and bake them in a preheated 400° F. oven for 5 to 10 minutes, or until they are golden. Serve the mushrooms warm or at room temperature. Makes about 14 stuffed mushrooms.

Mussels with Ham, Peppers, and Tomatoes

⅛ teaspoon saffron threads, crumbled
¼ cup dry white wine
2 pounds mussels, cleaned and steamed open
   (procedures on page 137)
1 onion, minced
2 ounces thickly sliced smoked ham, chopped
   fine
½ red bell pepper, chopped fine
½ green bell pepper, chopped fine
3 tablespoons olive oil
2 garlic cloves, minced
a 1-pound can tomatoes, drained well and
   chopped

In a small bowl let the saffron soak in the wine for 15 minutes. Transfer the mussels with a slotted spoon to a bowl, reserving the liquid, and strain the liquid through a fine sieve into another small bowl. In a large heavy skillet cook the onion, the ham, and the bell peppers in the oil over moderate heat, stirring, until the vegetables are softened, add the garlic, and cook the mixture, stirring, for 30 seconds. Add the tomatoes and cook the mixture, stirring, for 5 minutes, or until it is thickened. Add the saffron mixture and the reserved mussel liquid and boil the mixture until most of the liquid is evaporated. Season the sauce with salt and pepper and let it cool to room temperature. While the sauce is cooling remove the top shell from each mussel and loosen the mussels from the bottom shells. Spoon the sauce over the mussels on the half shell and arrange the mussels on a platter. Makes about 30 mussels.

Octopus Salad

8 pounds (about 4) octopus, thawed if frozen
1½ cups dry white wine
2 bay leaves
2 teaspoons salt
3 tablespoons fresh lemon juice
½ cup olive oil
¾ cup thinly sliced scallions

In a large kettle combine the octopus, the wine, the bay leaves, the salt, and 7 quarts water, or enough to cover the octopus by 4 inches, bring the liquid to a boil, and simmer the octopus, covered, for 2 hours, or until it is very tender. Remove the kettle from the heat and let the octopus cool in the liquid, uncovered. Drain the octopus in a large colander and, working with 1 octopus at a time, slip off the skin under cold water, reserving the large suckers if desired. Pat the tentacles dry and slice them thin diagonally. (If desired, the heads of the octopuses may be cut into thin strips.) In a small bowl whisk the lemon juice with salt and pepper to taste, add the oil in a stream, whisking, and whisk the dressing until it is emulsified. In a large bowl toss the octopus including the suckers if desired and the scallions with the dressing and salt and pepper to taste. *The salad may be made up to 1 day in advance and kept covered and chilled.* Serve the salad at room temperature. Makes about 5 cups.

Olive and Pecan Canapés

8 ounces cream cheese, softened
3 tablespoons mayonnaise
10 large pimiento-stuffed olives
½ cup pecans
12 slices of thin-sliced dense whole-grain
   bread, crusts removed

In a food processor blend the cream cheese, the mayonnaise, the olives, and the pecans until the olives and nuts are chopped fine. Spread the bread with the mixture and cut each slice into quarters. The canapés may be served at room temperature or hot. To serve the canapés hot broil them on a jelly-roll pan under a preheated broiler about 4 inches from the heat for 1 minute, or until the cream cheese mixture begins to bubble. Makes 48 canapés.

Marinated Black and Green Olives

1½ cups green olives (preferably small),
   pitted, stuffed, or unpitted as desired
1½ cups brine-cured black olives, preferably
   Niçoise (available at specialty foods shops)
   or Kalamata
¼ cup wine vinegar
6 garlic cloves, sliced
2 bay leaves
8 sprigs of fresh orégano or 1 teaspoon
   crumbled dried
8 sprigs of fresh thyme or 1 teaspoon
   crumbled dried
about 1½ cups olive oil

In 2 saucepans of boiling water blanch the green olives and the black olives separately for 1 minute each and drain them in 2 colanders. Pack the green and the black olives separately while they are still warm in two 2-cup glass jars and divide the vinegar, the garlic, the bay leaves, the orégano, and the thyme between the jars, pushing the garlic and herbs down the sides of the jars. Divide enough of the oil between the jars to cover the olives, seal the jars with the lids, and let them stand in a cool, dark place, shaking them daily, for at least 3 days. Remove the olives with a fork from the marinade. The olives keep, covered and chilled, indefinitely. Makes about 3 cups olives.

Peanut Butter and Bacon Canapés with Horseradish

½ cup smooth peanut butter
3 tablespoons drained bottled horseradish
2 tablespoons mayonnaise
a pinch of cayenne
6 slices of lean bacon, cut crosswise into
   thirds
9 slices of thin-sliced dense whole-grain
   bread, buttered lightly and crusts removed

In a bowl cream the peanut butter, the horseradish, the mayonnaise, and the cayenne until the mixture is smooth. Bake the bacon on a jelly-roll pan in a preheated 425° F. oven for 10 minutes, pour off the fat from the pan, and wipe the pan with paper towels. Spread the buttered bread with the peanut butter mixture and halve each slice. Arrange 1 piece of bacon on each canapé and bake the canapés on the jelly-roll pan in the 425° F. oven for 10 minutes, or until the bacon is crisp. Makes 18 canapés.

Spicy Light Peanut Butter Spread

¾ cup smooth peanut butter
¾ cup plain yogurt
½ to 1 bottled pickled *jalapeño* pepper, seeded
   (wear rubber gloves)

In a food processor blend the peanut butter with the yogurt and the *jalapeño* pepper, scraping down the sides, until the mixture is smooth. Use the spread as a filling for celery or with whole-wheat bread and crackers. Makes about 1½ cups.

Garlic Peanuts

12 large garlic cloves, sliced thick
½ teaspoon coarse salt plus additional to taste
2 cups vegetable oil, preferably safflower or corn oil
2 cups raw peanuts, with or without skins as desired (available at natural foods stores)
1 teaspoon Oriental sesame oil (available at Oriental markets, specialty foods shops, and many supermarkets)

In a bowl with a pestle mash 1 of the garlic slices with ½ teaspoon of the salt until a paste is formed. In a wok or deep skillet combine the vegetable oil and the remaining garlic and heat the mixture over moderately high heat until a deep-fat thermometer registers 300° F. Add the peanuts and fry them, stirring and increasing the heat until the thermometer registers 350° F., for 5 to 10 minutes, or until they are golden brown. Transfer the peanuts and the garlic with a slotted spoon to the bowl of garlic paste, drizzle them with the sesame oil, and stir the mixture until the peanuts are coated with the seasoning. Spread the peanut mixture on paper towels, season it with the additional salt, and let it cool completely. The peanuts improve in flavor if stored with the fried garlic slices in an airtight container overnight. *The peanuts may be made up to 1 week in advance and kept in an airtight container in a cool, dry place.* Makes 2 cups peanuts.

Pepperoni Mustard Spread

3½ ounces sliced pepperoni (about ¾ cup)
1 tablespoon coarse-grained mustard
1 teaspoon fresh lemon juice, or to taste
2 ounces cream cheese, softened
2 tablespoons snipped fresh dill

In a food processor blend the pepperoni with the mustard, the lemon juice, the cream cheese, and the dill, scraping down the sides, until the mixture is smooth. Use the spread as a filling for mushroom caps or with black bread and crackers. Makes about 1¼ cups.

Pork and Ham Meatballs in Sherry Pepper Sauce

For the meatballs
1 pound lean ground pork
¼ pound sliced smoked ham, chopped
½ cup minced onion
2 garlic cloves, minced
2 large eggs, beaten lightly
¾ cup fine fresh bread crumbs
1 tablespoon sweet paprika
1 teaspoon salt
½ teaspoon pepper
¼ teaspoon crumbled dried thyme
flour for dredging the meatballs
2 tablespoons olive oil
For the sauce
2 tablespoons olive oil
1 onion, minced
½ green bell pepper, sliced thin lengthwise
½ red bell pepper, sliced thin lengthwise
2 garlic cloves, minced
2 teaspoons sweet paprika
⅔ cup medium-dry Sherry
1 cup canned chicken broth
¼ cup minced fresh parsley leaves

Make the meatballs: In a bowl combine well the pork, the ham, the onion, the garlic, the eggs, the bread crumbs, the paprika, the salt, the pepper, and the thyme. (Test the seasoning by cooking a small amount of the meat mixture.) Form level tablespoons of the mixture into balls (about 40) and dredge the balls in batches in the flour, shaking off the excess. In a large heavy skillet heat the oil over moderately high heat until it is hot and in it brown the meatballs in batches, transferring them with a slotted spoon as they are browned to a bowl.

Make the sauce: Add the oil to the skillet in which the meatballs were browned, heat it over moderately low heat until it is hot, and in it cook the onion and the bell peppers, stirring, until the vegetables are softened. Add the garlic and cook the mixture, stirring, for 1 minute. Add the paprika and cook the mixture, stirring, for 30

seconds. Add the Sherry and the broth, whisking, and bring the mixture to a boil, whisking.

Add the meatballs to the sauce and simmer the mixture, covered, turning the meatballs occasionally, for 20 to 25 minutes, or until the meatballs are tender and the sauce is thickened slightly. Transfer the meatballs with a slotted spoon to a heated serving dish. (If the sauce seems thin, boil it, stirring, until it is thickened to the desired consistency.) Stir the parsley into the sauce, season the sauce with salt and pepper, and spoon it over the meatballs. Makes about 40 meatballs.

Rugola Horseradish Dipping Sauce with Crudités

4 cups packed chopped *rugola* leaves (about 4
  bunches) or 4 cups packed chopped
  watercress leaves
1 cup mayonnaise (page 232)
1 cup sour cream
¼ cup bottled horseradish
2 to 4 teaspoons fresh lemon juice
assorted *crudités,* such as carrot ovals, fennel
  sticks, and radishes

In a food processor or blender blend the *rugola,* the mayonnaise, the sour cream, the horseradish, and 2 teaspoons of the lemon juice, scraping down the sides several times with a rubber spatula, and add the remaining 2 teaspoons lemon juice if desired and salt and pepper to taste. Transfer the dipping sauce to a serving bowl and serve it with the *crudités* arranged on a serving tray. *Do not make the sauce more than 6 hours in advance.* Makes about 3 cups.

Double Salmon Canapés with Onion

a 3¾-ounce can salmon, drained and any gray
  portions discarded
2 tablespoons mayonnaise
1 tablespoon drained bottled horseradish
2 tablespoons snipped fresh dill
fresh lemon juice to taste
8 slices of thin-sliced dense pumpernickel,
  buttered lightly and crusts removed
3 ounces thinly sliced smoked salmon, cut
  into 32 pieces
1 small onion, sliced paper-thin
cracked black pepper to taste

In a food processor or blender blend the canned salmon, the mayonnaise, the horseradish, the dill, and the lemon juice until the mixture is smooth. Spread the buttered pumpernickel with the mixture, cut each slice into quarters, and top each canapé with a piece of the smoked salmon. Arrange the onion on top and sprinkle each canapé with some of the cracked pepper. Chill the canapés on a plate, covered with plastic wrap, for 1 hour. Makes 32 canapés.

Sardine Dip

a 4⅜-ounce can whole sardines, packed in oil
½ cup cottage cheese, forced through a sieve
3 tablespoons mayonnaise
1 tablespoon fresh lemon juice
2 teaspoons Dijon-style mustard
2 tablespoons snipped fresh dill
pita loaves, cut into wedges, or *crudités* for
  serving

In a bowl mash the sardines with their oil, add the cottage cheese, the mayonnaise, the lemon juice, the mustard, the dill, and salt and pepper to taste, and combine the mixture well. Transfer the mixture to a serving bowl and serve it with the *pita* wedges or the *crudités*. Makes about 2 cups.

Shrimp with Herbed Jalapeño Cheese

1 pound (about 25) shrimp
8 ounces cream cheese, softened
1 garlic clove, minced
2 pickled *jalapeño* chilies, seeded and
  chopped (wear rubber gloves)
2 tablespoons minced fresh coriander

Shell the shrimp, leaving the tail and the first joint of the shell intact, cut a deep slit down the length of the outside curve of each shrimp, and devein the shrimp. Plunge the shrimp into a large saucepan of boiling salted water and cook them for 45 seconds, or until they turn pink. Drain the shrimp in a colander, refresh them under cold water, and pat them dry. In a food processor or blender blend the cream cheese, the garlic, the chilies, the coriander, and salt and pepper to taste until the mixture is smooth, transfer the mixture to a bowl, and chill it, covered, for 30 minutes, or until it is just firm. Transfer the mixture to a pastry bag fitted with a small star tip and pipe it into the slit of each shrimp. Chill the shrimp on a platter, covered loosely, for 1 hour. Makes 25 hors d'oeuvres.

Garlic Shrimp

⅓ cup olive oil
4 garlic cloves, sliced
1 teaspoon red pepper flakes
1 pound unshelled shrimp (26 to 32 shrimp per
  pound)
2 teaspoons sweet paprika
¼ cup medium-dry Sherry
¼ cup minced fresh parsley leaves
fresh lemon juice to taste

In a large heavy skillet heat the oil over moderately
high heat until it is hot, add the garlic, and cook it, stirring, until it is pale golden. Add the red pepper flakes
and the shrimp and cook the mixture, stirring, for 1 minute, or until the shrimp are pink and just firm to the
touch. Sprinkle the shrimp with the paprika and cook
the mixture, stirring, for 30 seconds. Add the Sherry,
boil the mixture for 30 seconds, and sprinkle it with the
parsley. Season the mixture with the lemon juice and
salt and pepper to taste and transfer it to a bowl. *The
shrimp may be made up to 1 day in advance and kept
covered and chilled.* Serve the shrimp at room temperature. Makes 26 to 32 shrimp.

Smoked Oyster and Cucumber Canapés

a 3¾-ounce can smoked oysters, drained
1 teaspoon grated lemon rind
2 teaspoons fresh lemon juice, or to taste
2 tablespoons softened cream cheese
1 teaspoon Dijon-style mustard
8 slices of thin-sliced dense pumpernickel,
  buttered lightly and crusts removed
1 small cucumber, halved lengthwise, seeded,
  and 1 of the halves cut into thin slices,
  reserving the other half for another use
32 small sprigs of fresh dill

In a food processor or blender blend the oysters, the
lemon rind, the lemon juice, the cream cheese, and the
mustard until the mixture is smooth. Spread the buttered
pumpernickel with the mixture, cut each slice into quarters, and top each canapé with some of the cucumber
and 1 of the dill sprigs. Chill the canapés, covered with
plastic wrap, for 1 hour. Makes 32 canapés.

Smoked Salmon Biscuits with Salmon Roe

½ cup all-purpose flour
¾ teaspoon double-acting baking powder
1 tablespoon cold unsalted butter, cut into bits
1 ounce smoked salmon, minced (about 2
  tablespoons)
1 tablespoon snipped fresh dill
3 to 4 tablespoons heavy cream
1 tablespoon milk
2 heaping tablespoons sour cream
½ ounce (about 2 tablespoons) salmon roe
  (available at specialty foods shops)
fresh dill sprigs for garnish

Into a bowl sift together the flour, the baking powder,
and a pinch of salt and blend in the butter until the mixture resembles coarse meal. Stir in the smoked salmon,
the snipped dill, and enough of the heavy cream to make
a soft dough, form the dough into a ball, and on a lightly
floured surface roll or pat it out gently ½ inch thick. Cut
out 3 hearts with a 2½-inch heart-shaped cutter dipped
in flour, shaping and rerolling the dough as necessary,
and transfer them to a baking sheet. *The dough may be
made and cut 1 day in advance and kept covered and
chilled.* Brush the tops of the hearts with the milk and
bake the biscuits in the middle of a preheated 400° F.
oven for 15 to 17 minutes, or until they are puffed and
golden and a tester comes out clean. Gently halve the
biscuits horizontally with a serrated knife and transfer 3
hearts cut side up to each of 2 plates. Mound 1 teaspoon
of the sour cream onto each heart, top it with 1 teaspoon
of the roe, and garnish each plate with a dill sprig.
Serves 2.

Squid and Celery Salad

2 pounds squid, cleaned (procedure on page 137),
  the bodies cut crosswise into ¼-inch rings, the
  flaps cut into ¼-inch strips, and the tentacles
  halved lengthwise
1 cup dry white wine
2 teaspoons salt
1 bay leaf
3 tablespoons white-wine vinegar
⅓ cup olive oil
3 stalks of celery, sliced thin diagonally

In a large saucepan combine the squid, the wine, the
salt, the bay leaf, and enough water to cover the squid
by 2 inches, bring the liquid to a boil, and simmer the
squid, covered, for 40 to 50 minutes, or until it is tender.

Drain the squid in a colander, discarding the bay leaf, rinse it under cold water, and pat it dry. In a small bowl whisk the vinegar with salt and pepper to taste, add the oil in a stream, whisking, and whisk the dressing until it is emulsified. In a bowl combine the squid and the celery, drizzle the mixture with the dressing, and toss the salad with salt and pepper to taste. *The salad may be made up to 1 day in advance and kept covered and chilled.* Serve the salad at room temperature. Makes 4 cups.

Swiss Cheese and Caraway Spread

6 ounces Swiss cheese or Gruyère, cut into
    chunks
2 tablespoons mayonnaise
2 tablespoons softened unsalted butter
2 tablespoons coarse-grained mustard
1 teaspoon caraway seeds

In a food processor blend the cheese, the mayonnaise, the butter, the mustard, and the caraway seeds, scraping down the sides, until the mixture is smooth. Use the spread as a filling for cherry tomatoes and celery or with black bread and crackers. Makes about 1¼ cups.

Fresh Tortilla Chips

vegetable oil for deep-frying
12 corn tortillas, each cut into 6 wedges

In a large skillet heat ½ inch of the oil over moderate heat until it is hot, in it fry the tortilla wedges in batches, turning them, for 30 seconds to 1 minute, or until they are crisp and just golden, and transfer them with a slot-ted spoon as they are fried to paper towels to drain. Sprinkle the chips with salt to taste while they are still hot, let them cool, and transfer them to a portable container. Makes 72 tortilla chips.

Tuna Escabeche
(*Pickled Tuna with Vegetables*)

two 6½-ounce cans chunk light tuna packed in
    oil, drained
2 small onions, halved lengthwise and sliced
    thin crosswise
¼ cup olive oil
1 garlic clove, minced
½ cup minced carrot
¼ cup minced celery
¼ cup minced red bell pepper
1 teaspoon red pepper flakes, crumbled
½ cup white-wine vinegar
2 unwaxed cucumbers, sliced ¼ inch thick

Break the tuna into large flakes and arrange it in one layer in a shallow dish. In a skillet cook the onions in the oil over moderately low heat, stirring, until they are softened, add the garlic, and cook the mixture, stirring, for 1 minute. Add the carrot, the celery, the bell pepper, the red pepper flakes, and the vinegar, bring the liquid to a boil, and simmer the marinade, stirring occasionally, for 5 minutes. Add salt and pepper to taste, pour the marinade over the tuna, and let the tuna marinate, covered, for at least 1 day or up to 2 days. Top each cucumber slice with some of the tuna mixture and arrange the slices on a serving tray. Makes about 40 hors d'oeuvres.

BREADS

YEAST BREADS

Brioches

2½ teaspoons (a ¼-ounce package) active dry
    yeast
3 tablespoons sugar
¼ cup lukewarm milk
1½ teaspoons salt
2 to 2¼ cups all-purpose flour
3 large eggs, beaten lightly
1 stick (½ cup) unsalted butter, cut into bits
    and softened
an egg wash made by whisking 1 large egg
    yolk with 1 teaspoon water

In a large bowl proof the yeast with ¼ teaspoon of the sugar in the milk for 15 minutes, or until the mixture is foamy. Add the remaining sugar, the salt, 2 cups of the flour, the eggs, and the butter and stir the mixture until it forms a very soft, sticky dough. (The dough will be extremely loose.) Transfer the dough to a pastry board or other work surface and knead it, lifting it up and slapping it down on the board, for 10 minutes, or until it is soft, smooth, and silky, adding the additional ¼ cup flour if necessary. (The dough will become more firm as it is kneaded.) Transfer the dough to a buttered bowl, turn it to coat it with the butter, and let it rise, covered loosely with plastic wrap, in a warm place for 1 hour and 30 minutes, or until it is double in bulk. Punch down the dough and chill it, covered with plastic wrap, overnight, punching it down once after 3 hours.

Pull off three fourths of the dough, divide it into 6 pieces, and roll the pieces into balls. Set the balls into 6 well-buttered individual brioche molds and make a deep indentation in the center of each ball. Divide the remaining dough into 6 pieces, roll the pieces into pear shapes, and press them, gently, pointed ends down, into the indentations. Let the brioches rise, covered loosely with plastic wrap, in a warm place for 30 minutes, or until the larger portion of the dough has risen to the top of the molds. Brush the brioches with the egg wash, bake them in a preheated 450° F. oven for 15 to 20 minutes, or until they can be lifted out of the molds, and let them cool on a rack, unmolded, for 5 minutes. Makes 6 brioches.

Butter Fan Rolls

a ¼-ounce package (2½ teaspoons) active dry
    yeast
2 tablespoons sugar
2 cups milk
7 tablespoons unsalted butter
2 teaspoons salt
5½ to 6 cups all-purpose flour

In a small bowl proof the yeast in ¼ cup lukewarm water with a pinch of the sugar for 15 minutes, or until it is foamy. In a small saucepan heat the milk with the remaining sugar, 4 tablespoons of the butter, cut into bits and softened, and the salt, stirring, until the butter is melted and the milk is just warm. Transfer the milk mixture to a large bowl, stir in the yeast mixture and 3 cups of the flour, and beat the mixture for 2 to 3 minutes, or until it is smooth. Let the mixture stand, covered, in a warm place for 1 hour and stir in 2 cups of the remaining flour. Knead in enough of the remaining flour to form a soft dough and let the dough rest, covered, for 10 minutes. Knead the dough on a floured surface for 5 minutes, or until it is smooth and elastic, roll it into a 16- by 12-inch rectangle, and trim the edges to make the sides perfectly straight. Cut the dough lengthwise into 4 equal strips, spread the strips with the remaining 3 tablespoons butter, softened, and stack them. Cut the stack crosswise into 1-inch slices and arrange the slices cut side down in buttered muffin tins. Let the dough rise, covered with a lightly floured dish towel, in a warm place for 15 minutes and bake the rolls in a preheated 425° F. oven for 15 to 20 minutes, or until they are golden. *The rolls may be made up to 1 day in advance, kept in an airtight container, and reheated before serving. To reheat the rolls wrap them in foil and heat them in a preheated 375° F. oven for 15 to 20 minutes, or until they are hot.* Serve the rolls hot. Makes 14 to 16 rolls.

Italian Flatbread with Sage

2¼ to 2½ cups unbleached all-purpose flour
2½ teaspoons (a ¼-ounce package) quick-rise
 yeast (available at most supermarkets)
2 teaspoons olive oil plus additional for
 brushing the dough
½ teaspoon table salt
1½ teaspoons crumbled dried sage
¼ teaspoon kosher salt

In a food processor combine 1 cup of the flour and the yeast, with the motor running add ¾ cup hot water (125° to 130° F.) combined with 2 teaspoons of the oil, and turn the motor off. Add 1¼ cups of the remaining flour, the table salt, and 1¼ teaspoons of the sage and blend the mixture until it forms a ball. (If the dough is sticky add up to ¼ cup more of the flour, 1 tablespoon at a time, pulsing the dough until the flour is incorporated.) Transfer the dough to a lightly floured surface and knead it for 15 seconds to remove any air pockets. Put the dough on a lightly oiled baking sheet, pat it into a ½-inch-thick round, and prick it with a fork at 2-inch intervals. Brush the dough with the additional oil, sprinkle it with the remaining ¼ teaspoon sage and the kosher salt, and bake it in the middle of a preheated 500° F. oven for 13 to 15 minutes, or until it is golden. Makes 1 loaf.

Quick-Rise French Bread

2½ teaspoons (a ¼-ounce package) quick-rise
 yeast (available at most supermarkets)
a pinch of sugar
3½ to 3¾ cups all-purpose flour
2 teaspoons salt

In a food processor pulse the motor to combine the yeast, the sugar, and 1 cup of flour and with the motor running add 1¼ cups hot water (125° to 130° F.). Turn the motor off, add 2½ cups of the remaining flour and the salt, and process the mixture until it forms a ball. Knead the dough on a floured surface, kneading in enough of the remaining ¼ cup flour if necessary to keep it from sticking, for 5 minutes, or until it is smooth and elastic. Form the dough into a ball, put it in a well-buttered large bowl, turning it to coat it with the butter, and let it rise, covered with plastic wrap, in a warm place for 30 minutes, or until it is double in bulk. Punch down the dough and let it rise again, covered with plastic wrap, in a warm place for 30 minutes more, or until it is double in bulk. Punch down the dough and knead it

lightly on a floured surface several times. Halve the dough and let it rest, covered with plastic wrap, for 5 minutes. Form each piece of dough into a 12-inch rope and arrange the ropes on a lightly buttered baking sheet, preferably a heavy black steel sheet for a browner crust. Make diagonal cuts along both sides of the length of each rope with scissors and let the dough rest, covered with plastic wrap, in a warm place for 30 minutes. Bake the bread in the middle of a preheated 450° F. oven for 15 to 20 minutes, or until the crust is golden brown, and let it cool on a rack for 1 hour. *The bread may be cooled completely, wrapped in foil, and frozen. In the foil thaw the bread and reheat it.* Makes 2 loaves.

Slow-Rise French Bread

2½ teaspoons (a ¼-ounce package) active dry
 yeast
a pinch of sugar
3¼ to 3½ cups all-purpose flour
2 teaspoons salt

In the bowl of an electric mixer or in a large bowl proof the yeast with the sugar in ¼ cup lukewarm water for 10 to 15 minutes, or until it is foamy. Beat in 1 cup warm water, 2 cups of the flour, and the salt and beat the mixture until it is combined. With the dough hook of the electric mixer or by hand knead in the remaining 1¼ to 1½ cups flour, or enough to form a dough, and knead the dough with the dough hook for 5 minutes or by hand for 10 minutes, or until it is smooth and elastic. Form the dough into a ball, put it in a well-buttered large bowl, turning it to coat it with the butter, and let it rise, covered with plastic wrap, in a warm place for 2 hours, or until it is double in bulk. Punch down the dough and let it rise, covered with plastic wrap, in a warm place for 2 hours more, or until it is double in bulk. Punch down the dough and knead it lightly on a floured surface several times. Halve the dough and let it rest, covered with plastic wrap, for 5 minutes.

Form each piece of dough into a 12-inch rope and arrange the ropes on a lightly buttered baking sheet, preferably a heavy black steel sheet for a browner crust. Make diagonal cuts along both sides of the length of each rope with scissors and let the dough rest, covered with plastic wrap, in a warm place for 30 minutes. Bake the bread in the middle of a preheated 450° F. oven for 15 to 20 minutes, or until the crust is golden brown, and let it cool on a rack for 5 minutes. *The bread may be cooled completely, wrapped in foil, and frozen. In the foil thaw the bread and reheat it.* Makes 2 loaves.

Prosciutto Bread

2½ teaspoons (a ¼-ounce package) active dry yeast
a pinch of sugar
2 whole large eggs, beaten lightly
2 teaspoons fennel seeds
1 teaspoon salt
3 to 3½ cups all-purpose flour
1 cup minced onions
2 tablespoons olive oil
½ pound thinly sliced prosciutto, cut into thin strips
1 large egg yolk

In a small bowl proof the yeast in ¼ cup warm water with the sugar for 15 minutes, or until it is foamy. Transfer the mixture to a large bowl and stir in ½ cup warm water, the whole eggs, the fennel seeds, the salt, and enough of the flour to make a soft but not sticky dough. Knead the dough on a floured surface for 8 to 10 minutes, or until it is smooth and elastic, and form it into a ball. Put the dough in a lightly oiled bowl, turn it to coat it with the oil, and let it rise, covered with plastic wrap, in a warm place for 1 hour to 1 hour and 30 minutes, or until it is double in bulk.

In a skillet cook the onions in the oil over moderately low heat, stirring, until they are softened. Punch down the dough, knead in the onions and the prosciutto, and form the dough into a round loaf, tucking the seam under. Put the loaf on a baking sheet seam side down and let it rise, covered loosely with a dampened dish towel, for 30 minutes, or until it is double in bulk. In a small bowl whisk the egg yolk with 1 teaspoon water and brush the loaf evenly with the egg wash. Bake the bread in a preheated 350° F. oven for 30 to 40 minutes, or until it sounds hollow when the bottom is tapped, and let it cool on a rack. Makes 1 loaf.

Zucchini and Ricotta Bread

2 tablespoons active dry yeast
⅛ teaspoon honey or sugar
3 to 3½ cups unbleached all-purpose flour
¾ cup whole-wheat flour
¼ cup wheat germ, preferably raw (raw wheat germ is available at natural foods stores)
1 cup loosely packed grated zucchini
¾ cup whole-milk ricotta
¾ cup sour cream
1 tablespoon salt

In a large bowl proof the yeast in ½ cup warm water with the honey for 15 minutes, or until it is foamy. Stir in 3 cups of the unbleached flour, the whole-wheat flour, the wheat germ, and the zucchini and blend in the ricotta, the sour cream, and the salt to form a soft dough. Knead the dough on a floured surface, incorporating more of the remaining unbleached flour as necessary to keep the dough from sticking, for 8 to 10 minutes, or until it is smooth and elastic. Form the dough into a ball, put it in a lightly buttered bowl, and turn it to coat it with the butter. Let the dough rise, covered with plastic wrap, in a warm place for 1 hour, or until it is double in bulk.

Punch down the dough and form it into a loaf. Put the loaf in a loaf pan, 9 by 5 by 3 inches, and let it rise, covered with a dish towel, in a warm place for 30 to 45 minutes, or until it is double in bulk. Put a roasting pan on the lower rack of a cold oven, heat the oven to 375° F., and pour 1 cup water into the pan carefully. Bake the bread in the middle of the oven for 45 to 50 minutes, or until it sounds hollow when the bottom is tapped. Turn the bread out onto a rack and let it cool. Makes 1 loaf.

QUICK BREADS

Bacon Bread with Cheddar and Dill

½ pound lean bacon, chopped
2 cups all-purpose flour
½ cup yellow cornmeal (preferably
  stone-ground)
1 teaspoon salt
½ teaspoon baking soda
1½ teaspoons double-acting baking powder
1 cup finely grated sharp Cheddar
3 tablespoons snipped fresh dill
¼ cup vegetable shortening, softened
2 tablespoons sugar
2 large eggs, beaten lightly
1¼ cups buttermilk
1 teaspoon Worcestershire sauce

In a skillet cook the bacon over moderate heat, stirring, until it is crisp and transfer it with a slotted spoon to paper towels to drain. In a bowl combine well with a fork the flour, the cornmeal, the salt, the baking soda, and the baking powder, add the Cheddar and the dill, and toss the mixture until it is combined. In a large bowl stir together the shortening and the sugar, add the eggs, and combine the mixture well. Stir in the buttermilk and the Worcestershire sauce, combining the mixture well,

add the flour mixture and the bacon, and stir the batter until it is just combined. Divide the batter among 3 greased loaf pans, 5½ by 3⅛ by 2¼ inches, and bake it in the middle of a preheated 350° F. oven for 40 to 50 minutes, or until a skewer comes out clean. Let the loaves cool in the pans on a rack for 10 minutes. Loosen the edges with a knife, turn the loaves right side up onto the rack, and let them cool for 2 hours. *The bread keeps, wrapped tightly in foil and chilled, for up to 5 days or it may be frozen.* Serve the bread warm with soups and stews. Makes 3 loaves.

Tropical Banana Bread

1 cup dried currants
½ cup dark rum
3 cups all-purpose flour
1 teaspoon salt
1 teaspoon baking soda
1 teaspoon double-acting baking powder
2 teaspoons cinnamon
½ teaspoon freshly grated nutmeg
½ cup plus 2 tablespoons sweetened flaked
  coconut
½ cup vegetable shortening, softened
1 cup firmly packed dark brown sugar
2 large eggs, beaten lightly
⅓ cup buttermilk
1 cup mashed ripe banana
softened butter and apricot jam as
  accompaniments

In a small bowl let the currants steep in the rum, heated, for 1 hour. In a bowl combine well with a fork the flour, the salt, the baking soda, the baking powder, the cinnamon, the nutmeg, and ½ cup of the coconut. In a large bowl stir together the shortening and the brown sugar, add the eggs, and combine the mixture well. Stir in the buttermilk, the banana, and the currant mixture, combining the mixture well, add the flour mixture, and stir the batter until it is just combined. Spoon the batter into a greased loaf pan, 9¼ by 5¼ by 2¾ inches, sprinkle it with the remaining 2 tablespoons coconut, and bake it in the middle of a preheated 350° F. oven for 1 hour to 1 hour and 10 minutes, or until a skewer comes out clean. Let the loaf cool in the pan on a rack for 10 minutes. Loosen the edge with a knife, turn the loaf right side up onto the rack, and let it cool for 2 hours. *The bread keeps, wrapped tightly in foil and chilled, for up to 1 week or it may be frozen.* Serve the bread warm with the butter and the jam. Makes 1 loaf.

Carrot Bread with Caraway and Raisins

2 cups all-purpose flour
1 teaspoon salt
1 teaspoon baking soda
1 teaspoon double-acting baking powder
1 teaspoon cinnamon
¼ teaspoon ground allspice
⅛ teaspoon freshly grated nutmeg
⅛ teaspoon ground cloves
2 teaspoons caraway seeds
1 cup grated carrot (preferably with a food
   processor)
1 cup raisins
½ stick (¼ cup) unsalted butter, softened
1⅓ cups firmly packed dark brown sugar
1 large egg, beaten lightly
1 cup buttermilk
1 tablespoon freshly grated orange rind
softened cream cheese and orange marmalade
   as accompaniments

In a bowl combine well with a fork the flour, the salt, the baking soda, the baking powder, the cinnamon, the allspice, the nutmeg, the cloves, and the caraway seeds, add the carrot and the raisins, and toss the mixture to combine it. In a large bowl stir together the butter and the brown sugar, add the egg, and combine the mixture well. Stir in the buttermilk and the rind, combining the mixture well, add the flour mixture, and stir the batter until it is just combined. Divide the batter between 2 buttered loaf pans, 7¼ by 3½ by 2¼ inches, and bake it in the middle of a preheated 350° F. oven for 50 minutes to 1 hour, or until a skewer comes out clean. Let the loaves cool in the pans on a rack for 10 minutes. Loosen the edges with a knife, turn the loaves right side up onto the rack, and let them cool for 2 hours. *The bread keeps, wrapped tightly in foil and chilled, for up to 1 week or it may be frozen.* Serve the bread warm with the cream cheese and the marmalade. Makes 2 loaves.

Maple Pecan Corn Bread

1 cup all-purpose flour
1 cup yellow cornmeal (preferably
   stone-ground)
1 teaspoon salt
1 teaspoon baking soda
1 teaspoon double-acting baking powder
3 tablespoons unsalted butter, softened, plus
   additional as an accompaniment

2 tablespoons dark brown sugar
2 large eggs, beaten lightly
⅓ cup maple syrup
⅓ cup buttermilk
½ cup chopped pecans
maple sugar (available at specialty foods
   shops) as an accompaniment

In a bowl combine well with a fork the flour, the cornmeal, the salt, the baking soda, and the baking powder. In a large bowl stir together 3 tablespoons of the butter and the brown sugar, add the eggs, and combine the mixture well. Stir in the maple syrup and the buttermilk, combining the mixture well, add the flour mixture and the pecans, and stir the batter until it is just combined. Spoon the batter into a buttered loaf pan, 8½ by 4½ by 2⅝ inches, and bake it in the middle of a preheated 350° F. oven for 45 to 50 minutes, or until a skewer comes out clean. Let the loaf cool in the pan on a rack for 10 minutes. Loosen the edge with a knife, turn the loaf right side up onto the rack, and let it cool for 2 hours. *The bread keeps, wrapped tightly in foil and chilled, for up to 5 days or it may be frozen.* Serve the bread warm or toasted with the additional softened butter and the maple sugar. Makes 1 loaf.

Corn Sticks

lard or vegetable shortening for greasing the
   molds
1 cup yellow cornmeal (preferably
   stone-ground)
¾ cup all-purpose flour
2 teaspoons double-acting baking powder
2 teaspoons sugar
1 teaspoon salt
1 large egg, beaten lightly
1¼ cups heavy cream

Grease two 7-stick corn stick molds generously with the lard and heat them in a preheated 425° F. oven for 7 minutes. While the molds are heating, in a bowl whisk together the cornmeal, the flour, the baking powder, the sugar, and the salt. In a small bowl whisk together the egg and the cream, stir the egg mixture into the flour mixture, and stir the batter until it is just combined. Remove the molds from the oven, spoon the batter into them, spreading it evenly, and bake the corn sticks in the 425° F. oven for 15 minutes, or until they are golden. Invert the corn sticks immediately onto racks and serve them warm. Makes 14 corn sticks.

Corn Muffins

2 ears of corn, shucked
1 cup stone-ground white cornmeal (available at specialty foods shops)
1 cup all-purpose flour
1 tablespoon double-acting baking powder
1 teaspoon salt
½ teaspoon baking soda
½ teaspoon sugar
a pinch of cayenne
2 large eggs, beaten lightly
1¼ cups buttermilk
½ stick (¼ cup) unsalted butter, melted
⅓ cup freshly grated sharp Cheddar

With a serrated knife cut the corn kernels from the cobs into a bowl and with the back of the knife scrape the remaining corn from the cobs into the bowl. (There should be about 1 cup.) Into another bowl sift together the cornmeal, the flour, the baking powder, the salt, the baking soda, the sugar, and the cayenne. In a large bowl beat together the eggs and the buttermilk until the mixture is combined well and stir in the butter and the corn. Add the flour mixture to the buttermilk mixture and stir the batter gently until it is just combined. (The batter should be slightly lumpy.) Spoon the batter into 12 well-buttered ½-cup muffin tins, filling them three-fourths full, sprinkle the tops of the muffins with the Cheddar, and bake the muffins in a preheated 425° F. oven for 25 minutes, or until they are golden and a wooden pick comes out clean. Makes 12 muffins.

Cranberry Lemon Bread

2 cups all-purpose flour
1 teaspoon salt
1 teaspoon baking soda
1 teaspoon double-acting baking powder
¼ cup vegetable shortening, softened
1¼ cups sugar
2 large eggs, beaten lightly
½ cup buttermilk
½ teaspoon vanilla
1 tablespoon freshly grated lemon rind
1 cup fresh or unthawed frozen cranberries, picked over
softened butter as an accompaniment

In a bowl combine well with a fork the flour, the salt, the baking soda, and the baking powder. In a large bowl stir together the shortening and the sugar, add the eggs,

and combine the mixture well. Stir in the buttermilk, the vanilla, and the rind, combining the mixture well, add the flour mixture, and stir the batter until it is just combined. Stir in the cranberries gently but thoroughly, divide the batter among 6 greased loaf pans, 4½ by 2⅜ by 1½ inches, and bake it in the middle of a preheated 350° F. oven for 30 to 40 minutes, or until a skewer comes out clean. Let the loaves cool in the pans on a rack for 10 minutes. Loosen the edges with a knife, turn the loaves right side up onto the rack, and let them cool for 2 hours. *The bread keeps, wrapped tightly in foil and chilled, for up to 1 week or it may be frozen.* Serve the bread warm with the butter. Makes 6 loaves.

Molasses Cheddar Muffins

2 cups all-purpose flour
1 tablespoon double-acting baking powder
¼ teaspoon baking soda
1 teaspoon cinnamon
¼ teaspoon ground ginger
¼ teaspoon ground allspice
¼ teaspoon freshly grated nutmeg
1 teaspoon salt
1 tablespoon sugar
1 large egg, beaten lightly
½ cup milk
½ cup unsulphured dark molasses
½ stick (¼ cup) unsalted butter, melted and cooled
1¾ cups grated extra sharp Cheddar

Into a large bowl sift together the flour, the baking powder, the baking soda, the cinnamon, the ginger, the allspice, the nutmeg, the salt, and the sugar. In a small bowl combine well the egg, the milk, and the molasses, add the mixture to the flour mixture, and stir the mixture until it is just combined. Stir in the butter and the Cheddar and spoon the batter into 12 well-buttered ⅓-cup muffin tins. Bake the muffins in a preheated 425° F. oven for 15 minutes, or until a tester comes out with crumbs clinging to it. Serve the muffins immediately. Makes 12 muffins.

Oatmeal Molasses Bread

1 cup old-fashioned rolled oats
1 cup whole-wheat flour
1 cup all-purpose flour
1 teaspoon salt
1 teaspoon baking soda
1 teaspoon double-acting baking powder
¼ cup sugar

1 large egg, beaten lightly

⅓ cup unsulfured dark molasses

1¼ cups buttermilk

½ cup raisins

For the topping

1 tablespoon cold unsalted butter

2 tablespoons dark brown sugar

2 tablespoons flour

1 teaspoon cinnamon

3 tablespoons old-fashioned rolled oats

softened cream cheese or peanut butter as an
accompaniment

In a bowl combine well with a fork the rolled oats, the whole-wheat flour, the all-purpose flour, the salt, the baking soda, and the baking powder. In a large bowl stir together the sugar, the egg, and the molasses, add the buttermilk, and combine the mixture well. Add the flour mixture and the raisins and stir the batter until it is just combined. Divide the batter between 2 greased loaf pans, 7¼ by 3½ by 2¼ inches.

Make the topping: In a small bowl blend the butter with the brown sugar, the flour, the cinnamon, and the rolled oats until the mixture is crumbly and sprinkle the topping over the batter.

Bake the batter in the middle of a preheated 350° F. oven for 45 to 50 minutes, or until a skewer comes out clean. Let the loaves cool in the pans on a rack for 10 minutes. Loosen the edges with a knife, turn the loaves right side up onto the rack, and let them cool for 2 hours. *The bread keeps, wrapped tightly in foil and chilled, for up to 1 week or it may be frozen.* Serve the bread warm with the cream cheese or peanut butter. Makes 2 loaves.

Orange Poppy Seed Bread

2 cups all-purpose flour

1 teaspoon salt

2 teaspoons double-acting baking powder

2 tablespoons poppy seeds

2 tablespoons unsalted butter, melted

½ cup plus 2 tablespoons sweet orange
marmalade plus additional as an
accompaniment

1 large egg, beaten lightly

½ cup milk

1 tablespoon freshly grated orange rind

softened butter as an accompaniment

In a bowl combine well with a fork the flour, the salt, the baking powder, and the poppy seeds. In a large bowl

stir together the melted butter and ½ cup of the marmalade, add the egg, and combine the mixture well. Stir in the milk and the rind, combining the mixture well, add the flour mixture, and stir the batter until it is just combined. Spoon the batter into a buttered loaf pan, 8½ by 4½ by 2⅝ inches, and bake it in the middle of a preheated 350° F. oven for 45 to 50 minutes, or until a skewer comes out clean. Brush the top of the loaf with 2 tablespoons of the remaining marmalade and let the loaf cool in the pan on a rack for 10 minutes. Loosen the edge with a knife, turn the loaf right side up onto the rack, and let it cool for 2 hours. *The bread keeps, wrapped tightly in foil and chilled, for up to 5 days or it may be frozen.* Serve the bread warm with the softened butter and the additional marmalade. Makes 1 loaf.

Parmesan Herb Bread

2½ cups all-purpose flour

1¼ teaspoons salt

½ teaspoon baking soda

2 teaspoons double-acting baking powder

⅛ teaspoon cayenne

1 teaspoon crumbled dried sage

1 teaspoon coarsely ground pepper

1 cup freshly grated Parmesan

¾ cup minced fresh parsley leaves

¼ cup vegetable shortening, softened

2 tablespoons sugar

2 large eggs, beaten lightly

1¼ cups buttermilk

½ teaspoon Worcestershire sauce

In a bowl combine well with a fork the flour, the salt, the baking soda, the baking powder, the cayenne, the sage, the pepper, the Parmesan, and the parsley. In a large bowl stir together the shortening and the sugar, add the eggs, and combine the mixture well. Stir in the buttermilk and the Worcestershire sauce, combining the mixture well, add the flour mixture, and stir the batter until it is just combined. Divide the batter among 3 greased loaf pans, 5½ by 3⅛ by 2¼ inches, and bake it in the middle of a preheated 350° F. oven for 40 to 45 minutes, or until a skewer comes out clean. Let the loaves cool in the pans on a rack for 10 minutes. Loosen the edges with a knife, turn the loaves right side up onto the rack, and let them cool for 2 hours. *The bread keeps, wrapped tightly in foil and chilled, for up to 5 days or it may be frozen.* Serve the bread warm with soups and stews. Makes 3 loaves.

Pumpkin Chutney Bread

1¾ cups all-purpose flour
¾ teaspoon salt
1 teaspoon baking soda
½ teaspoon double-acting baking powder
1½ teaspoons cinnamon
¼ teaspoon freshly grated nutmeg
⅛ teaspoon ground allspice
⅓ cup vegetable shortening, softened
⅔ cup firmly packed dark brown sugar
2 large eggs, beaten lightly
¼ cup buttermilk
1 cup canned pumpkin purée
⅔ cup bottled mango chutney, large pieces
    chopped, plus additional as an
    accompaniment
½ cup chopped walnuts
½ cup raisins
softened cream cheese as an accompaniment

In a bowl combine well with a fork the flour, the salt, the baking soda, the baking powder, the cinnamon, the nutmeg, and the allspice. In a large bowl stir together the shortening and the brown sugar, add the eggs, and combine the mixture well. Stir in the buttermilk, the pumpkin purée, and ⅔ cup of the chutney, combining the mixture well, add the flour mixture, the walnuts, and the raisins, and stir the batter until it is just combined. Spoon the batter into a greased loaf pan, 9¼ by 5¼ by 2¾ inches, and bake it in the middle of a preheated 350° F. oven for 1 hour to 1 hour and 10 minutes, or until a skewer comes out clean. Let the loaf cool in the pan on a rack for 10 minutes. Loosen the edge with a knife, turn the loaf right side up onto the rack, and let it cool for 2 hours. *The bread keeps, wrapped tightly in foil and chilled, for up to 1 week or it may be frozen.* Serve the bread warm with the cream cheese and the additional chutney. Makes 1 loaf.

Sour Cherry Almond Bread

3 cups all-purpose flour
1¼ teaspoons salt
1 teaspoon baking soda
2 teaspoons double-acting baking powder
1 cup chopped almonds
¼ cup vegetable shortening, softened
1 cup plus 1 teaspoon sugar
2 large eggs, beaten lightly
1 cup buttermilk
1 teaspoon almond extract
1 cup drained canned pitted sour cherries,
    chopped coarse
2 tablespoons sliced almonds
softened butter and cherry jam as
    accompaniments

In a bowl combine well with a fork the flour, the salt, the baking soda, the baking powder, and the chopped almonds. In a large bowl stir together the shortening and 1 cup of the sugar, add the eggs, and combine the mixture well. Stir in the buttermilk and the almond extract, combining the mixture well, add the flour mixture, and stir the batter until it is just combined. Stir in the cherries gently but thoroughly and spoon the batter into a greased loaf pan, 9¼ by 5¼ by 2¾ inches. Sprinkle the batter with the sliced almonds and the remaining 1 teaspoon sugar and bake the batter in the middle of a preheated 350° F. oven for 1 hour to 1 hour and 10 minutes, or until a skewer comes out clean. Let the loaf cool in the pan on a rack for 10 minutes. Loosen the edge with a knife, turn the loaf right side up onto the rack, and let it cool for 2 hours. *The bread keeps, wrapped tightly in foil and chilled, for up to 5 days or it may be frozen.* Serve the bread warm with the butter and the jam. Makes 1 loaf.

Spiced Whole-Wheat Apple Bread

1½ cups all-purpose flour
1 cup whole-wheat flour
1 teaspoon salt
1 teaspoon baking soda
1 teaspoon double-acting baking powder
2 teaspoons cinnamon
¼ teaspoon ground ginger
¼ teaspoon freshly grated nutmeg
3 tablespoons vegetable shortening, softened
⅔ cup firmly packed dark brown sugar
2 large eggs, beaten lightly
1 cup buttermilk
½ cup chopped pecans
1 McIntosh apple, peeled, cored, and chopped
apple butter or softened butter and cinnamon
    sugar as an accompaniment

In a bowl combine well with a fork the all-purpose flour, the whole-wheat flour, the salt, the baking soda, the baking powder, the cinnamon, the ginger, and the nutmeg. In a large bowl stir together the shortening and the brown sugar, add the eggs, and combine the mixture well. Stir in the buttermilk, combining the mixture well, add the flour mixture, the pecans, and the apple, and stir the batter until it is just combined. Divide the batter between 2 greased loaf pans, 7¼ by 3½ by 2¼ inches, and bake it in the middle of a preheated 350° F. oven for 45 to 50 minutes, or until a skewer comes out clean. Let the bread cool in the pans on a rack for 10 minutes. Loosen the edges with a knife, turn the loaves right side up onto the rack, and let them cool for 2 hours. *The bread keeps, wrapped tightly in foil and chilled, for up to 5 days or it may be frozen.* Serve the bread warm with the apple butter or toasted with the butter and the cinnamon sugar. Makes 2 loaves.

TREVOR

Potato Biscuits

¾ cup firmly packed cooked, peeled, and
   mashed boiling potato (about ½ pound)
½ stick (¼ cup) unsalted butter, melted
1⅓ cups all-purpose flour
3 teaspoons double-acting baking powder
1 teaspoon baking soda
1 teaspoon salt
⅓ cup buttermilk or 1½ tablespoons dried
   buttermilk powder dissolved in ⅓ cup water
an egg wash made by beating 1 egg lightly
   with 1 tablespoon milk
sardine anchovy butter (recipe follows) as an
   accompaniment

Force the mashed potato through a ricer or a coarse sieve into a large bowl, stir in the butter, and blend the mixture well. Into the bowl sift together the flour, the baking powder, the baking soda, and the salt and toss the mixture until it is combined well. Add the buttermilk and stir the mixture until it just forms a dough. Knead the dough gently on a floured surface for 5 seconds and roll or pat it out ½ inch thick. With a 1½-inch round cutter dipped in flour cut out as many rounds as possible and transfer them to a baking sheet. Gather the scraps, reroll the dough, and cut out more rounds in the same manner. Brush the tops of the rounds with the egg wash, prick them with a fork, and bake the biscuits in the middle of a preheated 425° F. oven for 15 minutes, or until they are puffed and golden. Transfer the biscuits to a platter and serve them warm or at room temperature with the flavored butter. Makes about 33 biscuits.

Sardine Anchovy Butter

a 4⅜-ounce can sardines, including the oil
4 flat anchovy fillets
1 stick (½ cup) unsalted butter, softened
2 scallions, minced
1½ teaspoons Dijon-style mustard
1½ teaspoons fresh lemon juice, or to taste
½ teaspoon Worcestershire sauce

In a food processor purée the sardines with the anchovies and the butter, add the scallions, the mustard, the lemon juice, and the Worcestershire sauce, and blend the mixture well. Transfer the butter to a serving dish and chill it for 30 minutes. *The butter may be made up to 3 days in advance and kept covered and chilled.* Serve the butter at room temperature. Makes about 1¼ cups.

Rosemary Parmesan Muffins

¾ cup buttermilk
1 large egg
1½ tablespoons olive oil
1¼ cups all-purpose flour
1 teaspoon double-acting baking powder
½ teaspoon baking soda
¼ teaspoon salt
½ cup freshly grated Parmesan
1 teaspoon dried rosemary, or to taste,
   crumbled fine

In a bowl beat together the buttermilk, the egg, and the oil. Into a large bowl sift together the flour, the baking powder, the baking soda, and the salt, add ¼ cup of the Parmesan and the rosemary, and toss the mixture with a fork until it is combined well. Make a well in the center, add the buttermilk mixture, and stir the batter until it is just combined. (The batter should be lumpy.) Spoon the batter into 6 buttered ⅓-cup muffin tins, sprinkle the tops of the muffins with the remaining ¼ cup Parmesan, and bake the muffins in the upper third of a preheated 350° F. oven for 20 to 25 minutes, or until a tester comes out clean. Serve the muffins warm with soups or salads. Makes 6 muffins.

Scallion Drop Biscuits

2 cups cake flour (not self-rising)
1½ teaspoons double-acting baking powder
1 teaspoon baking soda
1 teaspoon salt
½ teaspoon sugar
1 stick (½ cup) cold unsalted butter, cut into
  bits
1 cup buttermilk
⅓ cup minced scallions

Into a bowl sift together the flour, the baking powder, the baking soda, the salt, and the sugar, add the butter, and blend the mixture until it resembles meal. Make a well in the center, add the buttermilk and the scallions, and stir the mixture until it just forms a dough. Drop the dough by rounded tablespoons onto an ungreased baking sheet and bake the biscuits in a preheated 425° F. oven for 10 to 12 minutes, or until they are pale golden. Makes about 24 biscuits.

Sesame Dill Biscuit Thins

½ cup all-purpose flour
½ teaspoon double-acting baking powder
⅛ teaspoon baking soda
⅛ teaspoon salt
¼ teaspoon dried dill
1½ tablespoons sesame seeds, toasted lightly
1 tablespoon cold unsalted butter, cut into bits
5 tablespoons plain yogurt
softened unsalted butter as an accompaniment

Into a bowl sift together the flour, the baking powder, the baking soda, and the salt, stir in the dill and the sesame seeds, and blend in the cold butter until the mixture resembles coarse meal. Make a well in the center, add the yogurt, and combine the mixture with a fork until it just forms a soft dough. Knead the dough gently on a lightly floured surface for 30 seconds and roll it out ⅛ inch thick. Cut out rounds of the dough with a floured biscuit cutter 2¼ inches in diameter and bake the biscuits on a buttered baking sheet in a preheated 450° F.

oven for 8 to 10 minutes, or until they are golden. Serve the biscuits warm with the softened butter. Makes about 10 biscuit thins.

TOASTS AND CROUTONS

Basil Pita Toasts

1 stick (½ cup) unsalted butter, softened
½ cup packed fresh basil leaves
¾ teaspoon cracked black pepper, or to taste
2 *pita* loaves, halved horizontally and each
  half cut into 4 pieces
¼ cup freshly grated Parmesan

In a small bowl cream the butter, add the basil, the pepper, and salt to taste, and blend the mixture well. Spread the butter on the *pita* quarters, sprinkle the quarters with the Parmesan, and bake them on a baking sheet in a preheated 400° F. oven for 5 to 8 minutes, or until the toasts are golden. Makes 16 toasts.

Large Croutons

½ loaf of Italian bread, crusts discarded, cut
  into ¾-inch cubes

Toast the cubes in one layer on a baking sheet in a preheated 350° F. oven for 15 minutes, or until they are pale golden, let them cool, and transfer them to a portable container. Makes about 2 cups croutons.

Fennel Seed and Pepper Toasts

1 large egg, beaten lightly
1 tablespoon vegetable oil
six ¾-inch diagonal slices of Italian bread
¾ teaspoon fennel seeds, ground coarse or
  crushed, plus ¼ teaspoon whole fennel
  seeds
¾ teaspoon coarsely ground pepper

In a shallow dish beat together the egg and the oil, dip the bread slices in the mixture, coating both sides and letting the excess drip off, and sprinkle both sides of the bread with the ground fennel seeds, the whole fennel seeds, and the pepper. Bake the bread slices on a buttered baking sheet in a preheated 350° F. oven, turning them every 10 minutes, for 30 minutes, or until they are golden brown. Makes 6 toasts.

Melba Toast Hearts

1 loaf of very thinly sliced homemade-type
  white or whole-wheat bread
1 loaf of large thin oval slices of pumpernickel
  or seedless rye bread

With a serrated bread knife remove the crusts from the white bread and positioning the slices so that a pointed end faces you trim the slices into rough heart shapes. Trim the bottom crusts from the pumpernickel bread, halve the slices crosswise, and with the pointed end facing you trim the slices into rough heart shapes, trimming the crusts at the same time. Dry the hearts in one layer on baking sheets in a preheated 300° F. oven, alternating the sheets on the oven racks every 15 minutes, for 30 minutes to 1 hour, or until the toasts are crisp and golden. Let the toasts cool and store them in an airtight container. *The toasts keep in the airtight container in a dry place for at least 4 days.* Makes about 50 Melba toast hearts.

Muffin Toasts with Golden Onions

2 cups thinly sliced onion
1 teaspoon minced peeled gingerroot
3 tablespoons unsalted butter
1 English muffin, cut horizontally into 4
  rounds
4 teaspoons sour cream

In a large heavy skillet cook the onion with the gingerroot in the butter over moderately low heat, stirring occasionally, for 20 to 25 minutes, or until it is golden. Toast the muffin rounds and spread them with the sour cream. Top the rounds with the onions and cut each round into quarters. Serves 2 as an hors d'oeuvre.

Parmesan Toasts

four ½-inch slices of homemade-type white
  bread, crusts removed and the slices
    quartered lengthwise
¾ stick (6 tablespoons) unsalted butter, melted
1¼ cups freshly grated Parmesan

Working with 1 strip at a time, with a fork roll the strips quickly in the butter, coating all sides and letting the excess drip off, and then in the Parmesan, coating all sides and patting the Parmesan onto them to help it adhere. Bake the strips on a lightly buttered jelly-roll pan in the upper third of a preheated 375° F. oven for 10

minutes, turn them, and bake them for 5 to 10 minutes more, or until they are golden and crisp. Transfer the toasts with tongs to paper towels to drain. *The toasts may be made up to 1 day in advance and kept, covered loosely, at room temperature. Reheat the toasts on a jelly-roll pan in a preheated 325° F. oven for 5 to 10 minutes, or until they are heated through.* Serve the toasts warm. Makes 16 toasts.

BREAKFAST ITEMS

Rice Corn Bread

1 cup yellow cornmeal (preferably stone-ground)
1 cup white cornmeal (preferably stone- ground)
1 teaspoon salt
1 teaspoon baking soda
2½ teaspoons double-acting baking powder
1 tablespoon unsalted butter, softened, plus
  additional as an accompaniment
1 tablespoon sugar
1 cup cooked rice, cooled to room temperature
3 large eggs, beaten lightly
2 cups buttermilk
maple syrup, heated, as an accompaniment

In a bowl combine well with a fork the yellow cornmeal, the white cornmeal, the salt, the baking soda, and the baking powder. In a large bowl stir together 1 tablespoon of the butter and the sugar, add the rice, mashing it slightly, and combine the mixture well. Stir in the eggs and the buttermilk, combining the mixture well, add the cornmeal mixture, and stir the batter until it is just combined. Spoon the batter into a buttered 8-inch-square cake pan and bake it in the middle of a preheated 400° F. oven for 30 to 35 minutes, or until a skewer comes out clean. Let the bread cool in the pan on a rack for 10 minutes and cut it into squares. Serve the bread warm with the additional butter and the maple syrup. Serves 6 to 8 as a breakfast dish.

Stuffed French Toast

½ Golden Delicious apple, peeled, cored, and
    chopped fine (preferably with a food
    processor)
1 ounce (about ¼ cup) dried apricots, chopped
    fine
2 tablespoons orange-flavored liqueur
1 large egg, beaten lightly
¼ cup milk
1 drop of almond extract
8 stale or toasted ¾-inch-thick diagonal slices
    of Italian or French bread
melted unsalted butter for brushing the griddle
maple syrup as an accompaniment

In a saucepan combine the apple, the apricots, the liqueur, and 2 tablespoons water and bring the liquid to a
boil. Simmer the mixture, covered, for 10 minutes, or
until the apple is tender, and chill it until it has cooled to
room temperature. In a bowl whisk together the egg, the
milk, and the almond extract. Spread 2 tablespoons of
the fruit mixture on 4 slices of the bread, leaving a ¼-
inch border all around, and top the mixture with the remaining 4 slices of bread to form 4 sandwiches. Soak
each sandwich in the egg mixture, turning it, for 3 minutes, or until it is softened. Heat a large griddle or skillet
over moderately high heat until it is hot, brush it with the
butter, and in it sauté the sandwiches, turning them, for
6 to 8 minutes, or until they are slightly puffed and gold-
en brown. Transfer the French toast to heated plates and
serve it with the maple syrup, heated. Serves 2.

Waffles

¾ cup all-purpose flour
1 tablespoon sugar
2 teaspoons double-acting baking powder
¼ teaspoon salt
1 large egg, beaten lightly
2 tablespoons unsalted butter, melted and cooled
¾ cup very fresh seltzer or club soda
vegetable oil for brushing the waffle iron
softened unsalted butter and maple syrup for
    serving

Into a bowl sift together the flour, the sugar, the baking powder, and the salt. In a small bowl whisk together
the egg and the melted butter, add the mixture to the
flour mixture with the seltzer, and stir the batter until it
is just combined. Heat a well seasoned or non-stick waffle iron until it is hot, brush it lightly with the oil, and
pour the batter into it, using ¼ cup of the batter for each
4-inch square waffle. Cook the waffles according to the
manufacturer's instructions, transferring them as they
are cooked to heated plates. Top the waffles with pats of
the softened butter and serve them with the syrup,
warmed. Makes 6 to 7 waffles, serving 2.

SOUPS

Avgolemono Soup with Broccoli
(Egg Lemon Soup with Broccoli)

2 cups chopped broccoli trimmings or
   chopped unpeeled broccoli stems
4 cups canned chicken broth
3 tablespoons long-grain rice
¼ cup fresh lemon juice
2 large eggs, beaten lightly
1 cup broccoli flowerets, blanched in boiling
   salted water for 1 minute, refreshed in a
   bowl of ice and cold water, and drained

In a saucepan combine the broccoli trimmings, the
broth, and 3 cups water, bring the liquid to a boil, and
simmer the broccoli for 30 minutes. Strain the liquid,
discarding the solids, measure it, and transfer it to another saucepan. There should be about 5 cups; if there is
more boil the liquid until it is reduced sufficiently; if
there is less add water. Add the rice and simmer the mixture for 15 minutes, or until the rice is tender. In a bowl
whisk together the lemon juice, the eggs, and salt and
pepper to taste, add 1 cup of the hot liquid in a stream,
whisking, and whisk the mixture into the remaining hot
liquid. Add the broccoli flowerets and heat the soup
over moderate heat, stirring constantly, until it is thickened slightly, but do not let it boil. Makes about 5 cups,
serving 4.

Bok Choy Soup
(Chinese Cabbage Soup)

1 large garlic clove, minced
1½ tablespoons olive oil
3 cups chopped *bok choy* (Chinese cabbage),
   including the leaves
2 cups canned chicken broth
freshly ground pepper to taste

In a large saucepan cook the garlic in the oil over
moderately low heat, stirring, for 1 minute, add the *bok
choy* and the broth, and simmer the mixture, covered,
for 3 to 5 minutes, or until the *bok choy* is tender. Season
the soup with the pepper and salt to taste. Makes about
2½ cups, serving 2.

Two-Bean and Bacon Soup

1 cup finely chopped onion
¾ cup finely chopped celery
2 tablespoons unsalted butter
3 garlic cloves, chopped
1½ cups cooked thawed frozen lima beans
2½ cups canned chicken broth
1 cup chopped cooked green beans
1 tablespoon snipped fresh dill
4 slices of lean bacon, cut crosswise into thin
   strips
small sprigs of dill for garnish

In a large saucepan cook the onion and the celery in
the butter over moderately low heat, stirring, until the
vegetables are softened, add the garlic, and cook the
mixture, stirring, for 1 minute. Add the lima beans, 1
cup water, and the broth, bring the liquid to a boil, and
simmer the mixture, covered, for 15 minutes. Purée the
mixture in a blender or food processor and return it to
the pan. Add the green beans, the snipped dill, and salt
and pepper to taste and heat the mixture, stirring, until it
is hot. While the soup is heating, in a small skillet cook
the bacon over moderate heat, stirring, until it is crisp
and transfer it with a slotted spoon to paper towels to
drain. Divide the soup among mugs or bowls, sprinkle
each serving with some of the bacon, and garnish the
soup with the dill sprigs. *The soup may be prepared up
to 1 day in advance and kept covered and chilled, but do
not add the bacon and the dill sprigs until serving.*
Makes about 6 cups, serving 6.

Minted Cantaloupe Soup

2½ cups peeled, seeded, and chopped
   cantaloupe
1½ teaspoons chopped fresh mint leaves or
   ½ teaspoon dried
1½ tablespoons sugar
3 tablespoons plain yogurt
¼ cup dry white wine
2 mint sprigs for garnish if desired

In a food processor or blender purée the cantaloupe
with the chopped mint and the sugar until the sugar is
dissolved, transfer the purée to a metal bowl, and whisk
in the yogurt and the wine. Set the bowl in a bowl of ice
and cold water and stir the soup until it is chilled well.
Ladle the soup into 2 chilled bowls and garnish each
bowl with a mint sprig if desired. Makes about 1½ cups,
serving 2.

Carrot and Parsnip Chowder

1 onion, chopped
1 boiling potato, peeled and diced
2 carrots, diced
2 parsnips, diced
2 tablespoons unsalted butter
2 cups canned chicken broth
2 tablespoons heavy cream
1 tablespoon snipped fresh dill

In a saucepan cook the onion, the potato, the carrots,
and the parsnips in 1 tablespoon of the butter, covered,
over moderately low heat, stirring occasionally, for 10
minutes, add the broth, and simmer the mixture, covered, stirring occasionally, for 10 to 15 minutes, or until
the vegetables are very tender. In a blender or food processor purée ⅔ cup of the mixture and stir the purée into
the remaining mixture. Add the cream, the dill, and salt
and pepper to taste and cook the chowder over moderate
heat, stirring, until it is hot. Ladle the chowder into
heated bowls and top each serving with ½ tablespoon of
the remaining butter. Makes about 2 cups, serving 2.

Purée of Carrot Top Soup

2 onions, chopped fine
½ stick (¼ cup) unsalted butter
½ pound potatoes
½ pound carrot tops, stems discarded, rinsed,
   spun dry, and chopped
6 cups chicken stock (page 119) or canned
   chicken broth
2 teaspoons fresh lemon juice
3 carrots, sliced thin crosswise, blanched for 3
   minutes, and drained, for garnish

In a kettle cook the onions in the butter over moderately low heat, stirring, until they are softened. Add the
potatoes, peeled and grated coarse, the carrot tops, and
the stock, bring the mixture to a boil, and simmer it,
covered, for 30 minutes. In a food processor purée the
mixture in batches until it is smooth and add the lemon
juice and salt and pepper to taste. In the kettle heat the
soup until it is hot and serve it garnished with the carrot
slices. Makes about 6 cups, serving 6.

Cauliflower Cheddar Soup

⅓ cup thinly sliced white part of scallion
1 tablespoon unsalted butter
1½ cups cauliflower flowerets
1½ cups canned chicken broth
1 cup grated extra-sharp Cheddar
2 tablespoons thinly sliced scallion greens

In a heavy saucepan cook the white part of scallion in
the butter over moderately low heat, stirring, until it is
softened. Add the cauliflower and the broth, bring the
liquid to a boil, and simmer the mixture, covered, for 12
to 15 minutes, or until the cauliflower is tender. Add the
Cheddar and salt and pepper to taste, cook the mixture,
stirring, until the Cheddar is melted, and purée the mixture in batches in a blender. Return the soup to the pan,

stir in the scallion greens, and heat the soup over moderate heat, stirring, until it is hot. Makes about 2 cups, serving 2.

Chilled Celery Soup with Yogurt

½ cup chopped scallions, including some of
   the green part
1 teaspoon vegetable oil
1½ cups chopped celery, including the leaves
2½ cups canned chicken broth
½ cup chilled plain yogurt
thinly sliced scallion greens for garnish

In a large saucepan cook the chopped scallions in the oil over moderately low heat, stirring, until they are softened. Add the celery, the broth, and salt and pepper to taste, bring the liquid to a boil, and boil the mixture for 5 to 7 minutes, or until the celery is tender. In a blender purée the mixture in batches, transfer it to a metal bowl set in a bowl of ice and cold water, and stir it until it is cold. Whisk in the yogurt, ladle the soup into 2 chilled bowls, and sprinkle it with the scallion greens. Makes about 2 cups, serving 2.

Cheddar Cheese Soup

4 slices of lean bacon, chopped
1 cup finely chopped onion
1 cup finely chopped celery, including some
   of the leaves
   carrot, chopped fine
3 tablespoons flour
½ teaspoon paprika
4 cups chicken stock (page 119) or canned
   chicken broth
1 cup half-and-half
¾ pound extra sharp Cheddar, grated
3 tablespoons minced fresh parsley leaves

In a kettle cook the bacon over moderate heat, stirring occasionally, until it is crisp and transfer it with a slotted spoon to paper towels. In the bacon fat remaining in the kettle cook the onion, the celery, and the carrot over moderately low heat, stirring occasionally, for 10 minutes, or until the vegetables are softened, add the flour and the paprika, and cook the mixture, stirring, for 3 minutes. Add the stock in a stream, whisking, bring the liquid to a boil, whisking, and simmer the mixture, stirring occasionally, for 10 minutes. Stir in the half-and-half and the Cheddar and cook the soup over low heat, stirring, until the cheese is melted, but do not let

the soup boil. Stir in the parsley and serve the soup in heated bowls garnished with the bacon. Makes about 6 cups, serving 6.

Clear Chicken Soup with
Chicken Balls, Watercress, and Mushrooms

For the chicken balls
½ pound skinless boneless chicken breast,
   trimmed and cut into ½-inch pieces
1 tablespoon lard
1 large egg white
¼ cup Chinese chicken broth (page 125) or
   canned chicken broth
1 tablespoon rice wine (available at Oriental
   markets and some liquor stores) or Scotch
½ teaspoon soy sauce
½ teaspoon salt
1 teaspoon Oriental sesame oil*
2 tablespoons minced scallion
2 tablespoons chopped fresh coriander

7 cups Chinese chicken broth or canned
   chicken broth
24 watercress sprigs
a 3½-ounce package fresh *enoki-daki*
   mushrooms,* the lower 1½ inches of stem
   discarded

*available at Oriental markets, some specialty
   foods shops, and some supermarkets

Make the chicken balls: In a food processor purée the chicken with the lard and the egg white, with the motor running add the broth, the rice wine, the soy sauce, the salt, the sesame oil, the scallion, and the coriander, and blend the mixture well. Transfer the purée to a pastry bag fitted with a ¼-inch plain tip and pipe about sixty ¾-inch mounds ½ inch apart into a lightly buttered skillet. With a finger dipped in cold water smooth the tops of the mounds. Pour enough boiling water carefully over the chicken balls to cover them and poach the balls at a bare simmer for 3 to 5 minutes, or until they are just firm. Transfer the balls with a slotted spoon to a bowl. *The balls may be made 1 day in advance and kept covered and chilled.*

In a large saucepan bring the broth to a simmer, add the chicken balls, the watercress, and the mushrooms, and simmer the soup for 30 seconds to 1 minute, or until the mixture is heated through. Ladle the soup into heated soup bowls. Makes about 9 cups, serving 8.

Chili con Queso Soup

1 small onion, chopped fine
1½ tablespoons unsalted butter
a 3-ounce can mild green chilies, drained,
    seeded, and chopped fine
a 14-ounce can plum tomatoes, drained,
    seeded, and chopped fine (about ⅔ cup)
3 ounces cream cheese, cut into bits
½ cup canned chicken broth
¾ cup half-and-half
2 teaspoons fresh lemon juice, or to taste
cayenne to taste

In a saucepan cook the onion in the butter over moderately low heat, stirring occasionally, until it is softened, add the chilies and the tomatoes, and cook the mixture over moderate heat, stirring occasionally, for 8 to 10 minutes, or until the liquid is evaporated. Stir in the cream cheese over moderately low heat and stir the mixture until the cheese is melted. Stir in the broth, the half-and-half, the lemon juice, the cayenne, and salt to taste and heat the soup over moderate heat until it is hot, but do not let it boil. Serve the soup with tortilla chips if desired. Makes about 2 cups, serving 2.

Corn Chowder with Thyme

3 tablespoons bacon fat or vegetable oil
½ pound smoked ham, cut into ½-inch dice
3 onions, chopped coarse
2 stalks of celery, chopped coarse
3 carrots, sliced thick
2 sprigs of thyme or ¼ teaspoon dried,
    crumbled
1 small bay leaf
1 pound boiling potatoes, cut into ½-inch dice
2 to 2½ cups canned chicken broth or water
¾ teaspoon salt
⅔ cup heavy cream
1½ to 1¾ cups milk
5½ cups corn with pulp (cut and scraped from
    about 10 ears of corn)
about 3 tablespoons unsalted butter if desired
fresh thyme leaves for garnish
diced raw or roasted (procedure follows) red
    bell pepper for garnish
pilot crackers or other bland white crackers as
    an accompaniment

In a large saucepan heat the fat over moderate heat until it is hot, in it cook the ham, stirring, until it is pale golden, and transfer it with a slotted spoon to a plate, reserving it. In the fat remaining in the pan cook the onions, the celery, the carrots, the thyme sprigs, and the bay leaf over moderate heat, stirring, for 10 minutes, or until the vegetables are wilted but not brown. Add the potatoes, enough of the broth to cover the vegetables, and the salt, bring the liquid to a boil, and simmer the mixture, covered, for 20 to 25 minutes, or until the potatoes are just tender. Skim any fat that has accumulated on the surface and discard the thyme sprigs and the bay leaf.

In a saucepan bring the cream and 1½ cups of the milk just to a boil, stir the liquid and the corn into the potato mixture, and simmer the mixture, covered partially, for 5 minutes. Transfer half the solids with a slotted spoon to a food processor or blender and purée them. Add the purée and the reserved ham to the mixture and simmer the mixture for 5 minutes. Add enough of the remaining ¼ cup milk to thin the chowder to a medium-thick consistency and season the chowder with salt and pepper. Ladle the chowder into heated bowls, top each serving with a thin pat of the butter if desired, and garnish it with the thyme leaves and the bell pepper. Serve the chowder with the crackers. Makes about 10 cups, serving 6.

To Roast Bell Peppers

Using a long-handled fork char the peppers over an open flame, turning them, for 2 to 3 minutes, or until the skins are blackened. (Or broil the peppers on the rack of a broiler pan under a preheated broiler about 2 inches from the heat, turning them frequently, for 20 to 25 minutes, or until the skins are blistered and charred.) Enclose the peppers in a plastic bag and let them steam until they are cool enough to handle. Keeping the peppers whole, peel them starting at the blossom end, cut off the tops, and discard the seeds and ribs.

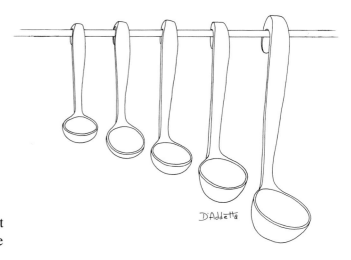

Purée of Fennel Soup

¾ pound onions, sliced thin
3 tablespoons unsalted butter
1½ pounds fennel bulbs, trimmed and sliced
    thin
1 tablespoon fresh lemon juice
½ pound boiling potatoes
4 cups chicken stock (page 119) or canned
    chicken broth
a 2-inch piece of fennel stalk, halved
    lengthwise and sliced thin on the diagonal,
    for garnish
1 tablespoon Pernod, or to taste
6 sprigs of fennel top for garnish

In a large saucepan cook the onions in 2 tablespoons of the butter over moderately low heat, stirring, until they are softened, add the fennel bulbs and the lemon juice, and cook the mixture, covered, stirring occasionally, for 10 minutes. Add the potatoes, peeled and sliced thin, and the stock, bring the stock to a boil, and simmer the mixture, covered, for 30 to 45 minutes, or until the potatoes are tender. While the mixture is simmering cook the fennel stalk in the remaining 1 tablespoon butter over moderately low heat, stirring, for 2 minutes and add salt and pepper to taste. In a blender purée the onion mixture in batches and transfer the purée to a saucepan. Add the Pernod and salt and pepper to taste and heat the soup over moderately low heat, stirring, until it is hot. *The soup may be made up to 1 day in advance, kept covered and chilled, and reheated.* Divide the soup among 6 heated bowls and garnish each serving with several slices of the fennel stalk and a sprig of the fennel top. Serves 6.

Green Pea and Snow Pea Soup

the white part of ½ pound leeks, quartered
    lengthwise, sliced crosswise, and washed
    well
2 tablespoons unsalted butter
¼ pound snow peas, trimmed, strings
    discarded, and cut crosswise into ½-inch
    pieces
1 cup frozen green peas
2 cups canned chicken broth
1 tablespoon minced fresh parsley leaves
a pinch of crumbled dried mint

In a large saucepan cook the leeks in the butter over moderately low heat, stirring occasionally, until they are softened and add the snow peas, the green peas, and the broth. Bring the liquid to a boil and simmer the mixture, covered, for 3 to 5 minutes, or until the vegetables are tender. Stir in the parsley, the mint, and salt and pepper to taste. Makes about 3 cups, serving 2.

Jerusalem Artichoke Soup with Lemon and Dill

½ pound Jerusalem artichokes
¼ cup fresh lemon juice
1 small boiling potato (about ¼ pound)
1 cup thinly sliced onion
2 cups canned chicken broth
For the garnish
2 tablespoons snipped fresh dill
2 tablespoons sour cream if desired

With a vegetable peeler peel the Jerusalem artichokes, dropping each one as it is peeled into a large bowl of cold water acidulated with 3 tablespoons of the lemon juice. Peel the potato and in a food processor chop it fine with the remaining 1 tablespoon lemon juice and the Jerusalem artichokes, drained. Transfer the mixture to a saucepan, add the onion and the broth, and bring the broth to a boil. Simmer the mixture, covered, stirring occasionally, for 25 to 30 minutes, or until the vegetables are tender. In a blender or food processor purée the mixture in batches, transfer the soup to a pan, and add salt and pepper to taste. Heat the soup over moderately low heat and garnish it with the dill and the sour cream if desired. Makes about 3 cups, serving 2.

Lima Bean and Bacon Soup

2 slices of lean bacon
1 small onion, minced
2 cups canned beef broth
a 10-ounce package frozen lima beans
½ cup heavy cream

In a heavy skillet cook the bacon over moderate heat, turning it, until it is crisp and transfer it to paper towels to drain. In the fat remaining in the skillet cook the onion over moderately low heat until it is softened and transfer it with a slotted spoon to a small saucepan. Add the broth to the pan and bring it to a boil. Add 1 slice of the bacon, crumbled, and the lima beans and simmer the mixture, covered, for 15 to 17 minutes, or until the beans are tender. In a blender purée the bean mixture with the cream, heated, divide the soup between heated bowls, and garnish it with the remaining slice of bacon, crumbled. Serves 2.

Mussel Scallion Soup

½ cup minced onion
1 teaspoon fennel seed
1 teaspoon crumbled dried thyme
1 small bay leaf, crumbled
1½ cups dry white wine
3 pounds mussels, cleaned (procedure on
    page 137)
1 cup chopped white part of scallions (about 3
    bunches)
2 tablespoons unsalted butter
1 cup peeled, seeded, and chopped tomato
1 cup heavy cream
½ cup chopped scallion greens
scallion and garlic purée (page 209) to spread
    on toast as an accompaniment if desired

In a large heavy stainless steel or enameled kettle combine the onion, the fennel seed, the thyme, the bay leaf, and the wine, bring the liquid to a boil, and simmer the mixture, covered, for 15 minutes. Add the mussels and steam them, covered, over high heat, shaking the kettle occasionally, for 4 to 6 minutes, or until the shells have opened and the mussels are just firm. Discard any unopened shells. Strain the cooking liquid through a fine sieve into a bowl, remove the mussels from the shells, discarding all but 2 of the shells, and, if desired, discard the tough black rims. Reserve the mussels, covered, and the 2 shells for garnish.

In a large heavy skillet cook the white part of the scallions in the butter over moderately low heat, stirring occasionally, for 5 minutes, add the tomato, and cook the mixture, stirring, for 10 minutes. Add the mussel liquid and the cream, bring the mixture to a boil, and simmer it for 10 minutes. Add the reserved mussels and the scallion greens, heat the soup over low heat until it is heated through, and garnish it with the reserved shells. Serve the soup with the scallion and garlic purée on toast if desired. Makes about 4 cups, serving 4.

Cream of Parsley Soup with Onion

4 cups chicken stock (page 119) or canned
    chicken broth
2 cups firmly packed fresh parsley leaves,
    minced
2 large egg yolks
1 cup half-and-half
1 small red onion, sliced thin and separated
    into rings
white pepper to taste

In a saucepan bring the stock to a boil over moderately high heat, add the parsley, and simmer the mixture for 10 minutes. In a bowl beat the egg yolks lightly and whisk in the half-and-half. Add ½ cup of the stock mixture to the cream mixture in a stream, whisking, and whisk the mixture back into the pan. Add the onion and simmer the soup, stirring, for 5 minutes, or until it is thickened slightly, but do not let it boil. Stir in the white pepper and salt to taste. Makes about 4 cups, serving 4.

Sorrel Soup with Salmon Quenelles

1 cup minced onion
½ stick (¼ cup) unsalted butter
1 pound fresh sorrel, stemmed, rinsed,
    drained, and shredded
4 cups canned chicken broth
½ cup half-and-half
¼ pound boneless fresh salmon, cut into
    chunks
¼ pound smoked salmon, chopped
a pinch of cayenne
½ cup heavy cream
¼ cup sour cream
4 teaspoons fresh salmon roe (available at
    specialty foods shops)
4 dill sprigs

In a kettle cook the onion in the butter over moderately low heat, stirring, until it is softened, add the sorrel, and cook the mixture, covered, stirring occasionally, for 10 minutes. Add the broth and salt and pepper to taste, bring the liquid to a boil, and simmer the mixture, covered, for 15 minutes. Add the half-and-half and cook the soup over moderately low heat until it is heated through, but do not let it boil.

In a food processor purée the fresh salmon and the smoked salmon for 20 seconds, or until the mixture is smooth, with the motor running add the cayenne and the heavy cream in a stream, and blend the mixture for 15 seconds. Transfer the mixture to a pastry bag fitted with a ¼-inch plain tip and pipe about forty ⅓-inch mounds into a lightly buttered large skillet. Ladle enough of the soup gently over the quenelles to just cover them and poach the quenelles at a bare simmer for 3 to 4 minutes, or until they are just firm. Transfer the quenelles and the soup they were poached in to the kettle and heat the soup over moderately low heat until it is heated through. Ladle the soup into 4 heated bowls and garnish each serving with 1 tablespoon of the sour cream topped with 1 teaspoon of the salmon roe and a dill sprig. Makes about 6 cups, serving 4.

Summer Squash Soup with Coriander Swirl

For the soup

6 onions, chopped

⅔ cup olive oil

6 pounds yellow summer squash, trimmed, quartered lengthwise, and cut into ½-inch pieces

6 cups fresh or thawed frozen corn kernels

three 35-ounce cans Italian plum tomatoes, drained

18 cups chicken stock (page 119) or canned chicken broth

For the coriander mixture

1 cup loosely packed chopped fresh coriander

1 small garlic clove, chopped

2 large egg yolks

½ cup olive oil or vegetable oil

½ cup buttermilk

Make the soup: In a very large kettle (or 2 smaller kettles) cook the onions in the oil over moderately low heat, stirring, until they are softened, add the squash, the corn, the tomatoes, and the stock, and bring the stock to a boil. Simmer the mixture, covered, for 20 to 25 minutes, or until the squash is tender, and in a blender or food processor purée it in batches, transferring it as it is puréed to a large bowl. Let the soup cool, uncovered, chill it, covered, for at least 3 hours, or until it is cold, and season it with salt and pepper. *The soup may be made up to this point 1 day in advance and kept covered and chilled.*

Make the coriander mixture: In a blender or food processor purée the coriander with the garlic and the egg yolks and with the motor running add the oil in a slow stream, blending the mixture until it is emulsified. With the motor still running add the buttermilk in a stream and season the mixture with salt and pepper. *The coriander mixture may be made 1 day in advance and kept covered and chilled. Just before serving stir the coriander mixture well.*

Stir the soup well, ladle it into chilled bowls, and transfer the coriander mixture to a small pitcher. Work-

ing with 1 serving at a time, drizzle about a tablespoon of the coriander mixture onto the soup in the center, making an arc design, and draw the end of a chopstick or skewer through the coriander mixture carefully to extend the arc into a swirl pattern. Makes about 40 cups, serving 20 generously.

Cold Tomato Soup with Basil

1½ pounds tomatoes, peeled, seeded, and chopped

¼ cup chopped fresh basil leaves

½ cup well chilled half-and-half

¾ teaspoon Tabasco, or to taste

In a food processor or blender purée the tomatoes with the basil. In a metal bowl whisk together the purée, the half-and-half, the Tabasco, and salt and pepper to taste, set the bowl in a bowl of ice and cold water, and stir the soup until it is cold. Ladle the soup into 2 chilled bowls. Makes about 2 cups, serving 2.

Cold Confetti Vegetable Soup

½ cup finely chopped onion

1 small garlic clove, minced

½ cup dry white wine

3 cups canned chicken broth

1 pound cucumbers, peeled, seeded, and grated coarse

½ red bell pepper, cut lengthwise into julienne strips and the strips halved crosswise

½ green bell pepper, cut lengthwise into julienne strips and the strips halved crosswise

2 ounces radishes, trimmed, halved lengthwise, and sliced thin

¼ teaspoon Tabasco, or to taste

1½ tablespoons fresh lemon juice

2 cups large croutons (page 108)

In a saucepan combine the onion, the garlic, the wine, and the broth, bring the liquid to a boil, and simmer the mixture for 5 minutes. Let the mixture cool and chill it, covered, for 1 hour, or until it is cold. In a large bowl combine the broth mixture, the cucumbers, the bell peppers, the radishes, the Tabasco, the lemon juice, and salt and pepper to taste and transfer the soup to a large thermos. *The soup may be made 1 day in advance and kept covered and chilled.* Serve the chilled soup in mugs with the croutons. Makes about 4½ cups, serving 4.

Winter Vegetable Soup

2 onions, chopped
2 garlic cloves, minced
2 carrots, chopped
2 stalks of celery, chopped
½ stick (¼ cup) unsalted butter
1 teaspoon dried marjoram
1 bay leaf
½ teaspoon dried basil
4 cups chicken stock (page 119) or canned
    chicken broth
1 cup canned tomato purée
a 10-ounce package frozen spinach
a 10-ounce package frozen peas
a 10-ounce package frozen corn
⅓ cup chopped fresh parsley leaves

In a kettle cook the onions, the garlic, the carrots, and the celery in the butter with the marjoram, the bay leaf, the basil, and salt and pepper to taste over moderately low heat, stirring occasionally, until the vegetables are softened, add the stock and the tomato purée, and bring the liquid to a boil. Add the spinach, the peas, and the corn, return the liquid to a boil, breaking up the vegetables, and simmer the soup for 5 minutes, or until the vegetables are just tender. Discard the bay leaf. In a food processor, pulsing the motor several times, purée the soup coarse in batches. *The soup may be prepared up to 3 days in advance and kept covered and chilled.* Return the soup to the kettle, bring it to a boil, and stir in the parsley. Makes about 9 cups, serving 6 to 8.

Zucchini and Orzo Soup

1 garlic clove, minced
1 onion, chopped fine
2 tablespoons olive oil
6 ounces zucchini, scrubbed, trimmed, and
    cut into ½-inch cubes (about 1⅓ cups)
2½ cups canned chicken broth
½ cup *orzo* (rice-shaped pasta)
3 tablespoons freshly grated Parmesan

In a saucepan cook the garlic and the onion in the oil over moderately low heat, stirring, until they are softened, add the zucchini and the broth, and bring the liquid to a boil over high heat. Stir in the *orzo*, boil the mixture, stirring occasionally, for 8 to 10 minutes, or until the *orzo* is *al dente*, and season the soup with salt and pepper. Ladle the soup into bowls and sprinkle it with the Parmesan. Makes about 3 cups, serving 2.

Zucchini Vegetable Broth

2 onions, chopped coarse
1 carrot, chopped coarse
2 tablespoons olive oil
1 cup chopped fresh parsley leaves
½ pound mushrooms, chopped coarse
3 pounds zucchini, cut into ½-inch pieces,
    plus ½ cup coarsely grated zucchini
two 2- by ½-inch strips of lemon rind
½ teaspoon crumbled dried thyme

In a kettle cook the onions and the carrot in the oil over moderate heat, stirring, for 3 to 5 minutes, or until the vegetables are browned lightly. Add 8 cups water, the parsley, the mushrooms, the zucchini pieces, the lemon rind, and the thyme, bring the water to a boil, and simmer the mixture for 30 minutes. Strain the mixture through a fine sieve lined with a double thickness of rinsed and squeezed cheesecloth into a large saucepan, bring the broth to a boil, and reduce it to about 4 cups. Season the broth with salt and pepper and stir in the grated zucchini. Makes about 4 cups, serving 4.

STOCKS

Brown Stock

2 pounds meaty beef shanks, sawed into
    1-inch slices
2 pounds meaty veal shanks, sawed into
    1-inch slices
2 unpeeled onions, quartered
1 carrot, quartered
2 stalks of celery
1½ teaspoons salt
a cheesecloth bag containing 4 sprigs of
    parsley, ½ teaspoon dried thyme, and
    1 bay leaf

Spread the beef shanks, the veal shanks, the onions, and the carrot in a flameproof baking pan, brown them well in a preheated 450° F. oven, and transfer them to a kettle. Add 2 cups water to the pan, deglaze the pan over high heat, scraping up the brown bits, and add the liquid to the kettle with 14 cups cold water, the celery, the salt, and the cheesecloth bag. Bring the water to a boil and skim the froth. Add ½ cup cold water, bring the mixture to a simmer, and skim any froth. Simmer the mixture, adding boiling water to keep the ingredients barely covered, for 5 to 6 hours, or until the stock is reduced to about 8 cups. Strain the stock through a fine sieve into a bowl, pressing hard on the solids, and let it cool. Chill the stock and remove the fat. The stock may be frozen. Makes about 8 cups.

Chicken Stock

a 4-pound fowl
the neck and giblets (excluding the liver), chopped
1 large onion stuck with 2 cloves
2 leeks, halved lengthwise and washed well
2 carrots
1 stalk of celery, halved
2 teaspoons salt
a cheesecloth bag containing 6 sprigs of parsley, ½ teaspoon dried thyme, 1 unpeeled garlic clove, and 1 bay leaf

In a kettle combine the fowl, the neck and the giblets, and 12 cups cold water, bring the water to a boil, and skim the froth. Add ½ cup cold water, bring the stock to a simmer, and skim any froth. Add the onion, the leeks, the carrots, the celery, the salt, and the cheesecloth bag and simmer the stock, skimming the froth, for 2 hours. Remove the fowl from the kettle, remove the meat and skin from the carcass, and reserve the meat for another use. Chop the carcass, return it and the skin to the kettle, and simmer the stock, adding boiling water if necessary to keep the ingredients barely covered, for 2 hours more. Strain the stock through a fine sieve into a bowl, pressing hard on the solids, and let it cool. Chill the stock and remove the fat. The stock may be frozen. Makes about 6 cups.

Turkey Breast Stock

the bones from 2 turkey breasts (procedure for boning on page 172)
2 carrots, sliced thick
1 stalk of celery, sliced thick
2 onions, quartered, and 3 of the quarters stuck with 1 clove each
1 teaspoon peppercorns
½ teaspoon crumbled dried thyme
1 bay leaf
12 parsley stems

Chop the bones with a cleaver and in a kettle combine them with the carrots, the celery, the onions, and 16 cups water. Bring the water to a boil, skimming the froth, add the peppercorns, the thyme, the bay leaf, and the parsley, and simmer the stock for 1 hour and 30 minutes. Strain the stock through a fine sieve into a large bowl, measure it, and, if necessary, boil it until it is reduced to 8 cups. Spoon off the fat or let the stock cool, chill it overnight, and remove the fat. Makes about 8 cups.

Wing Tip Consommé

5 cups wing tip stock (page 120)
the crushed shells of 2 large eggs
2 large egg whites, beaten lightly
2 scallions, chopped
3 tablespoons Madeira, or to taste
Worcestershire sauce to taste
white-wine vinegar to taste
¼ cup julienne strips of carrot, blanched in boiling water for 1 minute and drained
¼ cup julienne strips of celery, blanched in boiling water for 1 minute and drained

Clarify the stock: In a large heavy saucepan heat the stock, if necessary, over low heat, stirring, until it is liquid but not hot. Add the shells, the whites, and the scallions and bring the mixture just to a boil, stirring. Cook the mixture at a bare simmer, undisturbed, for 20 minutes and ladle it through a fine sieve lined with a double thickness of rinsed and squeezed cheesecloth into another large heavy saucepan. Stir in the Madeira, the Worcestershire sauce, the vinegar, and salt to taste and heat the consommé over moderate heat until it is hot. Divide the carrot and the celery strips among small soup bowls and ladle the consommé over them. Serves 6 as a first course.

Wing Tip Stock

2 pounds wing tips (about 100), thawed if
    frozen, and patted dry
chicken bones, such as those reserved from
    boning chicken thighs, if desired
2 onions, unpeeled and quartered
1 carrot, sliced thick
1 stalk of celery, sliced thick
3 garlic cloves, unpeeled
1 bay leaf
1 teaspoon peppercorns
½ teaspoon salt
4 sprigs of parsley
⅛ teaspoon crumbled dried thyme

Spread the wing tips, any other chicken bones, if desired, the onions, and the carrot in a flameproof baking pan and brown them well in a preheated 450° F. oven, stirring occasionally. (This could take as long as 1 hour.) Transfer the chicken and vegetables to a large saucepan, add 3 cups water to the baking pan, and deglaze the pan over high heat, scraping up the brown bits. Add the liquid to the saucepan with 7 cups water, the celery, the garlic, the bay leaf, the peppercorns, and the salt, bring the liquid to a boil, skimming any froth, and add ½ cup cold water. Bring the mixture to a simmer and skim any froth. Add the parsley and the thyme and simmer the mixture for 4 hours. Strain the stock through a fine sieve into a large bowl, pressing hard on the solids, and let it cool. Chill the stock and remove the fat. The stock may be frozen. Makes about 5 cups.

GARNISHES
FOR CLEAR SOUPS

Coriander Egg Sheets

3 large eggs
⅓ cup minced fresh coriander
¾ teaspoon salt
1½ teaspoons Oriental sesame oil (available at
    Oriental markets and some supermarkets)
vegetable oil for brushing the skillet

In a small bowl beat the eggs lightly with the coriander, the salt, the sesame oil, and 2 tablespoons water. Heat a 7-inch non-stick skillet over moderately high heat until it is hot but not smoking and brush it lightly with the vegetable oil. Half-fill a ¼-cup measure with the egg mixture, remove the skillet from the heat, and pour in the egg mixture, tilting and rotating the skillet quickly so that the mixture covers the bottom in a thin layer. Return the skillet to the heat, cook the egg sheet for 30 seconds, or until it is set, and loosen the edge with a rubber spatula. Turn the egg sheet, cook it for 15 seconds, and transfer it with the spatula to a plate. Make egg sheets with the remaining mixture in the same manner, brushing the skillet lightly with the oil as necessary. Cut the egg sheets into ½-inch strips. Makes enough garnish for 6 cups soup.

French-Toasted Croutons

2 large eggs, beaten lightly
¼ teaspoon Tabasco
¼ teaspoon salt
1 tablespoon minced fresh parsley leaves
enough day-old French bread, crusts
    discarded, cut into ½-inch cubes, to
    measure 2 cups
2 tablespoons unsalted butter

In a large bowl whisk together the eggs, the Tabasco, the salt, and the parsley, add the bread cubes, and let the mixture stand, stirring it once or twice, for 5 minutes, or until the cubes have absorbed the egg mixture. In a large heavy skillet heat the butter over moderately high heat until the foam subsides and in it sauté the bread cubes, stirring, until they are golden and crisp. Makes enough garnish for 6 cups soup.

Green Chili Custards

½ cup half-and-half
a 3-ounce can chopped green chili peppers,
    drained
1 large whole egg
1 large egg yolk
½ teaspoon salt

In a food processor or blender purée the half-and-half with the chili peppers. In a bowl whisk together the chili mixture, the whole egg, the egg yolk, and the salt and pour the custard into a buttered heavy 8-inch round cake pan lined with a buttered round of wax paper. Put the pan in an ovenproof deep skillet, add enough boiling water to the skillet to come halfway up the sides of the pan, and cover the skillet with foil. Bake the custard in the middle of a preheated 325° F. oven for 15 to 20 minutes, or until it is set, and let it cool for 5 minutes. Remove the foil, run a thin knife around the edge of the custard, and invert the pan carefully onto a buttered sheet of wax paper. Let the custard cool until it is warm, remove the round of wax paper, and with a 1-inch decorative cutter cut out shapes, or with a knife cut the custard into 1-inch pieces. Makes enough garnish for 6 cups soup.

Toasted Onion Crêpes

1½ cups chopped onion
2 tablespoons unsalted butter
½ cup all-purpose flour
⅓ cup plus 1 tablespoon milk
2 large eggs
½ teaspoon salt
vegetable oil for brushing the crêpe pan

In a skillet cook the onion in the butter over moderate heat, stirring, until it is golden brown. In a food processor or blender blend the flour with the milk, the eggs, the onion mixture, and the salt for 5 seconds. Turn off the motor and with a rubber spatula scrape down the bowl. Blend the batter for 20 seconds more, transfer it to a bowl, and let it stand, covered with plastic wrap, for 1 hour.

Heat a 6- to 7-inch crêpe pan (preferably iron) or nonstick skillet over moderately high heat until it is hot. Brush the pan lightly with the oil, heat the oil until it is hot but not smoking, and remove the pan from the heat. Stir the batter, half-fill a ¼-cup measure with it, and pour the batter into the pan. Tilt and rotate the pan quickly so that the batter covers the bottom in a thin layer and return any excess batter to the bowl. Return the pan to the heat, loosen the edge of the crêpe from the pan with a metal spatula, and cook the crêpe until the underside is browned lightly. Turn the crêpe, brown the other side, and transfer the crêpe to a plate or dish towel.

Make crêpes with the remaining batter in the same manner, brushing the pan lightly with the oil as necessary. *The crêpes may be prepared in advance, stacked, wrapped in plastic wrap, and chilled or frozen.* Cut the crêpes into ½-inch strips. Makes enough garnish for 12 cups soup.

Parmesan Tortilla Strips

¼ cup vegetable oil
six 7-inch corn tortillas (available at Hispanic markets, specialty foods shops, and some supermarkets), halved and cut crosswise into ½-inch strips
6 tablespoons fresh very finely grated Parmesan

In a large heavy skillet heat the oil over moderate heat until it is hot but not smoking and in it cook the tortilla strips in batches, stirring, for 30 seconds to 1 minute, or until they are golden and crisp, transferring them with a slotted spatula as they are fried to paper towels to drain. In a baking pan heat the strips in a preheated 250° F. oven for 10 minutes, sprinkle them with the Parmesan, tossing the strips to coat them evenly, and let the cheese melt on the strips in the oven for 5 minutes. Makes enough garnish for 6 cups soup.

FISH AND SHELLFISH

FISH

Anchovy Caper Toasts

4 anchovy fillets
1½ teaspoons drained capers
1 large egg yolk
2 teaspoons fresh lemon juice
5 tablespoons olive oil
six ½-inch slices of French bread

In a food processor or blender purée the anchovies, the capers, the egg yolk, the lemon juice, and pepper to taste, scraping down the sides with a rubber spatula, until the mixture is smooth. With the motor running add 3 tablespoons of the oil in a stream and blend the mixture until it forms a paste. Brush both sides of the bread with the remaining 2 tablespoons oil and toast the bread on the rack of a broiler pan under a preheated broiler about 4 inches from the heat, turning it once, until it is golden. Let the toasts cool until they can be handled and spread the paste on the tops. Return the toasts to the rack and broil them about 4 inches from the heat until they are bubbling and puffed. Serves 2 as an hors d'oeuvre.

Sautéed Flounder with Lime and Brown Butter

¾ pound flounder fillets, cut into 4 pieces
flour for dredging
1 large egg, beaten lightly
1½ tablespoons vegetable oil
3 tablespoons unsalted butter
1 tablespoon fresh lime juice
1 tablespoon minced fresh parsley leaves
lime slices for garnish

Season the flounder with salt and pepper, dredge it in the flour, shaking off the excess, and dip it in the egg. In a large heavy skillet heat the oil and 1 tablespoon of the butter over moderately high heat until it is hot but not smoking and in the fat sauté the flounder, turning it once, for 2 to 3 minutes, or until it just flakes. Transfer the flounder to a heated platter and drizzle it with the lime juice. Wipe the skillet clean and in it cook the remaining 2 tablespoons butter over moderately high heat, swirling the skillet occasionally, until the foam subsides and the butter is nut-brown. Pour the butter over the flounder, sprinkle the flounder with the parsley, and garnish it with the lime slices. Serves 2.

Steamed Stuffed Fish Rolls

For the fish rolls

3 tablespoons rice wine* or Scotch

½ teaspoon salt

the white part of 4 scallions, flattened with the flat side of a cleaver

6 slices of gingerroot, each about the size of a quarter, flattened with the side of a cleaver

4 small sole fillets (about 2 pounds in all), preferably gray sole, halved lengthwise

2 stalks of celery, cut into 2-inch fine julienne strips, blanched in boiling water for 1 minute, drained, and refreshed under cold water

1 large carrot, cut into 2-inch fine julienne strips, blanched in boiling water for 1 minute, drained, and refreshed under cold water

3 whole scallions, cut into 2-inch fine julienne strips

sixteen 6-inch-long scallion greens, halved lengthwise if wide, blanched in boiling water for 3 seconds, drained, and refreshed under cold water

For the sauce

1½ teaspoons cornstarch

½ cup Chinese chicken broth (recipe follows) or canned chicken broth

2 tablespoons rice wine* or Scotch

1½ teaspoons sugar

¼ teaspoon salt, or to taste

1½ tablespoons vegetable oil, preferably safflower or corn oil

⅓ cup minced scallions

¼ cup minced peeled gingerroot

*available at Oriental markets and some liquor stores

Make the fish rolls: In a large bowl combine the rice wine, the salt, the scallion whites, and the gingerroot, pressing the gingerroot and scallions to release their flavors, add the sole, turning it to coat it with the marinade, and let it marinate at room temperature for 30 minutes or covered and chilled for 2 hours. Discard the marinade and cut each fillet half crosswise into 2 pieces, making the piece with the thin, narrow end of the fillet slightly longer. Working with 1 piece at a time, arrange the sole skinned side up with a narrow end facing you on a work surface. Gather a few of the celery, the carrot, and the scallion strips into a small bunch, lay the bunch across the narrow end, and roll up the sole jelly-roll fashion around the vegetables. Tie the rolls with the strips of blanched scallion and arrange them, as they are filled and tied, in one layer on lightly oiled heatproof plates. *The rolls may be made up to this point 1 day in*

TREVOR

advance and kept covered tightly with plastic wrap and chilled.

Make the sauce: In a small bowl dissolve the cornstarch in the broth and add the rice wine, the sugar, and the salt. Heat a wok or small heavy skillet over high heat until it is hot, add the oil, and heat it until it is just smoking. Add the scallions and the gingerroot and stir-fry the mixture for 10 seconds, or until it is fragrant. Stir the broth mixture, add it to the wok, stirring, and bring it to a boil, stirring. Strain the sauce through a fine sieve into a small saucepan and keep it warm, covered.

Steam the fish rolls (procedure follows), 1 plate at a time, for 2 minutes, or until the fish just flakes when tested with a fork. Keep the cooked rolls warm, covered loosely, while steaming the remaining ones. Transfer the rolls carefully with a slotted spatula to a heated serving dish, arranging them decoratively. Bring the sauce to a boil and pour it over the fish. Serves 8.

Chinese Chicken Broth

6 pounds chicken wings and backs
¾ cup rice wine (available at Oriental markets
    and some liquor stores) or Scotch
8 large slices of gingerroot, each about ⅛ inch
    thick, flattened with the side of a cleaver
2 teaspoons salt, or to taste

Cut the chicken wings at the joints into thirds, discard the loose fat from the backs, and chop the backs into large pieces. In a kettle of boiling water blanch the chicken for 1 minute, drain it in a large colander, and rinse it under cold water. Rinse out the kettle, return the chicken to it, and add the rice wine, the gingerroot, the salt, and 24 cups cold water. Bring the liquid to a boil, skimming the froth, and simmer the mixture, skimming the froth, for 3 hours. Strain the broth through a large sieve lined with a triple thickness of rinsed and squeezed cheesecloth into a large bowl. Let the broth cool completely, uncovered, chill it, and remove the fat. *The broth may be made up to 3 days in advance and kept covered and chilled, or it may be frozen.* Makes about 12 cups.

To Steam Food Chinese Style

Arrange the food on the latticework trays of a bamboo steamer lined with oiled parchment paper. Stack the trays so that they interlock and cover the topmost tray with the lid. In a wok bring 2 inches of water to a vigorous boil over high heat. Set the bamboo steamer over the boiling water, making sure that the tray sits at least ½ inch above the water and the bottom of the rim rests in the water, and steam the food, adding more boiling water if necessary to maintain the level, until it is cooked. Turn off the heat, remove the lid carefully to allow the steam to disperse for a few seconds, and remove the steamer from the wok.

To steam on an improvised rack: In a deep pan bring 2 inches of water to a vigorous boil over high heat. Set a rack in the pan, making sure that it is elevated at least ½ inch above the water. Set the food either directly on the rack lined with oiled parchment paper or in a shallow heatproof dish on the rack and cover the pan with a lid. Steam the food, adding more boiling water if necessary to maintain the level, until it is cooked. Turn off the heat, remove the lid carefully to allow the steam to disperse for a few seconds, and remove the rack from the pan.

Halibut with Red Pepper Sauce

⅔ cup drained bottled roasted red peppers
2 tablespoons heavy cream
¼ teaspoon sugar, or to taste
2 teaspoons fresh lemon juice
1½ tablespoons unsalted butter
1 pound halibut steak
½ small green bell pepper, cut into julienne
    strips
½ small red or yellow bell pepper, cut into
    julienne strips
1 teaspoon vegetable oil

In a food processor purée the roasted peppers, transfer the purée to a small saucepan, and stir in the cream, the sugar, and enough water to thin the sauce to the desired consistency. Bring the sauce to a boil, stirring, and keep it warm, covered, over low heat. In another small saucepan combine the lemon juice, the butter, and salt and pepper to taste and heat the mixture over moderate heat until the butter is melted. Measure the thickness of the halibut and broil the halibut on the rack of a broiler pan under a preheated broiler about 4 inches from the heat, basting it with the lemon butter and turning it once, for 7 to 10 minutes per inch of thickness, or until it just flakes. While the halibut is broiling cook the bell pepper in the oil over moderately low heat, stirring, for 3 to 5 minutes, or until it is crisp-tender. Spoon the sauce onto a heated platter, arrange the halibut on the sauce, and scatter the bell pepper over it. Serves 2.

Salmon Steaks au Poivre with Lime Butter

For the lime butter
½ stick (¼ cup) unsalted butter, softened
¾ teaspoon grated lime rind
½ teaspoon fresh lime juice

four 1¼-inch-thick salmon steaks
¼ cup vegetable oil
1 teaspoon freeze-dried green peppercorns
    (available at specialty foods shops), crushed
    and minced
4 lime wedges
parsley sprigs for garnish if desired

Make the lime butter: In a bowl combine well the butter, the lime rind, and the lime juice, transfer the mixture to a sheet of wax paper, and top it with another sheet of wax paper. Pat out the mixture about ¼ inch thick and chill it for 30 minutes, or until it is very firm. Cut the lime butter into decorative shapes with a small fluted cutter or a knife and reserve it, covered and chilled, until the salmon is cooked.

Rub the salmon steaks on both sides with the oil, salt to taste, and the peppercorns. Heat a large non-stick skillet over moderate heat until it is hot and in it sear the salmon for 1 minute on each side. Reduce the heat to moderately low and cook the salmon for 8 minutes, or until it just flakes. Transfer the salmon steaks to a heated platter, top them with the lime butter and the lime wedges, and garnish the platter with the parsley if desired. Serves 4.

Sardine Pissaladières

about ⅓ cup olive oil
2 pounds onions, sliced thin
½ teaspoon crumbled dried rosemary
½ teaspoon crumbled dried thyme
½ teaspoon crumbled dried basil
2 garlic cloves, minced

two 1-pound cans tomatoes, drained and
  chopped fine
2 tablespoons white-wine vinegar
1 recipe pizza dough (recipe follows)
cornmeal for sprinkling the baking sheets
10 whole sardines (three 4⅜-ounce cans)
  packed in oil, drained, reserving the oil, and
  quartered lengthwise
22 medium pitted black olives, halved
  lengthwise

In a large heavy skillet heat ¼ cup of the olive oil over
moderately high heat until it is hot, add the onions, the
rosemary, the thyme, and the basil, stirring to coat the
onions with the oil, and cook the mixture, covered, over
low heat, stirring occasionally, for 30 minutes, or until
the onions are soft but not colored. Stir in the garlic, the
tomatoes, the vinegar, and salt to taste and cook the
mixture, covered, for 15 minutes. Remove the lid, cook
the mixture over moderately high heat, stirring constantly, for 10 minutes, or until the excess liquid is
evaporated, and let the mixture cool.

Divide the pizza dough into 4 balls, working with 1
ball at a time roll out each ball on a floured surface into a
6-inch round, leaving a slight rim, and stretch it gently
into a 7-inch round. Transfer the rounds carefully to 2
large baking sheets liberally sprinkled with the cornmeal and brush them lightly with some of the remaining
olive oil. Spread one fourth of the onion mixture over
each round, leaving a ½-inch border, and top each
round with 10 of the sardine pieces in a spoke pattern
and 11 of the olive halves. Drizzle about 1 teaspoon of
the reserved sardine oil over each *pissaladière* and bake
the *pissaladières*, 1 baking sheet at a time, on the floor
of a preheated 500° F. gas oven or on the lowest shelf of
a preheated 500° F. electric oven for 10 to 12 minutes,
or until the bottom of the crust is golden brown and
crisp. Serves 4.

Pizza Dough

2½ teaspoons (a ¼-ounce package) active dry
  yeast
¼ teaspoon sugar
¼ cup whole-wheat flour
2 tablespoons olive oil
2½ to 2¾ cups unbleached flour
1 teaspoon salt

In a large bowl proof the yeast with the sugar in ¼ cup
lukewarm water for 15 minutes, or until it is foamy. Stir

in ¾ cup more lukewarm water, the whole-wheat flour,
the oil, 2½ cups of the unbleached flour, and the salt and
blend the mixture until it forms a dough. Knead the
dough on a floured surface for 5 to 10 minutes, kneading
in more of the remaining unbleached flour, if necessary, until it is smooth and elastic. Put the dough in a
lightly oiled large bowl, turn it to coat it with the oil, and
let it rise, covered with plastic wrap, in a warm place for
1 hour, or until it is double in bulk. Punch down the
dough. The dough is now ready to be formed into pizzas. Makes enough dough for four 7-inch pizzas.

Sardine-Stuffed Lemon Halves

2 lemons, halved crosswise and juiced,
  reserving the juice and the lemon halves
a 4⅜-ounce can whole sardines packed in oil
2 tablespoons mayonnaise
⅓ cup minced celery
¼ cup minced scallions
1 tablespoon Dijon-style mustard
toast points for garnish and serving

Discard the membranes from the lemon halves and
cut a thin slice off the bottom of each half so it will stand
on end securely. In a small bowl mash the sardines with
their oil, add the mayonnaise, the celery, the scallions,
the mustard, and 1 tablespoon of the reserved lemon
juice, or to taste, and combine the mixture well. Season
the mixture with salt and pepper, spoon it into the lemon
shells, mounding it, and stand a toast point in each serving. Serves 4 as a first course.

Sardine Toasts

a 4⅜-ounce can whole sardines packed in oil,
  drained
½ cup mayonnaise (page 232)
2 teaspoons fresh lemon juice
¼ cup minced fresh parsley leaves
¼ teaspoon Worcestershire sauce
eighteen ¼-inch-thick slices of Italian or
  French bread

In a bowl mash the sardines with the back of a fork,
add the mayonnaise, the lemon juice, the parsley, the
Worcestershire sauce, and salt and pepper to taste, and
combine the mixture well. Spread about 1 tablespoon of
the mixture on each slice of the bread, covering the top
completely, and bake the toasts on baking sheets in a
preheated 425° F. oven for 10 minutes, or until the topping is puffed slightly and the bread is crisp. Makes 18
hors d'oeuvres.

Sashimi
(Assorted Raw Seafood)

For the dipping sauce
¼ cup soy sauce
2 tablespoons rice vinegar*
1 teaspoon minced scallion
½ teaspoon minced peeled gingerroot

1 tablespoon *wasabi** (powdered Japanese horseradish)

¼ pound very fresh sea scallops, halved and chilled
2 teaspoons rice vinegar*
½ teaspoon sugar
¼ pound very fresh skinless boneless tuna fillet, chilled
¼ pound very fresh skinless boneless salmon fillet or steak, chilled
4 snow peas, trimmed and strings discarded
pickled ginger*
shredded scallion greens and cucumber strips

*available at Oriental markets and some supermarkets

Make the dipping sauce: In a small bowl combine the soy sauce, the vinegar, the scallion, and the gingerroot, divide the sauce between 2 small shallow bowls, and arrange the bowls on 2 large serving plates.

In a small bowl combine the *wasabi* with 1½ teaspoons water to form a paste and put a pinch of the paste on each plate. (A small amount of the *wasabi* may also be stirred into the dipping sauce, a little at a time, to make a hotter sauce.)

In a bowl toss the scallops with the vinegar and the sugar until the sugar is dissolved, drain them, and divide them between the plates. Cut the tuna and the salm-on into bite-size pieces and divide them between the plates. Arrange the snow peas, the pickled ginger, and the scallion and cucumber strips on the plates decoratively. Serve the *sashimi* immediately. Serves 2.

Scrod with Broccoli Cream Sauce

1½ cups trimmed, peeled, and chopped broccoli plus ¼ cup small broccoli flowerets
1 red bell pepper, minced
2 tablespoons unsalted butter
four 6-ounce pieces scrod fillet
½ cup minced onion
1 cup dry white wine
¼ cup heavy cream

In a saucepan of boiling salted water cook the chopped broccoli until it is tender and drain it, reserving 3 cups of the cooking liquid. Refresh the broccoli in a bowl of ice and cold water and drain it.

In a saucepan cook the bell pepper in 1 tablespoon of the butter, covered, over moderately low heat, stirring occasionally, until it is softened and keep it warm, covered. In a skillet large enough to hold the scrod in one layer combine the onion, the wine, and the reserved cooking liquid, bring the liquid to a boil, and simmer the mixture for 10 minutes. Add the scrod and poach it, covered, at a bare simmer, turning it once, for 8 to 10 minutes, or until it just flakes. Transfer the scrod with a slotted spatula to a plate and keep it warm, covered. Strain ½ cup of the cooking liquid into a blender and purée it with the cooked broccoli, the cream, and salt and pepper to taste. Transfer the sauce to a saucepan and cook it over moderately low heat, stirring, until it is heated through.

In a small saucepan of boiling salted water blanch the broccoli flowerets for 1 minute, drain them, and in a small bowl toss them with the remaining 1 tablespoon

butter and salt and pepper to taste. Cover the bottom of a heated platter with a layer of the sauce, arrange the scrod on top, and garnish the platter with the broccoli flowerets and 2 tablespoons of the bell pepper. Add the remaining bell pepper to the remaining sauce and serve it with the scrod. Serves 4.

Seafood Sausage with Lemon Herb Sauce

For the seafood sausage

½ pound sole fillets, cut into 1-inch pieces
¼ pound shrimp, shelled, deveined, and
 chopped coarse
½ pound salmon steak, skinned, boned, and
 chopped coarse
2 large eggs
¼ cup heavy cream
¼ teaspoon salt
¼ teaspoon white pepper
1 teaspoon minced fresh parsley leaves

For the sauce

¼ cup dry white wine
1 tablespoon fresh lemon juice
1 teaspoon white-wine vinegar
1 stick (½ cup) unsalted butter, cut into bits
½ teaspoon freshly grated lemon rind
1 teaspoon minced scallion
1 teaspoon minced fresh parsley leaves
1 teaspoon snipped fresh dill
cayenne to taste

For the garnish

4 cooked shrimp, shelled, leaving the tails
 intact
shredded scallion greens soaked in cold water
 for 5 minutes and patted dry

Make the seafood sausage: In a food processor purée the sole, scraping down the sides of the bowl several times, and in a bowl chill the purée, covered, for 30 minutes. In another bowl chill the shrimp and the salmon, covered, for 1 hour and 30 minutes. In the food processor blend the sole purée, the eggs, the cream, the salt, and the pepper until the mixture is combined well, transfer the mixture to a bowl, and chill it, covered, for 1 hour. Fold the shrimp, the salmon, and the parsley into the sole mixture, divide the mixture between two 12-inch-square sheets of Saran wrap, and form it into 2 logs using the Saran wrap to roll it, twisting the ends securely. Wrap each sausage securely in foil and poach the sausages in a kettle of simmering water for 10 to 15 minutes, or until a metal skewer inserted into the center

comes out hot. Transfer the sausages to a cutting board and let them stand for 10 minutes.

Make the sauce: In a small heavy saucepan boil the wine, the lemon juice, and the vinegar until the mixture is reduced by half, reduce the heat to low, and whisk in the butter, bit by bit, lifting the pan from the heat occasionally to keep the butter from liquefying. Whisk in the lemon rind, the scallion, the parsley, the dill, the cayenne, and salt to taste.

Pour the sauce onto a platter, on it arrange the sausages, unwrapped and cut into ¾-inch-thick slices with a serrated knife, and garnish the dish with the shrimp and the scallion greens. Serves 4 as a first course.

Seafood Stew

3 large garlic cloves, minced
2½ cups chopped onions
⅓ cup vegetable oil
1 pound boiling potatoes, peeled and cut into
 ½-inch cubes
3 carrots, 4 lengthwise grooves cut with a
 channel knife and cut crosswise into ¼-inch
 slices
2 cups bottled clam juice
a 28-ounce can plum tomatoes, chopped,
 including the juice
1 cup dry white wine
1 large green bell pepper, cut into matchsticks
1 pound mussels, cleaned (procedure on page
 137)
1½ pounds *lotte* (monkfish), cut into 1-inch
 pieces
6 ounces small shrimp, shelled and deveined
1 teaspoon crumbled dried tarragon
2 tablespoons Pernod or other anise-flavored
 liqueur if desired

In a flameproof 4-quart casserole cook the garlic and the onions in the oil over moderately low heat, stirring, until they are softened. Add the potatoes, the carrots, the clam juice, the tomatoes, and the wine, bring the liquid to a boil, and simmer the mixture for 40 minutes, or until the carrots and potatoes are tender. Add the bell pepper and the mussels, return the liquid to a simmer, and simmer the mixture, covered, for 2 minutes, or until the mussels begin to open. Add the *lotte*, the shrimp, the tarragon, and salt and pepper to taste and simmer the stew, covered, for 5 minutes, or until the *lotte* is opaque. Discard any unopened mussels and stir in the Pernod if desired. Serves 4 to 6.

Tuna and Red Pepper Pizzas

1 recipe pizza dough (page 127)
cornmeal for sprinkling the baking sheets
about ⅓ cup olive oil
¾ pound whole-milk mozzarella, sliced thin
4 garlic cloves if desired, minced
1 teaspoon dried thyme
two 6½-ounce cans tuna packed in oil, drained
1 cup drained and sliced bottled roasted red
    peppers
¼ cup freshly grated Parmesan

Divide the pizza dough into 4 balls, working with 1 ball at a time roll out each ball on a floured surface into a 6-inch round, leaving a slight rim, and stretch it gently into a 7-inch round. Transfer the rounds carefully to 2 large baking sheets liberally sprinkled with the cornmeal, and brush them lightly with some of the oil. Arrange one fourth of the mozzarella slices in one layer on each round, leaving a ½-inch border, sprinkle one fourth of the garlic if desired over each round, and crumble the thyme over the tops. Arrange the tuna and the red pepper slices over the mozzarella, sprinkle the tops with the Parmesan, and drizzle each pizza with about 1 teaspoon of the remaining oil. Bake the pizzas, 1 baking sheet at a time, on the floor of a preheated 500° F. gas oven or on the lowest shelf of a preheated 500° F. electric oven for 10 to 15 minutes, or until the bottom of the crust is golden brown and crisp. Serves 4.

Dilled Tuna Gratin with Orzo and Artichoke Hearts

a 9-ounce package frozen artichoke hearts
2 cups chicken stock (page 119) or canned
    chicken broth
1 cup thinly sliced scallions
2 tablespoons olive or vegetable oil
½ pound mushrooms, sliced thin
2 garlic cloves, minced
a 6½-ounce can tuna packed in olive oil,
    drained
1 cup *orzo* (rice-shaped pasta), cooked in
    boiling salted water until *al dente* and
    drained
3 tablespoons unsalted butter
¼ cup all-purpose flour
3 tablespoons fresh lemon juice
¾ cup freshly grated Parmesan
2 tablespoons snipped fresh dill
½ cup fine fresh bread crumbs

In a small saucepan combine the artichokes and the stock, bring the stock to a boil, and boil the artichokes for 7 to 8 minutes, or until they are tender. Transfer the artichokes with a slotted spoon to a cutting board, reserving the stock, chop them coarse, and put them in a large bowl.

In a large heavy skillet cook the scallions in the oil over moderate heat, stirring, for 1 minute. Add the mushrooms and the garlic, cook the mixture, stirring, until the liquid from the mushrooms is evaporated, and add the mixture to the artichokes with the tuna and the *orzo*.

In a small heavy saucepan melt the butter over moderately low heat, add the flour, and cook the *roux*, stirring, for 3 minutes. Add the reserved stock in a stream, whisking, and bring the mixture to a boil, whisking. Simmer the mixture, stirring, for 5 minutes, remove the pan from the heat, and stir in the lemon juice and ¼ cup of the Parmesan. Add the sauce to the tuna mixture with the dill and salt and pepper to taste, combine the mixture well, and transfer it to a buttered 1½-quart gratin dish. In a small bowl combine the remaining ½ cup Parmesan and the bread crumbs, sprinkle the mixture evenly over the tuna mixture, and bake the gratin in the middle of a preheated 400° F. oven for 30 minutes, or until the topping is golden. Serves 4 to 6.

Tuna Melt Croustades

4 French rolls, halved horizontally
two 6½-ounce cans tuna packed in oil, drained
1 cup minced celery
⅔ cup thinly sliced scallions
¾ cup mayonnaise (page 232)
2 tablespoons Dijon-style mustard
1 tablespoon fresh lemon juice, or to taste
6 ounces Münster, cut into 8 slices

With a fork remove the soft crumb from the rolls, leaving a ¼-inch shell, and reserve it for another use. In a bowl combine well the tuna, the celery, the scallions, ½ cup of the mayonnaise, the mustard, the lemon juice, and salt and pepper to taste. Brush the insides of the rolls with the remaining ¼ cup mayonnaise, divide the tuna mixture among the rolls, mounding it slightly, and top each croustade with a slice of the Münster. Bake the croustades on a baking sheet in a preheated 350° F. oven for 25 minutes, or until the filling is puffed slightly and the Münster is bubbly. Serves 8 as a luncheon entrée.

Pan-Fried Brook Trout with Bacon

8 slices of lean bacon
four ¾-pound brook trout, cleaned
1 cup milk
1 cup crushed Triscuit cracker crumbs

In a large skillet cook the bacon over moderately low heat, turning it, until it is just crisp and transfer it to paper towels to drain. Dip the trout in the milk and dredge them in the crumbs, packing the crumbs well onto all sides to form a thick coating. In the fat remaining in the skillet sauté the trout over moderate heat for 5 to 6 minutes on each side, or until they are golden brown and just flake when tested, and serve them with the bacon, crumbled. Serves 4.

SHELLFISH

Portuguese Clams with Parsnips and Carrots

1 cup finely chopped onions
¼ cup olive oil
¼ pound carrots, grated coarse, preferably in a
  food processor
¼ pound parsnips, grated coarse, preferably in
  a food processor
2 garlic cloves, minced
1 cup dry white wine
2 cups chicken stock (page 119) or canned
  chicken broth
24 small hard-shelled clams
3 tablespoons chopped fresh coriander leaves
2 tablespoons fresh lemon juice

In a large kettle cook the onions in the oil over moderately low heat, stirring, until they are softened, add the carrots, the parsnips, and the garlic, and cook the mixture, stirring, for 3 minutes. Add the wine, 1 cup of the stock, and the clams and cook the mixture, covered, over high heat, transferring the clams to a bowl as they open, for 20 to 30 minutes, or until the clams are opened. Discard any unopened clams and return the opened clams to the kettle. Add the remaining 1 cup stock, the coriander, and the lemon juice and heat the mixture until it is hot. Transfer the clams to heated bowls and pour the liquid over them. Serves 4 as a first course or 2 as an entrée.

Lobster Stew sous Croûte

1 recipe *pâte brisée* (page 274)
1 cup chopped onion
¼ cup chopped carrot
¼ cup chopped celery
2 garlic cloves, crushed
1 teaspoon salt
2 cups dry white wine
1 teaspoon crumbled dried tarragon
a pinch of cayenne
1 tablespoon tomato paste
a 2-pound lobster
2 leeks, halved lengthwise, cut into 1-inch
    pieces, and rinsed well
½ pound Jerusalem artichokes, peeled, sliced,
    and reserved in a bowl of acidulated water
½ pound small mushrooms, cut into quarters
a 1-pound can plum tomatoes, drained,
    seeded, and chopped
2 tablespoons softened unsalted butter
3 tablespoons flour
3 tablespoons heavy cream
1 tablespoon fresh lemon juice
1 large egg yolk
2 tablespoons minced fresh parsley leaves

On a lightly floured surface roll out the dough ⅛ inch thick and cut out 4 decorative shapes. Transfer the dough shapes to a baking sheet and freeze them, covered with plastic wrap, for at least 30 minutes or overnight.

In a kettle combine the onion, the carrot, the celery, the garlic, the salt, the wine, the tarragon, the cayenne, the tomato paste, and enough water to measure 2 inches liquid and bring the liquid to a boil. Plunge the lobster headfirst into the liquid, return the liquid to a boil, and cook the lobster, covered, for 8 minutes. (The meat will not be completely cooked.) Transfer the lobster immediately with tongs to cold water to stop further cooking and, working over a bowl to catch and reserve the juices, remove all the meat from the claws and tail. Reserve the shells. Chop coarse the lobster meat and keep it covered and chilled. Discard the tomalley, the coral (if any), and the sac behind the head and chop coarse all the shells. Add the chopped shells and the reserved juices to the liquid in the kettle, bring the liquid to a boil, and simmer it, skimming it occasionally, for 1 hour, or until it is reduced to about 2 cups. Strain the stock through a fine sieve into a saucepan, pressing hard on the solids, and discard the solids. Add the leeks, the Je-

rusalem artichokes, drained, the mushrooms, and the tomatoes and simmer the mixture until the Jerusalem artichokes are tender. In a small bowl knead together the butter and the flour, bring the stock mixture to a boil, and into it whisk bits of the *beurre manié*, whisking the mixture until it is thickened slightly. Stir in 2 tablespoons of the cream and boil the mixture for 3 minutes. Add the lemon juice, the lobster meat, and salt and pepper to taste, cook the stew over moderately low heat, stirring, until the lobster is just heated through, and keep it warm. *The stew may be made up to 1 day in advance, kept covered and chilled, and reheated over low heat.*

In a small bowl whisk together the egg yolk and the remaining 1 tablespoon cream, brush the top of the dough shapes with the egg wash, and bake the pastry in a preheated 425° F. oven for 10 to 12 minutes, or until it is golden. Divide the stew between 2 heated dishes, sprinkle it with the parsley, and garnish it with the decorative pastry. Serves 2.

Fried Oysters with Tartar Sauce

1 cup all-purpose flour
1 teaspoon salt
¼ teaspoon cayenne, or to taste
1 cup beer
32 oysters, shucked (procedure on page 137),
    and, 40 of the half shells reserved, washed
    well, and dried
vegetable oil for frying
tartar sauce (recipe follows) as an
    accompaniment
flat-leafed parsley leaves for garnish

In a bowl whisk together the flour, the salt, and the cayenne, add the beer, and whisk the mixture until it is smooth. Let the batter stand, covered, at room temperature for at least 1 hour or up to 3 hours and stir it well.

Pat the oysters dry carefully on paper towels. In a large skillet heat ½ inch of the oil to 375° F. In batches dip the oysters in the batter, coating them well and letting any excess drip off, and fry them in the oil, turning them, for 1 minute, or until they are golden and crisp. Transfer the oysters with a slotted spoon as they are fried to paper towels to drain. Arrange 5 of the reserved oyster shells on each of 8 plates, top 4 of the shells on each plate with a fried oyster, and fill the remaining shells with the tartar sauce. Garnish the tartar sauce with the parsley and serve the oysters immediately. Serves 8 as a first course.

Tartar Sauce

1 large egg yolk at room temperature
2 teaspoons white-wine vinegar, plus
    additional to taste
2 teaspoons Dijon-style mustard, or to taste
¾ cup vegetable oil
2 sweet gherkins, minced
2 tablespoons minced scallion including the
    green tops
2 shallots, minced
1 tablespoon minced fresh parsley leaves
2 teaspoons minced capers
2 teaspoons grated onion
½ teaspoon crumbled dried tarragon
½ teaspoon sugar
½ teaspoon salt, or to taste
1 hard-boiled large egg yolk, chopped fine
white pepper to taste

Rinse a mixing bowl with hot water and dry it well. In the bowl combine the raw egg yolk, 1 teaspoon of the vinegar, and the mustard and beat the mixture vigorously with a whisk or an electric mixer at high speed until it is combined. Add ⅓ cup of the oil, drop by drop, beating constantly, add 1 teaspoon of the remaining vinegar, and add the remaining oil in a slow stream, beating constantly. Stir in the gherkins, the scallion, the shallots, the parsley, the capers, the onion, the tarragon, the sugar, and the salt, combine the mixture well, and fold in the hard-boiled egg yolk. Season the tartar sauce with the additional vinegar, the white pepper, and salt to taste. *The sauce may be made up to 2 days in advance and kept covered and chilled.* Makes about 1 cup.

Jalapeño Scallop Mousses with Shrimp

4 shrimp
½ pound sea scallops, rinsed and patted dry
½ teaspoon salt
a pinch of freshly grated nutmeg
1 cup well chilled heavy cream
1 tablespoon seeded and minced pickled
    jalapeño pepper (wear rubber gloves)
2 tablespoons minced scallion
1 tablespoon minced fresh parsley leaves
light tomato sauce (page 134) as an
    accompaniment

Into a saucepan of boiling water plunge the shrimp, boil them for 15 seconds, and drain them. Let the shrimp cool, shell them, and halve them horizontally, deveining them.

If necessary, discard the tough bit of muscle clinging to the side of each scallop and in a food processor purée the scallops with the salt and the nutmeg. With the motor running add the cream in a stream and blend the mixture until it is just smooth, scraping down the sides of the processor with a rubber spatula. Add the *jalapeño* pepper, the scallion, and the parsley and process the mixture until it is just combined.

Arrange 1 shrimp half, pink side down, in the bottom of each of 8 buttered ⅓-cup muffin tins and fill the tins with the scallop mousse, rapping the pan gently on a hard surface to expel any air bubbles and smoothing the tops. Cover the pan with a buttered piece of wax paper and a layer of foil, put it in a baking pan just large enough to hold it, and add enough hot water to the baking pan to come halfway up the sides of the muffin pan. Bake the mousses in a preheated 300° F. oven for 15 to 20 minutes, or until a skewer inserted in the center comes out clean. *The mousses may be made up to this point 1 day in advance and kept covered and chilled. Reheat the mousses in a pan of hot water in a preheated 300° F. oven for 10 minutes, or until they are heated through.* Run a thin knife around each mousse to loosen it, invert a baking sheet over the pan, and invert the mousses onto the sheet. Divide the mousses among 4 heated plates, transferring them with a slotted spatula, and spoon the tomato sauce around them. Serves 4.

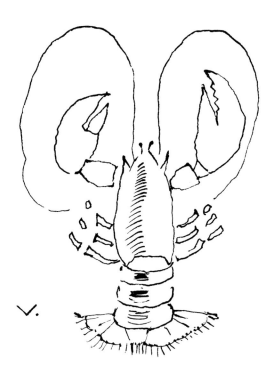

Light Tomato Sauce

¼ cup minced onion
¼ cup minced carrot
¼ cup minced celery
1 small garlic clove, minced
1½ tablespoons unsalted butter
¼ cup dry white wine
a 1-pound can tomatoes, puréed in a blender
    or food processor
¼ teaspoon crumbled dried basil
⅛ teaspoon crumbled dried thyme

In a heavy skillet cook the onion, the carrot, the celery, and the garlic in the butter, covered, over moderately low heat, stirring occasionally, for 5 minutes, or until the vegetables are softened. Add the wine, the tomatoes, the basil, the thyme, and salt and pepper to taste, bring the mixture to a boil, and simmer it, stirring occasionally, for 15 minutes. Purée the sauce in a blender or food processor and strain it through a fine sieve into a saucepan, pressing hard on the solids. Reheat the sauce over low heat, stirring, until it is heated through. *The sauce may be made up to 3 days in advance and kept covered and chilled.* Makes about 1⅓ cups.

Scallops with Shallots and Garlic

3 tablespoons unsalted butter
¾ pound sea scallops, rinsed, patted dry, and
    quartered
¼ teaspoon Worcestershire sauce
2 garlic cloves, minced
3 tablespoons minced shallots
¼ cup minced fresh parsley leaves
1 teaspoon fresh lemon juice

In a heavy skillet heat 1½ tablespoons of the butter over moderately high heat until the foam subsides, in it sauté the scallops in batches for 1 minute, and transfer them to a plate. To the skillet add the remaining 1½ tablespoons butter and the Worcestershire sauce and in the mixture cook the garlic, the shallots, and the parsley over moderately low heat, stirring, for 2 to 3 minutes, or until the shallots are softened. Stir in the lemon juice, the scallops, and salt and pepper to taste and heat the mixture, stirring, until the scallops are just heated through. Serves 2.

Shellfish in Saffron Broth

1 dozen small hard-shelled clams, scrubbed
1 dozen mussels, cleaned (procedure on
    page 137)
½ cup dry white wine
¼ cup chopped onion
1 garlic clove, minced
1 carrot, cut into julienne strips
1 stalk of celery, cut into julienne strips
¼ cup julienne red bell pepper strips
1 small boiling potato, peeled and diced
2 tablespoons unsalted butter
3 cups canned chicken broth
⅛ teaspoon crumbled saffron threads
    dissolved in ¼ cup hot water
¼ pound large shrimp
¼ pound sea scallops
1 tablespoon minced scallion
1 teaspoon minced fresh parsley leaves
1 tablespoon snipped fresh dill plus 2 dill
    sprigs for garnish
fennel seed and pepper toasts (page 108) as an
    accompaniment

In a large saucepan steam the clams and the mussels in the wine, covered tightly, over moderately high heat, shaking the pan occasionally, for 5 to 6 minutes, or until the clams and mussels have opened. Discard any unopened shells and reserve 4 clams and 4 mussels in their shells for garnish. Remove the remaining clams and mussels from their shells and reserve them in a small bowl. Strain the cooking liquid into another small bowl and reserve it. In the saucepan cook the onion, the garlic, the carrot, the celery, the bell pepper, and the potato in the butter, covered, over moderately low heat, stirring, for 10 minutes, or until the vegetables are tender, stir in the broth and the saffron mixture, and bring the liquid to a boil. Add the shrimp and the scallops, simmer the mixture for 2 to 3 minutes, or until the shrimp

are pink, and stir in the reserved shelled clams and mussels, the scallion, the parsley, the snipped dill, and the reserved cooking liquid to taste. (The cooking liquid may be very salty.) Ladle the mixture into heated shallow bowls, garnish it with the reserved clams and mussels in their shells and the dill sprigs, and serve it with the toasts. Serves 2.

Baked Spiced Shrimp

½ cup loosely packed fresh parsley leaves
1 small onion, chopped
1 garlic clove, chopped
½ teaspoon dried dill
½ teaspoon mustard seed
½ teaspoon ground coriander
¼ teaspoon cayenne
¼ teaspoon ground allspice
⅛ teaspoon ground cloves
½ teaspoon salt
2 tablespoons white-wine vinegar
⅓ cup olive oil
¾ pound (about 12) large shrimp
1 bay leaf
French bread as an accompaniment

In a food processor or blender blend well the parsley, the onion, the garlic, the dill, the mustard seed, the coriander, the cayenne, the allspice, the cloves, the salt, and the vinegar, scraping down the sides with a rubber spatula, with the motor running add the oil in a stream, and blend the mixture until it is emulsified. In a baking dish large enough to hold the shrimp in one layer toss together the shrimp, the spice mixture, and the bay leaf and bake the shrimp in a preheated 375° F. oven for 15 to 20 minutes, or until they are opaque. Discard the bay leaf and serve the shrimp with the bread. Serves 2.

Oriental-Style Shrimp with Radishes and Peas

⅓ cup long-grain rice
2 teaspoons soy sauce
1½ tablespoons Scotch
1 teaspoon Oriental sesame oil (available at many supermarkets, Oriental markets, and specialty foods shops)
2½ tablespoons canned chicken broth or water
½ teaspoon sugar
½ teaspoon salt
2 tablespoons vegetable oil
½ pound (about 22) small shrimp, shelled, deveined, and patted dry
the white part of 1 scallion, minced
2 ounces radishes, trimmed, halved lengthwise, and cut crosswise into very thin slices (about ½ cup)
½ cup frozen peas, thawed
the green part of 1 scallion, sliced thin

In a saucepan bring ⅔ cup water to a boil, stir in the rice, and simmer it, covered, for 20 minutes, or until it is tender and the liquid is absorbed. In a small bowl combine the soy sauce, the Scotch, the sesame oil, and the broth and in the mixture dissolve the sugar and the salt. In a large heavy skillet heat the vegetable oil over high heat until it is hot but not smoking, in it cook the shrimp, turning them once, for 1 minute, and transfer them to a bowl. Let the skillet cool for 1 minute, add the white part of the scallion and the radishes, and sauté the vegetables over high heat, stirring, for 20 seconds. Add the soy mixture, the shrimp, and any juices that have accumulated in the bowl, reduce the liquid to about ¼ cup, and stir in the peas and the green part of the scallion. Arrange the rice around the edges of 2 dishes and spoon the shrimp mixture into the center of the dishes. Serves 2.

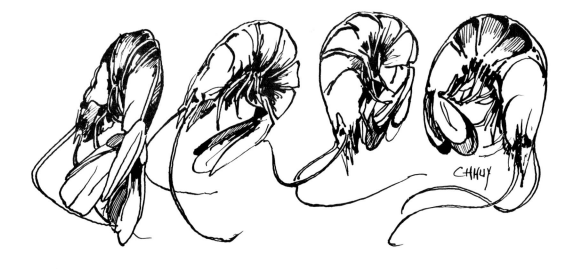

Spiced Shrimp with Papaya and Curry Mayonnaise

½ lemon, quartered
2 tablespoons salt
½ teaspoon cayenne
½ bay leaf
¾ pound (about 12) large shrimp
1½ teaspoons cider vinegar
¼ teaspoon honey
1 teaspoon curry powder
¾ cup quick mayonnaise (page 232)
3 cups thinly sliced iceberg lettuce
1 small papaya, peeled and sliced

To a large saucepan of cold water add the lemon, the salt, the cayenne, the bay leaf, and pepper to taste, bring the liquid to a boil, and boil the mixture for 1 minute. Add the shrimp, cook them for 2 to 3 minutes, or until they are just firm, and drain them well, discarding the lemon and the bay leaf. Let the shrimp cool until they can be handled, shell them, and halve them lengthwise, discarding the vein. In a small bowl whisk together the vinegar, the honey, 2 teaspoons water, and the curry powder until the honey is dissolved and whisk in the mayonnaise. On 2 chilled plates arrange the lettuce, the shrimp, and the papaya, spoon about one third of the curry mayonnaise on each plate, and serve the remaining mayonnaise in a sauceboat. Serves 2.

Rosemary Shrimp

2 garlic cloves, minced
2 tablespoons minced fresh rosemary leaves or
    1 tablespoon crumbled dried
¼ cup dry white wine
2 tablespoons fresh lemon juice
⅓ cup olive oil
1 pound medium shrimp, unshelled
lemon wedges and fresh rosemary sprigs for
    garnish
toasted *pita* triangles as an accompaniment

In a small bowl combine the garlic, the minced or crumbled rosemary, the wine, the lemon juice, and salt and pepper to taste. In a large skillet heat the oil over high heat until it is hot, in it sauté the shrimp, stirring, for 3 minutes, or until they have turned pink, and add the rosemary mixture. Transfer the mixture to a shallow baking dish large enough to hold the shrimp in one layer and let the shrimp marinate, covered and chilled, stirring occasionally, for at least 1 hour or overnight. Arrange the shrimp on a platter and garnish them with the

lemon wedges and the rosemary sprigs. Serve the shrimp at room temperature with the toasted *pita*. Serves 4.

Stir-Fried Shrimp and Snow Peas in Bird's Nest

¼ cup dried wood ears or tree ears*
For the shrimp
1½ pounds (about 42) shrimp, shelled,
    deveined, rinsed, and squeezed dry in a dish
    towel
1 tablespoon cornstarch
1 large egg white
¼ teaspoon salt
For the sauce
1 tablespoon cornstarch
1 cup Chinese chicken broth (page 125) or
    canned chicken broth
3 tablespoons rice wine (available at Oriental
    markets and some liquor stores) or Scotch
1 tablespoon soy sauce
¾ teaspoon sugar
¼ teaspoon salt

3 cups vegetable oil, preferably safflower or
    corn oil
2 ounces rice vermicelli,* broken into small
    handfuls
3 tablespoons minced scallion
2 tablespoons minced peeled gingerroot
1 tablespoon minced garlic
½ pound snow peas, strings discarded,
    blanched for 1 second in boiling water,
    drained, refreshed under cold water, and
    patted dry
a 15-ounce can baby corn,* drained, blanched
    in boiling water for 5 seconds, drained,
    refreshed under cold water, and halved
    lengthwise
2 teaspoons Oriental sesame oil*
2 teaspoons rice vinegar*

*available at Oriental markets, some specialty
    foods shops, and some supermarkets

In a small bowl let the wood ears soak in 2 cups hot water for 20 minutes, or until they are soft and spongy, and drain them. Cut off and discard any hard edges and chop the wood ears. *The wood ears may be prepared up to this point 1 day in advance and kept covered and chilled.*

Prepare the shrimp: In a bowl combine the shrimp, the cornstarch, the egg white, and the salt, stirring vigorously in one direction until the shrimp are coated well with the mixture, and chill the shrimp, covered, for at least 30 minutes. *The shrimp may be prepared up to this point 1 day in advance and kept covered tightly and chilled.*

Make the sauce: In a small bowl dissolve the cornstarch in the broth and add the rice wine, the soy sauce, the sugar, and the salt.

Heat a wok over high heat until it is hot, add the vegetable oil, and heat it until a deep-fat thermometer registers 425° F. Add a handful of the rice vermicelli and fry it for 1 to 2 seconds, or until it puffs and turns white. (The noodles will splutter and expand rapidly.) Transfer the noodles with a wire skimmer as they are fried to paper towels to drain and fry and drain the remaining noodles in the same manner. *The noodles may be fried up to 2 days in advance and kept in an airtight container or sealable plastic bag in a cool, dry place.* Just before serving, break up the noodles and arrange them in a large nest on a platter.

Pour off all but 1 cup of the oil in the wok and heat the remaining oil over high heat until a deep-fat thermometer registers 380° F. Add the shrimp and stir-fry them for 1 minute, or until they separate and turn pink. Transfer the shrimp with a slotted spoon to a large sieve set over a bowl. *The shrimp may be prepared up to this point 4 hours in advance and kept in a bowl, covered and chilled.* Pour off all but 3 tablespoons of the oil from the wok and heat the remaining oil over high heat until it is just smoking. Add the scallion, the gingerroot, and the garlic and stir-fry the mixture for 5 seconds, or until it is fragrant. Add the wood ears and stir-fry the mixture for 5 seconds. Stir the sauce, add it to the wok, stirring, and bring it to a boil, stirring. Add the snow peas, the corn, and the shrimp and cook the mixture, stirring, for 1 minute, or until it is heated through. Drizzle the mix-

ture with the sesame oil and the vinegar, toss it, and mound it in the center of the noodle nest. Serves 8.

PROCEDURES

To Clean Mussels

Scrub the mussels well in several changes of water, scrape off the beards, and rinse the mussels. If the mussels are exceptionally dirty, let them soak in cold water to cover, with ⅓ cup salt and 1 tablespoon cornmeal per gallon water, for 2 hours to help them disgorge any sand. Drain the mussels and rinse them well under cold water.

To Steam Open Mussels

In a kettle steam the mussels, covered, over high heat, shaking the kettle once or twice, for 5 to 6 minutes, or until the shells have opened. Discard any unopened shells.

To Shuck Oysters

Scrub the oysters thoroughly with a stiff brush under running cold water and break off the thin end of the shells. Hold each oyster in the palm of the hand with the hinged end facing you, force an oyster knife between the shells at the broken end, and twist it to force the shells apart, cutting the large muscle close to the flat upper shell. Break off and discard the flat shell and slide the knife under the oyster to release it.

To Clean Squid

Pull the head and body of the squid apart, cut off the tentacles just below the eyes, and reserve the tentacles and body sac. Discard the transparent quill from inside the body sac, rinse the body sac well, and peel off the purple membrane covering it. Pull off the flaps gently from the body sac to avoid tearing the sac and reserve them.

MEAT

BEEF

Beef and Broccoli Burritos with Monterey Jack Sauce

For the filling
a ½-pound piece of boneless chuck, cut into
　¼-inch cubes
1 tablespoon vegetable oil
1¼ cups finely chopped broccoli
1 small garlic clove, minced
1 small onion, minced
½ cup canned tomato purée
½ teaspoon chili powder, or to taste
¼ teaspoon ground cumin

For the sauce
3 ounces Monterey Jack, grated
½ cup sour cream
1 tablespoon drained, seeded, and chopped
　jalapeño pepper (wear rubber gloves)
2 teaspoons fresh lemon juice

four 8-inch flour tortillas

Make the filling: In a large heavy skillet cook the chuck in the oil over moderately high heat, stirring, until it is just browned, add the broccoli, the garlic, the onion, the tomato purée, the chili powder, the cumin, salt to taste, and ½ cup water, and cook the mixture, covered, over moderate heat for 15 to 17 minutes, or until the filling is thickened. Keep the filling warm, covered, over low heat.

Make the sauce: In a small saucepan combine the Monterey Jack, the sour cream, the *jalapeño* pepper, and the lemon juice, heat the mixture over moderately low heat, stirring occasionally, until the cheese is melted, and keep the sauce warm, covered, over low heat. Do not let the sauce boil.

Heat a dry 8-inch heavy skillet over moderately high heat until it is hot, in it heat 1 of the tortillas, turning it frequently, for 30 seconds, or until it is softened, and transfer it to a work surface. Spoon one fourth of the filling on the tortilla and roll up the *burrito*. Assemble the remaining *burritos* in the same manner, arrange them seam side down on a platter, and nap them with the sauce. Serves 2.

Moroccan Beef and Vegetable Stew with Couscous

2 acorn squash, halved and seeded
1 tablespoon vegetable oil
1 cup chopped celery including some of the
  leaves
2 onions, chopped
2 pounds boneless beef chuck, cut into 2-inch
  pieces
1 stick (½ cup) unsalted butter
3 parsley sprigs
3 coriander sprigs
a 3-inch cinnamon stick
⅛ teaspoon cayenne
a pinch of saffron threads, crumbled
a 35-ounce can plum tomatoes including the
  juice
6 carrots, cut into 1-inch pieces
4 small turnips, peeled and cut into 1-inch
  pieces
¾ cup raisins
2 red bell peppers, seeded and cut into 1-inch
  pieces
a 19-ounce can chick-peas, drained, rinsed,
  and, if desired, skins removed
4 small zucchini, cut crosswise into ¾-inch
  pieces
3 tablespoons minced fresh parsley leaves
3 tablespoons minced fresh coriander leaves
2½ cups couscous
Moroccan-style hot spiced oil (recipe follows)
  as an accompaniment if desired

In a shallow roasting pan arrange the acorn squash cut side up, drizzle it with the vegetable oil, and sprinkle it with salt and pepper. Bake the squash in a preheated 400° F. oven for 40 minutes, or until it is just tender, and let it cool. Quarter the squash, discard the skin, and reserve the squash, covered and chilled.

In a kettle cook the celery, the onions, and the chuck in the butter with salt and pepper to taste over moderately low heat, stirring occasionally, for 5 minutes. Tie together the parsley sprigs, the coriander sprigs, and the cinnamon stick, add the spice bundle to the kettle with the cayenne and the saffron, and cook the mixture, stirring occasionally, for 10 minutes. Add the tomatoes with their juice and 4 cups water, bring the liquid to a boil, and simmer the mixture, covered, skimming the froth, for 1 hour. Add the carrots and the turnips and simmer the mixture, stirring occasionally, for 30 minutes, or until the chuck is very tender. *The stew mixture*

may be prepared up to this point and kept covered and chilled for up to 3 days.

Bring the mixture to a boil and skim off 1¾ cups of the cooking liquid, reserving it for cooking the couscous. Stir in the raisins and the bell peppers and simmer the mixture for 5 minutes. Stir in the chick-peas and the zucchini and simmer the mixture for 5 minutes. Stir in the minced parsley, the minced coriander, and the acorn squash, simmer the stew until the squash is heated through, and discard the spice bundle.

In a large saucepan bring the reserved cooking liquid to a boil, stir in the couscous, and remove the pan from the heat. Let the couscous stand for 4 minutes and fluff it with a fork. Serve the couscous with the stew and drizzle the spiced oil over each serving if desired. Serves 6 to 8.

Moroccan-Style Hot Spiced Oil

1 teaspoon caraway seeds
2 tablespoons cayenne, or to taste
1 tablespoon ground cumin
1 garlic clove
½ teaspoon salt
½ cup olive oil

In a blender blend the caraway seeds, the cayenne, the cumin, the garlic, and the salt until the caraway seeds are ground fine, with the motor running add the oil in a stream, and blend the mixture for 30 seconds. Transfer the oil to a jar. *The spiced oil keeps, covered and chilled, for up to 1 week.* Stir the spiced oil before serving. Makes about ¾ cup.

Beef Pie with Corn Custard

2 tablespoons bacon fat or vegetable oil
1½ pounds very lean ground beef
2 onions, chopped
1 small red bell pepper, chopped
3 garlic cloves, minced
1½ teaspoons salt
1 teaspoon ground cumin
1 teaspoon cinnamon
½ teaspoon crumbled dried orégano
2 tablespoons red-wine vinegar
1 pound tomatoes, peeled, seeded, and
  chopped
⅓ to ½ cup beer
¼ teaspoon cayenne, or to taste
¼ cup raisíns
¼ cup (10 to 12) pimiento-stuffed olives,
  sliced thick
¼ cup minced fresh parsley leaves (or a
  mixture of fresh parsley and fresh
  coriander)
For the custard
4 cups corn (cut from about 7 ears of corn)
1 stick (½ cup) unsalted butter
2 teaspoons sugar
1 teaspoon salt
4 large eggs, beaten lightly

sweet paprika to taste

In a large skillet heat the fat over moderately high heat until it is hot but not smoking and in it cook the beef, stirring, for 2 to 3 minutes, or until half the beef is browned lightly. Add the onions and the bell pepper and cook the mixture over moderate heat, stirring, for 5 to 7 minutes, or until the onion is softened. Add the garlic, the salt, the cumin, the cinnamon, and the orégano, cook the mixture, stirring, for 2 minutes, and add the vinegar. Cook the mixture, stirring, until most of the liquid is evaporated, add the tomatoes, and simmer the mixture for 2 minutes. Add ⅓ cup of the beer, bring the liquid to a boil, and simmer the mixture, covered partially, for 10 minutes. The mixture should be thick but not dry. If the mixture is dry add the remaining beer. Add the cayenne, the raisins, the olives, the parsley, and salt to taste.

Make the custard: In a food processor or blender purée 3 cups of the corn. In a heavy saucepan melt the butter and in it cook the corn purée with the sugar and the salt over low heat, stirring, until the mixture is com-

bined. Add the remaining 1 cup corn, stir in the eggs, a little at a time, and cook the mixture over low heat, stirring, for 2 to 3 minutes, or until it is thickened slightly. Let the custard cool.

Spoon one third of the custard into a buttered 2-quart soufflé dish, smoothing the top, and add half the beef mixture. Continue to make layers, alternating the custard and the beef mixture and ending with the custard. Sprinkle the custard with the paprika and bake the pie in a preheated 375° F. oven for 40 to 45 minutes, or until it is golden and the custard is set. Let the pie stand for 10 minutes before serving. Serves 6 to 8.

Beef Stew with Root Vegetables

2 tablespoons vegetable oil
6 small white onions (about 1½ inches in
  diameter), blanched in boiling water for 30
  seconds and peeled
6 turnips, cut into 1½-inch pieces
3 large carrots, cut crosswise into 1½-inch
  pieces
1 tablespoon flour
¾ cup dry red wine
1½ cups brown stock (page 118) or canned
  beef broth
1 parsley sprig plus ¼ cup
  finely chopped fresh parsley leaves
½ bay leaf
½ teaspoon crumbled dried thyme
2 pounds boneless beef chuck, cut into 1-inch
  cubes

In a flameproof 4-quart casserole heat the oil over moderately high heat until it is hot but not smoking and in it brown the onions, the turnips, and the carrots in batches, transferring them with a slotted spoon as they are browned to a bowl. Remove the casserole from the heat, stir in the flour, and return the casserole to the heat. Stir in the wine, the stock, the parsley sprig, the bay leaf, the thyme, and the beef, bring the liquid to a boil, and bake the mixture, covered, in a preheated 325° F. oven for 30 minutes. Stir in the vegetables and bake the stew for 1 hour and 30 minutes, or until the meat is tender. (The stew improves in flavor if cooled to room temperature, uncovered, and chilled, covered, overnight.) Discard the bay leaf and stir in the chopped parsley and salt and pepper to taste. Serves 4 to 6.

Filets Mignons Persillés

For the persillé topping
¼ cup coarse fresh bread crumbs, toasted
¼ cup freshly grated Parmesan
1 tablespoon drained capers, minced
1 tablespoon minced pimiento
2 anchovy fillets, minced
½ teaspoon minced garlic
1 tablespoon olive oil
1 tablespoon unsalted butter
1 tablespoon minced fresh basil leaves
2 tablespoons minced fresh parsley leaves

4 slices of lean bacon
four 6-ounce filets mignons
2 tablespoons olive oil

Make the *persillé* topping: In a bowl combine the bread crumbs and the Parmesan. In a small saucepan combine the capers, the pimiento, the anchovies, the garlic, the oil, and the butter, cook the mixture over moderately low heat, stirring, until the butter is melted, and let it cool. Stir the mixture into the crumb mixture, add the basil and the parsley, and toss the topping.

Wrap a slice of the bacon around the edge of each filet mignon and secure it with kitchen string. In a heavy skillet heat the oil over moderately high heat until it is hot but not smoking and in it sear the filets for 1 minute on each side. Reduce the heat to moderate and cook the filets, turning them on their sides to cook the bacon, for 5 minutes more for rare meat. Transfer the filets to the rack of a broiler pan, top them with the *persillé* mixture,

and broil them under a preheated broiler about 3 inches from the heat for 2 to 3 minutes, or until the topping is golden. Discard the string just before serving. Serves 4.

Roast Prime Ribs of Beef with Cracked Pepper Crust

a 4-rib standing rib roast (trimmed weight about 10 to 10½ pounds)
1 tablespoon black peppercorns, ground coarse
2 teaspoons dried green peppercorns (available at specialty foods shops), ground coarse
1 teaspoon white peppercorns, ground coarse
4 whole allspice, ground coarse
½ teaspoon dried thyme
1 teaspoon coarse salt
¾ pound very small carrots, peeled, trimmed, blanched in boiling salted water for 4 minutes, and refreshed under cold water
1 head of garlic, separated into cloves, blanched in boiling water for 5 minutes, refreshed under cold water, and peeled
½ pound large shallots, blanched in boiling water for 3 minutes, refreshed under cold water, and peeled
For the sauce
½ cup dry red wine
2 cups canned beef broth
6 tablespoons Madeira
1 tablespoon arrowroot
2 tablespoons Dijon-style mustard

fresh thyme sprigs for garnish

Let the meat stand at room temperature for 1 hour. In a small bowl combine the black pepper, the green pepper, the white pepper, the allspice, the thyme, and the salt and rub the meat with the mixture. Roast the meat rib side down in a roasting pan in a preheated 500° F. oven for 30 minutes, reduce the heat to 350° F., and roast the meat for 1 hour and 45 minutes to 2 hours more, or until a meat thermometer inserted in the fleshy part of the meat registers 130° F. for medium-rare. Twenty minutes before the roast is done add to the pan the carrots, the garlic, and the shallots, all patted dry. (Remove the vegetables with a slotted spoon if they brown too quickly.) Transfer the roast to a heated platter, drain the vegetables on paper towels, and keep them warm, covered loosely. Let the roast rest for at least 20 minutes or up to 30 minutes before carving it.

Make the sauce: Skim the fat from the pan juices, add the red wine, and deglaze the pan over moderately high heat, scraping up the brown bits. Boil the liquid until it is reduced by half and transfer it to a saucepan. Add the broth and ¼ cup of the Madeira and boil the mixture for 5 minutes. In a small bowl stir together the remaining 2 tablespoons Madeira, the arrowroot, and the mustard and add the mixture to the pan in a stream, whisking. Bring the sauce to a boil, whisking, and boil it for 1 minute. Season the sauce with salt and pepper and transfer it to a heated sauceboat. Arrange the roasted vegetables around the roast with the fresh thyme and serve the roast with the sauce. Serves 8 generously.

Cajun-Style Round Steak with Rusty Gravy and Mashed Potatoes

½ pound boiling potatoes, peeled and cut into
   ¼-inch dice
2 tablespoons milk
1½ tablespoons unsalted butter
2 tablespoons vegetable oil
a ½-inch-thick piece of top round steak (about
   ½ pound), halved crosswise
3 tablespoons finely chopped green bell
   pepper
1 small onion, chopped fine
cayenne to taste

In a saucepan of boiling salted water cook the potatoes for 10 to 12 minutes, or until they are tender, drain them, and transfer them to a metal bowl. In a small saucepan heat the milk and the butter over moderate heat, stirring, until the butter is melted. With a fork mash the potatoes, leaving some lumps, and stir in the milk mixture and salt and pepper to taste. Keep the potatoes warm, covered, in the bowl set in another bowl of hot water.

In a heavy skillet heat the oil over moderately high heat until it is hot but not smoking and in it brown the steak for 2 to 3 minutes on each side. Transfer the steak to a plate and in the oil sauté the bell pepper and the onion, stirring, until they are softened. Return the steak and any juices that have accumulated on the plate to the skillet, add ¼ cup water, and cook the steak, covered, over moderately high heat until the liquid is reduced to a glaze. Add ¼ cup water, turn the steak, and cook it, covered, until the liquid is reduced to a glaze. Repeat this procedure, using ½ cup more water, ¼ cup at a time. Add an additional ¼ cup water, the cayenne, and salt to taste and cook the gravy until it returns to a boil. Arrange the steak on 2 heated plates. Mound half the pota-

toes on each plate, make a depression in each mound with the back of a spoon, and fill the depression with the vegetables and gravy. Serves 2.

Shepherd's Pie Crêpes

For the potato filling
1½ cups boiled and mashed baking potatoes
   (about 1 pound raw)
3 tablespoons unsalted butter, melted
¼ cup milk
1 large egg, beaten lightly
½ cup minced scallion
For the beef filling
1 onion, minced
1 tablespoon beef drippings or butter
2 cups (about ¾ pound) finely chopped
   leftover roast beef
¼ teaspoon crumbled dried thyme
2 teaspoons Worcestershire sauce
½ cup leftover beef gravy
½ cup thawed frozen peas

12 parsley crêpes (page 144)
melted unsalted butter for brushing the crêpes
honey-glazed carrots as an accompaniment
   (page 198)
winter tomato sauce as an accompaniment
   (page 239)

Make the potato filling: In a bowl combine well the potato, the butter, the milk, the egg, the scallion, and salt and pepper to taste.

Make the beef filling: In a skillet cook the onion in the beef drippings over moderately low heat, stirring, until it is softened, add the beef and the thyme, and cook the mixture over moderate heat, stirring, for 1 minute. Add the Worcestershire sauce and the gravy, bring the mixture to a simmer, and simmer it for 1 to 2 minutes, or until it is heated through. Stir in the peas and salt and pepper to taste and remove the skillet from the heat.

Working with 1 crêpe at a time, spread 2 tablespoons of the potato filling on each crêpe and spread 2 tablespoons of the meat mixture over it. Fold the crêpes into quarters and arrange them decoratively, overlapping them and leaving room for the carrots, on a lightly buttered ovenproof platter. Brush the crêpes lightly with the melted butter and bake them in a preheated 400° F. oven for 10 to 15 minutes, or until they are browned lightly and the edges are slightly crisp. Arrange the carrots decoratively on the platter and serve the crêpes with the tomato sauce. Serves 6.

Parsley Crêpes

1 cup all-purpose flour
½ cup milk
3 large eggs
2 tablespoons unsalted butter, melted and
  cooled
½ teaspoon salt
3 tablespoons minced fresh parsley leaves
vegetable oil for cooking the crêpes

In a blender or food processor blend the flour, ½ cup water, the milk, the eggs, the butter, and the salt for 5 seconds. Turn off the motor, with a rubber spatula scrape down the sides of the container, and blend the batter for 20 seconds more. Transfer the batter to a bowl, stir in the parsley, and let the batter stand, covered with plastic wrap, for 1 hour. *The batter may be made up to 1 day in advance and kept covered and chilled.*

Heat a crêpe pan or non-stick skillet measuring 6 to 7 inches across the bottom over moderate heat until it is hot. Brush the pan lightly with the oil, heat the oil until it is hot but not smoking, and remove the pan from the heat. Stir the batter, half-fill a ¼-cup measure with it, and pour the batter into the pan. Tilt and rotate the pan quickly to cover the bottom with a thin layer of batter and return any excess batter to the bowl. Return the pan to the heat, loosen the edge of the crêpe with a spatula, and cook the crêpe until the underside is browned lightly. Turn the crêpe, brown the other side lightly, and transfer the crêpe to a plate or dish towel. Make crêpes with the remaining batter in the same manner, brushing the pan lightly with oil as necessary. *The crêpes may be made in advance, stacked, wrapped in plastic wrap, and refrigerated for up to 3 days or frozen.* Makes about 16 crêpes.

Sliced Sirloin Steak with Chili Sauce

½ teaspoon cuminseed
2 teaspoons chili powder
1 teaspoon crumbled dried orégano
½ teaspoon sweet paprika (preferably
  Hungarian)
⅛ teaspoon cayenne
¾ pound boneless sirloin steak, trimmed and
  sliced at an angle across the grain into ½-
  inch-thick slices
flour seasoned with salt and pepper for
  dredging
3 tablespoons vegetable oil
1 cup sliced onion
1 green bell pepper, chopped coarse
1 garlic clove, minced
1 tablespoon tomato paste
1 teaspoon firmly packed dark brown sugar
1 teaspoon fresh lime juice
1 cup canned beef broth

In a small bowl combine the cuminseed, the chili powder, the orégano, the paprika, and the cayenne. In a bowl dredge the steak in the flour, put it in a large sieve, and shake it to remove the excess flour. In a large skillet heat the oil over high heat until it is hot but not smoking, in it brown the steak, and transfer it with a slotted spoon to a plate. To the skillet add the onion and the bell pepper and cook the mixture over moderate heat, stirring, for 5 minutes. Add the garlic and the spice mixture and cook the mixture, stirring, for 1 minute. Add the tomato

paste, the brown sugar, the lime juice, and the broth, bring the liquid to a boil, and simmer the mixture, stirring occasionally, for 5 minutes. Add the steak and any juices that have accumulated on the plate and simmer the mixture, stirring, until the steak is just heated through. Serves 2.

Swiss Steak Stew

6 tablespoons flour seasoned with salt and
    pepper
2 pounds round steak, 1½ inches thick
¼ cup vegetable oil
1 large onion, sliced thin
2 cups brown stock (page 118) or canned beef
    broth
1 teaspoon minced garlic
mashed potatoes as an accompaniment

With the edge of a heavy plate pound gently ¼ cup of the flour into both sides of the steak and cut the steak into 1-inch cubes. In a bowl toss the steak cubes with the remaining 2 tablespoons flour, coating them completely, and let them stand at room temperature for 30 minutes. In a large heavy skillet heat the oil over moderately high heat until it is hot but not smoking and in it brown the steak in batches, transferring it with a slotted spoon as it is browned to a 4-quart ovenproof casserole. In the oil remaining in the skillet sauté the onion over moderately high heat, stirring, until it is golden, add the stock and the garlic, and bring the liquid to a boil. Pour the stock mixture over the steak and bake the dish, covered, in a preheated 350° F. oven for 1 hour and 30 minutes to 2 hours, or until the steak is tender. (The stew improves in flavor if cooled to room temperature, uncovered, and chilled, covered, overnight.) Season the stew with salt and pepper and serve it with the mashed potatoes. Serves 4 to 6.

Calf's Liver with Mustard Sauce

2 slices of calf's liver, ¼ inch thick (about ½
    pound)
flour seasoned with salt and pepper for
    dredging
¼ cup vegetable oil
½ small onion, minced
1 tablespoon unsalted butter
⅓ cup heavy cream
1 tablespoon Dijon-style mustard
3 tablespoons minced fresh parsley leaves
1 teaspoon fresh lemon juice

Dredge the liver in the flour, shaking off the excess. In a heavy skillet heat the oil over moderately high heat until it is hot but not smoking and in it sauté the liver, turning it once, for 2 minutes, or until it is browned on the outside but still pink within. Transfer the liver with tongs to a heatproof platter and keep it warm in a preheated 200° F. oven. Discard the oil and wipe out the skillet. In the skillet cook the onion in the butter over moderately low heat, stirring, until it is softened, add the cream, and boil it until it is just thickened. Remove the skillet from the heat, stir in the mustard, the parsley, the lemon juice, and salt and pepper to taste, and spoon the sauce over the liver. Serves 2.

Calf's Liver with Sweet-and-Sour Leeks

about ½ pound white part of leeks, sliced thin,
    washed well, and drained
2 tablespoons unsalted butter
1 tablespoon dark brown sugar
¼ cup red-wine vinegar
¾ cup canned chicken broth
four ¼-inch-thick slices of calf's liver (about
    ¾ pound)
flour seasoned with salt and pepper for
    dredging
2 tablespoons vegetable oil

In a large heavy skillet cook the leeks in the butter, covered, over moderately low heat, stirring occasionally, for 20 minutes, or until they are softened. Add the brown sugar, 2 tablespoons of the vinegar, and ¼ cup of the broth and bring the liquid to a boil. Simmer the mixture, covered, stirring occasionally, for 10 minutes, or until the liquid is absorbed, and add salt and pepper to taste.

While the leeks are cooking prepare the liver: Pat the liver dry and dredge it in the flour, shaking off the excess. In a large skillet heat the oil over moderately high heat until it is hot but not smoking and in it sauté the liver, turning it once, for 3 minutes for medium-rare. Transfer the liver with a slotted spatula to a platter and keep it warm, covered.

Discard the oil in the skillet, add the remaining 2 tablespoons vinegar and the remaining ½ cup broth, and deglaze the skillet over moderately high heat, scraping up the brown bits. Bring the liquid to a boil and boil it until it is reduced to about ⅓ cup. Add the leeks, cook the mixture over moderately low heat, stirring, for 1 minute, or until it is just heated through, and mound the leeks on top of the liver. Serves 2.

VEAL

Veal and Macaroni with Parmesan Crumb Topping

½ cup elbow macaroni
¼ cup canned chicken broth
3½ tablespoons unsalted butter
cayenne to taste
2 teaspoons vegetable oil
½ pound veal scallops, flattened to ¼ inch
½ cup fine fresh bread crumbs
¼ cup freshly grated Parmesan
minced fresh parsley leaves for garnish
fresh lemon juice to taste

In a large saucepan of boiling salted water cook the macaroni for 7 minutes, or until it is almost *al dente,* drain it, and return it to the pan. Add the broth, 1 tablespoon of the butter, and the cayenne and cook the mixture, covered, over moderately low heat for 1 to 2 minutes, or until the macaroni is *al dente*. In a large heavy skillet heat 2 tablespoons of the remaining butter and the oil over moderately high heat until the fat is hot and in the fat sauté the veal in batches, turning it once, for 30 to 40 seconds, or until it is springy to the touch. Transfer the veal to an ovenproof platter and keep it warm in a preheated 200° F. oven.

In a small bowl combine well the bread crumbs and the Parmesan. Wipe the skillet clean, add the remaining ½ tablespoon butter, and in it cook the crumb mixture, stirring, until it is golden. Transfer the macaroni mixture to the platter with the veal and sprinkle it with some of the crumb mixture and some of the parsley. Sprinkle the veal with the remaining crumb mixture and the remaining parsley and drizzle it with the lemon juice. Serves 2.

Braised Veal Roast with Vegetables Provençale

For the veal

5 tablespoons unsalted butter
2 tablespoons olive oil
a 4- to 4¼-pound boneless veal shoulder roast, rolled and tied
1 large onion, chopped
1 carrot, chopped
2 garlic cloves, minced
a 35-ounce can tomatoes including the juice
½ cup chopped and drained bottled roasted red peppers
½ cup dry white wine
1 small bay leaf
½ teaspoon crumbled dried thyme

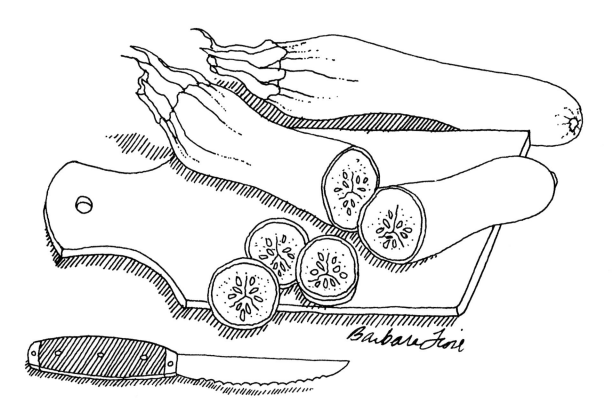

For the vegetables

4 small eggplants (about ½ pound in all), cut crosswise into ½-inch slices

½ pound small white onions

¼ cup olive oil

1 garlic clove

½ pound small mushrooms, trimmed

2 small zucchini (about ½ pound in all), cut crosswise into ½-inch slices

1 pint cherry tomatoes

3 tablespoons minced fresh parsley leaves

sugar to taste if desired

steamed rice (page 190) as an accompaniment

Prepare the veal: In a heavy casserole heat 2 tablespoons of the butter and the oil over moderately high heat until the fat is hot. Pat the veal dry, season it with salt and pepper, and brown it in the fat. Transfer the veal to a plate, pour off the fat, and wipe the casserole clean with a paper towel. In the casserole cook the onion, the carrot, and the garlic in the remaining 3 tablespoons butter over moderately low heat, stirring, until the vegetables are softened, stir in the tomatoes, breaking them up with a spoon, the tomato juice, the roasted peppers, the wine, the bay leaf, the thyme, and salt and pepper to taste, and bring the mixture to a boil. Add the veal to the casserole with any juices that have accumulated on the plate and braise it, covered, in a preheated 300° F. oven, basting it with the tomato mixture and turning it occasionally, for 1 hour and 45 minutes to 2 hours, or until it is tender when pierced with a fork. Transfer the veal to a carving board and let it stand, covered loosely with foil, for 20 minutes. While the veal roast is standing, reduce the tomato sauce in the casserole over high heat, skimming the fat and stirring occasionally, until it is thickened slightly and keep it warm. Carve the veal crosswise into thin slices, discarding the strings.

Prepare the vegetables while the veal is roasting: Sprinkle the eggplant generously with salt and let it drain in a colander for 1 hour. Rinse the eggplant and pat it dry. In a saucepan of boiling salted water blanch the onions for 8 minutes, or until they are just tender when tested with a knife, and refresh them under cold water. Peel the onions and pat them dry.

Just before serving the veal cook the vegetables: In a large heavy skillet heat 3 tablespoons of the oil with the garlic over moderately high heat until it is hot and discard the garlic. In the oil sauté the eggplant, stirring, until it is golden and tender and transfer it with a slotted spoon to a heated platter. Add the remaining 1 tablespoon oil to the skillet, heat it until it is hot, and in it sauté the onions and the mushrooms, stirring, until they are golden and the mushrooms are just tender. Transfer the vegetables with the slotted spoon to the platter. In the skillet sauté the zucchini, stirring, until it is golden and just tender and transfer it with the slotted spoon to the platter. In the skillet sauté the tomatoes, stirring, until they are just heated through and transfer them with the slotted spoon to the platter. Arrange the veal slices on the platter, brush them with the juices from the carving board, and sprinkle the dish with the parsley. Discard the bay leaf from the tomato sauce, season the sauce with the sugar if desired and salt and pepper, and transfer the sauce to a heated bowl. Serve the veal with the rice. Serves 8.

Veal Stew Provençale

3 onions, chopped

3 large garlic cloves, minced and mashed to a paste

¼ cup olive oil or vegetable oil

½ pound carrots, cut into 3- by ½-inch sticks

2 pounds boneless veal shoulder, cut into 1½- inch pieces

4 strips of orange rind, cut into julienne strips

a 28-ounce can plum tomatoes including the juice

1 cup dry white wine

¾ teaspoon crumbled dried thyme

¾ teaspoon crumbled dried rosemary

½ pound pearl onions, cooked in boiling water until tender and peeled

½ cup oil-cured black olives for garnish

a fresh rosemary sprig for garnish

In a flameproof 4-quart casserole cook the chopped onions and two thirds of the mashed garlic in the oil over moderately low heat, stirring, until they are softened. Add the carrots, the veal, the rind, the tomatoes, the wine, the thyme, and the crumbled rosemary, bring the liquid to a boil, and braise the mixture, covered, in a preheated 325° F. oven for 1 hour and 30 minutes, or until the veal is tender. Stir in the pearl onions, the remaining garlic, and salt and pepper to taste. (The stew improves in flavor if cooled to room temperature, uncovered, and chilled, covered, overnight.) Sprinkle the stew with the olives and garnish it with the rosemary sprig. Serves 4 to 6.

PORK

Bacon, Corn, and Tomato Mélange

3 slices of lean bacon, chopped
1 small onion, minced
1 cup corn (cut from about 2 ears)
1 tomato, peeled, seeded, and chopped
1 tablespoon minced fresh basil leaves

In a skillet cook the bacon over moderate heat, stirring, until it is crisp and transfer it with a slotted spoon to paper towels to drain. In the fat remaining in the skillet cook the onion and the corn over moderately low heat, stirring, for 5 minutes, stir in the tomato, salt and pepper to taste, and a pinch of sugar, and cook the mixture, covered, stirring occasionally, for 10 to 15 minutes, or until the corn is tender. Stir in the bacon and the basil leaves. Serves 2.

Oven Bacon

8 slices of lean bacon, preferably sliced thick

Arrange the slices of bacon on the rack of a broiler pan and bake them in the middle of a preheated 375° F. oven, turning them once, for 15 to 20 minutes, or until they are golden and crisp. Transfer the bacon to paper towels to drain. Serves 2.

Open-Faced Bacon, Mushroom, and Cheese Sandwiches

¼ pound mushrooms, sliced thin
2 teaspoons minced onion
1 tablespoon unsalted butter
1 teaspoon Worcestershire sauce, or to taste
4 slices (about 2 ounces) of Canadian bacon
2 English muffins, split and toasted
Dijon-style mustard to taste
4 slices (about ¼ pound) of Swiss cheese
cherry tomato slices for garnish

In a small skillet cook the mushrooms and the onion in the butter with the Worcestershire sauce over moderate heat, stirring occasionally, until the liquid the mushrooms give off is evaporated and season the mixture with salt and pepper. In a skillet heat the bacon over moderately high heat, turning it, until it is hot. Spread

the muffins with the mustard, put 1 slice of the bacon on each muffin half, and top it with some of the mushroom mixture. Arrange 1 slice of the cheese on each muffin half and broil the sandwiches on the rack of a broiler pan under a preheated broiler about 4 inches from the heat for 1 to 2 minutes, or until the cheese begins to melt. Top the sandwiches with the tomato slices. Serves 2.

Broccoli and Ham Gratin

¾ stick (6 tablespoons) unsalted butter
¼ cup all-purpose flour
2 cups milk
½ cup freshly grated Parmesan
½ cup grated Swiss cheese
1 pound broccoli, trimmed, cooked in boiling
  salted water until it is just tender, and
  chopped coarse (about 4¼ cups)
¼ pound cooked ham, chopped
1 cup coarse dry bread crumbs

In a saucepan melt 4 tablespoons of the butter over moderately low heat, add the flour, and cook the *roux*, stirring, for 3 minutes. Add the milk, heated, in a stream, whisking, bring the mixture to a boil, whisking, and simmer it, stirring, for 5 minutes. Stir in the Parmesan, the Swiss cheese, and salt and pepper to taste and cook the mixture, stirring, until the cheese is melted. In a well buttered 14-inch gratin dish combine the broccoli and the ham and pour the sauce over the mixture. Sprinkle the bread crumbs over the top, dot them with the remaining 2 tablespoons butter, cut into bits, and bake the gratin in a preheated 375° F. oven for 30 minutes, or until it is bubbling. Serves 6 to 8.

Ham Croustades

¼ teaspoon minced garlic
2 tablespoons unsalted butter
½ teaspoon finely crumbled dried orégano
2 French rolls, halved horizontally
2 teaspoons white-wine vinegar
1 teaspoon Dijon-style mustard
1 tablespoon vegetable oil
¼ pound ham steak, rinsed, patted dry, and
  cut into ¼-inch cubes
½ cup grated whole-milk mozzarella
2 tablespoons minced fresh parsley leaves

In a small heavy skillet cook the garlic in the butter over moderately low heat, stirring, until it is softened and stir in the orégano and salt and pepper to taste. Remove the soft crumb from the rolls with a fork, leaving a ¼-inch shell, brush the insides and rims with the butter mixture, and toast the shells on the rack of a broiler pan about 4 inches from the heat for 1 to 2 minutes, or until they are golden. In a small bowl whisk together the vinegar, the mustard, and salt and pepper to taste, add the oil in a stream, whisking, and whisk the mixture until it is emulsified. In a bowl combine the ham, the mozzarella, and the parsley, toss the mixture with the mustard mixture, and spoon the mixture into the shells, mounding it. Serves 2.

Ham Steak with Ginger Chutney Sauce

a ¾-pound ham steak, ½ inch thick
1 cup milk
a 1- by ½-inch piece of gingerroot, peeled and
    cut into julienne strips
1 tablespoon unsalted butter
¼ cup mango chutney, drained and chopped,
    reserving the liquid
¼ cup dry white wine
1 tablespoon vegetable oil

Rinse the ham under cold water and in a shallow dish let it soak in the milk at room temperature for 25 minutes. While the ham is soaking, in a small saucepan cook the gingerroot in the butter over moderately low heat, stirring occasionally, for 5 minutes, add the chutney, the chutney liquid, and the wine, and cook the mixture over moderately high heat, stirring occasionally, for 8 to 10 minutes, or until the sauce is thickened. Transfer the sauce to a sauceboat.

In a large heavy skillet heat the oil over high heat until it is hot and in it sauté the ham, drained and patted dry, turning it once, for 4 minutes. Transfer the ham to a platter and serve it with the sauce. Serves 2.

Pork and Eggplant Orientale

6 tablespoons peanut oil
1 small eggplant, cut into strips
1 tablespoon cornstarch
¾ pound boneless pork shoulder, trimmed and
    sliced thin
1 teaspoon minced peeled gingerroot
½ teaspoon minced garlic
4 scallions, minced
¼ red bell pepper, cut into strips
2 tablespoons red-wine vinegar
2 tablespoons soy sauce
2 teaspoons sugar
¼ pound snow peas, trimmed and strings
    discarded
1 tablespoon minced fresh coriander

Heat a wok or large heavy skillet over high heat until it is hot, add 4 tablespoons of the oil, and heat it until it is hot but not smoking. In a bowl toss the eggplant with the cornstarch to coat it well, fry it in the oil in batches, stirring constantly, until it is golden, and transfer it as it is cooked with a slotted spoon to paper towels to drain. Add the remaining 2 tablespoons oil to the wok, heat it until it is hot but not smoking, and in it cook the pork in batches, stirring constantly, for 1 to 2 minutes, or until it is browned on the outside but not quite cooked through. Transfer the pork as it is cooked with the slotted spoon to a bowl. Add to the wok the gingerroot, the garlic, the scallions, and the bell pepper and cook the mixture over moderately high heat, stirring constantly, for 15 seconds. Add the vinegar, the soy sauce, the sugar, and 2 tablespoons water and bring the liquid to a boil. Add the eggplant, the pork and any juices that have accumulated in the bowl, and the snow peas, bring the liquid to a boil, stirring constantly, and cook the mixture, stirring, for 1 minute. Sprinkle the dish with the coriander. Serves 2.

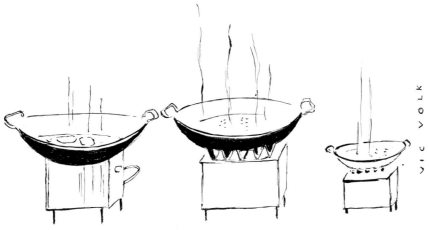

Spicy Pork and Peppers

For the pork
a 2-pound piece of boneless pork loin,
    trimmed of all fat, sliced thin crosswise,
    and the slices cut into ¼-inch strips
1½ tablespoons cornstarch
1 large egg white
1 tablespoon rice wine (available at Oriental
    markets and some liquor stores) or Scotch
2 teaspoons Oriental sesame oil*
1 teaspoon soy sauce
For the sauce
1½ teaspoons cornstarch
⅓ cup Chinese chicken broth (page 125) or
    canned chicken broth
2 tablespoons soy sauce
1 tablespoon rice wine or Scotch
1 teaspoon rice vinegar*
1 teaspoon sugar
2 teaspoons Oriental sesame oil*

3 cups vegetable oil, preferably safflower or
    corn oil
2 red bell peppers, cut lengthwise into ⅛-inch strips
2 green bell peppers, cut lengthwise into ⅛-inch strips
two 3-inch fresh green or red hot chili peppers
    (available at specialty produce markets and
    many supermarkets), seeded and minced
    (wear rubber gloves)
2 tablespoons minced garlic
½ teaspoon Szechwan peppercorns,* crushed
    lightly
1 tablespoon minced peeled gingerroot
2 teaspoons chili paste* (with or without garlic)
3 chili flowers for garnish (procedure follows)
    if desired
steamed lotus buns (recipe follows) as an
    accompaniment

*available at Oriental markets and specialty
    foods shops, and supermarkets

Prepare the pork: In a bowl combine the pork, the cornstarch, the egg white, the rice wine, the sesame oil, and the soy sauce, stir the mixture vigorously in one direction until the pork is coated well, and chill it, covered, for at least 30 minutes or overnight.

Make the sauce: In a small bowl dissolve the cornstarch in the broth and add the soy sauce, the rice wine, the rice vinegar, the sugar, and the sesame oil.

Heat a wok over high heat until it is hot, add the vegetable oil, and heat it until a deep-fat thermometer registers 400° F. Fry the pork in the oil in 4 batches, stirring, for 15 to 30 seconds, or until the strips separate and change color, and transfer it with a slotted spoon to a large sieve set over a bowl, making sure the oil returns to 400° F. before adding each new batch. *The pork may be fried up to 6 hours in advance and kept covered and chilled.*

Pour off all but 3 tablespoons of the oil in the wok, heat the remaining oil over high heat until it is hot, and in it stir-fry the red and green bell peppers for 10 to 20 seconds, or until they are softened slightly but still crisp. Transfer the peppers with a slotted spoon to a bowl. If necessary add more oil to the wok to measure a total of 3 tablespoons, heat the oil until it is hot, and in it stir-fry the chili peppers, the garlic, the peppercorns, the gingerroot, and the chili paste for 5 to 15 seconds, or until the mixture is fragrant. Stir the sauce, add it to the wok, stirring, and bring it to a boil, stirring. Add the pork and the peppers and cook the mixture, tossing it constantly, for 30 seconds to 1 minute, or until it is heated through. Transfer the mixture to a heated serving dish, garnish it with the chili flowers if desired, and serve it with the lotus buns. Serves 8.

To Make Chili Flowers for Garnish

fresh red or green chili peppers (available at
    specialty produce markets and many
    supermarkets)

Wearing rubber gloves and with a very sharp knife slit the chili peppers lengthwise from the tip end, at 4 equal intervals, leaving at least 1 inch of the stem end intact, and scrape out the seeds and ribs gently. Let the chili peppers stand in a bowl of ice and cold water for 1 hour, or until they are curled.

Steamed Lotus Buns

2 teaspoons active dry yeast
2 tablespoons sugar
about 2⅔ cups all-purpose flour
1 teaspoon double-acting baking powder
about ¼ cup Oriental sesame oil (available at
    Oriental markets, some specialty foods
    shops, and some supermarkets)

In a small bowl proof the yeast with the sugar in ¾ cup lukewarm water for 15 minutes, or until it is foamy. In a food processor blend 2⅔ cups of the flour, with the motor running add the yeast mixture in a stream, and blend the mixture until it forms a ball of dough, adding additional flour by tablespoons if the dough seems wet and additional warm water by tablespoons if the dough does not gather into a ball. Knead the dough in the processor for 30 seconds, turn it out onto a floured surface, and knead it for 1 to 2 minutes, or until it is smooth and elastic. Put the dough in an oiled bowl, turn it to coat it with the oil, and let it rise, covered with plastic wrap, in a warm place for 1 hour, or until it is double in bulk. *The dough may be made 1 day in advance, punched down well, and chilled, covered tightly with plastic wrap.*

Punch down the dough, make a shallow trench in it, and sprinkle the baking powder in the trench. Pinch the dough together to seal in the baking powder, return the dough to the processor, and blend it for 15 seconds, or until it is combined well. Halve the dough, keeping one half covered tightly with plastic wrap, roll the remaining half into an 8-inch log on a floured surface, and cut the log into 1-inch sections. Working with 1 section at a time and keeping the remaining dough covered, roll each section cut side down into a 3½-inch round, brush the rounds lightly with the sesame oil, and fold them to form half-moons. Score the buns in a crosshatch pattern with a razor blade or very sharp knife and with the blunt edge of a cleaver or knife make 2 indentations along the curved edge of each bun, pushing the dough in slightly to form a scalloped edge. Make buns with the remaining dough in the same manner.

Arrange the buns 1 inch apart on steamer trays or racks both lined with oiled parchment paper and let them rise, covered with a dish towel, in a warm place for 20 minutes, or until they are puffed slightly. Steam the buns (procedure on page 125) for 15 minutes, or until they are puffed and dry. *The buns may be made up to 1 day in advance and kept wrapped tightly in plastic wrap. Reheat the buns, wrapped in foil, in a preheated 300° F. oven for 15 minutes, or until they are heated through.* Serve the buns warm. Makes 16 buns.

Pork Chops with Shallot Sauce

two ½-inch-thick center-cut pork chops
2 teaspoons olive oil
1 tablespoon minced shallot
¼ cup dry white wine

Season the pork chops, patted dry, with salt and pepper. In a heavy skillet heat the oil over moderately high heat until it is hot but not smoking, in it sauté the chops,

turning them once, for 6 minutes, and transfer them to a heated platter. Add the shallot to the skillet and sauté it, stirring, for 1 minute. Add the wine, salt and pepper to taste, and any juices that have accumulated on the platter, cook the mixture, scraping up the brown bits, until it is reduced to about ¼ cup, and spoon the sauce over the pork chops. Serves 2.

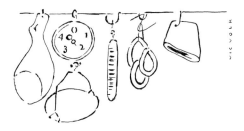

Zucchini-Stuffed Pork Chops with Mustard Sauce

¾ pound zucchini, grated coarse
1 tablespoon salt
1 tablespoon minced garlic
¼ cup olive oil
3 tablespoons freshly grated Parmesan
six ¾-inch-thick loin pork chops
1 small onion, chopped
⅓ cup dry white wine
½ cup heavy cream
1 tablespoon Dijon-style mustard

In a colander combine well the zucchini with the salt, let it drain for 30 minutes, and squeeze it dry. In a heavy skillet cook the zucchini with the garlic in 3 tablespoons of the oil over moderately low heat, stirring, for 8 to 10 minutes, or until it is just tender, stir in the Parmesan, and let the stuffing cool for 5 minutes.

Cut a deep pocket in each of the pork chops and fill the pockets with the stuffing. In a large heavy skillet heat the remaining 1 tablespoon oil over moderately high heat until it is hot but not smoking and in it sauté 3 of the chops, patted dry, turning them once, for 8 to 10 minutes, or until they are firm to the touch. Transfer the chops to an ovenproof platter and keep them warm in a preheated 200° F. oven. Sauté the remaining 3 chops in the same manner and transfer them to the platter.

In the oil remaining in the skillet sauté the onion over moderately high heat, stirring, for 1 minute, deglaze the skillet with the wine, scraping up the brown bits, and whisk in the cream, the mustard, any juices that have accumulated on the platter, and salt and pepper to taste. Strain the sauce through a fine sieve into a bowl, pressing hard on the solids, and spoon it around the pork chops. Serves 4 to 6.

Pork Stew with Prunes

2 pounds boneless pork shoulder, trimmed and
    cut into 1-inch cubes
¼ cup flour seasoned with salt and pepper
1½ tablespoons unsalted butter
1 tablespoon minced peeled gingerroot
2½ cups dry white wine
12 pitted prunes
¼ cup heavy cream
buttered noodles as an accompaniment

Dredge the pork in the flour. In a flameproof 4-quart
casserole heat the butter over moderately high heat until
the foam subsides and in it brown the pork in batches,
transferring it with a slotted spoon as it is browned to a
bowl. Return the pork to the casserole, add the gingerroot, and cook the mixture, stirring, for 1 minute. Stir in
the wine and the prunes and cook the mixture at a bare
simmer, covered, for 1 hour and 30 minutes, or until the
pork is tender. Stir in the cream and salt and pepper to
taste. (The stew improves in flavor if cooled to room
temperature, uncovered, and chilled, covered, overnight.) Serve the stew with the noodles. Serves 4 to 6.

Prosciutto and Avocado

½ avocado, peeled and sliced lengthwise into
    8 pieces
2 teaspoons fresh lime juice
2 ounces thinly sliced prosciutto
freshly ground black pepper

Divide the avocado slices evenly between 2 plates,
fanning them, and sprinkle them with the lime juice.
Drape the prosciutto decoratively over the avocado
slices and grind the pepper over it to taste. Serves 2.

Sausage in Pastry with Honey Mustard

For the dough
1⅓ cups all-purpose flour
½ teaspoon salt
1 stick (½ cup) cold unsalted butter, cut into
    bits
1 large egg, beaten lightly
1 tablespoon sour cream

1 pound *kielbasa* (Polish sausage)
an egg wash made by beating together 1 egg
    with 1 teaspoon water
fresh thyme sprigs for garnish if desired

For the honey mustard
⅓ cup Dijon-style mustard
3 tablespoons honey, or to taste
¼ teaspoon fresh thyme leaves, or to taste

Make the dough: Into a bowl sift together the flour
and the salt and blend in the butter until the mixture resembles coarse meal. In a small bowl whisk together the
egg and the sour cream, add the mixture to the flour
mixture, and stir the mixture until it forms a soft dough.
Form the dough into a ball, dust it with flour, and flatten
it slightly. Chill the dough, wrapped in wax paper, for at
least 1 hour or overnight.

Halve the *kielbasa* crosswise, trimming the ends of
each half and reserving them for another use, to form 2
fairly straight sausages. Prick the sausages with a fork
and cook them in a skillet in 1 inch of boiling water for 8
minutes. Drain the sausages, let them cool until they
can be handled, and peel off carefully the outer casing.
Let the sausages cool completely, wrapped in paper
towels to absorb any liquid.

Roll half the dough into a rectangle ⅛ inch thick on a
lightly floured surface, arrange 1 sausage in the center
of it, and trim the dough, leaving about 3 inches on each
side of the sausage and about 1½ inches at each end, or
enough to enclose the sausage. Bring 1 side of the dough
up around the sausage and brush the edge with some of
the egg wash. Bring the other side up to overlap it by
about 1 inch and press the edges together. Seal the ends
with some of the egg wash in the same manner to enclose the sausage completely and transfer the sausage
seam side down to a baking sheet. Brush the entire sausage package with some of the egg wash. Cut out decorative shapes, such as leaves, from the dough scraps
with a sharp knife, transfer them to the top of the sausage package, pressing them down firmly to make them
adhere, and brush them lightly with some of the egg
wash. Prepare the other sausage in the same manner
with the remaining dough and egg wash and chill the
sausages for 15 minutes. Bake the sausages in a preheated 375° F. oven for 25 to 30 minutes, or until the pastry
is golden and flaky. (Cover the decorations with small
pieces of foil if they begin to brown too quickly.) Transfer the sausage pastries to a platter and garnish the platter with the thyme sprigs if desired.

Make the honey mustard: In a small bowl whisk together the mustard, the honey, and the thyme and transfer the mixture to a small serving dish.

Cut the sausages with a serrated knife into ¾-inch
slices and serve them with the honey mustard. Serves 8.

Kidney Bean and Sausage Stew

2 cups dried kidney beans, picked over and
    rinsed
1 cup chopped celery including the leaves
½ cup chopped green bell pepper
1 cup chopped onion
2 garlic cloves, minced
1 pound hot smoked sausage, smoked sausage,
    or *kielbasa*, cut into ½-inch rounds
½ teaspoon Tabasco
2 teaspoons Worcestershire sauce
1 cup thinly sliced scallion greens
½ cup minced fresh parsley leaves
distilled white vinegar to taste if desired
cooked brown rice as an accompaniment

In a flameproof 4-quart casserole bring 7 cups water
to a boil, add the beans, and boil them for 2 minutes. Remove the casserole from the heat and let the beans soak
for 1 hour. Bring the liquid to a boil, stir in the celery,
the bell pepper, the onion, the garlic, the sausage, the
Tabasco, and the Worcestershire sauce, and simmer the
mixture, covered, for 50 minutes to 1 hour, or until the
beans are tender. (The stew improves in flavor if cooled
to room temperature, uncovered, and chilled, covered,
overnight.) Stir in the scallions, the parsley, and salt
and pepper to taste. Serve the stew, sprinkled with the
vinegar if desired, over the rice. Serves 4 to 6.

Smoked Sausage and Red Cabbage
with Mustard Dressing

3 tablespoons red-wine vinegar
1½ tablespoons Dijon-style mustard
3 tablespoons olive oil
4 cups thinly sliced red cabbage
½ pound *kielbasa* or other smoked sausage,
    cut into ¾-inch pieces
2 tablespoons thinly sliced scallion greens

In a bowl whisk together the vinegar, the mustard,
and salt and pepper to taste, add the oil in a stream,
whisking, and whisk the dressing until it is emulsified.
In a large saucepan of boiling salted water blanch the
cabbage for 5 to 7 minutes, or until it is crisp-tender,
drain it well, and transfer it to an ovenproof serving
dish. Keep the cabbage warm, covered loosely, in a
preheated 200° F. oven.
In a dry heavy skillet sauté the sausage over moderately high heat for 3 to 5 minutes, or until it is browned,
and transfer it to paper towels to drain. Add the sausage
and the scallions to the cabbage, add the dressing, and
toss the mixture well. Serves 2 as an entrée.

LAMB

Lamb Brochettes with Yogurt Marinade

½ cup plain yogurt
1 teaspoon minced peeled gingerroot
½ teaspoon curry powder
½ teaspoon salt
a large pinch of cayenne
½ pound boneless lamb shoulder, cut into ¾-
    inch pieces
½ large red bell pepper, cut into ¾-inch pieces
2 tablespoons olive oil
¼ pound eggplant, cut into ¾-inch pieces

In a shallow dish combine well the yogurt, the gingerroot, the curry powder, the salt, and the cayenne,
add the lamb, stirring to coat it with the mixture, and let
it marinate at room temperature for 15 minutes. In a
heavy skillet cook the bell pepper in the oil, stirring occasionally, for 3 minutes, add the eggplant, and cook
the vegetables, stirring occasionally, for 5 to 7 minutes,
or until they are just tender. Stir the vegetables into the
yogurt and lamb mixture. On each of four 8-inch metal
skewers thread 4 pieces of the bell pepper alternately
with 4 pieces of the eggplant and 4 pieces of the lamb,
setting the skewers as they are filled over a foil-lined
baking pan and reserving the marinade. Roast the bro-
chettes in a preheated 425° F. oven for 10 minutes,
brush them with the reserved marinade, and roast them
for 10 minutes more for medium-rare. Serves 2.

Lamb Chops Stuffed with Feta

½ cup minced onion
2 tablespoons olive oil
1 small garlic clove, minced
2 plum tomatoes peeled, seeded, and chopped
¼ pound Feta, crumbled
2 tablespoons minced fresh mint leaves
8 single-rib lamb chops, frenched
oil for brushing the chops
fresh mint sprigs for garnish

In a heavy skillet cook the onion in the olive oil over moderately low heat, stirring, until it is softened, add the garlic and the tomatoes, and cook the mixture, stirring, for 3 minutes. Add the Feta and cook the mixture, stirring, until the cheese is almost melted. Stir in the minced mint, add salt and pepper to taste, and let the mixture cool.

With a sharp paring knife make an incision about ¾ inch long along the fat side of each chop and cut a pocket in the chop by moving the knife back and forth carefully through the incision. Stuff each chop with ⅛ of the Feta mixture and close the pockets with wooden picks. Brush the chops with the oil and grill them on an oiled rack over glowing coals, turning them once, for 8 minutes for medium-rare meat. Season the chops with salt and pepper and discard the wooden picks. Arrange the chops on a heated platter and garnish them with the mint sprigs. Serves 4.

Lamb Chops with Olive and Tomato Sauce

four 1-inch-thick loin lamb chops, boned and tied
flour for dredging
1 tablespoon olive oil
¼ cup dry white wine
1 pound plum tomatoes, peeled, seeded, and chopped
⅓ cup drained pitted black olives, cut into slivers

Pat the chops dry, season with salt and pepper, and dredge them in the flour, shaking off the excess. In a large heavy skillet heat the oil over moderately high heat until it is hot and in it sauté the chops, turning them once, for 6 minutes for medium-rare. Transfer the chops to an ovenproof platter, discard the strings, and keep the chops warm in a preheated 200° F. oven. Deglaze the skillet with the wine, scraping up the brown bits, stir in the tomatoes and the olives, and cook the mixture over moderate heat, stirring occasionally, for 3 to 4 minutes, or until the liquid is almost evaporated. Season the sauce with salt and pepper and spoon it over the chops. Serves 2.

Middle Eastern Lamb Pie

For the filling
1 large onion, chopped fine
3 tablespoons olive oil
3 garlic cloves, minced
2 pounds ground lamb
a 1-pound can tomatoes, drained, reserving the juice, and chopped
⅔ cup raisins
1½ teaspoons crumbled dried mint
1 teaspoon cinnamon
¼ teaspoon ground allspice
about 1½ cups canned beef broth
1 cup *bulgur* (cracked wheat, available at natural foods stores, specialty foods shops, and some supermarkets)
For the crust
3 sheets of *phyllo,* halved crosswise, stacked between 2 sheets of wax paper, and covered with a dampened dish towel
½ stick (¼ cup) unsalted butter, melted and cooled slightly

Make the filling: In a large heavy skillet cook the onion in the oil over moderately low heat, stirring occasionally, until it is softened, add the garlic, and cook the mixture, stirring, for 1 minute. Add the lamb and cook it over moderate heat, stirring and breaking up the lumps, until it is no longer pink. Stir in the tomatoes, including the reserved juice, the raisins, the mint, the cinnamon, the allspice, 1½ cups of the broth, and salt and pepper to taste, bring the mixture to a boil, and simmer it, covered, for 10 minutes. Stir in the *bulgur* and simmer the mixture, covered, for 15 to 20 minutes, or until the *bulgur* is tender and has absorbed most of the liquid. Season the filling with salt and pepper, if necessary, and transfer it to a buttered baking dish, 11 by 8 by 1¾ inches, or a 2-quart shallow rectangular baking dish, smoothing the top. *The filling may be made 1 day in advance and kept covered and chilled. In this case, moisten the filling with about ¼ cup additional water or canned beef broth just before baking.*

Make the crust: Brush 1 sheet of the *phyllo* lightly with the butter, top it with another sheet of *phyllo,* and brush that sheet lightly with the butter. Continue stacking and buttering the remaining sheets of *phyllo* in the same manner, set the buttered *phyllo* stack over the lamb filling, turning under the overhanging edges, and with a sharp knife score the crust in a wide diamond or crosshatch design.

Bake the pie in a preheated 375° F. oven for 40 minutes, or until the crust is golden and the filling is hot. Serves 6 to 8.

Lamb Stew with Cabbage

2 pounds boneless lamb shoulder, trimmed
    and cut into 1-inch pieces
1½ cups chicken stock (page 119) or canned
    chicken broth
½ bay leaf
1 pound boiling potatoes, peeled and cut into
    ½-inch cubes
1 small cabbage, cut into ½-inch pieces (about
    6 cups)
⅓ cup minced fresh parsley leaves
2 teaspoons fresh lemon juice

In a flameproof 4-quart casserole combine the lamb, the stock, and 1 cup water, bring the liquid to a boil, and simmer the mixture, skimming the froth, for 10 to 15 minutes, or until there is no froth. Add the bay leaf and simmer the mixture, covered, for 1 hour. While the lamb is simmering, in a large saucepan bring 3 cups water to a boil, add the potatoes, and boil them for 13 to 15 minutes, or until they are very tender. Drain the potatoes well and mash them with the back of a fork. Stir the potatoes and the cabbage into the lamb mixture and simmer the mixture, covered, for 20 to 30 minutes, or until the lamb is tender and the stew is thickened. (The stew improves in flavor if cooled to room temperature, uncovered, and chilled, covered, overnight.) Season the stew with salt and pepper and stir in the parsley and the lemon juice. Serves 4 to 6.

POULTRY

CHICKEN

Roast Chicken with Rice and Cheese Stuffing

For the stuffing
1 garlic clove, minced
1 onion, minced
2 tablespoons unsalted butter
a 10-ounce package frozen chopped spinach,
　thawed and excess liquid squeezed out
freshly grated nutmeg to taste
2 cups steamed rice (page 190)
⅔ cup chopped or coarsely grated provolone
⅔ cup chopped or coarsely grated Swiss
　cheese
⅔ cup freshly grated Parmesan
2 large eggs, beaten lightly
1 cup sour cream

a 6-pound roasting chicken
1 slice of bread

Make the stuffing: In a skillet cook the garlic and the onion in the butter over moderately low heat, stirring, until the onion is softened, add the spinach, and cook the mixture, stirring, for 3 to 5 minutes, or until any liquid is evaporated. Transfer the mixture to a bowl and season it with the nutmeg and salt and pepper. Stir in the rice, the provolone, the Swiss cheese, the Parmesan, the eggs, and the sour cream, combine the mixture well, and let the stuffing cool completely.

Rinse the chicken, pat it dry, and trim the excess fat from the cavity, reserving it. Stuff the chicken loosely with some of the stuffing, cover the stuffing with the slice of bread, and truss the chicken. Put the chicken on a rack in a roasting pan, sprinkle it with salt and pepper to taste, and put the reserved fat on the center of the breast. Transfer the remaining stuffing to a small baking dish and cover it with foil. Roast the chicken in a preheated 325° F. oven, basting it occasionally, for 2 hours, or until the juices run clear when the fleshy part of a thigh is pricked with a skewer. During the last 30 to 45 minutes of roasting bake the remaining stuffing in the baking dish, covered, in the 325° F. oven until it is heated through and moisten it with some of the pan juices before serving. Serves 6 to 8.

Almond-Crusted Chicken Breast with Grapes

1 whole skinless boneless chicken breast
　(about ½ pound), halved lengthwise and
　flattened between sheets of dampened wax
　paper
flour seasoned with salt and pepper for
　dredging
1 large egg, beaten lightly
¾ cup sliced natural almonds
2 tablespoons vegetable oil
2 tablespoons minced shallots
¼ cup dry white wine
¼ cup heavy cream
⅓ cup seedless green grapes, halved
　lengthwise

Dredge the chicken in the flour, shaking off any excess, dip it in the egg, and coat it with the almonds. In a large heavy skillet heat the oil over moderate heat until it is hot, in it cook the chicken, turning it once, for 4 to 6 minutes, or until it is golden, and transfer it with tongs to an ovenproof platter, letting the excess oil drip off. Keep the chicken warm in a preheated 200° F. oven. Pour off the oil in the skillet, add the shallots, and cook them over moderate heat, stirring, for 1 minute. Add the wine and reduce it by half. Stir in the cream, the grapes, and salt and pepper to taste, cook the sauce, stirring, until it is thickened, and ladle it around the chicken. Serves 2.

Rolled Stuffed Chicken Breast with Hot Pepper Sauce

For the rolled stuffed chicken

½ pound hot Italian sausage, casings discarded

1 large egg, beaten lightly

2 pounds spinach, washed well and coarse
  stems discarded

2 tablespoons olive oil

1 garlic clove, minced

1 whole boneless chicken breast (about 1
  pound), skin removed in one piece and
  reserved

1 teaspoon fresh lemon juice

2 tablespoons vegetable oil

For the sauce

¼ cup chopped onion

2 tablespoons unsalted butter

1 large red bell pepper, chopped fine

1 large green bell pepper, chopped fine

½ cup chicken stock (page 119) or canned
  chicken broth

½ cup dry white wine

1 teaspoon seeded and minced pickled
  jalapeño pepper (available at Hispanic
  markets and some specialty foods shops and
  supermarkets), or to taste (wear rubber
  gloves)

1 teaspoon fresh lemon juice

Make the rolled stuffed chicken: In a skillet cook the sausage over moderate heat, stirring and breaking up the lumps, until it is no longer pink and let it cool. Transfer the sausage with a slotted spoon to a food processor, add the egg, and pulse the mixture for 30 seconds, or until the sausage is chopped fine but not puréed. In a large saucepan cook the spinach in the water clinging to the leaves, covered, over moderately high heat, stirring occasionally, for 3 to 5 minutes, or until it is wilted. Drain the spinach in a colander, refresh it under cold water, and squeeze it dry. Chop the spinach coarse and sprinkle it with salt and pepper. In a skillet heat the olive oil over moderate heat until it is hot but not smoking and in it cook the garlic, stirring, for 1 minute. Add the spinach, cook the mixture, stirring, for 2 minutes, and let it cool.

Flatten the chicken breast between sheets of dampened wax paper until it is about ¼ inch thick, form it into a rectangular shape skinned side down, and sprinkle it with the lemon juice and salt and pepper to taste. Spread the spinach evenly on top of the chicken, leaving a ½-inch border all around, spread the sausage mixture

evenly on top of it, and beginning with the long side roll the chicken jelly-roll fashion to enclose the stuffing, forming a log. Stretch the reserved chicken skin to form a rectangle 2 inches wider than the log and roll the skin around the chicken, covering as much of it as possible. Tie the chicken at 1-inch intervals with kitchen string, pat it dry, and season it with salt and pepper. In an oven-proof skillet heat the vegetable oil over moderately high heat until it is hot but not smoking and in it brown the chicken. Bake the rolled chicken, seam side down, in a preheated 350° F. oven for 30 minutes and let it stand, covered, for 10 minutes.

Make the sauce while the chicken is baking: In a skillet cook the onion in the butter over moderately low heat, stirring, until it is softened, add the bell peppers, and cook the mixture, covered, stirring occasionally, for 10 minutes. Add the stock and the wine, bring the liquid to a boil, and simmer the mixture, covered, for 10 minutes. Add the *jalapeño* pepper, the lemon juice, and salt and pepper to taste and purée the mixture in a blender. *The sauce may be made 1 day in advance and kept covered and chilled.*

Discard the strings from the chicken and cut the chicken crosswise into 12 or 16 slices. Pour about ⅓ cup of the sauce, heated, on each of 4 heated plates and arrange 3 or 4 of the chicken slices on each plate. Serves 4.

Stuffed Chicken Normandy
(Apple-Stuffed Chicken with Cider Sauce)

For the stuffed chicken

½ cup minced onion

½ stick (¼ cup) unsalted butter

1 Golden Delicious apple, peeled, cored, and
  chopped

1½ teaspoons minced fresh sage leaves or
  ½ teaspoon crumbled dried

1½ teaspoons minced fresh thyme leaves or
  ½ teaspoon crumbled dried

2 teaspoons fresh lemon juice

4 whole chicken breasts with the first joint of
  the wings attached, halved, boned, and
  skinned

flour for dredging

2 large eggs beaten with 2 teaspoons water

½ cup fine dry bread crumbs

½ cup finely chopped salted cashews

¼ cup vegetable oil

For the sauce

½ cup minced onion

¾ cup dry white wine

¾ cup apple cider

1 cup chicken stock (page 119) or canned
    chicken broth

1 cup heavy cream

2 tablespoons Calvados or apple brandy

4 fresh sage sprigs for garnish

Make the stuffed chicken: In a skillet cook the onion in the butter over moderately low heat, stirring, until it is softened, add the apple, the sage, the thyme, and salt and pepper to taste, and cook the mixture, covered, for 10 minutes, or until the apple is just tender. Stir in the lemon juice and let the mixture cool completely. "French" the chicken wing bones by scraping the meat off the bones with a sharp knife and reserving the meat for another use. Detach the fillet strip from each breast and flatten the breasts and the fillets between sheets of dampened wax paper until they are about ¼ inch thick. Arrange the chicken breasts skinned side down on a work surface, in the center of each mound 2 tablespoons of the apple mixture, and cover the mixture with a fillet strip. Fold up the sides of the breasts to enclose the stuffing, forming the chicken into a "chop." Dredge the chops carefully in the flour, shaking off the excess, dip them in the egg mixture, and dredge them in the bread crumbs combined with the cashews, patting the mixture onto the flesh. Arrange the chops on a rack set over a pan and chill them, uncovered, for at least 1 hour or overnight to let the crumbs dry. In a large heavy skillet heat the oil over moderate heat until it is hot but not smoking, in it brown the chops, transferring them as they are browned to a baking pan, and bake them in a preheated 350° F. oven for 20 minutes. *The chicken may be kept warm, covered loosely with foil for up to 10 minutes.*

Make the sauce while the chops are baking: Pour off the fat from the skillet, add the onion, the wine, and the cider, and boil the mixture until almost all the liquid is evaporated. Add the stock and boil the mixture until the liquid is reduced by half. Add the cream and the Calvados, boil the sauce until it is thickened slightly (there should be about 1⅓ cups), and strain it into a heated sauceboat. Transfer the chops, fitted with paper frills, to a heated platter, garnish them with the sage sprigs, and serve them with the sauce. Serves 4.

H. FEDERICO

Chicken with Brown Rice and Carrots

½ cup brown rice
1 tablespoon olive oil
7 ounces boneless skinless chicken breast, cut
    into ½-inch pieces
¾ cup dry white wine
1 cup canned chicken broth
2 carrots, cut into ½-inch pieces
the white part of 16 scallions, cut into ½-inch
    pieces
1 tablespoon soy sauce
2 teaspoons fresh lime juice, or to taste
¼ cup dry roasted unsalted peanuts, chopped
¼ cup thinly sliced scallion greens
cayenne to taste
thin slices of lime for garnish

Add the rice to a large saucepan of boiling salted water, boil it for 15 minutes, and drain it. In a small saucepan bring ⅓ cup water to a boil, add the rice, and cook it, covered, over moderately low heat for 15 minutes more, or until it is tender and the liquid is absorbed. Keep the rice covered until ready to use.

In a heavy skillet heat the oil over moderately high heat until it is hot, in it brown the chicken, patted dry, for 2 to 3 minutes, or until it is springy to the touch, and transfer the chicken to a small bowl. Add ¼ cup of the wine to the skillet and deglaze the skillet over moderately high heat, scraping up the brown bits. Add the remaining ½ cup wine, the broth, and the carrots and cook the carrots, covered, for 5 minutes. Add the scallion pieces, cook the vegetables, covered, over moderate heat for 15 minutes, or until the carrots are just tender, and stir in the chicken, the soy sauce, and the lime juice.

In a bowl combine the rice, the peanuts, the scallion greens, the chicken mixture, the cayenne, and salt to taste, toss the mixture well, and transfer it to a heated serving dish. Garnish the dish with the lime slices. Serves 2.

Chicken with Caper Tarragon Sauce

1 whole skinless boneless chicken breast,
    halved and flattened ¼ inch thick between
    pieces of plastic wrap
1½ teaspoons vegetable oil
⅓ cup heavy cream
2 teaspoons drained capers, chopped fine
¼ teaspoon finely crumbled dried tarragon
½ teaspoon fresh lemon juice, or to taste
1½ teaspoons unsalted butter, cut into bits and
    softened

Pat the chicken dry and season it with salt and pepper. In a heavy skillet heat the oil over moderately high heat until it is hot and in it sauté the chicken, turning it once, for 2 minutes. Transfer the chicken to a serving dish and keep it warm. Discard any oil remaining in the skillet, add to the skillet the cream, the capers, the tarragon, the lemon juice, and salt and pepper to taste, and bring the liquid to a boil, scraping up the brown bits. Remove the skillet from the heat, stir in the butter and any juices that have accumulated on the serving dish, stirring, until the butter is melted, and spoon the sauce over the chicken. Serves 2.

Beer-Batter Fried Chicken

12 ounces beer
1½ cups all-purpose flour
1 teaspoon salt
¼ teaspoon Tabasco
vegetable shortening for deep-frying
two 3½-pound chickens, cut into serving
    pieces
fresh thyme sprigs for garnish if desired

In a bowl whisk together the beer, the flour, sifted, the salt, and the Tabasco until the mixture is smooth and let the mixture stand, covered, at room temperature for 2 hours. In a large deep fryer heat 3 inches of the shortening to 335° F. Pat the chicken legs and wings dry, whisk the batter to combine it, and dip the chicken in it, letting the excess drip off and transferring the chicken to the deep fat immediately. Fry the legs and wings, turning them occasionally with tongs, for 8 minutes and transfer them to paper towels to drain. (It is important to maintain the temperature of the fat as close to 335° F. as possible at all times; if the deep fryer is not large enough to accommodate all the legs and wings at once, dip and fry them in batches, bringing the shortening back to 335° F. before frying each new batch.) In the same manner dip the breasts and thighs in the batter, fry them for 10 minutes, and transfer them to paper towels to drain. *The chicken may be made up to 8 hours in advance but keep at room temperature, covered loosely, for no more than 2 hours. To crisp the chicken heat it in one layer in jelly-roll pans in a preheated 425° F. oven for 5 minutes, or until it is crisp and sizzling. The chicken may also be made up to 3 days in advance, kept covered and chilled, and reheated in jelly-roll pans in a 425° F. oven for 10 to 15 minutes, or until it is crisp and heated through.* Serve the chicken at room temperature or hot and garnish it with the thyme sprigs if desired. Serves 6 generously.

Chicken in Succotash

a 3½-pound chicken, cut into serving pieces,
  including the neck, back, and giblets
  (excluding the liver)
2 tablespoons bacon fat or a mixture of
  1 tablespoon butter and 1 tablespoon
  vegetable oil
1 onion, chopped
¾ cup canned chicken broth
a 10-ounce package frozen baby lima beans,
  thawed, or 2 cups fresh shelled lima beans
1 sprig of thyme or ¼ teaspoon crumbled
  dried, plus additional sprigs for garnish if
  desired
1 sprig of chervil or ¼ teaspoon crumbled
  dried, plus additional sprigs for garnish if
  desired
1⅓ to 1½ cups heavy cream
1½ cups corn (cut from about 3 ears of corn)
fresh lemon juice to taste
2 tablespoons minced fresh parsley leaves
2 tablespoons snipped fresh chives
freshly baked biscuits as an accompaniment if
  desired

Pat the chicken dry and season it with salt and pepper.
In a large skillet heat the fat over moderate heat until it is
hot but not smoking, in it cook the chicken, including
the neck, back, and giblets, in batches for 10 to 12 minutes, or until it is golden on both sides, and transfer it to paper towels to drain. Pour off all but 1 tablespoon of the fat from the skillet, add the onion, and cook it over moderate heat, stirring, for 2 minutes. Add the broth and deglaze the skillet over high heat, scraping up any brown bits. Arrange the chicken in the skillet, putting the breast pieces on top, and simmer it, covered, over moderately low heat for 10 minutes. Add the lima beans, the thyme sprig, and the chervil sprig, and simmer the mixture, covered, for 8 to 10 minutes, or until the chicken is tender. Transfer the chicken with tongs to a platter, reserving the neck, back, and giblets for another use.

Add 1⅓ cups of the cream to the skillet, boil the liquid until it is thickened slightly, skimming any fat that has accumulated around the edge, and stir in the corn. Simmer the mixture for 1 minute, return the chicken to the skillet, and simmer the mixture for 3 to 5 minutes, or until the chicken is heated through. Discard the thyme and chervil sprigs, add enough of the remaining cream to thin the sauce to the desired consistency, and add the lemon juice and salt and pepper to taste. Remove the skillet from the heat and stir in the parsley and the chives. Transfer the mixture to a serving dish, garnish it with the additional thyme sprigs and chervil sprigs if desired, and serve it with the warm biscuits if desired. Serves 4.

Chicken Pies with Biscuit Crust

For the filling

3 cups chicken stock (page 119) or canned
    chicken broth
3 carrots, cut crosswise into ¼-inch pieces
¾ pound red potatoes, quartered and cut
    crosswise into ½-inch pieces
2 stalks of celery, cut crosswise into ½-inch
    pieces
2½ cups cubed cooked chicken (the meat from
    a 3-pound chicken)
1 onion, chopped
½ stick (¼ cup) unsalted butter
4 tablespoons all-purpose flour
¼ teaspoon crumbled dried thyme
¼ teaspoon freshly grated nutmeg, or to taste
½ cup minced fresh parsley leaves

For the biscuit crust

1⅓ cups all-purpose flour
1½ teaspoons double-acting baking powder
½ teaspoon baking soda
¾ teaspoon salt
2 tablespoons cold unsalted butter, cut
    into bits
2 tablespoons cold vegetable shortening, cut
    into bits
⅓ cup grated sharp Cheddar
1 large whole egg
about ⅓ cup buttermilk or 1 tablespoon dried
    buttermilk powder dissolved in ⅓ cup water
1 large egg yolk
1 tablespoon milk

Make the filling: In a saucepan bring the stock to a boil, add the carrots, the potatoes, and the celery, and simmer the vegetables for 10 minutes, or until they are tender. Transfer the vegetables with a slotted spoon to a large bowl, reserving the stock, and add the chicken to the bowl. In a heavy saucepan cook the onion in the butter over moderately low heat, stirring, until it is softened, add the flour, and cook the *roux,* stirring, for 3 minutes. Add 2 cups of the reserved stock in a stream, whisking, reserving the remaining stock for another use, and bring the mixture to a boil, whisking. Add the thyme and simmer the sauce, stirring, for 5 minutes. Stir in the nutmeg, the parsley, and salt and pepper to taste, pour the sauce over the chicken mixture, and stir the mixture gently to combine it. Divide the filling among four 2-cup individual shallow baking dishes or transfer all of it to a 2-quart shallow baking dish. *The filling may be made 1 day in advance and kept covered and chilled. Let the filling stand for 1 hour at room temperature before baking.*

Make the biscuit crust: Into a bowl sift together the flour, the baking powder, the baking soda, and the salt, add the butter and the shortening, and blend the mixture until it resembles meal. Add the Cheddar and toss the mixture to combine it. Into a liquid measuring cup break the whole egg, add enough buttermilk to measure a total of ½ cup, and beat the mixture with a fork. Add the egg mixture to the flour mixture, stirring until the mixture just forms a dough, gather the dough into a ball, and pat it out ½ inch thick on a floured surface. With a 1½-inch round cutter dipped in flour cut out as many rounds as possible, gathering the scraps and patting the dough out again in the same manner until there is a total of 24 biscuits. Divide the biscuits among the individual pies or arrange them all on the large pie.

In a small bowl beat the egg yolk with the milk, brush the tops of the biscuits with the egg wash, and prick the biscuits with a fork. Bake the pies in a preheated 450° F. oven for 15 to 25 minutes, or until the biscuits are puffed and golden and the filling is bubbly. Serves 4.

Louisiana Chicken Sauce Piquante

2 tablespoons vegetable oil
a 3- to 3¼-pound chicken, cut into serving
    pieces
1½ tablespoons unsalted butter, cut into bits
3 tablespoons flour
1½ tablespoons tomato paste
1 cup chopped onion
¾ cup chopped celery
2 cups chicken stock (page 119) or canned
    chicken broth
a 28-ounce can plum tomatoes including the
    juice
1 small green bell pepper, cut into ¼-inch
    pieces
¼ cup thinly sliced scallion greens
½ teaspoon cayenne, or to taste
cooked rice as an accompaniment

In a large heavy skillet, preferably cast iron, heat the oil over moderately high heat until it is hot but not smoking and in it brown the chicken, patted dry, in batches, transferring it with tongs as it is browned to a plate. Reduce the heat to moderately low, add the butter, and stir in the flour. Cook the *roux,* stirring, until it is the color of peanut butter, stir in the tomato paste, and add the onion and the celery. Cook the vegetables, stirring, until they are softened, stir in the stock and the tomatoes, breaking up the tomatoes, and bring the liquid to a boil. Add the chicken pieces and any juices that have accumulated on the plate and simmer the mixture, covered, for 30 minutes. Stir in the bell pepper, simmer the mixture, covered, for 20 to 30 minutes, or until the chicken is tender, and stir in the scallions, the cayenne, and salt and pepper to taste. (The stew improves in flavor if cooled to room temperature, uncovered, and chilled, covered, overnight.) Serve the stew over the rice. Serves 4 to 6.

Parmesan-Crumbed Drumsticks

½ cup freshly grated Parmesan
⅓ cup fine dry bread crumbs
1 garlic clove, pressed through a garlic press
2 teaspoons grated lemon rind
1½ teaspoons salt
1 teaspoon crumbled dried rosemary
1 teaspoon freshly ground pepper
¼ teaspoon cayenne
2½ pounds drumsticks, patted dry
7 tablespoons unsalted butter, melted

In a wide shallow bowl combine well the Parmesan, the bread crumbs, the garlic, the lemon rind, the salt, the rosemary, the pepper, and the cayenne. Working with 1 drumstick at a time, brush the drumsticks with some of the butter and dredge them in the Parmesan mixture, coating them completely. Chill the drumsticks, covered loosely, on a jelly-roll pan for at least 1 hour or up to 24 hours. Arrange the drumsticks in a lightly buttered roasting pan, drizzle them with the remaining butter, and bake them in a preheated 425° F. oven for 30 minutes, or until they are tender. Serve the drumsticks warm or at room temperature. Serves 4 to 6.

Chicken Legs "au Vin"
(Chicken Legs with Mushrooms and Onions in Red-Wine Sauce)

3 slices of lean bacon, chopped
3 pounds whole chicken legs, halved at the
   joint (or substitute all thighs or drumsticks)
1½ cups frozen small onions, thawed and
   patted dry
½ pound mushrooms, quartered
1½ cups dry red wine
1 tablespoon tomato paste
2 large garlic cloves, minced
¼ teaspoon crumbled dried thyme
1 bay leaf
1 cup canned chicken broth
beurre manié, made by kneading together 2
   tablespoons flour and 2 tablespoons
   softened unsalted butter
3 tablespoons minced fresh parsley leaves
noodles as an accompaniment

In a flameproof wide shallow casserole or large heavy ovenproof skillet cook the bacon over moderately low heat, stirring, until it is crisp and transfer it with a slotted spoon to paper towels to drain. In the fat remaining in the casserole brown the chicken, patted dry and seasoned with salt and pepper, in batches over moderately high heat, transferring it with tongs to a plate as it is browned. Add the onions to the casserole, sauté them, stirring, for 2 to 3 minutes, or until they are golden, and transfer them with a slotted spoon to a small bowl. Add the mushrooms, sauté them, stirring, for 4 minutes, or until the liquid they give off is evaporated, and transfer them to the bowl of onions. Add the wine and deglaze the casserole over high heat, scraping up the brown bits. Stir in the tomato paste, the garlic, the thyme, and the bay leaf and boil the mixture for 2 minutes. Add the broth, the bacon, and the chicken skin side up to the casserole and bring the liquid to a boil. Braise the chicken, covered, in a preheated 325° F. oven for 35 to 40 minutes, or until it is tender. Transfer the chicken with tongs to a serving dish and keep it warm, covered loosely. Add to the casserole the mushrooms and the onions, bring the mixture to a boil, and boil it for 1 minute. Whisk in bits of the *beurre manié*, whisking until the sauce is thickened slightly, add salt and pepper to taste, and discard the bay leaf. Spoon the sauce over the chicken, sprinkle the dish with the parsley, and serve it with the noodles. *The dish may be prepared up to 2 days in advance and kept covered and chilled.* Serves 6.

Broiled East Indian Chicken Legs

1 onion, chopped
4 garlic cloves, chopped
a 1½-inch cube peeled gingerroot, chopped
2 teaspoons ground cumin
2 teaspoons salt
½ teaspoon red pepper flakes
¼ cup fresh lemon juice
¼ cup vegetable oil
3 pounds whole chicken legs, halved at the
    joint (or substitute all thighs or drumsticks)

In a blender or food processor purée the onion with the garlic, the gingerroot, the cumin, the salt, the red pepper flakes, the lemon juice, and the oil, in a large bowl pour the mixture over the chicken, stirring to coat the chicken well, and let the chicken marinate, covered and chilled, for at least 2 hours or up to 24 hours. Transfer the chicken, letting the excess marinade drip off, to an oiled rack of a broiler pan, arranging it skin side down, and broil it under a preheated broiler 4 to 5 inches from the heat, turning it once, for 30 minutes, or until it is tender and the skin is crisp. Serve the chicken warm or at room temperature. Serves 6.

Chicken Legs Cacciatora
(Chicken Legs with Herbed Tomato Sauce)

2 tablespoons olive oil or vegetable oil
3 pounds whole chicken legs, halved at the
    joint (or substitute all thighs or drumsticks)
1 onion, chopped fine
1 carrot, cut into ⅛-inch slices
1 large stalk of celery, cut into ⅛-inch slices
1 large green bell pepper, cut into ½-inch
    pieces
4 garlic cloves, minced
1 teaspoon red pepper flakes
a 1-pound can tomatoes, drained and chopped,
    reserving the juice
½ cup dry white wine
¾ teaspoon crumbled dried orégano
2 tablespoons minced fresh parsley leaves

In a flameproof wide shallow casserole heat the oil over moderately high heat until it is hot and in it brown the chicken, patted dry and seasoned with salt and pepper, in batches, transferring it with tongs to a plate as it is browned. Add to the casserole the onion, the carrot, the celery, and the bell pepper and cook the vegetables over moderately low heat, stirring, until they are soft-ened. Add the garlic and the red pepper flakes and cook the mixture, stirring, for 1 minute. Add the chopped to-matoes and cook the mixture over moderately high heat, stirring, until the excess liquid is evaporated. Add the wine and boil the mixture, stirring, until it is reduced by half. Stir in the reserved tomato juice and the orégano, add the chicken, and bring the liquid to a boil. Cover the casserole and braise the chicken in a preheated 325° F. oven for 35 to 40 minutes, or until it is tender. Transfer the chicken to a platter, keep it warm, covered loosely, and boil the cooking liquid, stirring, until it is thickened slightly. Stir in the parsley and salt and pepper to taste and spoon the sauce over the chicken. *The dish may be prepared up to 2 days in advance and kept covered and chilled.* Serves 6.

Chicken Legs Paprikás
(Chicken Legs with Paprika Sour Cream Sauce)

3 tablespoons vegetable oil
3 pounds whole chicken legs, halved at the
    joint (or substitute all thighs or drumsticks)
1 onion, chopped fine
1½ tablespoons sweet paprika (preferably
    Hungarian)
a 1-pound can tomatoes, drained and chopped
    fine
1 cup canned chicken broth
½ cup sour cream
2 tablespoons all-purpose flour
fresh lemon juice to taste
1 green bell pepper, sliced thin
noodles or boiled potatoes as an accompaniment

In a wide flameproof casserole or large heavy oven-proof skillet heat 2 tablespoons of the oil over moderately high heat until it is hot and in it brown the chicken, patted dry and seasoned with salt and pepper, in batch-es, transferring it with tongs to a plate as it is browned. Add the onion to the casserole and cook it over moder-ately low heat, stirring, until it is softened. Add the pa-prika and cook the mixture, stirring, for 10 seconds. Add the tomatoes and cook the mixture, stirring, for 2 minutes. Add the broth, return the chicken skin side up to the casserole, and bring the liquid to a boil. Cover the casserole, braise the chicken in a preheated 325° F. oven for 35 to 40 minutes, or until it is tender, and trans-fer it with tongs to a plate.

Bring the cooking liquid to a boil over high heat and, if necessary, boil it, stirring, until it is reduced to about

2 cups. In a small bowl whisk together the sour cream and the flour until the mixture is smooth, whisk ½ cup of the cooking liquid into the sour cream mixture, and whisk the mixture into the remaining cooking liquid. Simmer the sauce, stirring, for 2 to 3 minutes, or until it is thickened slightly, season it with salt, pepper, and the lemon juice, and return the chicken to the sauce. *The chicken may be prepared up to this point 1 day ahead and kept covered and chilled.* Simmer the mixture, stirring, until the chicken is heated through.

In a small skillet heat the remaining 1 tablespoon oil over moderately high heat until it is hot and in it sauté the bell pepper, stirring, for 1 minute, or until it is softened. Transfer the chicken mixture to a heated serving dish and arrange the bell pepper slices over it. Serve the chicken with the noodles or the potatoes. Serves 6.

Chicken and Vegetable Stew

2 tablespoons vegetable oil
2 chicken legs, cut into thighs and drumsticks
2½ tablespoons all-purpose flour
1 small onion, chopped fine
¼ cup chopped green bell pepper
2 carrots, cut crosswise into ½-inch slices
2 small boiling potatoes
1 teaspoon finely crumbled dried marjoram
¼ cup thinly sliced scallion greens
cayenne to taste
buttered noodles as an accompaniment

In a heavy skillet heat the oil over moderately high heat until it is hot, in it brown the chicken, turning it, and transfer the chicken to a plate. Pour off all but 2 tablespoons of the fat, stir in the flour, and cook the *roux* over moderate heat, stirring, for 3 minutes, letting it brown. Add the onion, cook the mixture, stirring, for 1 minute, and stir in 2 cups water, the bell pepper, and the chicken and any juices that have accumulated on the plate. Bring the liquid to a boil, stirring occasionally,

and simmer the mixture, covered, for 10 minutes. Add the carrots, the potatoes, halved, and the marjoram and cook the mixture, covered, for 15 to 17 minutes, or until the vegetables are tender. Add the scallions, the cayenne, and salt to taste and serve the stew over the noodles. Serves 2.

Chicken Thigh Paillards with Tarragon Vinegar Sauce

2½ pounds (about 8) chicken thighs, skinned and boned
1½ tablespoons vegetable oil
5 shallots, minced
½ teaspoon crumbled dried tarragon
½ cup cider vinegar
1 cup canned chicken broth
beurre manié, made by kneading together 1½ tablespoons flour and 1 tablespoon softened unsalted butter
2 tablespoons minced fresh parsley leaves

Flatten the thighs between sheets of dampened wax paper to about ¼ inch thick, pat them dry, and season them with salt and pepper. In a large heavy skillet, preferably cast iron, heat the oil over high heat until it is very hot and in it sear the thighs in batches, covered, turning them once, for 3 minutes, or until they are golden and firm to the touch. Transfer the thighs as they are cooked to a platter and keep them warm, covered loosely. Remove the skillet from the heat, add the shallots, and cook them in the residual heat of the skillet, stirring, until they are softened slightly. Add the tarragon and the vinegar and deglaze the skillet over high heat, scraping up the brown bits. Boil the liquid until it is almost completely evaporated, add the broth and any juices that have accumulated on the platter, and bring the liquid to a boil. Whisk in bits of the *beurre manié*, whisking until the sauce is thickened slightly, stir in the parsley and salt and pepper to taste, and spoon the sauce over the chicken. Serves 4.

Buffalo Chicken Wings

vegetable shortening or vegetable oil for deep-
  frying
3 pounds chicken wings, wing tips cut off and
  reserved for another use such as wing tip
  consommé (page 119) and the wings halved at
  the joint
3 tablespoons unsalted butter
4 tablespoons Frank's Louisiana Hot Sauce
  (available at supermarkets), or to taste
1 tablespoon cider vinegar
blue cheese dressing (recipe follows) and
  celery sticks as accompaniments

In a deep fryer or deep heavy skillet heat 2 inches of
the shortening to 380° F. and in it fry the wings, patted
dry and seasoned with salt and pepper, in small batches
for 5 to 8 minutes, or until they are golden and crisp,
transferring them with a slotted spoon as they are fried
to paper towels to drain and making sure the shortening
returns to 380° F. before adding each new batch. In a
large skillet melt the butter with the Louisiana Hot
Sauce and the vinegar over low heat, stirring, add the
wings, and heat them, tossing them to coat them with
the mixture. Transfer the wings to a platter and serve
them warm or at room temperature with the blue cheese
dressing and the celery sticks. Serves 8 as an hors
d'oeuvre.

Blue Cheese Dressing

⅔ cup mayonnaise (page 232)
⅓ cup sour cream
⅓ cup crumbled blue cheese

In a bowl combine well the mayonnaise, the sour
cream, and the blue cheese. Makes about 1 ⅓ cups.

Crispy Chinese Chicken Wings

2 pounds chicken wings, wing tips cut off and
  reserved for another use such as wing tip
  consommé (page 119) and the wings halved at
  the joint
3 garlic cloves, crushed with the flat side of a
  cleaver
3 slices of peeled gingerroot, each the size of
  a quarter, flattened with the flat side of a
  cleaver
1 tablespoon Scotch
1 tablespoon soy sauce
¾ cup cornstarch
vegetable shortening or vegetable oil for deep-
  frying
finely minced scallions and Szechwan
  peppercorn salt (recipe follows) as
  accompaniments

In a bowl toss the wings with the garlic, the ginger-root, the Scotch, and the soy sauce and let them marinate at room temperature for 30 minutes or covered and chilled for up to 8 hours. Discard the garlic and the gingerroot and in a bowl dredge the wings in small batches in the cornstarch, transferring them as they are dredged to racks to dry. In a wok or deep fryer heat 3 inches of the shortening to 375° F. and in it fry the wings in small batches for 5 minutes, transferring them with a slotted spoon to paper towels to drain as they are fried and making sure the shortening returns to 375° F. before adding each new batch.

When all the wings are fried heat the oil to 425° F. and in it fry the wings in batches for 2 minutes more, or until they are golden and crisp, transferring them with the slotted spoon to the paper towels to drain as they are fried. (The second frying crisps the wings.) Serve the wings with small dishes of the scallions and the Szechwan peppercorn salt for dipping. Serves 4 to 6 as an hors d'oeuvre.

Szechwan Peppercorn Salt

1 teaspoon Szechwan peppercorns (available
   at Oriental markets and many supermarkets)
1 tablespoon salt

In a dry small skillet toast the peppercorns over moderately low heat, swirling the skillet, for 4 to 5 minutes, or until they are fragrant. Transfer the peppercorns to a mortar and crush them with a pestle or pulverize them in an electric coffee or spice grinder. In a small bowl combine the pulverized peppercorns with the salt. Makes about 1 tablespoon.

Deviled Chicken Wings

¼ cup mayonnaise
¼ cup Dijon-style mustard
1 teaspoon dry mustard
cayenne to taste if desired
½ cup fine fresh bread crumbs
3 tablespoons minced fresh parsley leaves
2 pounds chicken wings, wing tips cut off and
   reserved for another use such as wing tip
   consommé (page 119) and the wings
   patted dry

In a small bowl whisk together the mayonnaise, the Dijon-style mustard, the dry mustard, and the cayenne. In another bowl combine well the bread crumbs and the parsley. Arrange the wings skin side down on a foil-lined rack of a broiler pan and season them with salt and pepper. Brush the wings liberally with some of the mustard mixture and broil them under a preheated broiler 4 to 5 inches from the heat for 10 to 12 minutes, or until they are browned. Turn the wings, brush them with more of the mustard mixture, and broil them for 6 minutes more, or until they are tender. Brush the wings with the remaining mustard mixture, top them with the crumb mixture, patting it on, and broil them for 2 to 4 minutes, or until the topping is golden brown. Serves 4 to 6 as an hors d'oeuvre.

Dick Christensen's Chicken Wings
 (Marinated Roasted Chicken Wings)

3 garlic cloves, chopped
2 teaspoons peppercorns, cracked
2 teaspoons salt
1½ tablespoons Maggi Seasoning (available at
   supermarkets) or Worcestershire sauce
½ teaspoon dry mustard
¼ cup tarragon vinegar
⅓ cup vegetable oil
3 pounds chicken wings, wing tips cut off and
   reserved for another use such as wing tip
   consommé (page 119) and the wings halved at
   the joint

In a blender blend the garlic, the peppercorns, the salt, the Maggi Seasoning, the mustard, and the vinegar until the mixture is smooth, with the motor running add the oil in a stream, and blend the mixture until it is emulsified. In a bowl combine the wings with the marinade and let them marinate at room temperature for 1 hour or covered and chilled for up to 24 hours. Transfer the wings skin side up in one layer to a large baking pan, letting the excess marinade drip off, bake them in a preheated 475° F. oven for 30 minutes, and broil them under a preheated broiler about 2 inches from the heat for 2 to 4 minutes, or until the skin is crisp. Transfer the wings with a slotted spoon to a platter and serve them warm or at room temperature. Serves 8 as an hors d'oeuvre.

Brioches Stuffed with Brandied Chicken Livers

6 brioches (page 99), tops removed and
  reserved and centers hollowed out,
  reserving the crumbs for another use
½ pound mushrooms, trimmed and quartered
3 tablespoons unsalted butter
3 tablespoons clarified butter (procedure on
  page 278) or vegetable oil
1½ pounds chicken livers, trimmed and
  patted dry
flour for dredging
½ cup minced shallots or scallions
½ cup brandy
½ cup dry white wine
½ cup chicken stock (page 119) or canned
  chicken broth
1 cup heavy cream
1 tablespoon minced fresh thyme leaves or 1
  teaspoon crumbled dried
3 tablespoons Dijon-style mustard
⅓ cup minced fresh parsley leaves plus
  additional for garnish

Make the brioches and keep them, covered, in a
warm oven while the livers are being prepared. In a skillet cook the mushrooms in the unsalted butter over moderate heat, stirring, until all the liquid the mushrooms
give off is evaporated and reserve them. In a large skillet
heat the clarified butter over moderately high heat until
it is hot and in it sauté the livers, dredged in the flour, in
batches, stirring, for 5 to 6 minutes, or until they are
browned on the outside but still pink within, transferring them with a slotted spoon to a plate as they are
done. Pour off the fat, add the shallots, the brandy, the
wine, and the stock, and boil the mixture over high heat
until it is reduced by half. Add the cream and boil the
mixture until it is reduced by half and starts to thicken.
Add the livers and any juices that have accumulated on
the plate, the reserved mushrooms, the thyme, the mustard, the parsley, and salt and pepper to taste and cook
the mixture over moderate heat, stirring, for 3 minutes.
Spoon the mixture into the brioches and sprinkle it with
the additional parsley. Arrange the brioches and the reserved tops decoratively on a platter. Serves 6.

ASSORTED FOWL

Rock Cornish Game Hen with Mustard Lemon Butter

2 tablespoons unsalted butter, softened
½ teaspoon Dijon-style mustard
1 teaspoon fresh lemon juice
⅛ teaspoon salt
a 1½-pound Rock Cornish game hen, halved,
  backbone removed, and patted dry

In a small bowl blend together the butter, the mustard, the lemon juice, the salt, and pepper to taste. Loos-
en the skin carefully from the breast meat on each hen
half with your finger, rub the meat under the skin with
two thirds of the butter mixture, smoothing the skin
over the mixture, and rub the remaining butter mixture
over the skin. Roast the hen skin side up on the foil-lined
rack of a broiling pan in a preheated 425° F. oven for 30
minutes, or until the juices run clear when a thigh is
pricked with a skewer. Transfer the hen to a heated platter. Serves 2.

Deviled Roast Rock Cornish Game Hens

3 tablespoons soy sauce
2 tablespoons honey
1 tablespoon cider vinegar
two 1½-pound Rock Cornish game hens,
  halved, removing the backbones, and
  patted dry
1 tablespoon vegetable oil
2 tablespoons Dijon-style mustard
French fried sweet potatoes (page 208) as an
  accompaniment
watercress sprigs for garnish

In a large shallow bowl whisk together the soy sauce,
the honey, and the vinegar, add the hen halves, turning
them to coat them with the marinade, and let them marinate skin side down at room temperature for at least 30
minutes or covered and chilled overnight. Transfer the
hens skin side up to the foil-lined rack of a broiling pan,
reserving the marinade, rub them with the oil, and season them with salt and pepper. Roast the hens in a pre-

heated 425° F. oven for 15 minutes. While the hens are roasting, in a small saucepan bring the reserved marinade to a boil and boil it, stirring occasionally, until it is reduced by half. Remove the pan from the heat and whisk in the mustard. Brush the hens liberally with the mustard mixture and continue to roast them, basting them again with the mustard mixture, for 10 to 15 minutes, or until the juices run clear when a thigh is pricked with a skewer (170° F. on an instant-read meat thermometer). Transfer the hens to a heated platter with a slotted spatula, arrange the sweet potatoes on the platter, and garnish the dish with the watercress. Serves 4.

Roasted Rock Cornish Game Hens with Scallions

a 1½-pound Rock Cornish game hen, halved
   lengthwise and rinsed
1½ tablespoons vegetable oil
¼ cup dry white wine
½ teaspoon finely crumbled dried rosemary
½ bay leaf
8 scallions, including 1 inch of the green part
2 tablespoons cold unsalted butter, cut into
   bits
fresh lemon juice to taste
1 teaspoon minced scallion greens

Pat the hen dry. In a heavy ovenproof skillet heat the oil over moderately high heat until it is hot and in it brown the hen, turning it. Transfer the hen to a dish, deglaze the skillet with the wine, scraping up the brown bits, and arrange the hen skin side up in the skillet. Sprinkle the hen with the rosemary and salt and pepper to taste, add the bay leaf, and put the skillet in a preheated 450° F. oven. Reduce the heat to 375° F. and roast the hen, basting it once and adding a little water if necessary to keep ½ cup liquid in the skillet, for 10 minutes. Add the whole scallions and roast the hen, basting it once, for 20 minutes more. Transfer the hen and the scallions to a platter. Discard the bay leaf, bring the liquid in the skillet to a boil, and reduce it until it is thickened slightly. Whisk in the butter and the lemon juice and season the sauce with salt and pepper. Spoon the sauce over the hen and sprinkle the minced scallion over it. Serves 2.

Broiled Squabs with Grapes and Zinfandel Sauce

two ¾-pound squabs or 2 small (1 to 1¼
   pounds each) Rock Cornish game hens
1 tablespoon vegetable oil
2 tablespoons unsalted butter

½ cup chopped onion
¼ cup chopped carrot
½ cup chopped red grapes
½ teaspoon crumbled dried thyme
½ small bay leaf
½ cup Zinfandel or other dry, fruity red wine
¾ cup chicken stock (page 119) or 2 teaspoons
   unflavored gelatin combined with ¾ cup
   canned chicken broth
8 red grapes, halved and seeded
8 green seedless grapes, halved
2 teaspoons Dijon-style mustard
small clusters of red and green grapes for
   garnish

Cut and remove the backbones from the squabs and cut the backbones into several pieces. Flatten the squabs skin side up by breaking the wishbones and pressing down on the breastbones and reserve them, covered and chilled. In a large saucepan sauté the chopped backbones in the oil over moderately high heat, stirring, until they are browned on all sides, add 1 tablespoon of the butter, the onion, and the carrot, and cook the mixture, stirring, until the vegetables are browned lightly. Add the chopped red grapes, the thyme, the bay leaf, the Zinfandel, and the stock, bring the mixture to a boil, skimming it, and simmer it for 45 minutes, or until the liquid is reduced to about ⅔ cup. Strain the stock through a fine sieve into a saucepan, pressing hard on the solids, and discard the solids. *The stock may be made 1 day in advance, kept covered and chilled, and reheated.*

Season the reserved squabs with salt and pepper and broil them skin side down on a lightly oiled rack under a preheated broiler about 4 inches from the heat for 4 minutes, turn them, and broil them for 6 minutes more for medium-rare meat. (If using the hens, broil them, starting with the skin side down and turning them once, for a total of 20 to 25 minutes, or until the juices run clear when a thigh is pricked with a skewer.) Transfer the squabs to a heated platter and let them stand, covered loosely, for 5 minutes.

In a skillet cook the halved red and green grapes in the remaining 1 tablespoon butter over moderate heat, stirring, for 2 to 3 minutes, or until they are just softened, and stir in the stock and any juices from the squabs that have accumulated on the plate. Bring the mixture to a boil, cook it until the liquid is reduced to about ½ cup, and whisk in the mustard and salt and pepper to taste. Transfer the squabs to a heated platter, garnish them with the red and green grape clusters, and serve them with the sauce. Serves 2.

Roast Turkey with Smoked Sausage and Rosemary Stuffing

For the stuffing

12 stale slices of homemade-type white bread
½ pound smoked sausage (such as *kielbasa*), chopped
1 stick (½ cup) unsalted butter
1½ cups chopped onion
1½ cups chopped celery
2 large garlic cloves, minced
2 teaspoons crumbled dried rosemary
1 cup thinly sliced scallion including the green tops
⅓ cup minced fresh parsley leaves
1 teaspoon salt, or to taste
⅛ teaspoon cayenne, or to taste
½ teaspoon black pepper

a 14-pound turkey, reserving the neck and giblets (excluding the liver) for making turkey giblet stock (recipe follows)
1 slice of bread
2 sticks (1 cup) unsalted butter, softened

For the gravy

1 cup dry white wine
7 tablespoons all-purpose flour
4 cups turkey giblet stock (recipe follows), reserving the cooked giblets if desired

fresh rosemary sprigs for garnish

Make the stuffing: Bake the bread slices in one layer on baking sheets in a preheated 300° F. oven for 10 to 20 minutes, or until they are pale golden, and let them cool. Enclose the slices in a large plastic bag, with a rolling pin crush them coarse, and transfer the crumbs to a large bowl. In a large skillet cook the sausage over moderate heat, stirring, until some of the fat has been rendered and the sausage is golden. Transfer the sausage with a slotted spoon to the bowl of crumbs. Add the butter to the fat remaining in the skillet, melt it, and add the onion and the celery. Cook the mixture over moderately low heat, stirring, until the vegetables are softened, add the garlic and the rosemary, and cook the mixture, stirring, for 1 minute. Transfer the mixture with the butter to the bowl of crumbs, add the scallion, the parsley, the salt, the cayenne, and the black pepper, and combine the stuffing well. Let the stuffing cool completely. *The stuffing may be made up to 1 day in advance and kept covered and chilled.* Do not stuff the turkey in advance.

Rinse the turkey, pat it dry, and season it inside and out with salt and pepper. Pack the neck cavity loosely with some of the stuffing, fold the neck skin under the body, and fasten it with a skewer. Pack the body cavity loosely with the remaining stuffing, cover it with the slice of bread, and tie the drumsticks together with kitchen string. Spread the turkey with 1 stick of the butter, season it with salt and pepper, and roast it on the rack of a roasting pan in a preheated 425° F. oven for 30 minutes. Reduce the heat to 325° F., brush the turkey with the pan juices, and arrange a piece of cheesecloth soaked in the remaining 1 stick butter, melted and cooled, over it. Roast the turkey, basting it every 20 minutes, for 2 hours and 30 minutes to 3 hours more, or until the juices run clear when the fleshy part of a thigh is pricked with a skewer and a meat thermometer inserted in the fleshy part of a thigh registers 180° F. Discard the cheesecloth and the trussing strings and if desired transfer the stuffing to a heated serving dish. Transfer the turkey to a heated large platter and let it stand for 25 minutes.

Make the gravy: Skim the fat from the pan juices and reserve ⅓ cup of it. Add the wine to the pan juices in the roasting pan and deglaze the pan over high heat, scraping up the brown bits clinging to the bottom and sides. Boil the liquid until it is reduced by half and reserve it. In a saucepan combine the reserved fat and the flour and cook the *roux* over moderately low heat, whisking, for 3 minutes. Add the stock and the reserved wine mixture in a stream, whisking, bring the liquid to a boil, whisking constantly, and simmer the gravy, stirring occasionally, for 10 minutes. If desired add the reserved cooked giblets, chopped fine, season the gravy with salt and pepper, and transfer it to a heated sauceboat. Garnish the platter with the rosemary sprigs. Serves 8.

Turkey Giblet Stock

the neck and giblets (excluding the liver) of 1 turkey
4 cups chicken stock (page 119) or canned chicken broth
1 stalk of celery, halved crosswise
1 carrot, halved crosswise
1 onion stuck with 1 clove
1 bay leaf
¼ teaspoon crumbled dried thyme

In a large saucepan combine the neck and giblets, the stock, the celery, the carrot, the onion, and 4 cups water and bring the liquid to a boil, skimming the froth as it rises to the surface. Add the bay leaf and the thyme and cook the mixture at a bare simmer for 3 hours. Strain the stock through a fine sieve into a bowl, if desired reserve the giblets for the gravy or another use, and skim off the fat. The stock may be frozen. Makes about 4 cups.

Pistachioed Turkey Ballottine with Madeira Sauce

two 8-pound turkey breasts (thawed if frozen), boned (page 172), reserving the fillets and the trimmings for the stuffing and the bones for turkey breast stock (page 119)
½ teaspoon dried thyme
3 tablespoons dry vermouth
½ pound lean bacon, chopped
6 large eggs
2 cups well chilled heavy cream
1½ teaspoons salt
1 teaspoon freshly ground pepper
½ teaspoon freshly grated nutmeg
1 pound baked ham, ground coarse
1 pound lean ground pork
1⅓ cups shelled pistachio nuts, blanched and oven-dried (procedure on page 277)
1⅓ cups minced scallions
½ cup vegetable oil
For the Madeira sauce
2 cups dry white wine
8 cups turkey breast stock (page 119) or canned chicken broth
1½ cups Sercial Madeira
¼ cup arrowroot

Weigh the reserved turkey breast trimmings and if necessary trim off enough additional meat from the edges of the breasts to make 1 pound. Grind the trimmings in a meat grinder. Pat the breasts dry and arrange each one skin side down on a large piece of doubled cheesecloth. Crumble the thyme over the breasts and season the breasts well with pepper. Cut the reserved fillets lengthwise into ½-inch strips and in a bowl toss the strips with the vermouth and salt and pepper to taste.

In a food processor purée the bacon with the ground turkey, blend in the eggs, 1 at a time, and blend the mixture well. With the motor running add the cream in a stream with the salt, the pepper, and the nutmeg and blend the mixture until it is just smooth. In a large bowl combine well the ham, the pork, and the bacon mixture, add the pistachio nuts and the scallions, and combine the mixture well. Chill the filling, covered, for 30 minutes, or until it is stiffened.

Season one of the turkey breasts with salt. Divide the filling into 4 equal portions. Spread one portion of it over the turkey, leaving a 1-inch border all around, arrange half the fillet strips, drained and patted dry, lengthwise in one layer on the filling, pressing them gently into it, and spread one more portion of the remaining filling over them in an even layer. With a long side facing you and using the cheesecloth bring the 2 long edges of the turkey breast together to form a roll, enclosing the stuffing. Roll the cheesecloth edges together firmly along the length of the turkey roll and tie the roll at 1-inch intervals with kitchen string. Twist the ends of the cheesecloth together firmly and tie them with kitchen string. (The filling will ooze a bit at the ends and along the seam of the roll but the cheesecloth will contain it.) Stuff the remaining turkey breast in the same manner with the remaining filling and the remaining fillet strips.

In each of 2 roasting pans heat ¼ cup of the oil over moderately high heat until it is hot and in it brown the *ballottines* wrapped in the cheesecloth, patted dry and seasoned with salt and pepper. Roast the *ballottines* seam side down in a preheated 325° F. oven, rotating the placement of the pans from the upper third to the lower third of the oven and basting the *ballottines* every 30 minutes, for 1 hour and 45 minutes to 2 hours, or until a meat thermometer registers 160° F. Transfer the *ballottines* to a work surface, reserving the pan drippings in the roasting pans, discard the strings, and peel off the cheesecloth carefully. Let the *ballottines* stand for 20 minutes before carving. *The* ballottines *may be made up to this point 1 day in advance. Let the* ballottines *cool to room temperature and chill them, wrapped well in plastic wrap. Remove the plastic and reheat the* ballottines, *wrapped in foil, on a rack set over a pan of water in a preheated 350° F. oven for 45 minutes, or until they are heated through.*

Make the Madeira sauce: Spoon off the fat from the roasting pans, add 1 cup of the wine to each pan, and deglaze the pans over high heat, scraping up the brown bits. Reduce the liquid in the pans by half and transfer it to a large saucepan. Add the stock and 1 cup of the Madeira, bring the liquid to a boil, and boil it for 5 minutes. In a small bowl dissolve the arrowroot in the remaining ½ cup Madeira, whisk the mixture into the boiling sauce, and boil the sauce, whisking, for 2 minutes, or until it is thickened. Season the sauce with salt and pepper and strain it through a fine sieve into heated sauceboats. *The sauce may be made 1 day in advance and kept covered and chilled.* Makes about 9 cups.

Slice the *ballottines* ¼ to ⅓ inch thick, arrange the slices, overlapping slightly, on heated platters, and serve them with the sauce. Serves 20.

To Bone a Turkey Breast

With a sharp knife and the fingers cut and pull the wishbone from the turkey breast. Turn the breast skin side down on a work surface and, starting at the severed backbone and working toward the ridge of the breastbone, cut the meat of half the breast away from the carcass, keeping the blade of the knife angled against the bones and pulling the meat away from the bones as it is cut. Turn the breast around so that the other side of the severed backbone is facing you and cut the meat away from the bones in the same manner. With the knife angled against the breastbone sever the meat from the bone completely, being careful not to cut the skin. Reserve the bones. Lay the breast skin side down. Remove the fillets from the breast, trim them of any tendons and sinews, and reserve them. Cut the breast to a uniform 1-inch thickness by slicing horizontally into the thicker sections and laying the slices open like a book. Use some of the trimmings to patch those areas of the breast where there is little or no meat, reserving the remaining trimmings. Cover the breast with moistened wax paper and with a mallet or the flat side of a cleaver pound the meat to flatten it slightly.

Turkey Scaloppine with Cassis Cranberry Sauce

For the sauce
¼ cup red-wine vinegar
3 tablespoons sugar

3 cups chicken stock (page 119) or canned chicken broth
1 cup finely chopped onion
¼ cup finely chopped carrot
3 tablespoons unsalted butter
3 tablespoons all-purpose flour
1 cup fresh or thawed frozen cranberries, picked over
¼ cup *crème de cassis*

1½ pounds turkey breast cutlets or slices
flour seasoned with salt and pepper for dredging
3 tablespoons vegetable oil
watercress sprigs for garnish
savory bread pudding (recipe follows) as an accompaniment

Make the sauce: In a small saucepan combine the vinegar and the sugar and cook the mixture over moderately low heat, stirring, until the sugar is dissolved. Bring the mixture to a boil and simmer it until it is reduced by half. Add the stock carefully (the mixture will spatter) and simmer the mixture, stirring, for 5 minutes. In a skillet cook the onion and the carrot in the butter over moderate heat, stirring, until they are browned. Reduce the heat to moderately low, add the flour, and cook the mixture, stirring, for 3 minutes. Whisk in the stock mixture, bring the liquid to a boil, whisking, and simmer the mixture for 5 minutes. Strain the mixture

through a fine sieve into a saucepan, pressing hard on the solids, add the cranberries, the *crème de cassis*, and salt and pepper to taste, and simmer the sauce for 5 minutes, or until the cranberries have popped. *The sauce may be made up to 1 day in advance, kept covered and chilled, and reheated.*

Flatten the turkey about ¼ inch thick between dampened sheets of wax paper and dredge it in the flour, shaking off the excess. In a large skillet heat the oil over moderately high heat until it is hot but not smoking and in it sauté the turkey in batches, turning it once, for 2 minutes, or until it is just firm to the touch. Transfer the turkey with tongs to a plate and keep it warm, covered. Pour off the fat from the skillet, add the sauce, and boil it for 2 minutes, scraping up any brown bits. Arrange the turkey in the center of a heated platter, overlapping it in a circle, nap it with about ¼ cup of the sauce, mounding the cranberries in the center, and top the cranberries with the watercress. Serve the turkey with the bread pudding, sliced and arranged on the platter, and the remaining sauce. Serves 6.

Savory Bread Pudding

1 cup minced onion
½ stick (¼ cup) unsalted butter
½ pound mushrooms, halved and sliced thin
2 tablespoons Tawny Port
1 teaspoon crumbled dried thyme
1 teaspoon crumbled dried sage
½ cup finely chopped celery
1 loaf of Italian bread, torn into pieces (about 6 cups) and toasted in a baking pan in a preheated 350° F. oven, stirring occasionally, for 15 minutes, or until it is crisp but not browned
2 large eggs, beaten lightly
1½ cups chicken stock (page 119) or canned chicken broth
¼ cup minced fresh parsley leaves

Butter a loaf pan, 8½ by 4½ by 2⅜ inches, and line it with a buttered 15-inch-long sheet of wax paper, letting the wax paper hang over the long sides of the pan. In a skillet cook the onion in the butter over moderately low heat, stirring, until it is softened, add the mushrooms, and cook the mixture stirring, until all the liquid the mushrooms give off is evaporated. Add the Port, the thyme, and the sage and cook the mixture, stirring, for 3 minutes. Transfer the mixture to a large bowl, stir in the celery, the bread, the eggs, the stock, the parsley,

and salt and pepper to taste, and let the mixture stand, stirring occasionally, for 5 minutes. Pack the mixture firmly into the pan, fold the wax paper over the top, and press down hard on the mixture. Bake the pudding in a baking pan of hot water in a preheated 250° F. oven for 1 hour. *The pudding may be made up to 1 day in advance, kept covered and chilled, and reheated in a baking pan of hot water in a preheated 400° F. oven for 15 minutes, or until it is heated through.* Remove the wax paper gently. Serves 6.

Turkey Tetrazzini

¼ pound spaghetti
¼ pound mushrooms, sliced thin
⅓ cup coarsely chopped green bell pepper
3½ tablespoons unsalted butter
2 tablespoons flour
¾ cup milk
⅓ cup canned chicken broth
3 tablespoons heavy cream
1 large egg yolk
4 teaspoons medium-dry Sherry
enough cooked turkey meat, cut into ½-inch pieces, to measure 1¼ cups
½ cup grated sharp Cheddar

In a kettle of boiling salted water cook the spaghetti for 10 to 12 minutes, or until it is *al dente*, and drain it in a colander. Rinse the spaghetti and drain it well. While the spaghetti is cooking, in a skillet cook the mushrooms and the bell pepper in 1½ tablespoons of the butter over moderately low heat, stirring, until they are softened and reserve them.

In a heavy saucepan melt the remaining 2 tablespoons butter over moderately low heat, stir in the flour, and cook the *roux*, stirring, for 3 minutes. Add the milk and the broth in a stream, whisking, bring the mixture to a boil, whisking, and remove the pan from the heat. In a small bowl whisk together the cream and the egg yolk, add ½ cup of the hot milk mixture in a stream, whisking, and whisk the yolk mixture into the milk mixture. Return the pan to the heat, heat the sauce over low heat, stirring, until it is hot but not boiling, and stir in the Sherry and the turkey. Transfer the mixture to a large bowl and add the spaghetti, the vegetable mixture, and salt and pepper to taste. Toss the mixture well, transfer it to a 3-cup gratin dish, and sprinkle it with the Cheddar. Bake the mixture in a preheated 375° F. oven for 25 minutes, or until it is heated through and the Cheddar is bubbling. Serves 2.

CHEESE AND EGGS

CHEESE

Apple and Cheddar Gratin

2 pounds Granny Smith apples, peeled and cut
  into ¼-inch slices
½ cup raisins
½ teaspoon cinnamon
¼ cup fresh lemon juice
¾ cup firmly packed dark brown sugar
½ cup all-purpose flour
⅛ teaspoon salt
½ stick (¼ cup) cold unsalted butter, cut
  into bits
1 cup finely grated extra sharp Cheddar

In a well-buttered 1-quart shallow baking dish arrange the apple slices and sprinkle them with the raisins, the cinnamon, and the lemon juice. In a small bowl
combine the sugar, the flour, and the salt, blend in the
butter until the mixture resembles coarse meal, and toss
the mixture with the Cheddar. Sprinkle the Cheddar
mixture over the apple mixture and bake the gratin in the
upper third of a preheated 350° F. oven for 30 minutes,
or until the apples are tender. Serve the gratin as a dessert or as an accompaniment to roast pork or ham.
Serves 4 to 6.

Cheese Pudding

16 slices of homemade-type white bread,
  buttered
1 pound sliced Monterey Jack or Münster
  cheese
4 scallions, minced
5 large eggs, beaten lightly
1 tablespoon Dijon-style mustard
3 cups milk
1 teaspoon salt
¼ teaspoon cayenne
¼ cup fine fresh bread crumbs
⅓ cup freshly grated Parmesan
2 tablespoons cold unsalted butter, cut
  into bits

In a buttered 3-quart shallow baking dish arrange in
alternate layers the bread, the cheese, and the scallions.
In a bowl whisk the eggs with the mustard until the mixture is combined and whisk in the milk, the salt, and the
cayenne. Pour the egg mixture into the baking dish
slowly and let the mixture stand for 30 minutes. In a
small bowl combine the bread crumbs and the Parmesan, sprinkle the pudding evenly with the mixture, and
dot it with the butter. Bake the pudding in a preheated
350° F. oven for 50 minutes to 1 hour, or until it is
puffed and golden brown. Serves 6 as a light luncheon
entrée or 8 to 10 as a side dish.

Cream Cheese and Olive Ribbon Sandwiches

For the fillings

½ cup drained and chopped pitted black olives

6 ounces cream cheese, softened

3 tablespoons softened unsalted butter

½ cup drained and chopped pimiento-stuffed
    green olives

⅓ cup drained and chopped bottled roasted red
    pepper or pimiento

1 hard-boiled large egg yolk

8 very thin slices of whole-wheat bread

4 very thin slices of homemade-type white
    bread

4 very thin slices of pumpernickel bread

Make the fillings: In a food processor purée the black olives with 2 tablespoons of the cream cheese and 1 tablespoon of the butter and transfer the mixture to a small bowl. In the food processor purée the green olives with 2 tablespoons of the cream cheese and 1 tablespoon of the butter and transfer the mixture to another small bowl. In the food processor purée the red pepper with 2 tablespoons of the cream cheese, the remaining 1 tablespoon butter, and the egg yolk, and transfer the mixture to another small bowl.

Assemble the sandwiches: Spread a thin layer of the remaining cream cheese, softened well, on a slice of the whole-wheat bread and cover it with a thick layer of the black olive spread. Cover the black olive spread with a slice of the white bread and spread the bread thickly with the red pepper spread. Cover the red pepper spread with a slice of the pumpernickel and spread the pumpernickel with a thick layer of the green olive spread. Cover the green olive spread with another slice of the whole-wheat bread and wrap the sandwich in plastic wrap. Continue making sandwiches with the remaining breads and fillings in the same manner. Wrap the sandwiches in plastic wrap and chill them for at least 1 hour or overnight. Unwrap the sandwiches, trim the crusts, and cut each sandwich lengthwise into thirds. Arrange the sandwiches cut side up decoratively on a platter. Makes 12 ribbon sandwiches, serving 6.

Fried Feta with Orégano Vinaigrette

1 teaspoon white-wine vinegar

½ teaspoon crumbled dried orégano

1½ tablespoons olive oil

¼ pound Feta, cut into four ½-inch-thick slices

flour for dredging

1 large egg, beaten well

⅔ cup fine fresh bread crumbs

1½ tablespoons unsalted butter

In a small bowl whisk together the vinegar, the orégano, and pepper to taste and whisk in the oil. Dredge the Feta slices in the flour, brushing off any excess carefully, dip them in the egg, and roll them in the bread crumbs, patting the crumbs gently onto the sides. In a heavy skillet heat the butter over moderate heat until the foam subsides, in it cook the Feta, turning it once, for 3 to 5 minutes, or until it is golden, and divide it between 2 heated serving plates. Whisk the vinaigrette and drizzle it over the Feta. Serves 2 as a first course.

Goat Cheese in Cracked Peppers

1 teaspoon black peppercorns

½ teaspoon red pepper flakes

4 whole allspice

1 teaspoon white peppercorns

1 teaspoon dried green peppercorns (available
    at specialty foods shops)

a 7-ounce Montrachet or other goat cheese,
    halved crosswise into 2 rounds

assorted breads as an accompaniment

In an electric spice grinder grind coarse the black peppercorns, the red pepper flakes, the allspice, the white peppercorns, and the green peppercorns. Roll the cheese rounds in the ground pepper mixture, coating them well. *The cheese keeps, covered and chilled, for up to 4 days.* Serve the cheese at room temperature with the breads. Serves 6 to 8.

Grilled Gouda and Apple Sandwiches

½ Golden Delicious apple, halved lengthwise
    and cut into ¼-inch-thick slices

2 tablespoons unsalted butter

4 teaspoons Dijon-style mustard

4 slices of homemade-type white bread, crusts
    removed

2 teaspoons bottled mango chutney

two ¼-inch-thick slices of Gouda, cut to fit the
    bread

In a large heavy skillet cook the apple slices in 1 tablespoon of the butter over moderate heat, turning them, for 4 to 6 minutes, or until they are tender, and transfer them to paper towels to drain. Spread 1 tea-

spoon of the mustard on each slice of the bread and spread 1 teaspoon of the chutney on 2 of the slices. Cover the chutney with a slice of the Gouda, top the cheese with a layer of the apple slices, and top the apples with the remaining bread mustard side down. In the skillet melt the remaining 1 tablespoon butter over moderately high heat and in it cook the sandwiches, turning them once and flattening them with the back of a spatula, for 1 to 2 minutes, or until they are golden. Transfer the sandwiches to a cutting board, quarter them diagonally, and arrange the triangles on a platter. Serves 2 as a first course or light luncheon entrée.

Mexican Pizza

For the crust

1½ cups all-purpose flour

¼ teaspoon sugar

1¼ teaspoons quick-rise yeast (available at most supermarkets)

½ teaspoon salt

1 tablespoon olive oil

1 tablespoon yellow cornmeal plus additional for sprinkling the pan

For the topping

½ pound tomatoes, sliced thin crosswise and seeded

1 garlic clove, minced

5 ounces Monterey Jack, sliced thin

1 small onion, sliced thin and separated into rings

1 red bell pepper, sliced thin into rings

1 pickled *jalapeño* pepper (available at Hispanic markets and some specialty foods shops and supermarkets), or to taste, chopped (wear rubber gloves)

2 tablespoons minced fresh coriander

2 tablespoons freshly grated Parmesan

1 tablespoon olive oil

Make the crust: In a food processor combine ½ cup of the flour, the sugar, and the yeast, with the motor running add ½ cup hot water, and turn the motor off. Add the remaining 1 cup flour, the salt, the oil, and 1 tablespoon of the cornmeal and blend the mixture until it forms a ball. Pat the dough out on an oiled 11-inch black steel pizza pan sprinkled lightly with the additional cornmeal, making the crust slightly thicker around the edge.

Arrange the topping: Put the tomato slices on the dough, sprinkle them with the garlic and salt and pepper

to taste, and cover the pizza with an even layer of the Monterey Jack. Add the onion rings, the bell pepper rings, and the *jalapeño* pepper, sprinkle the pizza with the coriander and the Parmesan, and drizzle it with the olive oil. Bake the pizza in the lower third of a preheated 500° F. oven for 15 to 20 minutes, or until the crust is golden brown and the top is bubbling. Serves 2.

Mozzarella with Olive Pimiento Marinade

4 teaspoons white-wine vinegar

½ teaspoon finely crumbled dried basil

¼ cup minced pimiento-stuffed olives

3 tablespoons olive oil

¼ pound whole-milk mozzarella, sliced ¼ inch thick

crackers as an accompaniment

In a bowl whisk together the vinegar, the basil, the olives, and salt and pepper to taste, add the oil in a stream, whisking, and whisk the marinade until it is emulsified. Put the mozzarella slices in a shallow dish, pour the marinade over them, and let the mozzarella marinate at room temperature for 30 minutes. Serve the mozzarella with the crackers. Serves 2 as a first course.

Fried Mozzarella with Anchovy Butter Sauce

For the sauce
1 garlic clove, minced
¾ stick (6 tablespoons) unsalted butter
1 tablespoon minced anchovy fillets
1 tablespoon drained capers, minced
2 tablespoons minced fresh parsley leaves
2 teaspoons fresh lemon juice
coarsely ground pepper to taste

½ pound chilled mozzarella, cut crosswise
    with a serrated knife into 16 slices
32 slices of homemade-type white bread, cut
    into rounds with a 3-inch cutter (reserving
    the scraps for another use such as bread
    crumbs)
2 large eggs, beaten lightly
2 tablespoons milk
about 4 tablespoons vegetable oil
about ½ stick (¼ cup) unsalted butter

Make the sauce: In a small saucepan cook the garlic in
the butter over moderately low heat for 3 minutes, remove the pan from the heat, and stir in the anchovies,
the capers, the parsley, the lemon juice, and the pepper.

Sandwich each slice of the mozzarella between 2
bread rounds, flatten the sandwiches slightly, and pinch
the edges of the bread together securely to enclose the
mozzarella completely. In a shallow dish beat together
lightly the eggs and the milk and dip the sandwiches into
the mixture, coating them on all sides and letting the excess drip off. In a large skillet heat 2 tablespoons of the
oil and 2 tablespoons of the butter over moderate heat
until the fat is hot and in the fat fry the sandwiches in
batches, using the remaining 2 tablespoons butter and 2
tablespoons oil if necessary, for 1 minute on each side,
or until they are golden. Transfer the fried mozzarella to
a heated platter and drizzle it with the sauce, heated.
Serves 8 as a first course.

Herb-Marinated Mozzarella

1 pound whole-milk mozzarella, chilled and
    sliced ¼ inch thick with a serrated knife
3 tablespoons extra-virgin olive oil (available
    at specialty foods shops and some
    supermarkets)
3 tablespoons vegetable oil

1 tablespoon minced and drained bottled sun-
    dried tomatoes, plus 1 teaspoon of the oil
    (available at specialty foods shops and some
    supermarkets)
¼ teaspoon red pepper flakes
1 tablespoon minced fresh parsley leaves
1 teaspoon minced fresh basil leaves
1 teaspoon snipped fresh chives
¼ teaspoon minced garlic
fresh herbs for garnish if desired

In a wide shallow serving dish arrange overlapping
slices of the mozzarella. In a small bowl whisk together
the olive oil, the vegetable oil, the tomatoes with the tomato oil, the red pepper flakes, the parsley, the basil,
the chives, and the garlic and drizzle the mixture over
the mozzarella. Let the mozzarella marinate, covered,
at room temperature for 2 hours and serve it at room
temperature, garnished with the fresh herbs if desired.
Serves 8.

Parmesan Puffs

4 large egg whites at room temperature
¼ teaspoon salt
¼ teaspoon cream of tartar
cayenne to taste
2 cups freshly grated Parmesan
vegetable shortening for deep-frying

In a bowl with an electric mixer beat the egg whites
with the salt until they are frothy, add the cream of tartar, and beat the whites until they hold stiff peaks. Stir in
the cayenne and the Parmesan. In a deep fryer heat 2
inches of vegetable shortening to 370° F. and in it fry
teaspoons of the mixture, formed into balls, in batches,
turning them occasionally, for 2 to 3 minutes, or until
they are golden. Transfer the Parmesan puffs to paper
towels to drain and serve them hot as an hors d'oeuvre.
Makes about 48 Parmesan puffs.

Swiss Cheese Salad

1 pound Swiss cheese, cut into julienne strips
½ pound Belgian endive, cut into julienne
    strips
6 stalks of celery, cut into julienne strips
¾ cup Parmesan vinaigrette (recipe follows)

In a salad bowl combine the Swiss cheese, the endive, and the celery, add the vinaigrette, and toss the
salad gently to coat it well. Serves 6 to 8.

Parmesan Vinaigrette

1 teaspoon caraway seeds
¼ cup firmly packed fresh parsley leaves
2 tablespoons white-wine vinegar
2 teaspoons Dijon-style mustard
¼ cup olive oil
¼ cup vegetable oil
½ cup freshly grated Parmesan

In a blender pulverize the caraway seeds, add the parsley, and blend the mixture until the parsley is minced. Add the vinegar, the mustard, and salt and pepper to taste and blend the mixture well. With the motor running add the olive oil and the vegetable oil in a stream and blend the dressing until it is emulsified. Add the Parmesan and blend the vinaigrette until it is combined. Makes about ¾ cup.

EGGS

Curried Egg Salad with Radish

3 hard-boiled large eggs, chopped
3 tablespoons mayonnaise
½ teaspoon curry powder
⅛ teaspoon celery salt
3 to 4 dashes of Tabasco
1 tablespoon bottled chutney, minced
3 tablespoons minced celery
5 radishes, minced

In a bowl combine well the eggs, the mayonnaise, the curry powder, the celery salt, and the Tabasco. Stir in the chutney, the celery, the radishes, and salt and pep-

per to taste. Use the salad as a filling for cherry tomatoes and celery or with black bread and crackers. Makes about 1½ cups.

Parmesan Coddled Eggs

softened unsalted butter for the egg coddlers
2 large eggs
2 teaspoons heavy cream
2 teaspoons freshly grated Parmesan
freshly ground pepper to taste

Set 2 empty small ceramic egg coddlers in a deep saucepan, add enough water to the pan to cover the coddlers, and remove them. Bring the water to a boil. Butter generously the insides of the coddlers and break an egg carefully into each one. Top each egg with 1 teaspoon of the cream and 1 teaspoon of the Parmesan, sprinkle the eggs with the pepper and salt to taste, and screw on the lids. Submerge the coddlers in the boiling water, cover the pan, and boil the eggs for 7 minutes. Transfer the coddlers with tongs to a dish towel, wipe the outsides dry, and serve the eggs in the coddlers. Serves 2.

Horseradish-Stuffed Eggs

4 hard-boiled large eggs
3 tablespoons mayonnaise
¼ cup sour cream
4 teaspoons drained and squeezed bottled
   horseradish
1½ tablespoons minced fresh parsley leaves

Halve the eggs lengthwise, force the yolks through a sieve into a bowl, and blend in the mayonnaise, the sour cream, the horseradish, the parsley, and salt and pepper to taste. With a pastry bag fitted with a decorative tip pipe the mixture into the egg whites, mounding it. Makes 8 egg halves, serving 2.

Bacon and Potato Frittata

1 pound sliced bacon, chopped
1 pound baking potatoes, peeled, sliced thin,
   and patted dry
1 onion, sliced thin and patted dry
2 tablespoons minced fresh parsley leaves
10 large eggs, beaten lightly
1 cup half-and-half
3 tablespoons flour
½ teaspoon salt

In an ovenproof 12-inch skillet cook the bacon over moderate heat, stirring occasionally, until it is crisp, transfer it to paper towels to drain, and pour off all but 2 tablespoons of the fat. In the skillet layer half the potatoes, the onion, and the remaining potatoes and cook the mixture over moderate heat, tamping it down, for 10 minutes, or until the potatoes are tender. Sprinkle the potato mixture with the bacon. In a large bowl whisk together the parsley, the eggs, the half-and-half, the flour, and the salt, pour the mixture into the skillet, and bake the *frittata* in a preheated 450° F. oven for 15 to 20 minutes, or until it is puffed and golden. Serve the *frittata* cut into wedges. Serves 6.

Zucchini Quiche Provençale

For the dough
1¼ cups all-purpose flour
¼ teaspoon salt
3 tablespoons lard
For the filling
1½ pounds zucchini, cut into ¼-inch rounds
1 small onion, sliced thin crosswise
2 tablespoons olive oil
½ cup drained pitted black olives, quartered
   lengthwise
½ teaspoon crumbled dried marjoram
½ teaspoon crumbled dried orégano
½ teaspoon crumbled dried thyme
½ teaspoon crumbled dried summer savory
3 large eggs
1½ cups half-and-half
1 teaspoon Dijon-style mustard

Make the dough: Into a bowl sift together the flour and the salt and blend in the lard until the mixture resembles coarse meal. Add 7 to 8 tablespoons ice water, or enough to form a soft dough, dust the dough with flour, and chill it, wrapped in wax paper, for 1 hour. Roll the dough into a round ⅛ inch thick on a floured surface, fit it into a 9- by 1½-inch quiche pan, and crimp the edge decoratively. Chill the shell for 5 minutes.

Make the filling: In a large heavy skillet cook the zucchini and the onion in the oil over moderately low heat, stirring occasionally, for 20 minutes, or until it is just tender, stir in the olives, the marjoram, the orégano, the thyme, the summer savory, and salt and pepper to taste, and transfer the mixture to the shell. In a bowl whisk together the eggs, the half-and-half, the mustard, and salt and pepper to taste, pour the mixture over the zucchini mixture, and bake the quiche in a preheated 375° F. oven for 25 to 30 minutes, or until a knife inserted in the custard comes out clean. Serves 4 to 6.

Broccoli Horseradish Soufflé

½ cup chopped walnuts
2 onions, chopped fine
¾ stick (6 tablespoons) unsalted butter
6½ cups chopped cooked broccoli
3 tablespoons all-purpose flour
1 cup milk
4 large eggs, separated, at room temperature
3 tablespoons bottled horseradish
a pinch of cream of tartar

Coat the bottom and sides of a well buttered 1½-quart soufflé dish with the walnuts and chill the dish. In a skillet cook the onions in 2 tablespoons of the butter over moderately low heat, stirring, until they are softened. In a food processor blend the onion mixture with the broccoli until the mixture is a coarse purée. In a large saucepan melt the remaining 4 tablespoons butter over moderately low heat, add the flour, and cook the *roux*, stirring, for 3 minutes. Add the milk, heated, in a stream, whisking, bring the mixture to a boil, whisking, and simmer it, stirring, for 5 minutes. Whisk in the egg yolks, bring the mixture to a boil, stirring, and stir in the broccoli purée, the horseradish, and salt and pepper to taste.

In a large bowl beat the egg whites with a pinch of salt until they are frothy, add the cream of tartar, and beat the whites until they just hold stiff peaks. Stir one fourth of the whites into the broccoli mixture, add the broccoli mixture to the remaining whites, and fold the mixture together gently. Spoon the mixture into the soufflé dish. Put the soufflé dish in a baking pan, add enough hot water to the pan to come halfway up the sides of the dish, and bake the soufflé in a preheated 350° F. oven for 45 minutes, or until it is puffed and golden. Serves 4.

Eggplant Soufflé with Red Pepper, Tomato, and
Coriander Sauce

For the soufflé

1 large eggplant (about 1 pound), peeled and
   cut crosswise into ¼-inch slices
2 tablespoons vegetable oil
2 garlic cloves, minced
4 scallions, minced
½ stick (¼ cup) unsalted butter
5 tablespoons flour
1½ cups milk
5 large egg yolks
1 tablespoon Worcestershire sauce
6 large egg whites at room temperature
a pinch of cream of tartar
¼ cup fine fresh bread crumbs

For the sauce

1 small onion, minced
1 garlic clove, minced
2 tablespoons unsalted butter
a 6½-ounce jar roasted red peppers, drained
   and chopped
½ cup canned tomato purée
1 teaspoon minced fresh coriander leaves
a pinch of sugar

fresh whole coriander leaves for garnish

Make the soufflé: In a colander set over a bowl let the
eggplant slices stand, sprinkled with salt, for 1 hour.
Discard the liquid in the bowl, rinse the eggplant under
cold water, and pat it dry. Arrange the eggplant slices in
one layer on lightly oiled jelly-roll pans and brush them
lightly with the oil. Broil the eggplant under a preheated
broiler about 2 inches from the heat for 3 to 5 minutes,
or until it is browned lightly, turn it, and broil it for 3 to 5
minutes more, or until it is very tender. In a food processor or blender purée the eggplant.

In a heavy saucepan cook the garlic and the scallions
in the butter over moderately low heat, stirring, for 3
minutes, stir in the flour, and cook the mixture, stirring,
for 3 minutes. Whisk in the milk, heated, and simmer
the mixture, whisking, for 5 minutes. Transfer the mixture to a large bowl, let it cool for 5 minutes, and whisk
in the egg yolks, the Worcestershire sauce, the eggplant
purée, and salt and pepper to taste. In a bowl with an
electric mixer beat the egg whites with a pinch of salt
until they are frothy, add the cream of tartar, and beat
the whites until they just hold stiff peaks. Stir one third
of the whites into the eggplant mixture and fold in the
remaining whites. Butter a 1½-quart soufflé dish and
sprinkle it with the bread crumbs, shaking out the excess. Spoon the soufflé mixture into the dish and
smooth the top gently. *The soufflé may be chilled for up*
to 2 hours at this point.

Make the sauce: In a saucepan cook the onion and the
garlic in the butter over low heat, stirring, for 5 minutes,
add the red peppers, the tomato purée, and ½ cup water,
and simmer the sauce, stirring occasionally, for 3 minutes. Stir in the minced coriander, the sugar, and salt
and pepper to taste. *The sauce may be prepared 1 day in*
advance and kept covered and chilled.

Bake the soufflé in a preheated 400° F. oven for 40 to
45 minutes, or until a skewer comes out clean. Serve the
soufflé immediately with the sauce, heated, and garnished with the whole coriander leaves. Serves 6.

Parmesan Scallion Soufflés

1 cup finely chopped scallions
½ stick (¼ cup) unsalted butter
5 tablespoons flour
1½ cups milk
1¼ cups freshly grated Parmesan
⅓ cup minced fresh parsley leaves
5 large egg yolks
1 teaspoon Worcestershire sauce
a pinch of cayenne
½ teaspoon salt
6 large egg whites at room temperature
a pinch of cream of tartar

In a saucepan cook the scallions in the butter over moderately low heat, stirring, for 3 minutes, stir in the flour, and cook the mixture, stirring, for 3 minutes. Whisk in the milk, heated, and simmer the mixture, whisking occasionally, for 8 minutes. Transfer the mixture to a large bowl, let it cool for 5 minutes, and stir in 1 cup of the Parmesan, the parsley, the egg yolks, the Worcestershire sauce, the cayenne, and the salt. In a bowl with an electric mixer beat the egg whites with a pinch of salt until they are frothy, add the cream of tartar, and beat the whites until they just hold stiff peaks. Stir one third of the whites into the yolk mixture and fold in the remaining whites. Butter four 1½-cup soufflé dishes and sprinkle them with the remaining ¼ cup Parmesan. Spoon the soufflé mixture into the dishes and smooth the tops gently. *The soufflés may be chilled for up to 2 hours at this point.*

Bake the soufflés in a preheated 400° F. oven for 20 minutes, or until they are puffed and browned. Serve the soufflés immediately. Serves 4.

Zoë

Saga Blue Soufflés with Port Sauce

1 tablespoon fine dry bread crumbs
1 tablespoon freshly grated Parmesan
6 ounces Saga blue or Bavarian blue cheese,
   rind discarded, at room temperature
3 large eggs at room temperature, separated
a pinch of cream of tartar
For the sauce
½ cup Ruby Port
2 tablespoons minced shallots
1½ cups canned chicken broth combined with
   1 envelope of unflavored gelatin
2 tablespoons red currant jelly
1 teaspoon Dijon-style mustard
1 tablespoon softened unsalted butter
For the garnish
2 small clusters of green grapes
2 sprigs of watercress

In a small bowl combine the bread crumbs and the Parmesan. Coat the bottom and sides of 2 buttered 1-cup soufflé dishes with the crumb mixture, shaking out the excess, and chill the dishes. In a food processor blend the Saga blue until it is smooth and add the egg yolks. Blend the mixture well and transfer it to a bowl. In another bowl with an electric mixer beat the egg whites with a pinch of salt until they are frothy, add the cream of tartar, and beat the whites until they just hold stiff peaks. Stir one third of the whites into the cheese mixture and fold in the remaining whites gently. Spoon the soufflé mixture into the dishes and smooth the tops gently. Put the soufflés in a baking pan, add enough hot water to the pan to come halfway up the sides of the dishes, and bake the soufflés in a preheated 375° F. oven for 20 to 25 minutes, or until they are puffed and golden brown.

Make the sauce while the soufflés are baking: In a saucepan combine the Port and the shallots, bring the Port to a boil, and boil it until it is reduced to about 2 tablespoons. Add the broth mixture and boil the liquid until it is reduced to about ⅔ cup. Add the jelly and cook the mixture over moderately low heat, stirring, until the jelly is melted. Whisk in the mustard, the butter, and salt and pepper to taste and keep the sauce warm.

Let the soufflés stand for 2 minutes, lift them gently from the dishes, and transfer them to heated plates. Pour the sauce around the soufflés and garnish the soufflés with the grapes and the watercress. Serves 2 as a luncheon entrée.

PASTA AND GRAINS

PASTA

*Fettuccine with Broccoli, Carrots,
and Hot Peanut Sauce*

¾ cup peanut butter
1 garlic clove, minced
1 small onion, chopped coarse
1 teaspoon red pepper flakes
1 tablespoon brown sugar
3 tablespoons fresh lemon juice
2 tablespoons soy sauce
1½ cups canned chicken broth or water
3 tablespoons vegetable oil
6 cups broccoli flowerets, blanched in boiling
   salted water for 1 minute, refreshed in a
   bowl of ice and cold water, drained, and
   patted dry
2 large carrots, cut into julienne strips
¾ pound fettuccine
¼ cup chopped fresh coriander if desired

In a food processor blend together the peanut butter, the garlic, the onion, the red pepper flakes, and the brown sugar, add the lemon juice, the soy sauce, and ¼ cup of the broth, and blend the mixture until it is smooth. Transfer the mixture to a saucepan and stir in the remaining 1¼ cups broth. Heat the sauce over moderately low heat, stirring, until it is hot and keep it warm.

In a large skillet heat the oil over moderately high heat until it is hot but not smoking, in it sauté the broccoli and the carrots until they are just tender, and add salt and pepper to taste. In a kettle of boiling salted water cook the fettuccine for 3 to 12 minutes, or until it is *al dente*, drain it, and in a serving bowl toss it with the vegetables, the peanut sauce, and the coriander if desired. Serves 4 to 6.

Fettuccine with Uncooked Tomato Sauce

1½ tablespoons red-wine vinegar
3 tablespoons olive oil, or to taste
1 pound tomatoes, peeled, seeded, and
   chopped
¼ cup thinly sliced scallions
¼ cup thinly sliced pimiento-stuffed olives
¼ pound fettuccine

In a bowl whisk together the vinegar, the oil, and salt and pepper to taste and stir in the tomatoes, the scallions, and the olives. In a kettle of boiling salted water cook the fettuccine for 3 to 12 minutes, or until it is *al dente*, drain it well, and transfer it to a bowl. Add the sauce to the fettuccine and toss the mixture. Serves 2.

Scallion Fettuccine

For the dough

1¾ cups all-purpose flour
1 teaspoon salt
1 large egg, beaten lightly
1 cup minced scallions (about 1 bunch)

⅔ cup chopped scallions (about 1 small bunch)
2 tablespoons unsalted butter, cut into bits and
  softened
½ cup freshly grated Parmesan

Make the dough: In a bowl stir together the flour, the salt, the egg, the minced scallions, and 1½ tablespoons warm water and knead the mixture on a floured surface until it is smooth and can be formed into a ball. The dough will be very dry and crumbly at first, but the moisture from the scallions will eventually make it come together. If necessary, add an additional tablespoon of water. Let the dough rest, covered with an inverted bowl, for 1 hour. Makes about 1 pound.

Knead and roll the pasta dough to the second lowest notch and cut it into fettuccine (procedures follow).

In a kettle of boiling salted water boil the fettuccine for 3 minutes, or until it is just *al dente*, drain it well, and in a heated bowl toss it with the chopped scallions, the butter, the Parmesan, and salt and pepper to taste. Serves 4.

To Knead and Roll Pasta Dough

Set the smooth rollers of a pasta machine at the highest number. (The rollers will be wide apart.) Divide each pound of dough into 6 pieces and flatten 1 piece into a rough rectangle. Cover the remaining pieces with an inverted bowl. Dust the dough with flour and feed it through the rollers. Fold the dough in half and feed it through the rollers 8 or 9 more times, folding it in half each time and dusting it with flour if necessary to prevent it from sticking. Turn the dial down one notch and feed the dough through the rollers without folding. Continue to feed the dough through the rollers without folding, dusting it with flour if it sticks and turning the dial one notch lower each time, until the lowest or second-lowest notch is reached. The pasta dough should be a smooth long sheet about 4 or 5 inches wide and about 1/16 inch thick. Knead and roll the remaining pasta dough in the same manner.

To Cut Fettuccine

Use the blades of a pasta machine that will cut ¼-inch-wide strips. Feed 1 end of a sheet of pasta dough through the blades, holding the other end straight up from the machine. Catch the strips from underneath the machine before the sheet goes completely through the rollers and put the cut strips lightly across floured jelly-roll pans or let them hang over the top of straight-backed chairs. Let the strips dry for 30 minutes.

Fusilli and Broccoli with Gorgonzola Sauce

1 pound *fusilli* (corkscrew-shaped pasta)
1 bunch of broccoli, trimmed into small
  flowerets and the stems reserved for another use
1 cup heavy cream
½ pound Gorgonzola at room temperature,
  rind discarded
1 stick (½ cup) unsalted butter, softened
¼ cup freshly grated Parmesan, or to taste
⅓ cup minced fresh parsley leaves

In a large kettle of boiling salted water cook the *fusilli* until it is *al dente*. While the pasta is cooking, in a saucepan of boiling salted water cook the broccoli for 2 minutes, or until it is *al dente*, drain it in a colander, and refresh it under cold water. In a small saucepan bring the cream to a boil and boil it for 5 minutes. Stir in the Gorgonzola and ½ stick of the butter and cook the sauce over moderately low heat, stirring, until it is smooth. Drain the *fusilli* well and in the kettle toss it with the broccoli and the remaining ½ stick butter. Add the Parmesan and the parsley and toss the mixture until it is combined. Add the Gorgonzola sauce and toss the mixture well. Serve the pasta immediately. Serves 6.

Fusilli with Parsley Walnut Sauce

1 small garlic clove, or to taste, chopped
2 tablespoons chopped walnuts, toasted lightly
1 cup loosely packed fresh parsley leaves
½ cup (about 2 ounces) freshly grated
  Parmesan
½ cup olive oil
1¾ cups *fusilli* (corkscrew-shaped pasta)
fresh lemon juice to taste if desired

In a food processor purée the garlic, the walnuts, the parsley, the Parmesan, 2 tablespoons of the oil, and salt

and pepper to taste, with the motor running add the remaining 6 tablespoons oil in a stream, and blend the sauce until it is emulsified. In a kettle of boiling salted water cook the *fusilli* for 9 to 11 minutes, or until it is *al dente*, and drain it well. In a bowl toss the *fusilli* with the sauce, coating it well, and season it with the lemon juice if desired and salt and pepper. Serves 2 as a first course.

Linguine with Scallops and Herb Sauce

¼ pound *linguine*
½ stick (¼ cup) unsalted butter
½ pound bay scallops, halved crosswise if
    large
¼ cup dry vermouth
½ cup canned chicken broth
1 tablespoon fresh lemon juice
¼ cup minced scallions
¼ cup minced fresh parsley leaves
2 tablespoons snipped fresh dill
1 tablespoon drained capers

In a large kettle of boiling salted water cook the *linguine* for 10 to 12 minutes, or until it is *al dente*, and drain it well.

Make the sauce while the *linguine* is cooking: In a large skillet heat the butter over moderately high heat until the foam subsides and in it sauté the scallops, patted dry, stirring, for 2 minutes, or until they are just firm. Transfer the scallops with a slotted spoon to a plate. To the skillet add the vermouth, the broth, and the lemon juice and boil the liquid until it is reduced by half. Add the scallions, the parsley, the dill, and the capers and simmer the mixture for 1 minute. Add the scallops

and the *linguine* and cook the mixture over moderately high heat, stirring, until it is heated through. Serves 2.

Oriental Noodles with Peanut Sauce

a 5-ounce package *saifun** (Japanese bean
    thread noodles) or Chinese cellophane
    noodles*
1 tablespoon minced fresh coriander
½ teaspoon minced garlic
½ cup smooth peanut butter
½ cup canned chicken broth
2 tablespoons rice vinegar*
1 tablespoon Oriental sesame oil*
½ teaspoon sugar
1 tablespoon soy sauce
4 scallions, chopped

*available at Oriental markets and some
    supermarkets

In a large heatproof bowl cover the noodles with boiling water and let them stand, stirring occasionally, for 5 minutes, or until they are *al dente*. Drain the noodles in a colander and rinse them under cold water. Pat the noodles dry and transfer them to a serving bowl. In a food processor or blender blend the coriander, the garlic, and the peanut butter until the mixture is combined well. In a small bowl combine the broth, the vinegar, the oil, the sugar, and the soy sauce. With the motor running add the mixture to the peanut butter mixture, blend the sauce until it is smooth, and pour it over the noodles. Toss the noodles to coat them with the sauce, add the scallions, and combine the mixture well. Serves 2 generously.

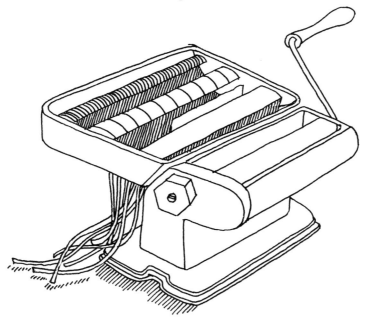

Pasta, Carrots, and Green Beans with Dill Vinaigrette

3 ounces green beans, sliced diagonally into
   ¼-inch pieces (about ½ cup)
½ cup coarsely grated carrots
2 cups *fusilli* (corkscrew-shaped pasta)
1 tablespoon white-wine vinegar
½ teaspoon Dijon-style mustard
1½ tablespoons snipped fresh dill plus dill
   sprigs for garnish
¼ cup olive oil

In a large saucepan of boiling salted water cook the green beans for 4 minutes, add the carrots, and cook the vegetables for 1 to 2 minutes, or until they are tender-crisp. Drain the vegetables, refresh them under cold water, and drain them on paper towels. In a kettle of boiling salted water cook the *fusilli* for 10 to 12 minutes, or until it is *al dente,* and drain it well. While the pasta is cooking, in a bowl whisk together the vinegar, the mustard, the snipped dill, and salt and pepper to taste, add the oil in a stream, whisking, and whisk the dressing until it is emulsified. In a large bowl toss the vegetables and the pasta with the dressing. Transfer the mixture to a serving dish and garnish it with the dill sprigs. Serves 2.

Pasta with Mushroom and Caper Sauce

1½ cups *rotelle* (corkscrew-shaped pasta)
1 cup finely chopped mushrooms (about 3
   ounces)
2 tablespoons olive oil
½ cup half-and-half
2 teaspoons drained capers, chopped
1 teaspoon tomato paste
1 tablespoon minced fresh parsley leaves
1 tablespoon minced scallion greens

In a large saucepan of boiling salted water cook the pasta for 5 to 7 minutes, or until it is *al dente,* drain it well, and transfer it to a serving bowl. While the pasta is cooking, in a heavy skillet cook the mushrooms in the oil over moderately low heat, stirring occasionally, for 7 minutes, or until most of the liquid the mushrooms give off is evaporated, and add the half-and-half, the capers, and the tomato paste, stirring. Bring the mixture to a boil over moderately high heat, reduce it to about 1 cup, and stir in the parsley, the scallion, and salt and pepper to taste. Spoon the sauce over the pasta and toss the mixture well. Serves 2 as a first course.

Spaghetti with Parsley Sauce

1½ cups firmly packed fresh parsley leaves
1 large garlic clove
2 hard-boiled large egg yolks
2 scallions, chopped coarse
¼ cup chopped walnuts
3 tablespoons softened unsalted butter
¾ teaspoon salt
½ cup olive oil
⅓ to ½ cup freshly grated Parmesan
¼ cup chopped roasted red pepper or pimiento
½ pound spaghetti, cooked

In a food processor purée the parsley, the garlic, the egg yolks, the scallions, the walnuts, the butter, and the salt and with the motor running add the oil in a stream. Transfer the mixture to a heated large serving bowl, stir in the Parmesan and the red pepper, and toss the sauce with the hot spaghetti. Serves 2 to 4.

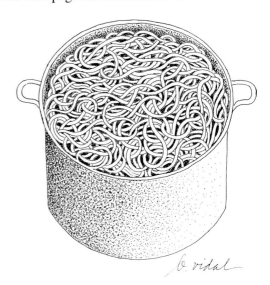

Spaghetti with Sardine Sauce

a 4⅜-ounce can whole sardines packed in oil
½ cup sour cream
¼ cup heavy cream
1 garlic clove, crushed and minced
½ teaspoon grated lemon rind
½ cup minced red onion
⅓ cup minced fresh parsley leaves
½ pound spaghetti
freshly ground pepper to taste

In a large bowl mash the sardines with their oil and stir in the sour cream, the heavy cream, the garlic, the lemon rind, the onion, and the parsley. In a large saucepan of boiling salted water boil the spaghetti, stirring

occasionally, until it is *al dente*, drain it, and add it to the bowl of sauce, tossing it to coat it well. Grind the pepper over the spaghetti. Serves 4 as a first course.

Spaghettini with Ham and Broccoli

½ pound spaghettini
2 cups small broccoli flowerets
2 tablespoons unsalted butter
½ cup heavy cream
¼ pound smoked ham, diced
½ cup freshly grated Parmesan
1 tablespoon minced fresh parsley leaves

In a kettle of boiling salted water cook the spaghettini for 8 to 10 minutes, or until it is *al dente*, add the broccoli to the kettle, and blanch it for 15 seconds. Reserve ⅓ cup of the cooking liquid and drain the spaghettini and the broccoli in a colander. Return the mixture to the kettle with the reserved liquid, add the butter and the cream, and bring the liquid to a simmer over moderate heat, stirring. Stir in the ham, the Parmesan, and the parsley, cook the mixture, stirring, until it is very hot, and season it with salt and pepper. Serves 2.

GRAINS

Bulgur and Wild Rice Pilaf

2 cups minced onions
1 stick (½ cup) unsalted butter
2 cups wild rice
7½ cups chicken stock (page 119) or canned chicken broth
2 cups *bulgur* (processed cracked wheat, available at natural foods stores, specialty food shops, and some supermarkets)
1 cup minced fresh parsley leaves

In a large heavy saucepan cook 1 cup of the onions in ½ stick of the butter over moderately low heat, stirring, until they are softened, add the wild rice, and stir it to coat it with the butter. Add 4 cups of the stock, bring it to a boil, and simmer the mixture, covered, for 45 minutes to 1 hour, or until the wild rice is tender and the liquid is absorbed.

While the wild rice is cooking, in a large deep skillet cook the remaining 1 cup onions in the remaining ½ stick butter over moderately low heat, stirring, until they are softened, add the *bulgur,* and stir it to coat it

with the butter. Add the remaining 3½ cups stock, bring it to a boil, and simmer the mixture, covered, for 10 minutes, or until the liquid is absorbed. Remove the skillet from the heat and let the *bulgur* stand, covered, for 10 minutes. In a large bowl combine the wild rice and the *bulgur,* tossing the mixture, and season the pilaf with salt and pepper. *The pilaf may be made up to this point 1 day in advance and kept covered and chilled. Reheat the pilaf in a buttered large shallow baking dish, covered tightly with foil, in a preheated 350° F. oven for 15 to 20 minutes, or until it is heated through.* Just before serving add the parsley, toss the pilaf well, and transfer it to heated serving dishes. Makes about 14 cups, serving 20.

Couscous Carbonara

3 ounces *pancetta* (cured pork belly, available at Italian markets and specialty foods shops), cut into ½-inch dice
½ stick (¼ cup) unsalted butter at room temperature
¼ cup heavy cream
2 garlic cloves, crushed slightly
1 cup couscous
1 large egg yolk at room temperature
3 tablespoons freshly grated Parmesan plus additional as an accompaniment

In a skillet cook the *pancetta* in 1 tablespoon of the butter over moderately low heat, stirring occasionally, for 6 to 7 minutes, or until it is golden brown, and keep the mixture warm, covered. In a small saucepan bring the cream to a simmer, add the garlic, and cook the mixture over low heat, swirling the pan occasionally, for 5 minutes. Remove the garlic with a slotted spoon, discard it, and keep the cream warm, covered.

In a saucepan bring ¾ cup water to a boil with 2 tablespoons of the remaining butter, cut into bits. Stir in the couscous with pepper to taste, cover the pan immediately, and let the couscous stand, off the heat, for 5 minutes. In a small bowl whisk together the cream and the egg yolk, pour the mixture over the couscous, and add the remaining 1 tablespoon butter, cut into bits. Let the couscous stand, covered, for 1 minute, fluff it with a fork to break up any lumps, and add the *pancetta* mixture, 3 tablespoons of the Parmesan, and pepper to taste. Toss the couscous until it is combined well and serve it with the additional Parmesan. Serves 4 as a first course.

Couscous with Chanterelles and Parmesan

5 ounces fresh chanterelles (available at
    specialty produce markets), rinsed, patted
    dry, trimmed, and cut into ½-inch slices
1 tablespoon vegetable oil
1 stick (½ cup) unsalted butter at room
    temperature
2 tablespoons minced shallots
1 cup chicken stock (page 119) or canned
    chicken broth
1 cup couscous
¼ cup freshly grated Parmesan

In a skillet sauté the chanterelles with salt and pepper
to taste in the oil and 2 tablespoons of the butter over
moderately high heat for 3 minutes, or until they give
off their liquid. Stir in the shallots and sauté the mixture
for 2 to 3 minutes, or until the chanterelles are golden
and tender.

In a saucepan bring the stock to a boil with 4 tablespoons of the remaining butter, cut into bits. Stir in the
couscous with salt and pepper to taste, cover the pan immediately, and let the couscous stand, off the heat, for 5
minutes. Scatter the remaining 2 tablespoons butter, cut
into bits, over the couscous and let the couscous stand,
covered, for 1 minute. Reheat the chanterelle mixture
over moderately low heat, stirring. Fluff the couscous
with a fork to break up any lumps, tossing it until the
butter is melted completely, and add the chanterelle
mixture and the Parmesan. Toss the mixture until it is
combined well and season it with salt and pepper.
Serves 4 as a first course or side dish.

Couscous with Red Pepper, Walnuts, and Basil

2 teaspoons vegetable oil
½ cup walnuts
1 small red bell pepper, cut into ¼-inch strips
4 tablespoons olive oil
1 cup couscous
1 teaspoon fresh lemon juice, or to taste
3 tablespoons minced fresh parsley leaves
3 tablespoons chopped fresh basil leaves, or to
    taste, plus basil sprigs for garnish if desired

In a small skillet heat the vegetable oil over moderate
heat until it is hot, add the walnuts with a pinch of salt,
and cook them, stirring, for 2 minutes, or until they are
golden brown. Transfer the walnuts with a slotted spoon
to paper towels to drain.

In a large skillet cook the bell pepper in 2 tablespoons
of the olive oil over moderately low heat, stirring, until
it is softened, add the couscous, and stir it to coat it with
the oil. Remove the skillet from the heat, shaking it to
spread the couscous in an even layer, pour 1 cup boiling
water evenly over the couscous, and cover the skillet
immediately. Let the mixture stand for 5 minutes, fluff
it with a fork to break up any lumps, and drizzle the remaining 2 tablespoons olive oil and the lemon juice over
it, tossing the mixture. Add the parsley, the chopped basil, the walnuts, and salt and pepper to taste and toss the
mixture well. Transfer the couscous to a serving dish,
garnish it with the basil sprigs if desired, and serve it
warm or at room temperature. Serves 4 as a first course
or side dish.

Fried Couscous with Scallions and Ginger

1¼ cups couscous
1 large carrot, cut into 2-inch julienne strips
2 tablespoons soy sauce
2 tablespoons *mirin* (Japanese rice wine,
    available at Oriental markets)
1 tablespoon Oriental sesame oil (available at
    most supermarkets, Oriental markets, and
    specialty foods shops)
3 tablespoons vegetable oil
3 large scallions, sliced thin
2 tablespoons minced peeled gingerroot
omelet strips (recipe follows)
1 tablespoon sesame seeds, toasted lightly
1 tablespoon minced fresh parsley leaves

In a saucepan bring 1 cup water to a boil. Stir in the
couscous with pepper to taste, cover the pan immediately, and let the couscous stand, off the heat, for 5 minutes. Transfer the couscous to a bowl, breaking up any
lumps with a fork, rub the grains between the fingers
gently, and let the couscous cool completely.

In a saucepan of boiling salted water cook the carrot
for 4 to 5 minutes, or until it is just tender, and drain it in
a colander. Refresh the carrot under cold water and
drain it well. In a small bowl combine the soy sauce, the
mirin, and the sesame oil. In a large skillet heat the vegetable oil over moderately high heat until it is hot and in
it sauté the scallions and the gingerroot, stirring, for 2
minutes. Stir in the carrot and the couscous and cook the
mixture over moderate heat, stirring gently, until it is
combined well and heated through. Remove the skillet
from the heat, stir in the soy sauce mixture and half the
omelet strips, and season the mixture with salt and pep-

per. Transfer the couscous to a platter and sprinkle it with the sesame seeds, the remaining omelet strips, and the parsley. Serves 4.

Omelet Strips

2 teaspoons vegetable oil
2 large eggs

In a 10-inch omelet pan or non-stick skillet heat the oil over moderate heat until it is hot. In a small bowl beat the eggs lightly with salt and pepper to taste, add them to the pan, tilting the pan to coat the bottom evenly, and cook them, loosening the edges to allow any uncooked egg to flow under the omelet, for 1 to 2 minutes, or until the omelet is set but still moist on top. With a metal spatula cut the omelet in half, loosen it, and turn each half. Cook the omelet for 15 seconds more and slide it onto a plate. Let the omelet cool briefly and cut each half crosswise into ¼-inch strips.

Cinnamon Oatmeal with Maple Cream

1 cup heavy cream at room temperature
½ cup maple syrup at room temperature
2 cups quick-cooking oats
¾ teaspoon salt
½ teaspoon cinnamon, or to taste

In a small bowl combine the cream and the syrup and transfer the mixture to a small pitcher. In a saucepan combine the oats, 4 cups cold water, and the salt, bring

the water to a boil, stirring occasionally, and simmer the mixture for 1 minute. Remove the pan from the heat and let the oatmeal stand, covered, for 2 minutes. Stir in the cinnamon and serve the oatmeal with the maple cream. Serves 6.

Polenta with Tuna Tomato Sauce

For the polenta
1½ cups yellow cornmeal
1½ teaspoons salt
¾ stick (6 tablespoons) unsalted butter
⅔ cup freshly grated Parmesan
For the sauce
1 onion, minced
2 tablespoons olive oil
2 garlic cloves, minced
1 teaspoon crumbled dried basil
½ teaspoon crumbled dried thyme
two 1-pound cans tomatoes, drained and
    chopped fine
a 6½-ounce can chunk light or Italian-style
    tuna packed in olive oil, drained and flaked

Make the polenta: In a large heavy saucepan bring to a simmer 5 cups water, sprinkle in gradually the cornmeal, whisking constantly, and the salt, and cook the mixture over moderately low heat, stirring constantly with a wooden spoon, for 30 to 40 minutes, or until it is very thick and cleans the sides of the pan. Remove the pan from the heat, add 4 tablespoons of the butter, cut into pieces, and ⅓ cup of the Parmesan, and stir the mixture until the butter is melted into it. Spread the mixture quickly in a lightly buttered 13- by 9-inch baking pan, smoothing the top with a rubber spatula dipped in cold water, dot the top with the remaining 2 tablespoons butter, cut into bits, and sprinkle it with the remaining ⅓ cup Parmesan. Bake the polenta in a preheated 375° F. oven for 30 minutes, or until it is lightly golden.

Make the sauce while the polenta is baking: In a heavy skillet cook the onion in the oil, covered, over moderately low heat, stirring occasionally, for 5 minutes, or until it is softened well. Add the garlic, the basil, and the thyme and cook the mixture, uncovered, stirring, for 1 minute. Add the tomatoes and simmer the mixture, stirring, for 10 minutes, or until it is thickened slightly. Add the tuna and simmer the mixture, stirring, for 2 to 3 minutes, or until the sauce is heated through. Cut the polenta into 6 pieces and serve each piece topped with the sauce. Serves 6.

Steamed Rice

1 tablespoon salt
2 cups unconverted long-grain rice

In a large saucepan bring 5 quarts water to a boil with the salt. Sprinkle in the rice, stirring until the water returns to a boil, and boil it for 10 minutes. Drain the rice in a large colander and rinse it. Set the colander over a saucepan of boiling water and steam the rice, covered with a dish towel and the lid, for 15 minutes, or until it is fluffy and dry. Makes about 6 cups.

Risotto with Tuna and Green Peppers

5 cups chicken stock (page 119) or canned
  chicken broth
1 onion, minced
1 green bell pepper, cut into ½-inch pieces
3 tablespoons olive oil
1½ cups unconverted long-grain rice
½ cup dry white wine
a 6½-ounce can tuna packed in oil, drained
⅔ cup freshly grated Parmesan

In a saucepan bring the stock to a simmer and keep it at a bare simmer. In a heavy 3-quart saucepan cook the onion and the bell pepper in the oil over moderately low heat, stirring, until the onion is softened. Stir in the rice and cook the mixture, stirring with a wooden spatula, until the rice is coated well with the oil. Add the wine and cook the mixture over moderately high heat, stirring, until the wine is absorbed. Add about ⅔ cup of the simmering stock and cook the mixture, stirring, until the stock is absorbed. Continue adding the stock, about ⅔ cup at a time, stirring constantly and letting each portion be absorbed before adding the next, until the rice is not quite *al dente*. Stir in the tuna and more stock, about ½ cup at a time, stirring constantly and letting each portion be absorbed before adding the next, until the rice is tender but still *al dente*. (The rice should take about 18 minutes to become *al dente*.) Remove the pan from the heat and stir in the Parmesan immediately with salt and pepper to taste. Serves 4 to 6.

Saffron Rice Timbales

1½ cups canned chicken broth
½ teaspoon crumbled saffron threads
1 cup minced onion
2 tablespoons unsalted butter
¾ cup long-grain rice
4 fresh coriander sprigs for garnish

In a saucepan heat the broth over moderate heat until it is hot and stir in the saffron. Remove the pan from the heat and let the mixture stand for 10 minutes. In a large heavy saucepan cook the onion in the butter over moderately low heat, stirring, until it is softened, add the rice, and cook the mixture, stirring, until the rice is coated well with the butter. Stir in the saffron mixture and salt and pepper to taste, bring the liquid to a boil, and cook the mixture, covered, at a bare simmer for 17 minutes, or until the rice is tender. Pack the rice into 4 well-buttered and chilled ½-cup timbale molds, invert the timbales onto plates, and garnish each rice timbale with a coriander sprig. Serves 4.

VEGETABLES

Artichoke Bottoms with Lemon and Orégano

½ lemon
3 large artichokes, trimmed into bottoms
    (procedure follows)
1 tablespoon minced onion
1 small garlic clove, minced
1 tablespoon olive oil
⅓ cup canned chicken broth
2 teaspoons fresh lemon juice
a pinch of crumbled dried orégano
freshly ground pepper to taste
1 tablespoon minced fresh parsley leaves

In a kettle of boiling salted water acidulated with the
juice of the lemon half cook the artichoke bottoms for
12 to 14 minutes, or until they are tender, drain them,
and remove the chokes. Cut each bottom into 8 pieces.
In a heavy skillet cook the onion and the garlic in the oil
over moderately low heat, stirring, until the onion is
softened, add the broth, the lemon juice, the orégano,

the pepper, and the artichoke pieces, and bring the liquid to a boil. Reduce the liquid to about 2 tablespoons,
stir in the parsley, and season the mixture with salt.
Serves 2 as a first course or side dish.

To Trim Artichokes into Artichoke Bottoms

large artichokes
1 lemon, halved

Break off and discard the stems of the artichokes.
Bend the outer leaves back until they snap off close to
the base and remove several more layers of leaves in the
same manner until the pale inner leaves are reached.
Trim the bases and sides with a stainless steel knife, cut
through each artichoke 1 ½ inches from the bottom, and
rub the cut surfaces with 1 of the lemon halves, dropping the artichoke bottoms as they are trimmed into a
bowl of cold water acidulated with the juice of the remaining lemon half.

Artichokes Gribiche
(Artichokes with Caper and Egg Sauce)

4 large artichokes
2½ lemons
3 hard-boiled large eggs
1 tablespoon Dijon-style mustard
2 tablespoons fresh lime juice
½ cup vegetable oil
⅓ cup finely chopped red onion
2 tablespoons drained capers
¼ cup snipped fresh dill
4 dill sprigs for garnish

Break off and discard the stems and tough outer leaves of the artichokes. Cut off the top quarter of each artichoke with a very sharp stainless steel knife, snip off the sharp tips of the leaves with scissors, and rub the cut surfaces with ½ lemon. Trim the bases, dropping the artichokes as they are trimmed into a bowl of cold water acidulated with the juice of 1 of the remaining lemons. In a stainless steel or enameled kettle of boiling salted water combine the artichokes, drained, with the juice of the remaining lemon and simmer them for 35 to 45 minutes, or until their bottoms are tender and a leaf pulls away easily. Let the artichokes drain upside down on a rack until they are just cool enough to handle.

Spread the leaves of the artichokes apart gently, pull out the tender center leaves in one piece, reserving them, and remove the chokes with a small spoon. Invert the center leaves and put them back in the center of the artichokes.

Halve the eggs and force the yolks through a sieve into a bowl, reserving the whites. Add the mustard, the lime juice, and salt and pepper to taste and stir the mixture until it is combined well. Add the oil in a stream, whisking, and whisk the mixture until it is emulsified. Stir in the onion, the capers, the snipped dill, and the reserved egg whites, chopped fine. Fill the inverted center leaves of each artichoke with the sauce and garnish the artichokes with the dill sprigs. Serves 4.

Asparagus with Garlic Mayonnaise and Pine Nuts

2 large garlic cloves, unpeeled
1 large egg yolk
1 teaspoon Dijon-style mustard
¼ teaspoon salt
1 tablespoon white-wine vinegar, or to taste
½ cup olive oil
1 pound asparagus, trimmed and the bottom 2 inches of each stalk peeled
2 tablespoons pine nuts, toasted lightly and chopped fine

In a small saucepan of boiling salted water cook the garlic for 10 minutes and drain it. Peel the garlic and mash it with the back of a fork. While the garlic is cooking, in a metal bowl whisk together the egg yolk, the mustard, the salt, 1 teaspoon of the vinegar, and pepper to taste and heat the mixture set over the pan of boiling water and garlic, whisking vigorously, for 2 to 3 minutes, or until it thickens. Remove the bowl from the pan

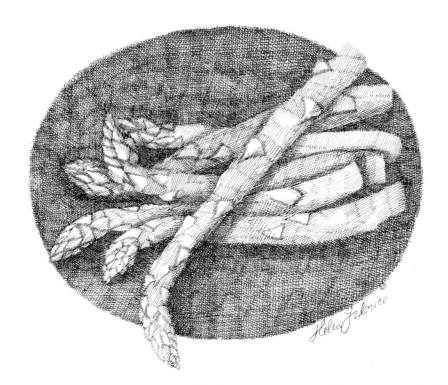

and add to the egg mixture ¼ cup of the oil, drop by drop, whisking constantly. Add the remaining 2 teaspoons vinegar and the remaining ¼ cup oil in a stream, whisking constantly, and whisk in the garlic and 1 to 2 tablespoons warm water to thin the mayonnaise to the desired consistency.

In a deep wide skillet of boiling salted water cook the asparagus for 4 to 6 minutes, or until the stalks are tender but not limp, and drain it well. Transfer the asparagus to a heated serving dish, spoon the mayonnaise over it, and sprinkle it with the pine nuts. Serves 2.

Asparagus Custards with Canadian Bacon and Maltaise Sauce

3 pounds asparagus, trimmed and peeled
1 cup chopped onion
2 cups chicken stock (page 119) or canned chicken broth
½ cup milk
3 large eggs, beaten lightly
1 teaspoon fresh lemon juice, or to taste
6 thin slices (about 3 ounces) of Canadian bacon
thin orange slices for garnish
1½ cups Maltaise sauce (recipe follows)

Cut off the asparagus tips, reserving the stems, and in a saucepan of boiling salted water blanch them for 3 minutes. Drain the tips, refresh them in a large bowl of ice water, and drain them again. *The asparagus tips may be blanched 1 day in advance and kept in a bowl covered and chilled.* In a saucepan combine the reserved asparagus stems, chopped coarse, the onion, and the stock, bring the stock to a boil, and simmer the mixture, covered, for 15 minutes, or until the asparagus is tender. Cook the mixture, uncovered, over moderately high heat, stirring occasionally, for 20 minutes, or until almost all the liquid is evaporated. (There will be about 2 cups of the mixture.)

In a food processor or blender purée the asparagus mixture until it is smooth. In a bowl stir together the purée, the milk, the eggs, the lemon juice, and salt and pepper to taste and divide the custard among 6 well-buttered ½-cup ramekins. Line a baking pan just large enough to hold the ramekins snugly with a kitchen towel for insulation. Arrange the ramekins on the towel, add enough hot water to the pan to come just halfway up the sides of the ramekins, and bake the custards in the middle of a preheated 325° F. oven for 35 to 40 minutes, or

until a thin knife inserted in the center comes out clean. Remove the ramekins from the pan and let them cool for 10 minutes. *The custards may be made 1 day in advance, kept in the ramekins, covered and chilled, and reheated in a preheated 325° F. oven for 20 minutes, or until they are heated through.*

Bake the bacon in one layer on a baking sheet in a preheated 325° F. oven for 15 minutes, or until it is heated through. Run a thin knife around the edge of each ramekin to loosen the custard, arrange a bacon slice on top of each custard, and on a small plate invert the custards onto the bacon (the bacon base will make it easier to transfer the custards). Transfer the custards and the bacon with a metal spatula to a heated platter and garnish the top of each custard with 2 small asparagus tips and a small triangular piece of orange slice. Garnish the platter with the orange slices and the remaining asparagus tips and serve the custards with the Maltaise sauce. Serves 6.

Maltaise Sauce (Orange-Flavored Hollandaise)

1 orange (preferably a blood orange, available seasonally at produce markets)
2 tablespoons white-wine vinegar
¼ teaspoon salt
freshly ground white pepper to taste
3 large egg yolks, beaten lightly
2 sticks (1 cup) unsalted butter at room temperature, cut into 12 pieces

Blanch the whole orange in a saucepan of boiling water for 3 minutes, drain it, and let it cool. Grate fine the rind and squeeze the orange to extract 2 tablespoons of the juice, reserving the remaining juice for another use.

In a small heavy stainless steel or enameled saucepan combine the vinegar, 2 tablespoons water, the salt, and the pepper and reduce the liquid over moderately high heat to about 2 tablespoons. Remove the pan from the heat and add 1 tablespoon cold water. Add the egg yolks, cook the mixture over very low heat, whisking, until it is thick, and whisk in the butter, 1 piece at a time, over low heat, lifting the pan occasionally to cool the mixture and making certain that each piece is melted before adding the next. Cook the sauce, whisking, until it is thick and add the grated rind and the juice. *The sauce may be kept warm for 1 hour, covered with a buttered round of wax paper, set in a pan of warm water.* Makes about 1½ cups.

Gazpacho-Filled Avocado

1½ tablespoons finely chopped onion
¼ cup seeded and finely chopped tomato
3 tablespoons peeled, seeded, and finely
    chopped cucumber
3 tablespoons finely chopped green bell
    pepper
½ teaspoon minced bottled pickled *jalapeño*
    pepper (wear rubber gloves), or to taste
2 teaspoons fresh lemon juice, plus additional
    for brushing the avocado
1 avocado (preferably California)
corn tortilla chips as an accompaniment

In a small bowl combine the onion, the tomato, the cucumber, the bell pepper, the *jalapeño* pepper, the lemon juice, and salt to taste. Halve and pit the avocado. Brush the avocado halves with the additional lemon juice, divide the filling between them, and serve the avocado with the tortilla chips. Serves 2.

Avocado Mousse with Salmon Roe

1 envelope unflavored gelatin
2 cups peeled, pitted, and chopped avocado
    (preferably California)
2 tablespoons fresh lemon juice, or to taste
1½ cups buttermilk
4 garlic cloves, cooked in boiling salted water
    for 15 minutes, drained, and peeled
½ teaspoon ground cumin, or to taste
½ teaspoon Tabasco, or to taste
about 4 ounces salmon roe (available at
    specialty foods shops)
Melba toast hearts (page 109) as an
    accompaniment

In a small heavy saucepan sprinkle the gelatin over ½ cup cold water and let it soften for 10 minutes. Heat the mixture over low heat, stirring, until the gelatin is melted and remove the pan from the heat. In a blender or food processor purée the avocado with the lemon juice, the buttermilk, the garlic, ½ cup water, the cumin, the Tabasco, and the gelatin mixture and season the purée with salt. Transfer the mousse to serving bowls and chill it, covered, for at least 2 hours, or until it is set (it will not be firm). *The mousse may be made up to 6 hours in advance and kept covered and chilled.* Just before serving spoon the salmon roe decoratively on the mousse and serve the mousse with the Melba toast hearts. Makes about 4 cups, serving 20 as an hors d'oeuvre.

Green Beans and Lima Beans with Herb Butter

1½ pounds green beans, trimmed, boiled in
    salted water for 5 minutes, and refreshed
    under cold water
two 10-ounce packages frozen small lima
    beans, boiled in salted water for 5 minutes,
    or until they are tender, and refreshed under
    cold water
1 stick (½ cup) unsalted butter
3 tablespoons minced fresh parsley leaves
4 scallions, minced
2 tablespoons snipped fresh dill
2 stalks of celery including the green leaves,
    minced
1 garlic clove, minced

Pat dry the green beans and the lima beans. Divide the butter between 2 large saucepans, heat it over moderate heat until it is melted, and cook the beans separately in the 2 pans, stirring to coat them with the butter, until they are just heated through. In a bowl combine the parsley, the scallions, the dill, the celery, and the garlic, divide the mixture between the pans, and cook the beans, stirring, for 2 minutes more. Season the beans with salt and pepper. Serves 8 generously.

Green Beans Vinaigrette with Red Onion and Coriander

1 small red onion, chopped fine
1 pound green beans, trimmed
2 tablespoons balsamic vinegar (available at
    specialty foods shops and some
    supermarkets) or wine vinegar
¼ cup olive oil
2 tablespoons chopped fresh coriander leaves
    or fresh basil leaves or minced fresh parsley
    leaves

Put the onion in a large bowl. In a steamer set over boiling water steam the green beans, covered, for 4 to 6 minutes, or until they are just tender, and add them to the onion. In a small bowl whisk together the vinegar and salt and pepper to taste, add the oil in a stream, whisking, and whisk the dressing until it is emulsified. Drizzle the dressing over the beans, add the coriander, and toss the mixture well. Serve the beans warm or at room temperature. Serves 4.

Sautéed Green Beans with Garlic Crumbs

½ pound green beans, trimmed
1 tablespoon olive oil
2 tablespoons unsalted butter
1 garlic clove, minced
5 anchovy fillets, minced
½ cup coarse fresh bread crumbs

In a skillet cook the green beans in the oil over moderately high heat, stirring, for 4 to 5 minutes, or until they are crisp-tender, reduce the heat to moderate, and stir in the butter, the garlic, the anchovies, and the bread crumbs. Cook the mixture, stirring, until the bread crumbs are golden and season it with salt and pepper. Serves 2.

Bean Curd with Black Bean Sauce

½ pound bean curd, drained and patted dry
1 teaspoon cornstarch plus additional for
    dredging
1 egg, beaten lightly
vegetable oil for frying
1 teaspoon sugar
½ cup canned chicken broth
2 tablespoons soy sauce
2 tablespoons white-wine vinegar
¼ cup drained canned black beans, rinsed,
    drained, and mashed
1 garlic clove, chopped
2 tablespoons minced scallion greens

Cut the bean curd into 1½-inch squares, ½ inch thick, dredge the squares in the cornstarch, coating them completely, and dip them in the egg. In a large heavy skillet heat ¼ inch of the oil to 350° F., in it fry the bean curd, turning it once, for 6 to 8 minutes, or until it is golden, and transfer it to paper towels to drain. Keep the bean curd warm on an ovenproof platter in a preheated 225° F. oven. Pour off all but 1 tablespoon of the oil and let the skillet cool slightly.

In a small bowl dissolve the 1 teaspoon cornstarch and the sugar in the broth and stir in the soy sauce, the vinegar, and the beans. In the skillet cook the garlic over moderate heat, stirring, for 30 seconds and stir in the cornstarch mixture. Cook the mixture over moderately high heat, stirring, until it is thick and smooth, strain the sauce through a fine sieve, pressing hard on the solids, and pour it around the bean curd. Sprinkle the bean curd with the scallions. Serves 2.

Bean Curd Noodles with Celery and Carrot

four 3-inch squares firm bean curd,* about 1
    inch thick
2 stalks of celery, strings discarded and the
    stalks cut into 2-inch fine julienne strips
1 carrot, cut into 2-inch fine julienne strips
1 teaspoon salt
4 teaspoons Oriental sesame oil,* or to taste

*available at Oriental markets, some specialty
    foods shops, and some supermarkets

In a saucepan of boiling salted water blanch the bean curd for 15 seconds, drain it carefully in a colander, and let it cool. Pat the bean curd dry, set the squares in one layer between several thicknesses of paper towels, and weight them evenly with a 5-pound weight for at least 2 hours and up to 5 hours.

While the bean curd is being weighted toss the celery and the carrot in separate bowls, each with ½ teaspoon of the salt, and let the vegetables stand for 20 minutes. Drain the vegetables and pat them dry. Holding a cleaver or large sharp knife parallel to the cutting surface, cut each square of bean curd carefully into thirds horizontally and cut the slices crosswise into thin noodle-like strips. In a bowl toss the bean curd noodles gently with the celery, the carrot, the sesame oil, and salt to taste. *The noodles may be made 1 day in advance and kept covered and chilled.* Serve the noodles at room temperature. Serves 8 as a first course.

Sesame Broccoli Flowerets

3 tablespoons vegetable oil

8 cups broccoli flowerets, blanched in boiling
    salted water for 1 minute, refreshed in a
    bowl of ice and cold water, drained, and
    patted dry

½ teaspoon sugar

2 garlic cloves, minced

1½ teaspoons minced peeled gingerroot

1½ tablespoons soy sauce, or to taste

2 tablespoons Oriental sesame oil (available at
    Oriental markets, specialty foods shops, and
    many supermarkets)

2 tablespoons sesame seeds, toasted lightly

Heat a wok over high heat until it is hot, add the vegetable oil, and heat it until it is just smoking. In the oil stir-fry the broccoli with the sugar for 2 minutes, add the garlic and the gingerroot, and stir-fry the mixture for 1 minute. Add the soy sauce, the sesame oil, the sesame seeds, and salt and pepper to taste and toss the mixture well. Serves 4.

Glazed Broccoli Stems

7 broccoli stems about 1½ inches in diameter,
    trimmed, peeled, and cut crosswise into
    ¾-inch slices

1 cup canned chicken broth

1 tablespoon fresh lemon juice

2 tablespoons unsalted butter, softened

1 tablespoon chopped fresh parsley leaves

In a saucepan combine the broccoli and the broth, bring the broth to a boil, and simmer the mixture, covered, for 10 to 12 minutes, or until the broccoli is just tender. Transfer the broccoli with a slotted spoon to a bowl, add the lemon juice to the pan, and boil the liquid until it is reduced to about ¼ cup. Whisk in the butter, the parsley, and pepper to taste, add the broccoli, and stir the broccoli to coat it with the glaze. Serves 4.

Sautéed Brussels Sprouts with Bacon

2 pounds Brussels sprouts, trimmed and an X
    cut into the base of each sprout

6 slices of lean bacon, chopped fine

2 tablespoons unsalted butter

In a large kettle of boiling salted water boil the Brussels sprouts for 8 to 10 minutes, or until they are just tender, and drain them. Refresh the Brussels sprouts in a bowl of ice and cold water, drain them, and pat them dry. *The Brussels sprouts may be prepared up to this point 1 day in advance and kept covered and chilled.*
In a large skillet cook the bacon over moderate heat, stirring occasionally, until it is crisp and transfer it with a slotted spoon to paper towels to drain. Add the butter to the skillet, heat the fat over moderately high heat until the foam subsides, and in it sauté the Brussels sprouts, stirring, until they are heated through. Add the bacon and salt and pepper to taste. Serves 6.

Caraway Cabbage

¾ stick (6 tablespoons) unsalted butter

a 2-pound cabbage, quartered, cored, and cut
    crosswise into ¼-inch strips

1 tablespoon caraway seeds

1 tablespoon distilled white vinegar, or to
    taste

In a heavy kettle heat the butter over moderately high heat until the foam subsides and in it sauté the cabbage, sprinkled with the caraway seeds and salt to taste, tossing it, for 1 to 2 minutes, or until it is coated well with the butter. Cook the cabbage, covered, over moderate heat for 2 to 3 minutes, or until it is just wilted. Transfer the cabbage to a heated serving dish, sprinkle it with the vinegar, and toss it. Serves 8.

Napa Cabbage with Sesame Seeds

1 tablespoon olive oil

½ pound Napa cabbage (celery cabbage),
    sliced thin

1 tablespoon white-wine vinegar, or to taste

1 tablespoon sesame seeds, toasted lightly

In a large heavy skillet heat the oil over moderately high heat until it is hot and in it cook the cabbage over moderate heat, stirring, for 3 to 5 minutes, or until it is crisp-tender. Add the vinegar, the sesame seeds, and salt and pepper to taste and toss the mixture. Serves 2.

Sweet-and-Sour Braised Red Cabbage

½ cup raspberry vinegar (available at specialty
    foods shops) or red-wine vinegar
3 tablespoons firmly packed dark brown sugar
1 cup chicken stock (page 119) or canned
    chicken broth
1 teaspoon caraway seeds
1 large (about 2 pounds) red cabbage, tough
    outer leaves discarded, cored and shredded

In a kettle combine the vinegar, the brown sugar, the
stock, the caraway seeds, the cabbage, and salt and pepper to taste, bring the liquid to a boil, and simmer the
mixture, covered, stirring occasionally, for 50 minutes,
or until the cabbage is just tender. Remove the lid, bring
the liquid to a boil, and boil it until almost all of it is
evaporated. *The braised cabbage may be made 1 day in
advance, kept covered and chilled, and reheated.*
Serves 4.

Carrot "Fettuccine"

1 pound carrots
3 tablespoons unsalted butter
½ cup minced onion
¼ pound sliced cooked ham (preferably
    smoked), cut into thin strips
2 garlic cloves, minced
½ cup dry white wine
1 cup heavy cream
1 cup frozen peas, thawed
1 tablespoon Dijon-style mustard

With a swivel-bladed vegetable peeler shred the carrots into fettuccine-like strands. In a large skillet heat
the butter over moderately high heat until the foam begins to subside and in it cook the onion and the ham, stirring, for 3 minutes. Add the carrot strands, the garlic,
and the wine and cook the mixture, covered, over moderately low heat, stirring occasionally, for 10 minutes,
or until almost all the liquid is evaporated and the carrots are almost tender. Add the cream and the peas,
bring the mixture to a boil, and simmer it, covered, for 5
minutes, or until the liquid is reduced by half. Stir in the
mustard and salt and pepper to taste. Serves 4 as a first
course or 2 as an entrée.

Lacy East Indian Carrot Fritters

¾ cup all-purpose flour
1½ teaspoons ground cumin
1½ teaspoons ground coriander
½ teaspoon turmeric
¼ teaspoon cayenne
1½ teaspoons salt
½ cup beer
1 large egg, beaten lightly
1 bunch of scallions (about 6 to 8) including
    the green tops, chopped
¼ pound carrots, grated coarse, preferably in a
    food processor
vegetable shortening or oil for deep-frying

Into a bowl sift together the flour, the cumin, the coriander, the turmeric, the cayenne, and the salt, add the
beer and the egg, stirring the mixture until it is just combined, and stir in the scallions and the carrots. In a deep
fryer fry heaping tablespoons of the mixture in batches
in 2 inches of 375° F. shortening, turning them, for 2 to
3 minutes, or until they are golden and crisp, and transfer them to paper towels to drain. Makes 12 fritters.

Susan Riecken

Pickled Carrot Sticks

1 pound carrots, cut into 3½- by ⅓-inch sticks
1 cup cider vinegar
¼ cup sugar
2 garlic cloves, crushed lightly
1½ tablespoons dill seeds
1½ tablespoons salt

In a large saucepan of boiling salted water blanch the carrots for 1 minute, drain them in a colander, and refresh them under cold water. Pack the carrot sticks upright in two 1-pint heatproof jars. In a saucepan combine the vinegar, 1¼ cups water, the sugar, the garlic, the dill seeds, and the salt, bring the mixture to a boil, and simmer it for 2 minutes. Pour the mixture over the carrots, filling the jars to within ¼ inch of the top and making sure that 1 garlic clove is in each jar, and chill the carrots, covered, for at least 24 hours or up to 1 week. Makes 2 pints.

Honey-Glazed Carrots

1¼ pounds carrots
2 tablespoons unsalted butter
1½ teaspoons honey, or to taste
1 teaspoon fresh lemon juice, or to taste

With a swivel-bladed vegetable peeler shred the carrots lengthwise into fettuccine-like strands. In a saucepan of boiling salted water boil the carrot strands for 1 to 2 minutes, or until they are barely tender. Drain the carrots in a colander, refresh them under cold water, and drain them again. *The carrots may be prepared up to this point 1 day in advance and kept covered and chilled.* In a skillet melt the butter with the honey and the lemon juice over moderately low heat, stirring, add the carrots, and heat the mixture, stirring and tossing the strands, for 1 to 3 minutes, or until the carrots are heated through and coated well with the honey mixture. Season the carrots with salt. Serves 6.

Pickled Cauliflower

4 cups small cauliflower flowerets
1⅓ cups cider vinegar
2 garlic cloves, crushed lightly
1½ tablespoons dill seeds
1½ tablespoons salt

In a large saucepan of boiling salted water blanch the cauliflower for 1 minute, drain it in a colander, and refresh it under cold water. Pack the cauliflower in a 1-quart heatproof jar. In a saucepan combine the vinegar, 1⅓ cups water, the garlic, the dill seeds, and the salt, bring the mixture to a boil, and simmer it for 2 minutes. Pour the mixture over the cauliflower, filling the jar to within ¼ inch of the top, and chill the cauliflower, covered, for at least 24 hours or up to 1 week. Makes 1 quart.

Spicy Indian Cauliflower Sauté

3 tablespoons vegetable oil
½ small head of cauliflower, broken into flowerets and sliced thin, with any green leaves chopped
a 2-inch piece of gingerroot, peeled and cut into 12 to 15 paper-thin slices with a vegetable peeler
1 garlic clove, minced
½ teaspoon turmeric
4 fresh plum tomatoes, peeled, seeded, and chopped, or 4 canned plum tomatoes, seeded and chopped
2 tablespoons dry white wine
½ bunch of scallions (about 3) including the green tops, chopped

In a large skillet heat the oil over moderately high heat until it is hot but not smoking and in it sauté the cauliflower with the leaves, stirring the mixture once, for 3 minutes, or until it is golden brown. Add the gingerroot, the garlic, and the turmeric and cook the mixture, stirring, for 30 seconds. Add the tomatoes, the wine, and ¼ cup water and bring the liquid to a boil. Simmer the mixture for 8 to 10 minutes, or until the cauliflower is just tender, and stir in the scallions and salt and pepper to taste. Serves 2.

Corn on the Cob with Basil Butter

½ cup loosely packed fresh basil leaves
1½ sticks (¾ cup) unsalted butter, softened
12 ears of corn, shucked
fresh basil sprigs for garnish if desired

In a food processor mince the basil leaves, add the butter and salt and pepper to taste, and blend the mixture until it is combined well. Transfer the butter to a small serving dish. *The basil butter may be made up to 3 days in advance, kept covered and chilled, and softened before serving.* In a kettle of boiling water cook the corn,

covered, for 3 to 5 minutes, or until it is just tender, and drain it. Garnish the corn with the basil sprigs if desired and serve it with the basil butter. Serves 6.

Layered Corn, Cheese, and Jalapeño Custard

2 onions, sliced
½ stick (¼ cup) unsalted butter
2 garlic cloves, minced
2 fresh or pickled *jalapeño* peppers, halved
    lengthwise, seeded, and cut crosswise into
    thin strips (wear rubber gloves)
1⅓ cups corn (cut from about 3 ears of corn)
freshly ground pepper to taste
1 cup coarsely grated Monterey Jack
⅔ cup coarsely grated sharp Cheddar
7 large eggs, beaten lightly
½ cup milk

In a 10-inch non-stick ovenproof skillet cook the onions in 2 tablespoons of the butter over moderately low heat, stirring occasionally, until they are softened but not brown. Add the garlic and the *jalapeño* peppers, cook the mixture, stirring, for 2 minutes, and stir in the corn, the ground pepper, and salt to taste. Cook the mixture, stirring, for 1 minute, or until it is combined, transfer two thirds of it to a bowl, and add the remaining 2 tablespoons butter to the skillet. In a small bowl combine the Monterey Jack and the Cheddar, sprinkle one third of the cheese over the corn mixture in the skillet, and cover it with half the remaining corn mixture, spreading it gently in an even layer. Add another third of the cheese and top it with the remaining corn mixture. In

another bowl beat together the eggs, the milk, and salt and pepper to taste and pour the custard gently into the skillet. Sprinkle the remaining third of the cheese over the mixture and bake the mixture in a preheated 350° F. oven for 20 to 25 minutes, or until it is puffed and golden and a knife comes out clean. Serve the custard hot or at room temperature, cut into wedges. Serves 4 to 6.

Corn Oysters

2 ears of corn, shucked
1 teaspoon milk if necessary
2 tablespoons sifted flour
freshly ground pepper to taste
1 large egg, separated
1 tablespoon vegetable shortening or bacon fat
1 tablespoon unsalted butter

With a serrated knife cut the corn kernels from the cobs into a bowl and with the back of the knife scrape the remaining corn from the cobs into the bowl. (There should be about 1 cup.) If the corn is not milky add the milk. Add the flour, the pepper, the egg yolk, and salt to taste and stir the mixture until it is combined. In a small bowl beat the egg white until it just holds stiff peaks and fold it into the corn mixture. In a large skillet heat the shortening and the butter over moderately high heat until it is hot but not smoking and in the fat cook heaping tablespoons of the corn mixture in batches for 3 minutes on each side, or until they are golden brown, transferring them as they are cooked to paper towels to drain. Keep the corn oysters warm in a preheated 200° F. oven. Makes about 10 corn oysters.

TREVOR

Corn Bread and Broccoli Pie

For the filling

2 onions, chopped
3 tablespoons olive oil
½ pound small mushrooms, halved
2 garlic cloves, minced
a 28-ounce can plum tomatoes, drained and
    chopped, reserving the juice
¼ cup Madeira
1½ pounds broccoli, trimmed, separated into
    flowerets, and stems halved horizontally
    and chopped (about 7 cups total)

For the crust

1 cup cornmeal (preferably stone-ground)
1 cup all-purpose flour
2 teaspoons double-acting baking powder
½ teaspoon baking soda
1 teaspoon salt
2 large eggs, beaten lightly
½ stick (¼ cup) unsalted butter, melted and
    cooled
½ cup milk
½ cup sour cream
2 teaspoons honey
4 ounces sharp Cheddar, grated coarse

Make the filling: In a large skillet cook the onions in the oil over moderately low heat, stirring, until they are softened, add the mushrooms, and cook the mixture, stirring occasionally, until all the liquid the mushrooms give off is evaporated. Add the garlic and cook the mixture, stirring, for 2 minutes. Add the tomatoes, the reserved juice, the Madeira, the broccoli, and salt and pepper to taste, bring the liquid to a boil, and simmer the mixture, covered, stirring occasionally, for 15 minutes. Strain the liquid through a sieve into a saucepan and transfer the mixture to a baking pan, 11½ by 8 by 2 inches. Boil the liquid until it is reduced to about ¾ cup and pour it over the mixture.

Make the crust: In a bowl combine well the cornmeal, the flour, the baking powder, the baking soda, and the salt, add the eggs, the butter, the milk, the sour cream, the honey, and the Cheddar, and stir the batter until it is just combined. Spread the batter evenly over the top of the broccoli mixture and bake the pie in a preheated 400° F. oven for 30 minutes, or until a tester inserted in the corn bread comes out clean. Serves 8 to 10.

Bread-and-Butter Pickles

1¼ pounds pickling cucumbers, such as
    Kirby, cut into ¼-inch slices
1 onion, sliced very thin
2 tablespoons coarse salt
1 cup cider vinegar
1 cup sugar
¼ teaspoon turmeric
1 tablespoon mustard seeds
½ teaspoon celery seeds
¼ teaspoon cayenne, or to taste

In a large bowl combine the cucumbers and the onion, sprinkle them with the salt, and toss the mixture well. Add about 2 cups ice cubes and chill the mixture, covered, overnight. Drain the mixture in a colander and rinse it under cold water. In a large saucepan combine the vinegar, the sugar, the turmeric, the mustard seeds, the celery seeds, and the cayenne and bring the liquid to a boil, stirring. Add the cucumber mixture, bring the liquid just to a simmer, stirring, and transfer the mixture to a bowl. Let the mixture cool and chill it, covered, for 24 hours. The pickles keep, covered and chilled, for up to 7 days. Makes about 1 quart.

Szechwan Pickled Cucumbers

1 pound small pickling (Kirby) cucumbers,
    scrubbed, cut lengthwise into 8 wedges, and
    seeded, or 1 large seedless cucumber, cut
    crosswise into 2-inch sections and each
    section cut lengthwise into 8 wedges and cored
2 teaspoons salt
1½ tablespoons sugar
2 tablespoons rice vinegar*
⅓ cup Oriental sesame oil*
a 1-inch cube peeled gingerroot, shredded fine
eight 1-inch dried hot chili peppers,* stemmed
    and seeded (wear rubber gloves)
1 teaspoon Szechwan peppercorns*

*available at Oriental markets, some specialty
    foods shops, and some supermarkets

In a bowl toss the cucumbers with the salt and let the mixture stand for 20 minutes. Drain the cucumbers in a sieve, rinse them under cold water, and pat them dry. In a bowl dissolve the sugar in the vinegar, stirring, add the cucumber, and toss it to coat it with the mixture.

In a wok or small deep skillet heat the sesame oil over moderately high heat until it is just smoking, add the gingerroot, the chili peppers, and the peppercorns, and stir-

fry the mixture for 3 to 5 seconds, or until the spices are fragrant and the chili peppers are very dark. Remove the wok from the heat and let the mixture cool completely. Pour the spiced oil over the cucumbers, toss the mixture, and let it marinate at room temperature for 3 hours or covered and chilled overnight. *The pickles may be made up to 4 days in advance and kept covered and chilled, stirring occasionally. The cucumbers will increase in hotness the longer they stand.* Makes about 3 cups.

Baked Eggplant and Rice Custard

¼ cup long-grain rice
½ pound eggplant, sliced into ¼-inch rounds
5 tablespoons olive oil
1 small onion, minced
1 large garlic clove, minced
½ cup half-and-half
1 large egg
⅓ cup freshly grated Parmesan

In a saucepan of boiling salted water boil the rice for 12 minutes, or until it is tender, drain it well, and transfer it to a small bowl.

In a large heavy skillet heat 2½ tablespoons of the oil over moderate heat until it is hot and in it cook the eggplant in batches, turning it once and adding the remaining 2½ tablespoons oil as necessary, for 5 to 6 minutes, or until it is browned, transferring it as it is browned to paper towels to drain. Let the skillet cool for 1 minute, in the oil remaining in it cook the onion and the garlic over moderately low heat until they are softened, and toss them with the rice.

In a bowl beat together the half-and-half, the egg, and the Parmesan. In an oiled shallow 3-cup baking dish put 1 eggplant slice, spoon some of the rice mixture on it, and overlap it with another eggplant slice, covering the rice mixture. Assemble the remaining rice mixture and eggplant in the same manner, spoon the Parmesan mixture around the eggplant, and bake the dish in a preheated 375° F. oven for 15 to 17 minutes, or until the top is golden. Serves 2 as a side dish.

Eggplant Rollatini with Three Cheeses

For the sauce
½ cup finely chopped carrots
½ cup finely chopped white part of leek,
    rinsed well and drained
1 cup finely chopped onions
3 tablespoons olive oil
2 garlic cloves, minced
a 35-ounce can plum tomatoes, chopped,
    including the juice
1 bay leaf
1 teaspoon crumbled dried thyme
For the rollatini
two 1½-pound eggplants, peeled and sliced
    lengthwise ¼ inch thick
½ pound Feta
1 cup whole-milk ricotta
1 large egg, beaten lightly
¾ cup freshly grated Parmesan
1 tablespoon fresh lemon juice
¼ cup plus 1 tablespoon minced fresh parsley
    leaves
½ cup minced scallions
oil for brushing

Make the sauce: In a large heavy skillet cook the carrots, the leeks, and the onions in the oil over moderately low heat, stirring, until the vegetables are softened, add the garlic, and cook the mixture, stirring, for 2 minutes. Add the tomatoes, the bay leaf, and the thyme, bring the mixture to a boil, and simmer it, stirring occasionally, for 45 minutes. Add salt and pepper to taste and discard the bay leaf.

Make the *rollatini*: Sprinkle the eggplant slices lightly with salt on both sides and let them drain in a colander for 30 minutes. In a food processor chop fine the Feta, add the ricotta, the egg, ½ cup of the Parmesan, and the lemon juice, and blend the mixture until it is smooth. Add ¼ cup of the parsley and the scallions and process the mixture for 10 seconds. Transfer the eggplant slices to paper towels and pat them dry. Arrange one third of the eggplant slices in one layer on a jelly-roll pan, brushed with the oil, and brush the tops with the oil. Cook the eggplant slices under a preheated broiler about 4 inches from the heat, turning them once and brushing them again with the oil, for 8 to 10 minutes, or until they are browned lightly on both sides, transfer them to paper towels to drain, and cook the remaining slices in the same manner. Put 2 tablespoons of the cheese mixture at the wide end of each slice and roll up the slices to enclose the filling.

Spread ¼ cup of the sauce in a 10- by 7-inch baking pan and arrange the egglant rolls in one layer on the sauce. Pour the remaining sauce over the rolls and sprinkle it with the remaining ¼ cup Parmesan. Bake the *rollatini* in a preheated 350° F. oven for 30 to 40 minutes, or until they are heated through, and sprinkle them with the remaining 1 tablespoon parsley. Serves 4.

Sautéed Kale with Red Bell Peppers

1 small head of kale, washed well, stems
discarded, and leaves chopped, reserving 6
whole leaves
2 tablespoons unsalted butter
1 red bell pepper, cut into 1- by ⅛-inch strips

In a large saucepan of boiling salted water blanch the
chopped and whole kale leaves for 30 seconds, transfer
the kale to a colander, and refresh it under cold water.
Drain the kale and pat it dry. *The kale may be blanched
1 day in advance and kept covered and chilled.* In a skillet heat the butter over moderately high heat until the
foam begins to subside and in it sauté the bell pepper,
stirring, for 2 minutes, or until it is just softened. Add
the chopped kale and salt and pepper to taste and cook
the mixture, stirring, for 3 minutes, or until it is heated
through. Line a heated small dish with the whole leaves
and mound the chopped mixture on top. Serves 2.

Mushroom Charlottes with Port and Currant Sauce

For the filling

3 garlic cloves
2 onions, quartered
2 tablespoons unsalted butter
1½ pounds mushrooms
¼ teaspoon crumbled dried thyme
½ cup firmly packed fresh parsley leaves
1 large egg
4 ounces cream cheese, softened
¼ cup heavy cream
½ cup freshly grated Parmesan

1 stick (½ cup) unsalted butter
a 1-pound loaf very thinly sliced homemade-
type white bread
For the sauce
½ cup plus 1 tablespoon Tawny Port
¼ cup dried currants
½ cup canned beef broth
2 tablespoons currant jelly
2 teaspoons red-wine vinegar
1 tablespoon arrowroot

flat-leafed parsley sprigs for garnish

Make the filling: Drop the garlic through the feed
tube into a food processor with the motor running and
mince it fine. Add the onions and chop them fine, puls-

ing the motor. In a kettle cook the onion mixture in the
butter over moderately low heat, stirring, until the onion is softened. In the food processor chop the mushrooms in 3 batches, pulsing the motor, and add them to
the kettle with the thyme and salt and pepper to taste.
Cook the mixture, stirring occasionally, for 15 to 20
minutes, or until most of the liquid the mushrooms give
off is evaporated, and let the mixture cool for 15 minutes. Transfer the mixture to a dish towel, squeeze out 1
cup of liquid, reserving the liquid for the sauce, and
transfer the mushroom mixture to a bowl. In the food
processor mince the parsley and add it to the bowl. In
the food processor blend the egg, the cream cheese, and
the cream until the mixture is smooth and stir it into the
mushroom mixture with the Parmesan and salt and pepper to taste. *The mushroom filling may be made 1 day in
advance and kept covered and chilled.*

In a small saucepan melt the butter and let it cool for 5
minutes. Cut 8 slices of the bread into rounds the same
size as the bottoms of eight ½-cup metal charlotte molds
or ovenproof dishes, brush the rounds lightly on both
sides with some of the butter, and fit them into the bottoms of the molds. Cut out 8 more rounds the same size
as the tops of the molds and reserve them. (The bread
scraps may be reserved for another use, such as bread
crumbs.) Trim the crusts from the remaining slices and
cut each slice into 4 squares. Brush both sides of the
squares lightly with some of the butter and line the sides
of the molds with the squares, overlapping the squares
slightly. (You will need approximately 5 squares for
each mold. Any leftover squares may be reserved for
another use.) Press the squares gently against the sides
of the molds to keep them in place and spoon the mushroom filling into the molds, tamping it down and filling
the molds just to the top of the bread lining. Brush both
sides of the reserved bread rounds lightly with the remaining butter and top each mold with a round, pressing
it down securely to cover the filling completely. Bake
the charlottes on a baking sheet in a preheated 425° F.
oven for 15 minutes, or until the bread is golden.

Make the sauce while the charlottes are baking: In a
small saucepan combine ½ cup of the Port and the currants, bring the Port to a boil, and boil it until it is reduced to about 3 tablespoons. Add the reserved
mushroom liquid and the broth, bring the liquid to a
boil, and boil it until it is reduced to about ¾ cup. Whisk
in the jelly and the vinegar and boil the sauce, whisking,
until the jelly is dissolved. In a small bowl stir together
the remaining 1 tablespoon Port and the arrowroot and
whisk the mixture into the sauce. Boil the sauce, whisk-

ing, for 1 minute, add salt and pepper to taste, and keep it warm.

Invert the charlottes onto individual serving plates, spoon the sauce around them, and garnish the charlottes with the parsley sprigs. Serves 8 as a first course.

Braised Black Mushrooms

2 ounces (about 12) dried large Chinese black
  mushrooms or dried *shiitake* mushrooms
  (available at Oriental markets, specialty
  foods shops, and some supermarkets)
1 tablespoon vegetable oil
1½ tablespoons soy sauce
1 teaspoon sugar
1 tablespoon sesame seeds, toasted lightly
coriander sprigs for garnish

In a bowl let the mushrooms soak in 3 cups hot water, stirring occasionally, for 20 minutes, or until they are soft and spongy. Drain the mushrooms, cut away and discard the stems, and pat the mushrooms dry.

Heat a wok or heavy skillet over high heat until it is hot, add the oil, and heat it until it is very hot but not smoking. Add the mushrooms and stir-fry them for 30 seconds to 1 minute, or until they are darkened slightly. Add 1½ cups water, the soy sauce, and the sugar and boil the mixture, turning the mushrooms occasionally, until almost all the liquid is evaporated and the mushrooms are glazed. Transfer the mixture to a bowl and let it cool completely. *The mushrooms may be made up to this point 1 day in advance and kept covered and chilled.* Holding a sharp knife at a forty-five-degree angle, cut the mushrooms crosswise into thin slices and arrange the slices decoratively in small shallow dishes. Sprinkle the mushrooms with the sesame seeds and garnish them with the coriander sprigs. Serves 8 as a first course.

Crisp Fried Okra in Curry Batter

1 large egg
1½ tablespoons fresh lemon juice
1 garlic clove, minced
1 teaspoon turmeric
1 teaspoon curry powder
½ teaspoon salt
⅛ teaspoon cayenne, or to taste
¼ pound okra, halved lengthwise
flour for dredging
1 cup fine fresh bread crumbs
vegetable oil for deep-frying

In a bowl whisk together the egg, the lemon juice, the garlic, the turmeric, the curry powder, the salt, and the cayenne. Dredge the okra in the flour, shaking off the excess, dip it in the egg mixture, letting the excess drip off, and roll it in the bread crumbs. In a large deep skillet heat 1 inch of the oil to 360° F. and in it fry the okra in batches, turning it, for 2 minutes, or until it is golden, transferring it with a slotted spoon as it is fried to paper towels to drain. Keep the okra warm on a baking sheet lined with paper towels in a preheated 200° F. oven. Serves 2.

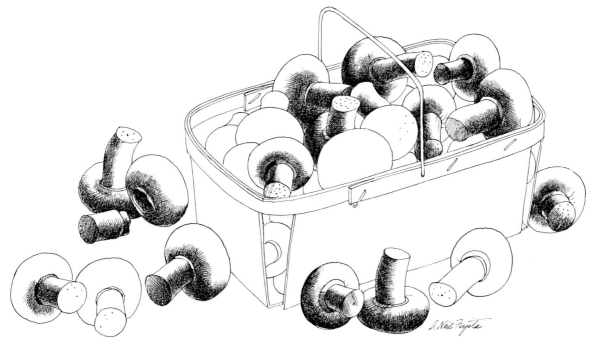

Spicy Okra Ratatouille

¼ cup vegetable oil
1 pound small okra, trimmed
1 cup chopped red onions
4 teaspoons minced peeled gingerroot
2 teaspoons minced garlic
2 teaspoons grated orange rind
½ cup fresh orange juice
½ pound plum tomatoes, seeded and chopped
1 pound yellow squash, cut into 2- by ½-inch
    pieces
2 tablespoons fresh lemon juice
3 tablespoons chopped fresh coriander

In a large heavy skillet heat the oil over high heat until it is hot, in it sauté the okra, stirring, for 4 minutes, and transfer it with a slotted spoon to a bowl. Add the onions to the skillet and cook them over moderately low heat, stirring, for 5 minutes. Add the gingerroot, the garlic, and the orange rind and cook the mixture, stirring, for 2 minutes. Add the orange juice and the tomatoes, bring the mixture to a boil, and add salt and pepper to taste. Add the okra and simmer the mixture, covered, for 10 minutes. Add the squash and simmer the mixture, covered, for 5 minutes, or until the vegetables are just tender. *The mixture may be made up to this point 1 day in advance and kept covered and chilled.* Let the mixture cool, stir in the lemon juice, the coriander, and salt and pepper to taste, and transfer the mixture to a portable container. Makes about 6 cups.

Mint-Marinated Grilled Red Onions

3 red onions, sliced crosswise into twelve
    ½-inch-thick slices
2 teaspoons crumbled dried mint
2 teaspoons crumbled dried orégano
½ teaspoon salt
1 teaspoon sugar
¼ cup distilled white vinegar
2 tablespoons olive oil
oil for brushing the onions

In a shallow dish large enough to hold the onions in one layer whisk together the mint, the orégano, the salt, the sugar, the vinegar, and the olive oil. Add the onions and let them marinate, covered, turning them occasionally, for at least 3 hours or, covered and chilled, overnight. Remove the onions from the marinade, discarding the marinade, and brush them with the oil. Grill the onions on an oiled rack over glowing coals,

turning them once with a metal spatula, for 8 minutes, or until they are just tender, transfer them to a heated platter, and season them with salt and pepper. Serves 4.

Parsley Dumplings with Brown Butter

¾ cup cake flour (not self-rising)
¼ cup all-purpose flour
1 teaspoon double-acting baking powder
½ teaspoon salt
2 tablespoons lard, melted and cooled
1 large egg, beaten lightly
¼ cup sour cream
⅔ cup firmly packed fresh parsley leaves
½ stick (¼ cup) unsalted butter

Into a bowl sift together the flours, the baking powder, and the salt. In a small bowl beat together lightly the lard, the egg, and the sour cream, add the mixture to the flour mixture with the parsley, and stir the batter until it is just combined. With a tablespoon dipped in hot water drop heaping tablespoons of the batter about 2 inches apart onto a buttered heatproof plate and steam the dumplings on the plate on a rack set over simmering water, covered, for 10 minutes. While the dumplings are steaming heat the butter in a small saucepan over moderate heat, swirling the pan, until it is deep golden. Transfer the dumplings to a serving dish and pour the butter over them. Serves 2.

Puréed Parsnips

1 cup finely chopped onions
2 tablespoons unsalted butter
2 pounds parsnips, sliced thin
2 teaspoons fresh lemon juice
½ cup milk

In a large saucepan cook the onions in the butter over moderately low heat, stirring, until they are softened and add the parsnips, 1½ cups water, and salt and pepper to taste. Bring the liquid to a boil and simmer the mixture, covered with a buttered round of wax paper and a lid, stirring occasionally, for 30 minutes, or until the parsnips are very tender. If there is any liquid left in the pan increase the heat to moderately high and cook the mixture, stirring, until all the liquid is evaporated. (The mixture should be very dry.) Mash the mixture with a fork or purée it in a food mill into a bowl. Stir in the lemon juice, salt and pepper to taste, and the milk, heated. Makes 3½ cups, serving 6 to 7.

Buttered Peas in Tomato Cups

4 plum tomatoes
1 cup fresh peas (about 1 pound unshelled)
2 tablespoons softened unsalted butter

Trim a thin slice from the bottom of each tomato to form a flat base, trim the top ¼ inch from each tomato, and with a small spoon scoop out the centers to form "cups." In a small baking dish heat the tomatoes in a preheated 325° F. oven for 10 to 15 minutes, or until they are heated through. In a saucepan of boiling salted water cook the peas for 3 to 8 minutes, or until they are just tender, drain them, and toss them in the pan with the butter and salt and pepper to taste. Fill the tomato cups with the peas. Serves 4.

Minted Peas and Onions

1½ pounds onions, halved lengthwise and
   sliced thin
½ stick (¼ cup) unsalted butter
4 cups (about 4 pounds unshelled) cooked
   fresh peas (procedure follows) or two
   10-ounce packages frozen peas, thawed and
   drained
¼ cup minced fresh mint leaves or 1
   tablespoon crumbled dried

In a large skillet cook the onions in the butter, covered, over moderately low heat, stirring, until they are softened. Add the peas, the mint, and salt and pepper to taste and cook the mixture, stirring, until the peas are heated through. Serves 6.

To Cook Fresh Peas

To simmer fresh peas: For each cup of shelled fresh peas bring to a boil 1 cup water with 4 empty pea pods, ¼ teaspoon salt, and the peas and simmer the peas for 3 to 8 minutes, or until they are tender. Drain the peas in a colander, discard the pods, and refresh the peas gently under running cold water.

To steam fresh peas: In a steamer set over boiling salted water steam the shelled peas, covered partially, for 4 to 12 minutes, or until they are tender, transfer them to a colander, and refresh them gently under running cold water.

Buttered Sugar Snap Peas and Carrots

3 pounds carrots, trimmed and cut into 2- by
   ¼-inch sticks
3 pounds sugar snap peas, trimmed and strings
   discarded
1 stick (½ cup) unsalted butter

In a kettle of boiling salted water boil the carrots for 3 to 4 minutes, or until they are just tender, drain them in a large colander, and refresh them under cold water. *The carrots may be prepared up to this point 6 hours in advance and kept covered and chilled.* In another kettle of boiling salted water boil the sugar snap peas for 15 seconds, drain them in a large colander, and refresh them under cold water. In 2 large skillets cook the carrots and the sugar snap peas separately in the butter with salt and pepper to taste over moderate heat for 3 minutes, or until they are heated through. Arrange the vegetables decoratively on heated platters. Serves 20.

Potato "Brioches"

3¼ pounds boiling potatoes, peeled and
  quartered
3 teaspoons salt
1 stick (½ cup) unsalted butter, cut into
  pieces, at room temperature
4 large egg yolks
white pepper to taste
2 teaspoons milk

16 well-buttered miniature brioche molds
  measuring 2½ inches across the top, chilled
  (available at kitchenware shops)

In a kettle cover the potatoes with cold water and
bring the water to a boil. Add 2 teaspoons of the salt and
simmer the potatoes for 12 to 15 minutes, or until they
are tender. Drain the potatoes and force them through a
ricer into a bowl. Stir in the butter, 3 of the egg yolks,
the remaining 1 teaspoon salt, and the white pepper and
let the mixture cool for at least 20 minutes or up to 2
hours.

Transfer ¼ cup of the potato mixture to a lightly
floured surface, with lightly floured hands pinch off a
piece about the size of a marble, and reserve it. With
lightly floured hands roll the larger portion into a
smooth ball and drop it gently into one of the chilled
molds. Make a shallow indentation gently in the top of
the ball, form the reserved marble-sized portion into a
smooth ball, and fit it gently into the indentation. Make
15 more brioches in the same manner. In a small bowl
combine the remaining egg yolk with the milk and brush
the egg wash gently over the brioches, being careful not
to let it drip down into the molds. Bake the brioches on a
baking sheet in a preheated 425° F. oven for 25 to 30
minutes, or until they are golden brown. Let the bri-

oches cool on a rack in the molds for 20 minutes. Loos-
en the edges with a metal skewer if necessary and invert
the brioches carefully to remove them from the molds.
*The potato brioches may be made 1 day in advance, kept
covered and chilled, and reheated on a baking sheet in a
400° F. oven for 15 minutes, or until they are heated
through.* Makes 16 "brioches," serving 8.

Lacy Potato Pancakes

2 large eggs
⅓ cup beer
½ cup all-purpose flour
1 teaspoon salt
freshly ground pepper to taste
1 onion, halved lengthwise and sliced thin
2 large russet (baking) potatoes (about 1¼
  pounds), peeled and reserved in a bowl of
  cold water
vegetable oil for frying

In a large bowl whisk together the eggs, the beer, the
flour, the salt, and the pepper and add the onion. In a
food processor fitted with the fine julienne blade and
filled with 2 inches cold water julienne the potatoes.
Drain the potatoes well, add them to the batter, and toss
the mixture to combine it well. In a large heavy skillet
heat ½ inch of the oil over moderately high heat until it is
hot. Working over the bowl, form a handful of the potato mixture into a loose patty and add it to the oil. Make
additional pancakes in the same manner, fry them in
batches, turning them once, for 4 to 5 minutes, or until
they are golden, and drain them on paper towels. *The
potato pancakes may be made several hours in advance
and reheated on a baking sheet in a preheated 350° F.
oven for 10 to 15 minutes, or until they are hot.* Makes
about 12 potato pancakes, serving 4 to 6.

Roasted Potato Skins with Scallion Dip

4 pounds baking potatoes, scrubbed well and
  patted dry
coarse salt to taste
For the dip
1 small garlic clove
¼ cup chopped scallions
½ cup chopped fresh parsley leaves
½ cup sour cream
½ cup mayonnaise (page 232)
1 teaspoon Worcestershire sauce, or to taste

With a paring knife peel the skin from the potatoes lengthwise into ¾-inch-wide strips, removing a thin layer of the flesh with each strip, and in a bowl of cold water reserve the potatoes for another use. Arrange the strips skin side up in one layer in well-buttered jelly-roll pans and bake them in a preheated 450° F. oven for 15 to 20 minutes, or until they are crisp and golden. Toss the potato skins with the salt, transfer them to racks, and let them cool. *The potato skins may be made up to 1 day in advance, kept in an airtight container, and served at room temperature or reheated in a preheated 450° F. oven for 5 minutes, or until they are hot.*

Make the dip: In a food processor or blender mince the garlic, the scallions, and the parsley, add the sour cream and the mayonnaise, and blend the mixture until it is smooth. Blend in the Worcestershire sauce and salt and pepper to taste, transfer the mixture to a bowl, and chill it, covered, overnight to allow the flavors to develop. *The dip may be made up to 3 days in advance and kept covered and chilled.* Serve the potato skins with the scallion dip. Serves 6 as an hors d'oeuvre.

Baked Sesame Caraway Potato Sticks

2 tablespoons unsalted butter
1 boiling potato (about ½ pound), peeled and
    cut into ¼-inch-thick sticks
1½ tablespoons caraway seeds, crushed fine
¼ cup sesame seeds

In a small saucepan melt the butter over moderately low heat and season it with salt and pepper. Remove the pan from the heat and add the potato sticks, coating them well with the butter. In a shallow dish combine the caraway and the sesame seeds and roll the potato sticks in the mixture. Bake the potato sticks on a baking sheet in a preheated 400° F. oven for 20 to 25 minutes, or until they are tender. Serves 2.

Mashed Potatoes with Scallions and Cheddar

4 russet (baking) potatoes
1 cup milk
½ cup grated sharp Cheddar
3 tablespoons unsalted butter, cut into bits
1 cup chopped scallions (about 1 bunch)

Peel the potatoes and cut them into ½-inch pieces, dropping them as they are cut into a bowl of cold water. Drain the potatoes and in a vegetable steamer set over boiling water steam them, covered, for 12 to 15 minutes, or until they are very tender. Rice the potatoes or purée them through a food mill into a large saucepan, adding some of the milk if necessary to facilitate ricing them. Stir in the milk, scalded, and the Cheddar, heat the mixture over low heat, stirring, until the Cheddar is melted, and beat in the butter, the scallions, and salt and pepper to taste. Serves 6.

Riced Mashed Potatoes

3 pounds russet (baking) potatoes, scrubbed
    well
1½ sticks (¾ cup) unsalted butter, cut into
    pieces and softened
⅔ cup milk
sweet paprika for garnish

In a large saucepan combine the potatoes and enough salted cold water to cover them by 2 inches, bring the water to a boil, and simmer the potatoes, covered, for 40 to 50 minutes, or until they are tender. Drain the potatoes in a colander, let them cool until they can be handled, and while they are still warm peel them. Force the potatoes through a ricer into the saucepan and add the butter. Stir in the milk, heated, heat the mixture over low heat, stirring, until the butter is melted and the potatoes are heated through, and season the potatoes with salt and pepper. *The potatoes may be prepared up to this point 1 day in advance and kept covered and chilled. Reheat the potatoes in the top of a double boiler set over simmering water, stirring occasionally, until they are hot.* Just before serving force the potatoes through the ricer into a heated serving dish and sprinkle them with the paprika. Serves 8.

Oven-Fried Potatoes

4 russet (baking) potatoes, peeled and sliced
    diagonally ⅛ inch thick
½ stick (¼ cup) unsalted butter, melted
coarse salt to taste

Pat the potatoes dry between paper towels and arrange them in one layer in 2 buttered jelly-roll pans. Brush the potatoes with the butter, bake them in a preheated 500° F. oven for 15 to 20 minutes, or until the edges are golden brown, and sprinkle them with the salt. Serves 4.

Pan-Roasted Potatoes with Garlic

1 large garlic clove, sliced thin
½ pound boiling potatoes, peeled and cut
    crosswise into ¼-inch rounds
1½ tablespoons unsalted butter

In a small saucepan of boiling water blanch the garlic
for 2 minutes, drain it, and pat it dry. In a heavy skillet
large enough to hold the potatoes in one layer cook the
potatoes in the butter over moderate heat, turning them,
for 13 to 15 minutes, or until they are golden and tender.
Add the garlic and salt and pepper to taste and cook the
mixture, shaking the pan occasionally, for 1 minute.
Serves 2.

Sweet Potatoes Duchesse

1 pound sweet potatoes, scrubbed
1 russet (baking) potato (about ½ pound),
    scrubbed
2 tablespoons softened unsalted butter
1 large whole egg, beaten lightly
1 large egg yolk, beaten lightly
melted unsalted butter for drizzling over the
    potatoes

Bake the sweet potatoes and the russet potato in a preheated 400° F. oven for 1 hour, or until they are tender.
Halve the potatoes lengthwise, scrape the flesh from the
skins, and force it through a ricer or food mill into a
large bowl. Beat in the softened butter, the whole egg,
the egg yolk, and salt and pepper to taste and beat the
mixture until it is smooth. Transfer the mixture to a pastry bag fitted with a large decorative tip, pipe it into
2-inch rosettes onto a buttered baking sheet, and drizzle
the rosettes with the melted butter. *The rosettes may be
prepared up to this point and kept, covered loosely and
chilled, for several hours or overnight.* Bake the rosettes in a preheated 350° F. oven for 10 to 15 minutes if
at room temperature or 25 to 30 minutes if chilled, or
until they are heated through, put the baking sheet under
a preheated broiler about 6 inches from the heat, and
broil the rosettes until the tops are browned lightly.
Makes about 8 rosettes, serving 4.

French Fried Sweet Potatoes

vegetable shortening or oil for deep-frying
1 pound sweet potatoes, peeled

In a deep fryer at least 5 inches deep heat 1½ inches of
the shortening to 380° F. While the shortening is heat-

ing, in a food processor fitted with the coarse grating
disk grate coarse the sweet potatoes or, with a sharp
knife, cut them into ¼-inch-thick sticks. Fry the potato
sticks in small batches in the shortening for 45 seconds
to 1 minute, or until the bubbles in the fat have subsided,
making sure the potatoes don't brown. (The potatoes
will seem limp in the hot fat but will become crisp as
they cool.) Transfer the potatoes as they are fried to paper towels to drain, making sure the shortening returns
to 380° F. before adding each new batch, and sprinkle
the potatoes with salt to taste. *The French fried potatoes
may be made up to 2 hours in advance and reheated on a
baking sheet in a preheated 300° F. oven for 10 minutes.*
Serves 4.

Riced Sweet Potatoes

2 pounds sweet potatoes, scrubbed well
1 pound russet (baking) potatoes, scrubbed
    well
1 stick (½ cup) unsalted butter, cut into pieces
    and softened
¼ teaspoon freshly grated orange rind
lightly toasted sesame seeds for garnish

In a large saucepan combine the sweet potatoes, the
russet potatoes, and enough salted cold water to cover
the potatoes by 2 inches, bring the water to a boil, and
simmer the potatoes, covered, for 20 to 30 minutes, or
until the sweet potatoes are tender. Transfer the sweet
potatoes with a slotted spoon to a colander and simmer
the russet potatoes, covered, for 10 to 20 minutes more,
or until they are tender. While the russet potatoes are
simmering, let the sweet potatoes cool until they can be
handled and while they are still warm peel them. Drain
the russet potatoes in a colander, let them cool until they
can be handled, and while they are still warm peel them.
Force the sweet potatoes and the russet potatoes through
a ricer into the pan and add the butter and the rind. Heat
the mixture over low heat, stirring, until the butter is
melted and the potatoes are heated through and season

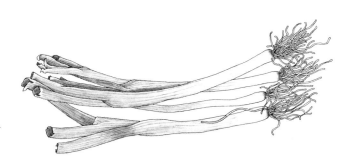

the potatoes with salt and pepper. *The potatoes may be prepared up to this point 1 day in advance and kept covered and chilled. Reheat the potatoes in a heavy saucepan over low heat, stirring, until they are hot.* Just before serving force the potatoes through the ricer into a heated serving dish and sprinkle them with the sesame seeds. Serves 8.

Radish Hearts

½ cup minced radishes
¼ cup minced fresh parsley leaves
12 very thin slices of homemade-type white
    bread
1 stick (½ cup) unsalted butter, softened well
about 8 radishes, sliced very thin

On a cutting board combine the minced radishes and the parsley, mince fine the mixture, and transfer it to a shallow bowl. Spread 1 side of each slice of bread with some of the butter and with a 2¼-inch heart-shaped cutter cut out 2 hearts from each slice (reserving the scraps for another use such as bread pudding). Arrange a layer of the sliced radishes on the buttered side of each heart, sprinkle the radishes with salt to taste, and sandwich the hearts together to form 12 hearts. Seal the edges of the hearts generously with the remaining butter and roll the edges in the minced radish mixture to coat them. Chill the sandwiches in one layer on plates, covered tightly with plastic wrap, for at least 1 hour or up to 3 hours and arrange them on a platter. Makes 12 radish heart sandwiches, serving 6.

Scallion and Garlic Purée

6 bunches of scallions
5 garlic cloves, inner green cores, if any,
    discarded
3 tablespoons olive oil
1 teaspoon fresh lemon juice or to taste
thirty-six ¼-inch-thick slices of French or
    Italian bread, toasted

Starting at the root end, cut off 4 inches of the white part of the scallions, reserving the greens for another use. Trim off the roots and chop the scallions coarse. In the center of a large piece of foil combine the scallions, the garlic, and the oil, wrap the foil around the mixture, and bake the mixture in a preheated 400° F. oven for 1 hour. In a food processor purée the mixture with the lemon juice and salt to taste until it is very smooth. Serve the purée either warm or at room temperature

with the toasts as an accompaniment to mussel scallion soup (page 116) or as an hors d'oeuvre. To serve the purée warm, spread it generously on the toasts and heat the toasts on a baking sheet in a preheated 375° F. oven for 10 minutes. *The purée keeps, covered and chilled, for up to 3 days.* Makes about ¾ cup.

Sautéed Scallions and Radishes with Ginger

3 bunches of scallions
3 tablespoons unsalted butter
1½ tablespoons peeled and grated fresh
    gingerroot
¾ pound radishes, sliced

Trim the root ends of the scallions and cut off the top 2 inches of the greens. Cut the white part of the scallions diagonally into ½-inch slices and chop the remaining scallion greens. In a large skillet heat the butter over moderately high heat until it is hot and in it sauté the white part of the scallions, stirring, for 2 minutes. Add the gingerroot and sauté the mixture for 1 minute. Add the radishes and the scallion greens, sauté the mixture, stirring, for 4 minutes, or until the radishes are just tender, and add salt and pepper to taste. Serves 4.

Creamed Spinach Gratin

¾ pound fresh spinach, washed well and
    coarse stems discarded
4 teaspoons unsalted butter
½ cup heavy cream
freshly grated nutmeg to taste
6 tablespoons freshly grated Parmesan
1 tablespoon minced scallion
1 tablespoon minced fresh parsley leaves
½ cup coarse fresh bread crumbs

In a saucepan steam the spinach in the water clinging to the leaves, covered, over moderate heat, stirring occasionally, until it is wilted, remove the lid, and cook the spinach over moderately low heat, stirring, until the water is evaporated. Stir in 3 teaspoons of the butter, the cream, and the nutmeg and simmer the mixture until it is thickened. Stir in 4 tablespoons of the Parmesan, the scallion, the parsley, and salt and pepper to taste and transfer the mixture to a buttered 7½-inch gratin dish. Sprinkle the mixture with the bread crumbs and the remaining 2 tablespoons Parmesan and dot it with the remaining 1 teaspoon butter. Bake the gratin in a preheated 400° F. oven for 20 minutes, or until the top is golden brown. Serves 2.

Crisp-Baked Acorn Squash Rings

2 large eggs, beaten lightly
¼ cup milk
2 teaspoons honey
¾ cup yellow cornmeal
1½ cups fine fresh bread crumbs
2 acorn squash, sliced crosswise into
    ½-inch-thick rounds and seeded
3 tablespoons unsalted butter, melted

In a shallow dish whisk together the eggs, the milk, and the honey. In another shallow dish stir together the cornmeal, the bread crumbs, and salt and pepper to taste. Dip the squash rings into the egg mixture and then into the crumb mixture, coating them well and patting the crumbs on well. Arrange the squash rings in one layer in 2 well buttered jelly-roll pans, drizzle them with the butter, and bake them in a preheated 400° F. oven, turning them once, for 30 minutes, or until they are tender. Sprinkle the squash with salt to taste and arrange it on a heated platter. Serves 6.

Butternut Squash Purée

1 onion, sliced
2 tablespoons unsalted butter
2 pounds butternut squash, peeled, seeded,
    strings discarded, and sliced thin
½ teaspoon ground cardamom

In a large heavy saucepan cook the onion in the butter, covered, over moderately low heat, stirring occasionally, until it is softened. Add the squash, the cardamom, and ½ cup water and bring the water to a boil. Cook the mixture, covered with a buttered round of wax paper and a lid, over low heat, stirring occasionally and adding a small amount of water if the mixture begins to stick to the bottom of the pan, for 30 minutes, or until the squash is very tender. In a food processor blend the mixture in batches until it is very smooth and add salt and pepper to taste. *The squash purée may be made 1 day in advance, kept covered and chilled, and reheated in a double boiler.* Transfer the purée to a bowl and smooth the top. Serves 2 generously.

Summer Squash with Pepperoni and Parmesan

two 6-inch yellow summer squash
1 tablespoon vegetable oil
1½ teaspoons unsalted butter
1 small onion, chopped fine
2 tablespoons finely chopped sliced pepperoni
¼ cup freshly grated Parmesan
3½ tablespoons fine fresh bread crumbs
1 tablespoon minced fresh parsley leaves
2 tablespoons unsalted butter

Halve the squash lengthwise, scoop out the pulp, leaving ¼-inch shells, and chop it fine. In a skillet cook the shells in the oil, covered, over moderately high heat, turning them once, for 4 to 5 minutes, or until they are just tender. Transfer the shells to a rack, let them cool until they can be handled, and pat them dry. Add the butter to the oil remaining in the skillet and in the fat cook the chopped squash and the onion over moderately low heat, stirring occasionally, until the onion is softened. Stir in the pepperoni, 1 tablespoon of the Parmesan, 1½ tablespoons of the bread crumbs, the parsley, and salt and pepper to taste and divide the mixture among the shells. In a small bowl toss together the remaining 3 tablespoons Parmesan and the remaining 2 tablespoons bread crumbs, sprinkle the mixture over the filling, and dot the filling with the butter. Broil the squash on the rack of a broiler pan under a preheated broiler about 4 inches from the heat for 2 to 4 minutes, or until the tops are golden. Serves 2 as a first course.

Turnip and Carrot Julienne

4 turnips, peeled and cut into fine julienne
    strips (preferably using a food processor)
4 carrots, peeled and cut into fine julienne
    strips (preferably using a food processor)
2 tablespoons unsalted butter
1 tablespoon minced fresh parsley leaves

In a skillet cook the turnips and the carrots in ½ cup boiling salted water until they are tender and most of the liquid is evaporated. Stir in the butter, the parsley, and salt and pepper to taste and cook the mixture over moderate heat, stirring, until the butter is melted. Serves 4.

Turnip and Potato Patties with Sausage

½ pound turnips, peeled and cut into ¼-inch
　　cubes (about 1⅓ cups)
6 ounces boiling potato, peeled and cut into
　　½-inch cubes (about 1 cup)
2½ tablespoons thinly sliced scallion greens
1 egg, beaten lightly
¼ cup all-purpose flour
vegetable oil for frying
very fresh parsley sprigs, patted dry
　　thoroughly and coarse stems discarded, for
　　garnish
3 tablespoons mayonnaise
1 teaspoon drained bottled horseradish
6 breakfast sausage links, cooked, as an
　　accompaniment

In a large saucepan of boiling salted water cook the
turnip and potato cubes for 15 to 17 minutes, or until
they are tender, and drain them. In a bowl mash the vegetables with the back of a fork and stir in the scallions,
the egg, the flour, and salt and pepper to taste.

In a large heavy skillet heat ½ inch of the oil to
360° F., spoon ¼-cup mounds of the batter into it, flattening them into ½-inch patties with the back of a spatula, and fry the patties, turning them once, for 4 minutes,
or until they are golden. Transfer the patties to paper
towels to drain. Heat the oil remaining in the skillet to
375° F. and in it fry carefully the parsley sprigs, stirring, for 3 to 5 seconds, or until the oil stops sizzling.
(The oil will splatter considerably.) Transfer the parsley
carefully to paper towels to drain and sprinkle it with
salt to taste.

In a small bowl combine well the mayonnaise and the
horseradish. Arrange the patties and the sausage on a
platter, garnish the platter with the fried parsley, and
serve the patties with the horseradish mayonnaise.
Serves 2 for brunch or as a light dinner entrée.

Vegetable "Pasta" with Tomato Concassé

1 cup minced onion
5 tablespoons unsalted butter
2 pounds tomatoes, peeled, seeded, and chopped
½ pound carrots, peeled
1½ pounds small yellow summer squash
3 large bunches of chives, rinsed and drained well
½ cup freshly grated Parmesan

In a skillet cook the onion in 2 tablespoons of the butter over moderately low heat, stirring, until it is softened, add the tomatoes, and cook the mixture, stirring
occasionally, for 15 minutes, or until most of the liquid
the tomatoes give off is evaporated. Season the mixture
with salt and pepper and keep it warm, covered, over
low heat.

In a saucepan of boiling salted water boil the carrots
for 5 minutes, or until they are just tender, drain them in
a colander, and refresh them under cold water. With a
mandoline or sharp knife cut the carrots and the squash
lengthwise into ¼-inch strips. In a large skillet heat the
remaining 3 tablespoons butter over moderately high
heat until it is hot and in it sauté the carrots and the
squash, stirring, for 5 minutes, or until they are just
tender. Add the chives and salt and pepper to taste and
cook the mixture, stirring, until the chives are just wilted. Divide the mixture among 4 heated plates, top each
serving with one fourth of the tomato *concassé*, and
sprinkle it with about 1 tablespoon of the Parmesan.
Serve the remaining Parmesan separately. Serves 4 as a
first course.

Vegetarian Tamale Pie

½ cup finely chopped green bell pepper
½ cup finely chopped onion
2 tablespoons vegetable oil
⅓ cup frozen corn
⅓ cup drained pitted black olives, quartered
an 8-ounce can tomato sauce
1 teaspoon chili powder, or to taste
¼ teaspoon salt
cayenne to taste
2 ounces sharp Cheddar, grated
1 cup drained and rinsed canned kidney beans
⅓ cup yellow cornmeal
1 teaspoon unsalted butter

In a deep heavy skillet cook the bell pepper and the
onion in the oil over moderately low heat, stirring occasionally, until they are softened, add the corn, the olives, the tomato sauce, the chili powder, the salt, and
the cayenne, and cook the mixture, stirring occasionally, for 5 to 7 minutes, or until it is thickened slightly.
Add the Cheddar, stirring until it is melted, and stir in
the beans. In a small saucepan combine well the cornmeal, 1 cup cold water, and salt to taste, bring the mixture to a boil, stirring constantly, and cook it over low
heat, stirring, until it is thick. Add the butter and stir the
mixture until the butter is melted. Spoon the bean mixture into an oiled shallow 3-cup baking dish, spread the
cornmeal mixture over it, and bake the tamale pie in a
preheated 375° F. oven for 20 minutes. Serves 2.

Stir-Fried Watercress

6 large bunches of watercress
3 tablespoons vegetable oil, preferably
   safflower or corn oil
1 teaspoon sugar
1½ teaspoons salt
2 teaspoons Oriental sesame oil (available at
   Oriental markets, some specialty foods
   shops, and some supermarkets), or to taste

Rinse the watercress, spin it dry, and discard the coarse stems. *The watercress may be prepared up to this point 1 day in advance and kept sealed tightly in plastic bags and chilled.* Heat a wok over high heat until it is hot, add half the oil, and heat it until it is just smoking. Add half the watercress, half the sugar, and half the salt and stir-fry the mixture for 1 minute, or until the watercress is wilted. Transfer the watercress with a wire skimmer or slotted spoon to a heated serving bowl. Stir-fry the remaining watercress in the same manner, transferring it to the bowl. Drizzle the watercress with the sesame oil and toss the mixture well. Serves 8.

Sherried Yams with Walnuts

½ pound yams, peeled and cut into ¼-inch
   pieces
2 tablespoons unsalted butter, cut into bits
2 tablespoons light brown sugar
⅛ teaspoon cinnamon
2 tablespoons medium-dry Sherry
1 tablespoon chopped walnuts, toasted lightly
fresh lemon juice to taste if desired

In a steamer set over boiling water steam the yams, covered, for 3 to 5 minutes, or until they are just tender.

In a heavy skillet combine the butter, the brown sugar, and the cinnamon, heat the mixture over moderate heat, stirring, until the butter is melted, and stir in the Sherry. Cook the sauce over moderate heat until it is thickened, stir in the yams, the walnuts, and salt and pepper to taste, and coat the mixture with the sauce. Sprinkle the dish with the lemon juice if desired. Serves 2.

Zucchini and Mushroom Biscuit Pizzas

½ pound zucchini, scrubbed, quartered
   lengthwise, and sliced thin crosswise (about
   2 cups)
¼ pound mushrooms, sliced thin (about
   1¾ cups)
¼ cup olive oil
¼ cup drained finely chopped pimiento-
   stuffed olives
2 tablespoons minced fresh parsley leaves
½ teaspoon crumbled dried orégano
½ teaspoon red pepper flakes, or to taste
¼ cup buttermilk
1 cup all-purpose flour
1 teaspoon double-acting baking powder
¼ teaspoon baking soda
¼ teaspoon salt
½ stick (¼ cup) cold unsalted butter, cut into
   bits
6 ounces whole-milk mozzarella, cut into
   ¼-inch-thick slices

In a heavy skillet cook the zucchini and the mushrooms in 2 tablespoons of the oil over moderate heat, stirring occasionally, for 7 to 8 minutes, or until the liquid the vegetables give off is evaporated, and stir in the olives, the parsley, the orégano, the red pepper flakes, and salt to taste.

In a small bowl whisk together the remaining 2 tablespoons oil and the buttermilk. Into a bowl sift together the flour, the baking powder, the baking soda, and the salt and blend in the butter until the mixture resembles coarse meal. Make a well in the center, add the oil mixture, and combine the mixture with a fork until it just forms a soft dough. Knead the dough lightly on a floured surface for 30 seconds, halve it, and roll each half into an 8-inch round. Transfer the rounds carefully to a baking sheet and form a ¼-inch rim around the edge of each round. Divide the zucchini mixture between the rounds, top it with the mozzarella, and bake the pizzas in a preheated 450° F. oven for 12 to 15 minutes, or until the crust is golden and crisp. Serves 2.

Fried Zucchini and Summer Squash

1 zucchini, scrubbed and cut lengthwise into
    ¼-inch-thick slices
1 yellow summer squash, cut lengthwise into
    ¼-inch-thick slices
1 teaspoon salt
1 large egg, beaten lightly
¼ teaspoon Dijon-style mustard
¾ cup flour
1½ cups fine dry bread crumbs
vegetable oil for deep-frying

In a colander toss the zucchini and the summer squash slices with the salt, let them drain for 15 minutes, and pat them dry. In a bowl whisk together the egg and the mustard. Dredge the slices in the flour, shaking off the excess, dip them in the egg mixture, letting the excess drip off, and roll them in the bread crumbs. In a large deep skillet heat 1 inch of the oil to 375° F. and in it fry the slices in batches, turning them, for 2 minutes, transferring them with a slotted spoon as they are fried to paper towels to drain. Keep the squash warm on a baking sheet lined with paper towels in a preheated 200° F. oven. Serves 2.

Zucchini Fans with Herb Butter

1 tablespoon fine fresh bread crumbs
2 tablespoons freshly grated Parmesan
¾ stick (6 tablespoons) unsalted butter,
    softened
½ teaspoon crumbled dried tarragon
2 tablespoons minced fresh parsley leaves
four 6-inch zucchini

In a small bowl toss the bread crumbs with the Parmesan. In another small bowl cream together the butter, the tarragon, the parsley, and salt and pepper to taste. Keeping the stem attached, cut each zucchini lengthwise into four ¼-inch-thick slices, spread some of the herb butter carefully between the layers, and press the slices together lightly. Separate the slices slightly to form a fan and bake the fans with ¼ cup water in a buttered baking pan, 15½ by 10½ by 1 inches, in a preheated 400° F. oven for 20 minutes, or until they are just tender. Sprinkle the fans with the bread crumb mixture and broil them under a preheated broiler about 4 inches from the heat for 1 to 2 minutes, or until they are golden. Serves 4.

Zucchini Moussaka with Feta

1 onion, chopped fine
2 tablespoons olive oil plus additional oil for
    brushing the zucchini
1 garlic clove, minced
1 pound lean ground lamb
½ cup dry red wine
a 14-ounce can plum tomatoes, drained
1 bay leaf
½ teaspoon crumbled dried oregano
¼ cup minced fresh parsley leaves
⅛ teaspoon freshly grated nutmeg
1¼ pounds zucchini, cut lengthwise into
    ¼-inch slices
3 tablespoons unsalted butter
3 tablespoons all-purpose flour
1 cup milk
1 large egg, beaten lightly
½ pound Feta, crumbled

In a large heavy skillet cook the onion in 2 tablespoons of the oil over moderately low heat, stirring, until it is softened, add the garlic, and cook the mixture, stirring, for 1 minute. Add the lamb and cook the mixture, stirring and breaking up the lumps, until the lamb is no longer pink. Add the wine, the tomatoes, the bay leaf, and the orégano and cook the mixture over moderate heat, stirring, for 20 minutes. Stir in the parsley and the nutmeg, cook the mixture for 10 minutes, or until it is thickened, and discard the bay leaf. (The lamb mixture improves in flavor if chilled, covered, overnight.)

Brush the zucchini with the additional oil, broil the slices in batches on the rack of a broiler pan under a preheated broiler about 4 inches from the heat, turning them once, for 8 to 10 minutes, or until they are soft and golden, and transfer them to paper towels to drain. In a small saucepan melt the butter over low heat, stir in the flour, and cook the *roux*, stirring, for 3 minutes. Add the milk in a stream, whisking, bring the mixture to a boil, whisking, and simmer it, stirring, for 5 minutes. Remove the pan from the heat and whisk in the egg.

In a 12-cup shallow glass baking dish arrange half the zucchini in one layer, cover it with half the lamb mixture, and sprinkle half the Feta over the lamb. Layer the remaining zucchini, lamb mixture, and Feta in the same manner, pour the sauce over the Feta, smoothing the top with a spatula, and bake the *moussaka* in the middle of a preheated 350° F. oven for 40 to 45 minutes, or until it is golden. Let the *moussaka* stand for 15 minutes before serving. Serves 6 to 8.

SALADS AND
SALAD DRESSINGS

ENTRÉE SALADS

Korean Beef Salad

For the marinated beef
1 pound sirloin steak, trimmed
½ pound onions, chopped coarse
6 tablespoons *sake* or dry Sherry
6 tablespoons soy sauce
3 tablespoons Oriental sesame oil*
1½ teaspoons coarsely ground pepper
For the dressing
1 garlic clove, minced
1 tablespoon Dijon-style mustard
2 teaspoons honey
3 tablespoons rice vinegar*
3 tablespoons soy sauce
3 tablespoons Oriental sesame oil*
6 tablespoons vegetable oil

2 tablespoons vegetable oil
½ pound small mushrooms
½ pound snow peas, blanched in boiling salted
   water for 3 seconds, drained, and patted
   dry, and strings discarded

pita pockets for serving
2 cups alfalfa sprouts as an accompaniment

*available at Oriental markets

Prepare the marinated beef: In a baking dish large
enough to hold the beef and the onions in one layer

whisk together the *sake*, the soy sauce, the sesame oil,
and the pepper, add the beef and the onions, and let the
mixture marinate, covered and chilled, stirring the onions and turning the beef several times, for at least 3
hours or overnight.

Make the dressing: In a large bowl combine the garlic, the mustard, the honey, the vinegar, and the soy
sauce, add the sesame oil and the vegetable oil in a
stream, whisking, and whisk the dressing until it is
emulsified. *The dressing may be made 1 day in advance
and kept covered and chilled.*

Remove the beef and the onions from the marinade
and reserve half the marinade. In a large skillet heat the
2 tablespoons oil over moderately high heat until it is hot
and in it sauté the beef, patted dry, turning it once, for 8
to 10 minutes for medium-rare meat. Transfer the beef
to a cutting board and let it stand for 10 minutes. *The
beef may be cooked 1 day in advance and kept covered
and chilled.* In the skillet cook the onions over moderately high heat, stirring, for 5 minutes, or until they are
tender but still slightly crisp, and transfer them with a
slotted spoon to the bowl containing the dressing. Add
the mushrooms with the reserved marinade to the skillet, cook them over moderate heat, stirring, until almost
all the liquid is evaporated, and transfer them to the
bowl. *The vegetable mixture may be made 1 day in advance and kept covered and chilled.*

Holding a knife at a 45-degree angle slice the beef
thin across the grain. Add the beef to the vegetable mixture with the snow peas and toss the mixture well.
Transfer the salad to a portable container and serve it in
the *pita* pockets with the sprouts. Makes about 6 cups.

Mexican Bluefish Salad with Chili Peppers

2 pounds bluefish fillet
1 cup bottled clam juice
1 tablespoon fresh lemon juice
1 onion, sliced
1 carrot, sliced
1 green bell pepper, chopped
3 tablespoons vegetable oil
two 3-inch hot green chili peppers, seeded and
    minced (wear rubber gloves)
1 garlic clove, crushed
12 coriander stems
¼ teaspoon ground cumin
1 small bay leaf
½ cup dry white wine
¼ cup white-wine vinegar
1 tablespoon olive oil
1 tablespoon fresh lime juice
1 pound plum tomatoes, seeded, halved
    lengthwise, and sliced
2 tablespoons minced fresh coriander leaves
1 head of romaine, shredded
coriander sprigs and lime slices for garnish

In a buttered shallow flameproof baking dish arrange the bluefish in one layer, add the clam juice, the lemon juice, and enough water, if necessary, to just cover the bluefish, and cover the dish with a buttered piece of wax paper. Bring the liquid to a bare simmer and poach the bluefish in a preheated 350° F. oven for 8 to 10 minutes, or until it just flakes when tested with a fork. Drain the bluefish and let it cool.

In a large skillet cook the onion, the carrot, and the bell pepper in the vegetable oil over moderately low heat, stirring occasionally, until the vegetables are softened, add half the minced chili peppers, the garlic, the coriander stems, the cumin, the bay leaf, the wine, and the vinegar, and combine the mixture well. In a shallow dish pour the marinade over the bluefish and chill the mixture, covered, overnight.

Discard the vegetables, the garlic, the coriander stems, and the bay leaf with a slotted spoon, drain the bluefish, reserving the liquid in a small bowl, and flake the bluefish into a large bowl, discarding the skin. Into the liquid whisk the olive oil and the lime juice, pour the mixture over the bluefish, and add the remaining chili peppers, the tomatoes, the coriander leaves, and salt and pepper to taste. Toss the salad gently, serve it on a platter lined with the romaine, and garnish it with the coriander sprigs and the lime slices. Serves 4 to 6.

Tropical Chicken Salad

2 tablespoons honey
2 tablespoons minced peeled gingerroot
¼ teaspoon ground cardamom
3 tablespoons fresh lime juice
½ cup mayonnaise (page 232)
½ cup plain yogurt, drained in a fine sieve for
    15 minutes
2 whole skinless boneless chicken breasts,
    poached (procedure follows) and cut into
    1-inch pieces (about 3 cups)

HECHTLINGER

1 mango, peeled and chopped coarse,
   reserving a few chunks for garnish
½ honeydew melon, cut into balls with a
   ¾-inch melon-ball cutter, reserving a
   few balls for garnish
3 tablespoons minced fresh mint leaves
   pita pockets for serving
1 bunch of watercress, coarse stems
   discarded, as an accompaniment

In a bowl whisk together the honey, the gingerroot, the cardamom, the lime juice, and salt and pepper to taste and stir in the mayonnaise and the yogurt. Add the chicken, the mango, the melon, and the mint leaves, toss the salad well, and transfer it to a portable container. *The salad may be made 1 day in advance and kept covered and chilled.* Garnish the salad with the reserved mango and the reserved melon and serve it in the *pita* pockets with the watercress. Makes about 4 cups.

To Poach Chicken Breasts

whole boneless chicken breasts, halved
chicken stock (page 119), canned chicken
   broth, or water

In a skillet large enough to hold the chicken breasts in one layer add enough stock to cover the chicken and bring it to a boil. Add the chicken and cook it at a bare simmer, turning it once, for 7 minutes. Remove the skillet from the heat and let the chicken cool in the stock for 30 minutes.

Chicken Tarragon Salad with Pine Nuts

1 tablespoon raspberry vinegar (available at
   specialty foods shops and some
   supermarkets)
1 teaspoon crumbled dried tarragon
2 tablespoons plain yogurt
1 tablespoon mayonnaise
1 cup finely chopped cooked chicken
2 tablespoons pine nuts, toasted and chopped
   coarse

In a small saucepan combine the vinegar and the tarragon, bring the vinegar to a boil, and cook the mixture over moderately high heat, stirring, until the vinegar is reduced to about 1 teaspoon. In a bowl combine the tarragon mixture, the yogurt, and the mayonnaise and stir in the chicken, the pine nuts, and salt and pepper to

taste. Use the salad as a filling for cherry tomatoes or with whole-wheat bread. Makes about 1¼ cups.

Crab Salad with Napa Cabbage and Lime Sauce

1 turnip (about ¼ pound), peeled and cut into
   ¼-inch cubes
1 tablespoon fresh lime juice, or to taste
1 tablespoon safflower oil or flavorless
   vegetable oil
½ pound Napa cabbage (celery cabbage)
2 teaspoons cider vinegar
1 teaspoon honey
½ cup quick lime mayonnaise (recipe follows)
¼ cup plain yogurt
cayenne to taste
¾ pound frozen Alaskan king crab meat,
   thawed, picked over, and patted dry, or
   lump crab meat, picked over
1½ tablespoons minced scallion greens
Napa cabbage leaves for garnish
lime slices for garnish

In a saucepan of boiling salted water cook the turnip for 2 to 4 minutes, or until it is *al dente,* drain it in a colander, and refresh it under cold water. Drain the turnip and pat it dry gently. In a small bowl whisk together the lime juice and salt to taste and whisk in the oil. Slice the cabbage thin and in a large bowl toss it with the lime dressing. In a small bowl whisk together the vinegar and the honey and whisk in the lime mayonnaise, the yogurt, and the cayenne. In a bowl combine the turnip, the crab meat, and the scallion greens and toss the mixture well with the mayonnaise mixture. Arrange the cabbage leaves decoratively on a platter, put the sliced cabbage mixture in the center, and spoon the crab-meat mixture onto it. Arrange the lime slices decoratively on the platter. Serves 2.

Quick Lime Mayonnaise

1 large egg at room temperature
5 teaspoons fresh lime juice, or to taste
1 teaspoon Dijon-style mustard
¼ teaspoon salt, or to taste
1 cup safflower oil or flavorless vegetable oil

In a food processor or blender with the motor on high blend the egg, the lime juice, the mustard, and the salt, add the oil in a stream, and blend the mayonnaise until it is emulsified. Season the mayonnaise with salt and lime juice to taste. Makes about 1 cup.

Lobster Horseradish Salad

2 tablespoons distilled white vinegar
3 tablespoons bottled horseradish
⅔ cup vegetable oil
two 1½-pound live lobsters, cooked and
    shelled (procedure follows) and chopped
    coarse
2 plum tomatoes, seeded and chopped
1½ cups cooked corn kernels, cut from the cob
¼ cup chopped scallion greens
pita pockets for serving

In a large bowl combine the vinegar, the horseradish, and salt and pepper to taste, add the oil in a stream, whisking, and whisk the dressing until it is emulsified. *The dressing may be made 1 day in advance and kept covered and chilled.* To the dressing add the lobster, the tomatoes, the corn, the scallions, and salt and pepper to taste, toss the salad well, and transfer it to a portable container. Serve the salad in the *pita* pockets. Makes about 5½ cups.

To Cook and Shell Lobsters

3 tablespoons salt
two 1½-pound live lobsters

In a kettle bring to a boil 2 inches water with the salt and plunge the lobsters head-first into the water. When the water returns to a boil cover the kettle and cook the lobsters for 7 minutes. Plunge the lobsters immediately into cold water to stop further cooking. Twist off the tail section, break off the 5 fins at the tip, and extract the slivers of meat from each. Push out the tail meat in 1 piece with the fingers or slit the underside of the tail and break the shell apart. Break off the claws at the body,

break them apart at the joints, and extract the meat. Twist off the legs and reserve them for another use.

Mediterranean Monkfish Salad
with White Beans and Fennel

1½ pounds monkfish fillet
1 cup bottled clam juice
1 cup dry white wine
1 tablespoon white-wine vinegar
a 16-ounce can *cannellini* (white kidney
    beans), rinsed and drained
20 black olives, cut into slivers
1 pound fennel bulb, sliced thin
3 scallions, minced
3 stalks of celery, sliced thin
2 tablespoons minced fresh parsley leaves
For the dressing
½ teaspoon fennel seeds
1 garlic clove
4 tablespoons white-wine vinegar
2 tablespoons Dijon-style mustard
¾ cup vegetable oil

fresh lemon juice to taste
chopped seeded tomato for garnish

In a buttered flameproof baking dish just large enough to hold the monkfish combine the monkfish, the clam juice, the wine, the vinegar, and enough water, if necessary, to just cover the monkfish and cover the dish with a buttered piece of wax paper. Bring the liquid to a simmer over moderate heat and poach the monkfish in a preheated 350° F. oven for 10 to 12 minutes, or until it just flakes when tested with a fork. Drain the monkfish, let it cool, and discard any tough membranes. Flake the monkfish into a large serving bowl and combine it with

the beans, the olives, the fennel, the scallions, the celery, and the parsley.

Make the dressing: In a blender blend the fennel seeds, the garlic, the vinegar, the mustard, and salt and pepper to taste, with the motor running add the oil in a stream, and blend the dressing until it is emulsified.

Pour the dressing over the monkfish mixture and toss the salad gently to combine it. Add the lemon juice and salt and pepper to taste and garnish the salad with the tomato. Serves 4 to 6.

Curried Mussel and Rice Salad

3 pounds mussels, cleaned (procedure on page 137)
1 cup dry white wine
1½ cups unconverted long-grain rice
1½ cups cooked fresh peas or thawed frozen
4 scallions, minced
3 tablespoons minced fresh coriander leaves
1 red bell pepper, roasted (procedure on page 114) and chopped
For the dressing
2 garlic cloves, minced
¾ cup vegetable oil
2 teaspoons curry powder
1 teaspoon ground cumin
¼ cup white-wine vinegar
2 tablespoons Dijon-style mustard, or to taste

fresh lemon juice to taste

In a kettle steam the mussels in the wine, covered, over high heat, shaking the kettle occasionally, for 4 to 5 minutes, or until they are opened, and discard any unopened ones. Let the mussels cool until they can be handled, remove the meat, and reserve it, covered, discarding the cooking liquid and the shells. In a large saucepan of boiling salted water cook the rice, stirring occasionally, for 10 minutes, drain it in a colander, and rinse it. Set the colander over a saucepan of boiling water and steam the rice, covered with a folded dish towel and the lid, for 15 minutes, or until it is fluffy and dry. In a large serving bowl combine the reserved mussels, the rice, the peas, the scallions, the coriander leaves, and the bell pepper.

Make the dressing: In a small skillet cook the garlic in 1 tablespoon of the oil over moderately low heat, stirring, for 3 to 5 minutes, or until it is softened, add the curry powder and the cumin, and cook the mixture, stirring, for 1 minute. Stir in the remaining oil. In a small bowl whisk together the vinegar, the mustard, and salt and pepper to taste, add the oil mixture in a stream, whisking, and whisk the dressing until it is emulsified.

Pour the dressing over the mussel mixture and toss the salad gently to combine it. Let the salad cool, covered, and chill it for at least 2 hours or overnight to allow the flavors to develop. Stir in the lemon juice and serve the salad at room temperature. Serves 4 to 6.

Scrod Salad with Avocado and Red Peppers

1½ pounds scrod fillet
1 cup bottled clam juice
1 cup dry white wine
1 tablespoon white-wine vinegar
⅓ cup black olives, chopped
2 avocados
2 red bell peppers, roasted (procedure on page 114) and chopped
3 scallions, minced
For the dressing
2 tablespoons fresh lemon juice
1 tablespoon white-wine vinegar
1 tablespoon Dijon-style mustard
⅓ cup vegetable oil

cayenne to taste
lettuce leaves
black olives for garnish

In a buttered shallow flameproof baking dish arrange the scrod in one layer, folding under the tail(s) of the fillet(s) to make it an even thickness throughout, add the clam juice, the wine, the vinegar, and enough water, if necessary, to just cover the scrod, and cover the dish with a buttered piece of wax paper. Bring the liquid to a bare simmer and poach the scrod in a preheated 350° F. oven for 8 to 10 minutes, or until it just flakes. Drain the scrod, let it cool, and flake it into a large bowl. Add the chopped olives, the avocados, peeled, pitted, and cut into ½-inch pieces, the bell peppers, and the scallions and toss the mixture to combine it.

Make the dressing: In a small bowl whisk together the lemon juice, the vinegar, the mustard, and salt and pepper to taste, add the oil in a stream, whisking, and whisk the dressing until it is emulsified.

Drizzle the scrod mixture with the dressing, toss the salad gently to combine it, and season it with the cayenne. Serve the salad on a platter lined with the lettuce and garnish it with the olives. Serves 4 to 6.

Mediterranean Tuna Salad

a 6½-ounce can chunk light tuna packed in oil,
   drained
10 Kalamata or other brine-cured olives,
   pitted and chopped
⅓ cup minced celery
⅓ cup minced bottled roasted red pepper,
   drained
3 tablespoons plain yogurt
2 tablespoons mayonnaise
2 teaspoons fresh lemon juice, or to taste
2 tablespoons minced fresh parsley leaves

In a bowl combine well the tuna, the olives, the celery, the red pepper, the yogurt, the mayonnaise, the lemon juice, the parsley, and salt and pepper to taste. Use the salad as a filling for cherry tomatoes, a topping for sliced cucumbers, or with black bread and crackers. Makes about 1⅔ cups.

SALADS WITH GREENS

*Boston Lettuce and Radicchio Salad
with Orange Vinaigrette*

2 heads of Boston lettuce, washed, patted dry,
   and the large leaves torn into bite-size
   pieces
1 small head of *radicchio*, washed, patted
   dry, and torn into bite-size pieces
For the dressing
1 teaspoon Dijon-style mustard
1 tablespoon fresh lemon juice
3 tablespoons fresh orange juice
1 teaspoon grated orange rind
2 tablespoons minced fresh parsley leaves
¼ cup vegetable oil
2 tablespoons olive oil

1 small red onion, halved and sliced paper thin
8 large green olives, cut into slivers
1 teaspoon grated orange rind for garnish if
   desired
1 tablespoon minced fresh parsley leaves for
   garnish if desired

In a shallow salad bowl combine the Boston lettuce and the *radicchio* and chill the lettuces, covered with a dampened paper towel. *The lettuces may be prepared several hours in advance.*

Make the dressing: In a small bowl whisk together the mustard, the lemon juice, the orange juice, the orange rind, the parsley, and salt and pepper to taste, whisk in the vegetable oil and the olive oil, and whisk the dressing until it is emulsified. *The dressing may be prepared several hours in advance and kept covered.*

Toss the lettuces with the dressing to combine the salad well. Sprinkle the salad with the onion and the olives and, if desired, with the orange rind and the parsley. Serves 8.

Boston Lettuce with Sun-Dried Tomato Vinaigrette

¼ cup drained sun-dried tomatoes in oil
   (available at specialty foods shops)
2 tablespoons red-wine vinegar
1 teaspoon Dijon-style mustard
½ teaspoon pepper
⅓ cup olive oil
2 heads of Boston lettuce, separated into
   leaves

In a blender or food processor blend the tomatoes with the vinegar, the mustard, and the pepper until they are minced. With the motor running add the oil in a stream and blend the dressing until it is emulsified. In a salad bowl toss the lettuce with the dressing. Serves 6.

Cucumber and Green Pepper Salad with Lime

4 cucumbers, peeled, halved lengthwise,
   seeded, and sliced diagonally
¼ cup fresh lime juice
1 teaspoon grated lime rind
1 tablespoon olive oil
2 green bell peppers, seeds and ribs discarded,
   the peppers chopped fine, and the excess
   liquid squeezed out

In a bowl combine well the cucumbers, the lime juice, the rind, the oil, and salt and pepper to taste. *The salad may be prepared up to this point 1 day in advance and kept covered and chilled.* Just before serving add the bell peppers and toss the salad. Serves 6.

Endive and Walnut Salad

2 teaspoons raspberry vinegar* or red-wine
    vinegar
2½ tablespoons walnut oil* or safflower oil
2 large Belgian endives, cut into julienne
    strips and reserved in a bowl of ice water
¼ bunch of watercress, coarse stems discarded
2 tablespoons chopped walnuts

*available at specialty foods shops

In a small bowl combine the vinegar and salt and pepper to taste, add the oil in a stream, whisking, and whisk the dressing until it is emulsified. In a bowl toss the endives, drained and patted dry, with the dressing and divide the mixture between 2 plates. Garnish the salads with the watercress and sprinkle them with the walnuts. Serves 2.

Endive, Watercress, and Beet Salad with Orange Caraway Vinaigrette

For the dressing
1 teaspoon caraway seeds
2 teaspoons Dijon-style mustard
3 tablespoons white-wine vinegar
1 tablespoon fresh orange juice
½ cup vegetable oil
½ cup olive oil
1 teaspoon freshly grated orange rind
1 tablespoon minced shallot
3 tablespoons minced fresh parsley leaves
5 heads of Belgian endive (about 1 pound),
    trimmed and separated into leaves,
    reserving 40 leaves whole and slicing the
    remaining leaves thin crosswise
2 bunches of watercress (about 1¼ pounds),
    rinsed, coarse stems discarded, and
    patted dry
2 cups cooked small beets or a 9½-ounce jar
    cooked beets, drained and sliced thin

Make the dressing: In a blender grind fine the caraway seeds, add the mustard, the vinegar, the orange juice, and salt and pepper to taste, and blend the mixture well. With the motor running add the oils in a stream and blend the dressing until it is emulsified. Add the rind, the shallot, and the parsley and blend the dressing for 5 seconds. *The dressing may be made 1 day in advance and kept covered and chilled.*

On each of 8 chilled salad plates arrange 5 whole endive leaves in a spoke pattern, top them with the watercress and sliced endive, and arrange the beet slices on the watercress. Whisk the dressing well and spoon it over the salads. Serves 8.

Green Salad with Creamy Mustard Vinaigrette

1 small head of Boston lettuce, torn into bite-
    size pieces
½ small head of curly soft-leafed lettuce or
    red-leafed lettuce, torn into bite-size pieces
2 scallions, sliced thin crosswise
1 large egg yolk
1 tablespoon white-wine vinegar
2 teaspoons Dijon-style mustard
¼ cup olive oil

In a salad bowl combine the Boston lettuce, the curly lettuce, and the scallions. In a small stainless steel bowl whisk together the egg yolk and 1 tablespoon water and heat the mixture over low heat, whisking constantly, for 1 to 3 minutes, or until it is foamy and thickened, being careful not to scramble the yolk. Remove the bowl from the heat and whisk in the vinegar, the mustard, and salt and pepper to taste. Add the oil in a stream, whisking constantly, and whisk the dressing until it is emulsified. Before serving, drizzle the dressing over the salad and toss the salad. Serves 4.

Romaine and Avocado Salad with Lemon Soy Dressing

5 cups loosely packed torn romaine, rinsed
    and patted dry
½ avocado (preferably California), cut into
    ½-inch pieces
⅓ cup thinly sliced radish
2 teaspoons hulled sunflower seeds, toasted
    lightly
1½ teaspoons fresh lemon juice
1½ teaspoons soy sauce
2 tablespoons olive oil

In a large bowl toss together the romaine, the avocado, the radish, and the sunflower seeds and divide the mixture between 2 chilled salad plates. In a small bowl whisk together the lemon juice, the soy sauce, and pepper to taste, whisk in the oil, and drizzle the dressing over the salads. Serves 2.

Romaine and Watercress Salad with Feta Dressing

2 tablespoons red-wine vinegar
2 ounces Feta, crumbled (about 5 tablespoons)
¼ cup olive oil
3 cups torn romaine, rinsed and patted dry
3 cups watercress leaves, rinsed and patted dry
¼ cup walnuts, chopped and toasted lightly
1 small cucumber, peeled, quartered
 lengthwise, seeded, and cut crosswise into
 ½-inch pieces
French bread as an accompaniment

In a bowl combine the vinegar, the Feta, and salt and pepper to taste, add the oil in a stream, whisking, and whisk the dressing until it is emulsified. In a large bowl combine the romaine, the watercress, the walnuts, and the cucumber and toss the mixture with the dressing. Serve the salad with the bread. Serves 2.

Shredded Romaine with Garlic Vinaigrette

2 garlic cloves
¼ teaspoon salt
1 teaspoon Dijon-style mustard
2 tablespoons white-wine vinegar
½ cup olive oil
1 large head of romaine, rinsed, spun dry, and
 shredded
freshly ground pepper to taste
¼ cup freshly grated Parmesan
¼ cup pine nuts, toasted lightly

In a small saucepan of boiling water boil the garlic for 10 minutes, drain it well, and in a large salad bowl mash it to a paste with the salt. Whisk in the mustard and the vinegar, add the oil in a stream, whisking, and whisk the dressing until it is emulsified. Add the romaine, toss the salad to combine it well, and season it with the pepper. Sprinkle the salad with the Parmesan and the pine nuts. Serves 6.

Rugola Salad

1 teaspoon Dijon-syle mustard
1½ tablespoons balsamic vinegar (available at
 specialty foods shops) or red-wine vinegar
freshly ground pepper to taste
⅓ cup olive oil
2 bunches of *rugola,* stems discarded, rinsed,
 and spun dry

In a small bowl whisk together the mustard, the vinegar, the pepper, and salt to taste, add the oil in a stream, whisking, and whisk the dressing until it is emulsified. In a bowl toss the *rugola* with the dressing and divide the salad among chilled plates. Serves 4.

Spinach Romaine Salad
with Creamy Horseradish Dressing

For the dressing
3 tablespoons sour cream
1½ tablespoons drained bottled horseradish
1 tablespoon distilled white vinegar
1 teaspoon Dijon-style mustard
3 tablespoons vegetable oil

½ pound spinach, washed, spun dry, and
 stems discarded
½ head of romaine, cut crosswise into 2-inch
 sections, rinsed well, and spun dry

Make the dressing: In a bowl whisk together the sour cream, the horseradish, the vinegar, the mustard, and salt and pepper to taste, add the oil in a stream, whisking, and whisk the dressing until it is emulsified.

In a salad bowl toss together well the spinach, the romaine, and the dressing. Serves 6.

VEGETABLE SALADS
AND SLAWS

Broccoli Stem and Swiss Cheese Salad
with Caraway Dressing

5 broccoli stems about 1½ inches in diameter,
 trimmed, peeled, and cut into julienne strips
 (about 2 cups)
½ teaspoon Dijon-style mustard
2 teaspoons caraway seeds
1 tablespoon cider vinegar
3½ tablespoons vegetable oil
¼ pound Swiss cheese, cut into julienne strips

In a saucepan of boiling salted water blanch the broccoli for 20 seconds and drain it. Refresh the broccoli in a bowl of ice and cold water, drain it, and pat it dry.

In a large bowl whisk together the mustard, the caraway seeds, the vinegar, and salt and pepper to taste, add the oil in a stream, whisking, and whisk the dressing until it is emulsified. Add the broccoli and the Swiss cheese and toss the salad well. Serves 4.

Carrot Salad with Lemon Dill Dressing

¾ pound carrots, cut into long julienne strips
1 teaspoon Dijon-style mustard
1 tablespoon fresh lemon juice, or to taste
½ cup olive oil
2 teaspoons snipped fresh dill
2 heads of Belgian endive, separated into
    leaves, for garnish
dill sprigs for garnish

In a saucepan of boiling salted water blanch the carrots for 15 seconds, drain them in a colander, and refresh them under cold water. In a bowl whisk together the mustard, the lemon juice, and salt and pepper to taste, add the oil in a stream, whisking, and whisk the dressing until it is emulsified. Pat the carrots dry, toss them with the dressing, and let them marinate at room temperature for 1 hour, or chill the mixture, covered, overnight. Toss the carrots with the snipped dill and serve them at room temperature garnished with the endive and the dill sprigs. Serves 4.

Spicy Carrot, Daikon, and Napa Cabbage Salad

1½ cups shredded carrots
1½ cups shredded *daikon** (Oriental white
    radish), patted dry
1½ cups shredded Napa cabbage (celery
    cabbage)
2 tablespoons minced fresh coriander
2 tablespoons rice vinegar*
½ teaspoon sugar
1 tablespoon Oriental sesame oil*
½ teaspoon Chinese chili oil* or Chinese chili
    paste*
¼ cup safflower oil

*available at Oriental markets and some
    supermarkets

In a large bowl toss together the carrots, the *daikon*, the cabbage, and the coriander. In a small bowl whisk together the vinegar, the sugar, the sesame oil, the chili oil, and the safflower oil and whisk the dressing until it is emulsified. Pour the dressing over the vegetable mixture, add salt and pepper to taste, and toss the salad until it is combined well. Serves 2 generously.

Sautéed Carrot Salad with Mint

⅓ cup minced red onion
½ teaspoon Dijon-style mustard
1 tablespoon plus 1 teaspoon distilled white
    vinegar
3 tablespoons vegetable oil
½ pound carrots, grated coarse (preferably
    with a food processor)
1 teaspoon crumbled dried mint
½ bunch of watercress, coarse stems
    discarded, rinsed, drained, and patted dry

In a small bowl let the onion soak in cold water while preparing the salad. In a bowl combine well the mustard, 1 teaspoon of the vinegar, and salt and pepper to taste and whisk in 1 tablespoon of the oil. In a large skillet heat the remaining 2 tablespoons oil over high heat until it is hot but not smoking and in it sauté the carrots, stirring them once, for 2 minutes, or until they are browned lightly. Add the mint and cook the mixture, stirring, for 1 minute. Remove the skillet from the heat, stir in the remaining 1 tablespoon vinegar and salt and pepper to taste, and let the mixture cool to room temperature. Drain the onion, pat it dry, and stir it into the carrot mixture. Whisk the dressing to combine it, add the watercress, and toss the mixture to coat the watercress. Arrange the watercress around the edges of 2 plates and mound the carrot mixture in the center of the plates. Serves 2.

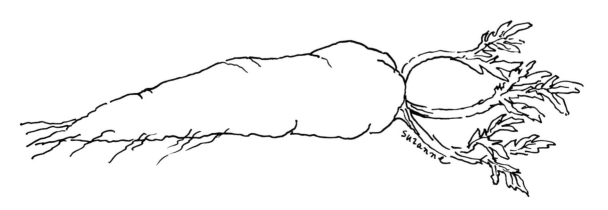

Corn Salad with Creamy Basil Dressing

2 ears of corn, shucked
1 large head of Bibb lettuce or ½ head of
   Boston lettuce, torn into bite-size pieces
   (about 4 cups)
3 tablespoons heavy cream
2½ teaspoons fresh lemon juice, or to taste
¼ teaspoon salt
1 tablespoon minced fresh basil leaves
2 teaspoons olive oil

In a large saucepan cover the corn with water, bring the water to a boil, and remove the pan from the heat. Drain the corn and let it stand until it is cool enough to handle. Cut the kernels from the cobs with a serrated knife, scrape the remaining corn from the cobs with the back of the knife, and put the corn and the lettuce in a large serving bowl. In a small bowl whisk together the cream, the lemon juice, the salt, the basil, and pepper to taste until the mixture is frothy, add the oil in a stream, whisking, and whisk the dressing until it is emulsified. Pour the dressing over the corn mixture and toss the salad well. Serves 2.

Fireworks Coleslaw

½ pound white cabbage, cored and sliced thin
   (about 4 cups)
½ pound red cabbage, cored and sliced thin
   (about 4 cups)
1 red bell pepper, sliced thin
1 yellow bell pepper, sliced thin
1 green bell pepper, sliced thin
a 4-inch green hot chili pepper, seeded and
   sliced thin (wear rubber gloves)
1 carrot, sliced thin lengthwise with a vegetable
   peeler
1 scallion, sliced thin
3 tablespoons minced fresh parsley leaves
2 tablespoons snipped fresh dill
For the dressing
1 small garlic clove
1 teaspoon caraway seeds
½ teaspoon ground cumin
½ cup sour cream
½ cup plain yogurt

In a large serving bowl combine the white and red cabbages, the red, yellow, and green bell peppers, the chili pepper, the carrot, the scallion, the parsley, and the dill. *The vegetables may be prepared up to 3 days in advance and kept covered and chilled.*

Make the dressing: In a blender or food processor blend the garlic and the caraway seeds until the garlic is minced and the seeds are ground, add the cumin, the sour cream, and the yogurt, and blend the mixture until it is combined well. *The dressing may be prepared up to 3 days in advance and kept covered and chilled.*

Just before serving pour the dressing over the vegetables, toss the coleslaw until it is combined well, and season it with salt and pepper. Serves 6.

Warm Lima Bean Salad

¼ cup minced red onion
2 teaspoons Dijon-style mustard
1½ tablespoons fresh lemon juice
¼ cup olive oil
2 cups shelled baby lima beans or a 10-ounce
   package frozen
2 ounces thinly sliced prosciutto or smoked
   ham, cut into ½-inch pieces
2½ teaspoons minced fresh tarragon leaves or
   1 teaspoon crumbled dried
rugola leaves for garnish

In a small bowl let the onion soak in cold water to cover for 30 minutes, drain it well, and pat it dry. In a large bowl stir together the mustard, the lemon juice, and salt and pepper to taste, add the oil in a stream, whisking, and whisk the dressing until it is emulsified. In a kettle of boiling salted water boil the fresh lima beans for 8 to 16 minutes, or until they are tender, or boil the frozen lima beans for 2 minutes, or until they are tender. Drain the beans well and pat them dry. Toss the beans while they are still warm with the dressing, the prosciutto, the onion, the tarragon, and salt and pepper to taste. Divide the salad among 4 chilled plates and garnish it with the *rugola* leaves. Serves 4.

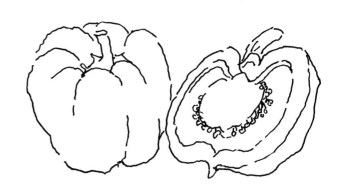

Orange, Radish, and Scallion Salad

6 navel oranges, peel and pith discarded and
    the flesh cut into sections
14 radishes, chopped coarse and excess liquid
    squeezed out
3 scallions, minced
¼ cup fresh lemon juice
2 tablespoons sugar, or to taste
2 tablespoons olive oil
coarsely ground pepper to taste
curly leaf lettuce

In a large bowl combine the orange sections, the radishes, the scallions, the lemon juice, the sugar, the oil, the pepper, and salt to taste, toss the salad gently, and serve it in a bowl lined with the lettuce. *The orange mixture may be prepared 1 day in advance and kept covered and chilled.* Serves 6.

Pepper Cabbage Slaw

4 cups thinly sliced cabbage
2 green bell peppers, sliced thin
½ red onion, sliced thin
3 tablespoons cider vinegar
1 teaspoon ground cumin
½ teaspoon sugar
⅓ cup vegetable oil

In a salad bowl combine the cabbage, the bell peppers, and the onion. In a small bowl whisk together the vinegar, the cumin, the sugar, and salt and pepper to taste, add the oil in a stream, whisking, and whisk the dressing until it is emulsified. Drizzle the dressing over the salad and toss the salad well. *The salad may be made up to 2 hours in advance and kept covered.* Serves 6.

Rosemary New Potato Salad with Roquefort

2 pounds small new potatoes, rinsed well
¼ cup plus 1 tablespoon white-wine vinegar
1½ tablespoons minced fresh rosemary leaves
    or 1½ teaspoons crumbled dried
1 tablespoon Dijon-style mustard
½ cup olive oil
¼ pound Roquefort, crumbled
rosemary sprigs for garnish if desired

In a saucepan cover the potatoes with cold salted water, bring the water to a boil, and simmer the potatoes

for 15 minutes, or until they are just tender. Drain the potatoes and transfer them to a large bowl. Add ¼ cup of the vinegar and the minced or crumbled rosemary, toss the mixture, and let the potatoes cool until they are lukewarm. In a bowl whisk together the remaining 1 tablespoon vinegar, the mustard, and salt and pepper to taste, add the oil in a stream, whisking, and whisk the dressing until it is emulsified. Add the dressing and the Roquefort to the potatoes, toss the salad well, and transfer it to a portable container. Garnish the salad with the rosemary sprigs if desired. Makes about 6 cups.

Bacon and Potato Salad

4 pounds baking potatoes, peeled (reserving
    the peels if desired for another use, such as
    roasted potato skins with scallion dip,
    page 206), halved lengthwise, and cut
    crosswise into ½-inch slices
3 cups sliced celery
½ cup chopped scallions
¼ cup minced fresh parsley leaves
½ pound sliced lean bacon, cut crosswise into
    ½-inch pieces
1 large egg
5 teaspoons fresh lemon juice
1 tablespoon Dijon-style mustard
½ teaspoon salt
¼ teaspoon pepper
½ cup vegetable oil

In a kettle cover the potatoes with cold water, bring the water to a boil, and add salt to taste. Simmer the potatoes for 10 to 12 minutes, or until they are just tender when pierced with a fork, and drain them. Transfer the potatoes to a serving bowl and add the celery, the scallions, and the parsley. In a skillet cook the bacon over moderate heat, stirring, until it is crisp and transfer it with a slotted spoon to paper towels to drain. Reserve ¼ cup of the fat and let it cool for 15 minutes. In a blender or food processor blend the egg, the lemon juice, the mustard, the salt, and the pepper for 5 seconds, with the motor running add the oil and the reserved bacon fat in a stream, and blend the mixture until it is emulsified. With the motor running add 1½ tablespoons warm water. Pour the dressing over the potato mixture, add the bacon, and toss the salad until it is combined. Sprinkle the salad with salt and pepper to taste and serve it at room temperature. *The salad may be made up to 3 days in advance and kept covered and chilled.* Serves 6.

GRAIN SALADS

Barley Corn Salad

1 cup barley
2 cups cooked fresh corn kernels cut from the
    cob, or a 10-ounce package frozen corn,
    thawed and drained
½ cup thinly sliced scallions
1 large tomato, seeded and chopped fine
one to two 4-inch fresh green hot chili peppers,
    seeded and minced (wear rubber gloves)
2 garlic cloves, cooked in boiling water for
    10 minutes, drained, and peeled
3 tablespoons white-wine vinegar
½ teaspoon ground cumin
⅓ cup olive oil or vegetable oil
¼ cup minced fresh coriander, or to taste

Into a large saucepan of boiling salted water sprinkle the barley, stirring, and boil it, skimming the froth, for 30 minutes, or until it is just tender. In a colander drain the barley, rinse it under cold water, and let it drain until it is cool. Transfer the barley to a large bowl, add the corn, the scallions, the tomato, and the chili peppers, and toss the mixture well. In a blender or food processor purée the garlic with the vinegar, the cumin, and salt and pepper to taste, add the oil in a stream, and blend the dressing until it is emulsified. Drizzle the salad with the dressing, sprinkle it with the coriander and salt and pepper to taste, and toss it well. *The salad may be made 1 day in advance and kept covered and chilled but do not add the coriander until just before serving.* Serve the salad at room temperature. Serves 4 to 6.

Brown Rice and Lentil Salad with Pepperoni

1 cup long-grain brown rice
1 cup lentils, picked over, rinsed, and drained
¾ cup chopped thinly sliced pepperoni (about
    3½ ounces)
⅔ cup finely chopped celery
½ cup finely chopped red onion
2 garlic cloves, cooked in boiling water for 10
    minutes, drained, and peeled
¼ cup red-wine vinegar, or to taste
1 tablespoon Dijon-style mustard
⅓ cup olive oil

Into a large saucepan of boiling salted water sprinkle the rice, stirring, and boil it for 25 minutes, or until it is just tender. In a colander drain the rice, refresh it under cold water, and let it drain until it is cool. In a saucepan combine the lentils and 4 cups water, bring the water to a boil, and simmer the lentils, covered, for 15 to 20 minutes, or until they are just tender but not mushy. Drain the lentils and in a bowl combine them with the rice, the pepperoni, the celery, and the onion. In a blender or food processor purée the garlic with the vinegar, the mustard, and salt and pepper to taste, add the oil in a stream, and blend the dressing until it is emulsified. Drizzle the salad with the dressing, toss it well, and add salt and pepper to taste. *The salad may be made 1 day in advance and kept covered and chilled.* Serve the salad at room temperature. Serves 4 to 6.

Buckwheat Noodle and Green Bean Salad
with Scallion Vinaigrette

For the salad
½ pound green beans, trimmed and cut on the
    diagonal into ¼-inch slices
½ pound *soba* (Japanese buckwheat noodles,
    available at Oriental markets and natural
    foods stores)
¼ cup thinly sliced scallion
⅓ cup finely chopped radishes
2 tablespoons snipped fresh dill, or to taste
For the scallion vinaigrette
¼ cup thinly sliced scallion
3 tablespoons rice vinegar (available at
    Oriental markets, natural foods stores, and
    some supermarkets) or distilled white
    vinegar
1 teaspoon honey
⅓ cup vegetable oil

Make the salad: In a steamer set over boiling water steam the green beans, covered, for 2 minutes, or until they are just tender, and transfer them to a bowl. In a large saucepan of boiling salted water boil the noodles, stirring occasionally, for 3 to 5 minutes, or until they are just tender, drain them in a colander, and refresh them under cold water. Drain the noodles well again, add them to the bowl of green beans with the scallion, the radishes, and the dill, and toss the mixture well.

Make the vinaigrette: In a blender purée the scallion with the vinegar, the honey, and salt and pepper to taste, add the oil in a stream, and blend the vinaigrette until it is emulsified. Drizzle the salad with the vinaigrette, toss it well, and add salt and pepper to taste. Serve the salad at room temperature. Serves 4.

Bulgur Salad with Dates and Walnuts

1 cup *bulgur* (processed cracked wheat,
    available at natural foods stores and some
    supermarkets)
⅓ cup minced scallion
½ cup minced celery
⅓ cup finely chopped dates
⅓ cup walnuts, toasted lightly and chopped
3 tablespoons fresh lemon juice
⅛ teaspoon cinnamon
⅓ cup olive oil

Into a large saucepan of boiling salted water sprinkle the *bulgur*, stirring, and boil it for 5 to 10 minutes (depending on the coarseness of the grains), or until it is just tender. In a large fine sieve drain the *bulgur*, rinse it under cold water, and let it drain until it is cool. Transfer the *bulgur* to a bowl, fluffing it with a fork, add the scallion, the celery, the dates, and the walnuts, and toss the mixture. In a small bowl whisk together the lemon juice, the cinnamon, and salt and pepper to taste, add the oil in a stream, whisking, and whisk the dressing until it is emulsified. Drizzle the salad with the dressing, toss it well, and add salt and pepper to taste. *The salad may be made 1 day in advance and kept covered and chilled.* Serve the bulgur salad at room temperature. Serves 4 to 6.

Couscous Salad with Tomatoes, Pine Nuts, and Mint

2 tablespoons fresh lemon juice plus additional
    to taste
6 tablespoons olive oil
1 cup couscous
2 tomatoes, diced
2 stalks of celery, chopped fine
3 scallions, chopped fine
3 tablespoons minced fresh mint leaves
3 tablespoons minced fresh parsley leaves
2 tablespoons pine nuts, toasted lightly
soft-leafed lettuce for lining the platter if
    desired
cherry tomatoes and mint sprigs for garnish
    if desired

In a bowl whisk 2 tablespoons of the lemon juice with salt and pepper to taste, add the oil in a stream, whisking, and whisk the dressing until it is emulsified. In a saucepan bring ⅔ cup water to a boil. Stir in the couscous, cover the pan immediately, and let the couscous stand, off the heat, for 5 minutes. Whisk the dressing,

drizzle 2 tablespoons of it over the couscous, and let the couscous stand, covered, for 2 minutes. Transfer the couscous to a bowl, fluff it with a fork to break up any lumps, and let it cool. Drizzle the remaining dressing over the couscous, add the diced tomatoes, the celery, the scallions, the minced mint, the parsley, and additional lemon juice, salt, and pepper to taste, and toss the salad. Chill the salad, covered, for at least 1 hour or overnight. Just before serving add the pine nuts and toss the salad well. Serve the salad on a platter lined with the lettuce if desired and garnish it with the cherry tomatoes and the mint sprigs if desired. Serves 4.

Kasha Tabbouleh
(Kasha Salad with Parsley and Mint)

1 cucumber, peeled, quartered lengthwise,
   seeded, and cut crosswise into ½-inch
   pieces
1 teaspoon salt
1 large egg, beaten lightly
1 cup whole kasha (toasted buckwheat groats,
   available at natural foods stores and many
   supermarkets)
½ cup vegetable oil
2 cups minced fresh parsley leaves
1 cup minced fresh mint leaves
⅓ cup minced scallion
1 tomato, seeded and chopped
5 tablespoons fresh lemon juice, or to taste

In a bowl toss the cucumber with ½ teaspoon of the
salt and let it stand for 30 minutes. In a sieve drain the
cucumber, rinse it under cold water, and drain it well
again. In a bowl stir together the egg and the kasha. In a
skillet heat 1 tablespoon of the oil over moderate heat
until it is hot and in it cook the kasha mixture, stirring
constantly, for 3 minutes, or until the grains are separated and appear dry. Add 1¾ cups water and the remaining ½ teaspoon salt, bring the liquid to a boil, and
simmer the kasha, covered, for 10 minutes, or until it is
just tender and the liquid is absorbed. Transfer the mixture to a bowl and let it cool, fluffing it occasionally
with a fork. Add the parsley, the mint, the scallion, the
cucumber, and the tomato and toss the mixture well.

In a bowl whisk the lemon juice with salt and pepper
to taste, add the remaining 7 tablespoons oil in a stream,
whisking, and whisk the dressing until it is emulsified.
Drizzle the salad with the dressing and toss it well. *The
salad may be made 1 day in advance and kept covered
and chilled.* Serve the salad at room temperature.
Serves 4 to 6.

Gingered Millet Salad with
Snow Peas, Water Chestnuts, and Carrots

For the salad
1 cup millet (available at natural foods stores)
¼ pound snow peas, strings discarded, cut on
   the diagonal into ½-inch slices, blanched in
   boiling water for 2 seconds, and drained
½ cup drained canned water chestnuts,
   blanched in boiling water for 30 seconds,
   drained, and sliced thin
½ cup thinly sliced scallions
½ cup grated carrot
For the dressing
3 tablespoons rice vinegar* or distilled white
   vinegar
2½ tablespoons soy sauce, or to taste
2 teaspoons peeled and grated gingerroot
1¼ teaspoons Oriental chili paste (preferably
   with garlic)*
1 teaspoon sugar
3 tablespoons Oriental sesame oil,* or to taste
3 tablespoons vegetable oil

*available at Oriental markets, natural foods
   stores, and some supermarkets

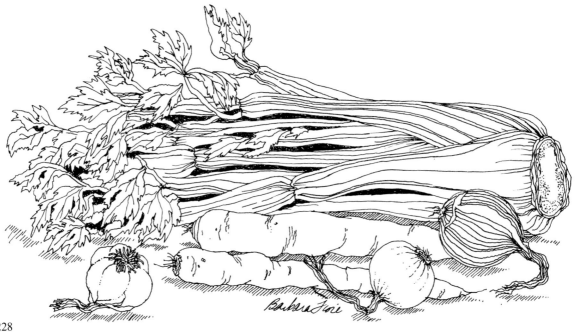

Barbara Fiore

Make the salad: Into a kettle of boiling salted water sprinkle the millet, stirring, and boil it for 12 minutes. In a large fine sieve drain the millet and rinse it under cold water. Set the sieve in a kettle over 1 inch boiling water and steam the millet, covered with a dish towel and the lid, for 10 minutes, or until it is tender. Transfer the millet to a large bowl, fluff it with a fork, and let it cool. Add the snow peas, the water chestnuts, the scallions, and the carrot and toss the mixture well.

Make the dressing: In a bowl whisk together the vinegar, the soy sauce, the gingerroot, the chili paste, and the sugar until the sugar is dissolved, add the sesame oil and the vegetable oil in a stream, whisking, and whisk the dressing until it is blended well. Drizzle the salad with the dressing, toss it well, and add salt and pepper to taste. *The salad may be made 1 day in advance, but do not add the snow peas until just before serving or they will discolor.* Serves 4 to 6.

Assumption Day Salad
(Rice Salad with Peppers, Tomatoes, Olives, and Raisins)

1½ cups long-grain rice
1 small red bell pepper, sliced thin lengthwise
1 small green bell pepper, sliced thin lengthwise
½ pound tomatoes, seeded and chopped
½ cup pitted black olives, quartered
½ cup golden raisins, plumped in a bowl of hot water for 10 minutes and drained
1 cup cooked fresh peas, or frozen peas, thawed
½ cup heavy cream
3 tablespoons fresh lemon juice, or to taste
¼ cup olive oil or vegetable oil

Into a kettle of boiling salted water sprinkle the rice, stirring, and boil it for 16 to 18 minutes, or until it is just tender. In a colander drain the rice, rinse it under cold water, and let it drain until it is cool. In a large bowl toss together the rice, the bell peppers, the tomatoes, the olives, the raisins, and the peas. In a small bowl whisk together the cream, the lemon juice, and salt and pepper to taste and add the oil in a stream, whisking. Drizzle the salad with the dressing, toss it well, and add salt and pepper to taste. *The salad may be made 1 day in advance and kept covered and chilled but do not add the peas until just before serving or they will discolor.* Serve the salad at room temperature. Serves 6 to 8.

Panzanella
(Italian Bread Salad)

3 cups ½-inch cubes of stale crusty Italian or French bread, toasted lightly
2 tomatoes (about ¾ pound), seeded and cut into ½-inch pieces
1 cucumber, peeled, quartered lengthwise, seeded, and cut crosswise into ½-inch pieces
½ cup finely chopped red onion
1 cup firmly packed fresh basil leaves
1 small garlic clove, minced
¼ cup red-wine vinegar
½ cup olive oil

In a bowl combine the bread, the tomatoes, the cucumber, and the onion, add salt and pepper to taste, and toss the mixture well. In a blender or food processor blend the basil, the garlic, the vinegar, and the oil until the basil is puréed and the dressing is emulsified. Drizzle the salad with the dressing and toss it well. The salad may be served at this point if a crunchy texture is desired. The longer the salad stands, the softer it becomes, as the bread absorbs the dressing and vegetable juices. Serve the salad at room temperature. Serves 4.

Lemon Rice Salad

2 teaspoons grated lemon rind
2 tablespoons fresh lemon juice
1 teaspoon Dijon-style mustard
¼ cup olive oil
1½ cups long-grain rice
1 bunch of radishes, sliced thin (about 1 cup)
¼ pound green beans, trimmed, frenched or sliced thin, and blanched until just tender
¼ cup snipped fresh dill
2 hard-boiled large eggs

In a large bowl whisk together the lemon rind, the lemon juice, the mustard, and salt and pepper to taste, add the oil in a stream, whisking, and whisk the dressing until it is emulsified.

In a kettle of boiling salted water cook the rice for 15 minutes, or until it is just tender, and drain it in a colander. Rinse the rice under lukewarm water and drain it well. Add the rice to the dressing, toss the mixture well, and let it marinate, covered, for 1 to 2 hours. Add the radishes, the beans, the dill, 1 of the eggs, sieved, and salt and pepper to taste, toss the salad well, and sprinkle it with the remaining egg, sieved. Serves 4.

FRUIT SALADS

Cantaloupe Salad with Cardamom-Yogurt Dressing

¼ cup plain yogurt
¼ teaspoon ground cardamom
1 teaspoon honey, or to taste
2 teaspoons fresh lime juice, or to taste
1 cantaloupe, scooped into balls with a melon-
 ball cutter

In a serving bowl whisk together the yogurt, the cardamom, the honey, and the lime juice. Add the cantaloupe and stir the salad gently to combine it. Serves 4.

Honeydew and Raspberry Salad with Lime Dressing

3 tablespoons fresh lime juice
1 teaspoon grated lime rind
1 tablespoon sugar
½ honeydew melon, scooped into balls with a
 melon-ball cutter
½ pint raspberries
2 teaspoons minced fresh mint leaves

In a serving bowl combine the lime juice, the rind,
and the sugar and stir the mixture until the sugar is dissolved. Add the melon, the raspberries, and the mint
and stir the salad gently to combine it well. Serves 4.

Honeydew Waldorf Salad

¼ honeydew melon, chilled and cut into
 bite-size pieces (about 1½ cups)
1 stalk of celery, chopped and strings
 discarded
1 teaspoon fresh lime juice, or to taste
1 teaspoon honey
¼ cup mayonnaise
¼ cup walnuts, chopped, toasted lightly, and
 cooled
lettuce leaves for garnish

In a bowl combine the melon and the celery and chill
the mixture for 20 minutes. In a small bowl stir together
the lime juice and the honey until the honey is dissolved
and whisk in the mayonnaise. Drain the melon mixture,
add the walnuts, and toss the mixture with the dressing.
Arrange the lettuce on 2 serving dishes, spoon the salad
onto it, and serve it immediately. Serves 2.

Kiwi, Orange, and Banana Salad with Honey-Nutmeg Dressing

¼ cup plain yogurt
1 teaspoon honey
a pinch of freshly grated nutmeg, or to taste
2 navel oranges, peel and pith removed with a
 serrated knife and the fruit cut into sections
2 bananas, halved lengthwise and cut
 crosswise into ½-inch slices
3 kiwis, peeled, halved length wise, and cut
 crosswise into ½-inch slices

In a serving bowl whisk together the yogurt, the honey, and the nutmeg. Add the oranges, the bananas, and
the kiwis and stir the salad gently to combine it well.
Serves 4.

Raspberry, Orange, and Green Grape Salad with Rum-Raspberry Dressing

1 pint raspberries
1 tablespoon confectioners' sugar
1 tablespoon dark rum
2 navel oranges, peel and pith removed with a
 serrated knife, sectioned, and the fruit cut
 into bite-size pieces
1 cup halved seedless green grapes
1 tablespoon minced fresh mint leaves

In a blender or food processor purée ¼ cup of the
raspberries with the confectioners' sugar and the rum
and pour the mixture into a serving bowl. Add the oranges, the grapes, the remaining raspberries, and the
mint and stir the salad gently to combine it. Serves 4.

Strawberry, Papaya, and Raspberry Salad with Honey-Lime Dressing

¼ cup raspberries
2 tablespoons fresh lime juice
1 tablespoon honey, or to taste
1 pint strawberries, hulled and halved
 lengthwise
1 papaya, peeled, halved lengthwise, and cut
 crosswise into ½-inch pieces

In a blender or food processor purée the raspberries
with the lime juice and the honey and pour the mixture
into a serving bowl. Add the strawberries and the papaya and stir the salad gently to combine it well. Serves 4.

SALAD DRESSINGS

Bacon Scallion Dressing

2 tablespoons white-wine vinegar
1 teaspoon bottled horseradish
1 scallion, chopped
3 slices of bacon, cooked until crisp, drained,
   and crumbled
⅓ to ½ cup vegetable oil, or to taste

In a blender or food processor blend the vinegar, the horseradish, the scallion, the bacon, and salt to taste, scraping down the sides with a rubber spatula, until the mixture is smooth. With the motor running add the oil in a stream and blend the dressing until it is emulsified. Makes about ⅔ cup.

Basil-Lime Vinaigrette

1 cup firmly packed fresh basil leaves
1 tablespoon fresh lime juice
1½ teaspoons white-wine vinegar
½ teaspoon Dijon-style mustard
1 small garlic clove if desired
½ cup olive oil

In a food processor or blender purée the basil with the lime juice, the vinegar, the mustard, the garlic if desired, and salt and pepper to taste. With the motor running add the oil in a stream and blend the dressing until it is emulsified. Serve the dressing with sliced tomatoes or pasta salads. Makes about ¾ cup.

Curry Dressing

2 tablespoons plain yogurt
1 teaspoon mayonnaise
1 teaspoon Dijon-style mustard
1½ tablespoons rice vinegar
1 teaspoon curry powder
¼ cup vegetable oil

In a blender or food processor blend the yogurt, the mayonnaise, the mustard, the vinegar, and the curry, scraping down the sides with a rubber spatula, until the mixture is smooth. With the motor running add the oil in a stream and blend the dressing until it is emulsified. Makes about ½ cup.

Garlic Mint Dressing

1 garlic clove
2 tablespoons fresh lime juice
1 teaspoon Dijon-style mustard
½ teaspoon dried mint
⅛ teaspoon sugar
¼ teaspoon salt
⅓ cup vegetable oil

In a blender or food processor blend the garlic, the lime juice, the mustard, the mint, the sugar, and the salt, scraping down the sides with a rubber spatula, until the mixture is smooth. With the motor running add the oil in a stream and blend the dressing until it is emulsified. Makes about ½ cup.

TREVOR

Herbed Cottage Cheese Dressing

½ cup cottage cheese
1 to 2 tablespoons fresh lemon juice, or
    to taste
¼ teaspoon dried tarragon
a pinch of dried thyme
⅛ teaspoon celery salt
⅓ cup vegetable oil

In a blender or food processor blend the cottage cheese, the lemon juice, the tarragon, the thyme, the celery salt, and 2 tablespoons water, scraping down the sides with a rubber spatula, until the mixture is smooth. With the motor running add the oil in a stream and blend the dressing until it is emulsified. Makes about ¾ cup.

Mayonnaise

2 large egg yolks at room temperature
2 teaspoons wine vinegar
1 teaspoon Dijon-style mustard
¼ teaspoon salt
white pepper to taste
1½ cups olive oil, vegetable oil, or a
    combination of both
fresh lemon juice to taste
cream to thin the mayonnaise if desired

Rinse a mixing bowl with hot water and dry it well. In the bowl combine the egg yolks, 1 teaspoon of the vinegar, the mustard, the salt, and the white pepper, beat the mixture vigorously with a whisk or with an electric mixer at high speed until it is combined, and add ½ cup of the oil, drop by drop, beating constantly. Add the remaining 1 teaspoon vinegar and the remaining 1 cup oil in a stream, beating constantly. Add the lemon juice and white pepper and salt to taste and thin the mayonnaise, if desired, with the cream or water. Makes about 2 cups.

Basil Mayonnaise

2 cups firmly packed fresh basil leaves
1 large egg
1 tablespoon fresh lemon juice plus additional
    to taste
½ cup olive oil
½ cup vegetable oil

In a saucepan of boiling water blanch the basil for 5 seconds, drain it in a colander, and refresh it under cold water. Squeeze out as much moisture from the basil as possible and in a food processor or blender blend the basil with the egg and 1 tablespoon of the lemon juice until the mixture is combined well. With the motor running add the olive oil and the vegetable oil in a slow stream, blend the mayonnaise until it is smooth, and season it with the additional lemon juice and salt and pepper to taste. Transfer the mayonnaise to a small bowl and chill it, covered tightly with plastic wrap, until ready to serve. The mayonnaise keeps, covered tightly and chilled, for up to 3 days. Makes about 1¼ cups.

Quick Mayonnaise

1 large egg at room temperature
5 teaspoons fresh lemon juice
1 teaspoon Dijon-style mustard
¼ teaspoon salt
¼ teaspoon white pepper
1 cup olive oil, vegetable oil, or a
    combination of both
heavy cream to thin the mayonnaise if desired

In a food processor or blender with the motor on high blend the egg, the lemon juice, the mustard, the salt, and the pepper, add the oil in a stream, and turn the motor off. Thin the mayonnaise, if desired, with the cream or water. Makes about 1 cup.

Oriental Dressing

2 tablespoons mayonnaise
1 teaspoon soy sauce
2 teaspoons Oriental sesame oil (available at most supermarkets, Oriental markets, and specialty foods shops)
2 tablespoons rice vinegar
a pinch of cayenne
¼ cup vegetable oil

In a blender or food processor blend the mayonnaise, the soy sauce, the sesame oil, the vinegar, and the cayenne, scraping down the sides with a rubber spatula, until the mixture is smooth. With the motor running add the vegetable oil in a stream and blend the dressing until it is emulsified. Makes about ½ cup.

Scallion Horseradish Dressing

2 teaspoons egg yolk
2 tablespoons bottled horseradish
½ cup vegetable oil
¼ cup buttermilk
½ cup minced scallions (about ½ bunch)

In a bowl whisk together the egg yolk, the horseradish, and salt and pepper to taste, add the oil in a stream, beating, and beat the mixture until it is emulsified. Stir in the buttermilk and the scallions. Makes about 1 cup.

Sherry Walnut Dressing

2 tablespoons walnut pieces
1½ tablespoons Sherry vinegar (available at specialty foods shops)
1 tablespoon medium-dry Sherry
1 tablespoon blue cheese
⅓ to ½ cup vegetable oil, or to taste

In a blender or food processor blend the walnuts, the vinegar, the Sherry, the blue cheese, and salt to taste, scraping down the sides with a rubber spatula, until the mixture is smooth. With the motor running add the oil in a stream and blend the dressing until it is emulsified. Makes about ½ cup.

Tahini Dressing

1 garlic clove
2 tablespoons fresh lemon juice
2 tablespoons *tahini* (sesame seed paste, available at specialty foods shops and some supermarkets), stirred well
⅛ teaspoon salt
a pinch of cayenne

In a blender or food processor blend the garlic, the lemon juice, the *tahini*, the salt, and the cayenne, scraping down the sides with a rubber spatula, until the mixture is smooth. With the motor running add ¼ cup water in a stream and blend the dressing until it is emulsified. Makes about ½ cup.

Tarragon Honey Dressing

1 tablespoon Dijon-style mustard
2 tablespoons rice vinegar
1½ teaspoons honey
½ teaspoon dried tarragon
⅓ cup vegetable oil

In a blender or food processor blend the mustard, the vinegar, the honey, and the tarragon, scraping down the sides with a rubber spatula, until the mixture is smooth. With the motor running add the oil in a stream and blend the dressing until it is emulsified. Makes about ½ cup.

SAUCES

SAVORY SAUCES

Barbecue Sauce

6 pitted prunes
2 teaspoons Chinese chili paste (available at
    Oriental markets and specialty foods shops)
⅓ cup fresh lemon juice
1 large onion, chopped coarse
½ stick (¼ cup) unsalted butter, melted and
    cooled
1 tablespoon Worcestershire sauce
2 teaspoons dry mustard
½ cup ketchup
1 large garlic clove, chopped coarse

In a food processor blend the prunes, the chili paste, and the lemon juice until the mixture is combined well. Add the onion, the butter, the Worcestershire sauce, the mustard, the ketchup, and the garlic and pulse the processor until the onion is chopped fine. Transfer the sauce to a saucepan, add salt to taste, and simmer the sauce, stirring occasionally, for 30 minutes. Use the sauce for basting grilled chicken or pork. Makes about 1⅔ cups.

Basil Butter

2 unpeeled garlic cloves
½ cup firmly packed fresh basil leaves
1 stick (½ cup) unsalted butter, softened
1 teaspoon Dijon-style mustard
½ teaspoon grated lemon rind, or to taste
white pepper to taste

In a small saucepan of boiling water boil the garlic for 10 minutes, transfer it to a plate, and let it cool. Add the basil to the boiling water and blanch it for 10 seconds. Drain the basil well, pat it dry, and mince it. In a small bowl cream the butter, add the garlic, peeled and mashed, the basil, the mustard, the lemon rind, the pepper, and salt to taste, and blend the mixture well. Let the butter stand, covered tightly with plastic wrap, in a cool place for 1 hour or chilled overnight. Serve the butter with steamed vegetables or grilled meats or fish. Makes about ⅔ cup.

Curry Pan Sauce

the pan juices from a roast chicken
1 small onion, minced
2 garlic cloves, minced
¼ cup all-purpose flour
1 tablespoon curry powder
2 cups chicken stock (page 119) or canned
    chicken broth
⅓ cup heavy cream
2 teaspoons fresh lemon juice

Skim all but 3 tablespoons of the fat from the pan juices in the roasting pan, add the onion and the garlic, and cook them over moderately low heat, stirring, until they are softened. Add the flour and cook the *roux,* stirring, for 2 minutes. Add the curry powder and cook the mixture, stirring, for 1 minute. Stir in the stock, bring the mixture to a boil, whisking, and simmer it for 5 minutes. Strain the mixture through a fine sieve into a heavy saucepan, stir in the cream, and bring the mixture to a boil. Simmer the mixture for 3 minutes, stir in the lemon juice and salt and pepper to taste, and transfer the sauce to a heated sauceboat. Makes about 2 cups.

Dill Tofu Sauce

3 garlic cloves, unpeeled
4 ounces tofu, patted dry and cut into pieces
¼ cup fresh lemon juice, or to taste
2 teaspoons Dijon-style mustard
¼ cup fresh dill
½ cup safflower oil

In a small saucepan combine the garlic with water to cover, bring the water to a boil, and simmer the garlic for 10 minutes. Drain the garlic and slip off the skins. In a food processor blend the garlic, the tofu, the lemon juice, the mustard, the dill, and salt to taste until the mixture is smooth. With the motor running add the oil in a stream and blend the sauce until it is emulsified. Serve the sauce with cooked green vegetables such as green beans and asparagus. Makes about 1 cup.

Green Chile Goat Cheese Sauce

¾ cup dry white wine
¾ cup heavy cream
a 4-ounce can green *chiles,* including the
    liquid
2 ounces goat cheese, such as Montrachet, at
    room temperature
2 tablespoons softened unsalted butter

In a small saucepan reduce the wine over high heat to about 1 tablespoon. Add the cream, reduce it over moderately high heat by half, and keep the mixture warm. In a food processor combine the *chiles,* the goat cheese, and the butter, with the motor running add the cream mixture in a stream, and blend the sauce until it is smooth. Serve the sauce with grilled meats or cooked vegetables. Makes about ¾ cup.

Green Peppercorn Pan Sauce

the pan juices from a roast beef
2 shallots, minced
½ cup Cognac
2 cups brown stock (page 118) or canned
    beef broth
beurre manié made by kneading together 2
    tablespoons all-purpose flour and
    2 tablespoons softened unsalted butter
2 tablespoons drained green peppercorns
    (available at specialty foods shops)
⅓ cup heavy cream

Skim all but 1 tablespoon of the fat from the pan juices in the roasting pan, add the shallots, and cook them over moderate heat, stirring, until they are softened. Add the Cognac and deglaze the pan over moder-

ately high heat, scraping up the brown bits. Add the stock, bring the liquid to a boil, stirring, and reduce it to about 1½ cups. Strain the mixture through a fine sieve into a heavy saucepan, bring it to a boil, and whisk in bits of the *beurre manié* until the mixture is thickened. Flatten 1 tablespoon of the peppercorns with the flat side of a large knife, add them with the remaining 1 tablespoon peppercorns to the mixture, and stir in the cream. Simmer the sauce for 3 minutes, add salt and pepper to taste, and transfer the sauce to a heated sauceboat. Makes about 1¾ cups.

Quick Mint Sauce

1 cup firmly packed fresh mint leaves
3 tablespoons sugar
⅓ cup rice vinegar (available at Oriental
    markets and some supermarkets)
1½ teaspoons cornstarch dissolved in 2
    teaspoons water

In a food processor chop the mint coarse. In a small saucepan combine the sugar and ¼ cup water, bring the water to a simmer, stirring to dissolve the sugar, and with the motor running add the syrup and the vinegar to the processor. Transfer the mixture to the pan, bring the liquid to a boil, and stir in the cornstarch mixture. Simmer the sauce for 3 minutes, or until it is thickened slightly. Transfer the sauce to a sauceboat and let it stand for 30 minutes to develop the flavors. Serve the sauce with roast lamb. Makes about ⅔ cup.

Mustard Pan Sauce

the pan juices from a roast beef, roast ham, or
    roast venison
¼ cup all-purpose flour
⅔ cup dry white wine
2¼ cups brown stock (page 118) or canned
    beef broth
3 tablespoons Dijon-style mustard
½ teaspoon Worcestershire sauce

Skim all but 3 tablespoons of the fat from the pan juices in the roasting pan, add the flour, and cook the *roux* over moderately low heat, stirring, for 3 minutes. Whisk in the wine and the stock, bring the liquid to a boil, stirring, and boil it, stirring, for 3 minutes. Stir in the mustard, the Worcestershire sauce, and salt and pepper to taste and strain the sauce through a fine sieve into a heated sauceboat. Makes about 2½ cups.

Onion Raisin Cranberry Confit

⅔ cup golden raisins
⅔ cup dark raisins
2 pounds small white onions, blanched in
    boiling water for 30 seconds and peeled
¾ stick (6 tablespoons) unsalted butter
½ cup sugar
¾ cup white-wine vinegar, or to taste
1½ cups dry white wine
3 garlic cloves, minced
¼ teaspoon crumbled dried thyme
1 teaspoon salt, or to taste
1⅔ cups fresh or frozen cranberries, picked
    over

In a small bowl let the raisins soak in 2 cups hot water for 10 minutes. In a large heavy saucepan cook the onions in the butter over moderate heat, stirring, until they are coated well with the butter, add the sugar and 1 tablespoon of the vinegar, and cook the mixture, stirring, until the sugar is dissolved and turns a golden caramel. Add the remaining 11 tablespoons vinegar and the wine and boil the mixture for 2 minutes. Add the raisins with the soaking liquid, the garlic, the thyme, the salt, and 1 cup water, or enough to just cover the solids, bring the liquid to a boil, and simmer the onions, covered, for 1 hour, or until they are tender. Add the cranberries and boil the mixture, uncovered, stirring occasionally, for 15 to 30 minutes, or until the liquid is reduced and the *confit* is thickened. Season the *confit* with salt, transfer it to a bowl, and let it cool. *The* confit *may be made up to 3 days in advance and kept covered and chilled. Reheat the* confit *in a saucepan over low heat, stirring, until the butter is just melted.* Serve the *confit* at room temperature. Makes about 4 cups.

Parsley Butter

2 tablespoons minced shallots
¼ cup dry white wine
1 stick (½ cup) unsalted butter, softened
3 tablespoons minced fresh parsley leaves
1 teaspoon fresh lemon juice
white pepper to taste

In a small saucepan simmer the shallots in the wine over moderately low heat, stirring occasionally, until the wine is evaporated. Transfer the shallots to a small bowl, let them cool, and combine them well with the butter, the parsley, the lemon juice, the white pepper, and salt to taste. Chill the butter, covered, for at least 1 hour. Serve the butter on grilled meat, poultry, or fish. Makes about ⅔ cup.

Peanut Sauce with Crudités

¼ cup unsalted dry-roasted peanuts
7 tablespoons plain yogurt
1 teaspoon fresh lemon juice, or to taste
⅛ teaspoon minced garlic
cayenne to taste
crudités as an accompaniment

In a food processor blend the peanuts until they form a smooth paste. In a bowl whisk together the peanut paste, the yogurt, the lemon juice, the garlic, the cayenne, and salt to taste. Serve the sauce with the *crudités*. Makes about ½ cup, serving 2.

Pesto
(Basil, Parmesan, and Pine Nut Sauce)

4 cups coarsely chopped fresh basil leaves
1 cup pine nuts
½ cup olive oil
1 cup freshly grated Parmesan
½ stick (¼ cup) unsalted butter, cut into bits
  and softened
2 garlic cloves, crushed

In a blender in batches or in a food processor purée the basil with the pine nuts, the oil, the Parmesan, the butter, the garlic, and salt to taste. Transfer the *pesto* to a small bowl and put plastic wrap directly on the surface of the *pesto* to prevent discoloring. *The* pesto *keeps, covered and chilled, for up to 2 weeks.* Serve the *pesto* with pasta or steamed or raw vegetables. Makes about 1½ cups.

Salsa Verde
(Green Sauce)

2 cups firmly packed fresh parsley leaves
1 large garlic clove
1 hard-boiled large egg
2 anchovy fillets, rinsed and patted dry
1 tablespoon drained capers
1 small onion, chopped coarse
⅓ cup red-wine vinegar
1 cup olive oil

In a food processor purée the parsley, the garlic, the egg, the anchovies, the capers, the onion, and the vinegar, with the motor running add the oil in a stream, and add salt and pepper to taste. Serve the sauce with steamed broccoli, green beans, cauliflower, or asparagus. Makes about 1⅔ cups.

Shiitake Mushroom Pan Sauce

1 ounce dried *shiitake* mushrooms (available
  at Oriental markets and some specialty
  foods shops)
¼ pound fresh mushrooms, sliced
1½ tablespoons unsalted butter
2½ cups brown stock (page 118) or canned
  beef broth
the pan juices from a roast beef
¼ cup minced shallots
1 cup Sercial Madeira
4 teaspoons arrowroot dissolved in
  2 tablespoons cold water

In a small bowl let the *shiitake* mushrooms soak in 2 cups hot water for 30 minutes, squeeze out the excess liquid, and reserve the soaking liquid in the bowl. Discard the stems and slice the caps thin. Strain the reserved liquid through a fine sieve into a bowl. In a heavy skillet sauté the fresh mushrooms in the butter over moderately high heat, stirring, for 1 minute, add the *shiitake* mushrooms, and sauté the mixture, stirring, for 1 minute. Add the stock and the reserved mushroom liquid, bring the liquid to a boil, and reduce it to about 2½ cups. Skim all but 1 tablespoon of the fat from the pan juices in the roasting pan, add the shallots, and cook them over moderately low heat, stirring, until they are softened. Add the Madeira and deglaze the pan over moderately high heat, scraping up the brown bits. Reduce the Madeira by half, strain it through a fine sieve into the mushroom mixture, and bring the mixture to a boil. Stir the arrowroot mixture, add it to the mushroom mixture, stirring, and simmer the sauce for 3 minutes, or until it is thickened. Add salt and pepper to taste and transfer the sauce to a heated sauceboat. Makes about 3 cups.

Sun-Dried Tomato and Olive Sauce

6 Kalamata olives, pitted
3 drained bottled sun-dried tomatoes
    (available at specialty foods shops and some
    supermarkets), cut into pieces
¼ cup firmly packed flat-leafed parsley leaves
2 to 3 tablespoons fresh lemon juice, or to
    taste
¼ cup olive oil

In a food processor blend the olives, the tomatoes, the parsley, and the lemon juice until the mixture is chopped fine. With the motor running add the oil in a stream and blend the mixture until the sauce is emulsified. Serve the sauce with grilled fish or chicken. Makes about ¾ cup.

Tarragon Pan Sauce

the pan juices from a roast chicken or small
    roast turkey
¼ cup minced shallots
½ cup white-wine vinegar
⅔ cup dry white wine
1 teaspoon dried tarragon
2 cups chicken stock (page 119) or canned
    chicken broth
beurre manié made by kneading together 3½
    tablespoons all-purpose flour and 3
    tablespoons softened unsalted butter

Skim all but 1 tablespoon of the fat from the pan juices in the roasting pan, add the shallots, and cook them over moderately low heat, stirring, until they are softened. Add the vinegar, the wine, and the tarragon and deglaze the pan over moderately high heat, scraping up the brown bits. Reduce the mixture by half, add the stock, and bring the liquid to a boil. Strain the mixture through a fine sieve into a heavy saucepan, bring it to a boil, and stir in bits of the *beurre manié* until the sauce is thickened. Simmer the sauce for 5 minutes, add salt and pepper to taste, and transfer the sauce to a heated sauceboat. Makes about 2½ cups.

Winter Tomato Sauce

1 onion, minced
⅓ cup minced celery
¼ cup minced carrot
2 tablespoons olive oil
3 garlic cloves, minced
a 28-ounce can Italian plum tomatoes
    including the juice, puréed coarse in a
    blender or food processor
1 bay leaf
½ teaspoon sugar, or to taste
¼ teaspoon crumbled dried thyme

In a large heavy skillet cook the onion, the celery, and the carrot in the oil over moderately low heat, stirring, until the vegetables are softened. Add the garlic and cook the mixture, stirring, for 1 minute. Add the tomatoes, the bay leaf, the sugar, the thyme, and salt and pepper to taste, bring the mixture to a boil, and simmer it, stirring occasionally, for 10 to 15 minutes, or until it is thickened slightly. Discard the bay leaf, purée the sauce through a food mill into a bowl, and season it with sugar, salt, and pepper to taste. *The sauce may be made up to 3 days in advance and kept covered and chilled or frozen.* In a small saucepan heat the sauce over moderately low heat, stirring, until it is heated through and transfer it to a heated sauceboat. Makes about 2 cups.

DESSERT SAUCES

Frangelico Chocolate Sauce

1 cup sugar
6 ounces unsweetened chocolate, chopped
1 cup half-and-half
⅓ to ½ cup Frangelico (hazelnut-flavored
    liqueur), or to taste

In a heavy saucepan combine the sugar and 1 cup water, bring the mixture to a boil, stirring until the sugar is dissolved, and remove the pan from the heat. Add the chocolate, stirring, and stir the mixture until the chocolate is melted and the mixture is smooth. Stir in the half-and-half and the Frangelico, let the sauce cool to room temperature, and transfer it to a sauceboat or bowl. Makes about 2⅔ cups.

Mocha Sauce

6 ounces unsweetened chocolate, cut into pieces
½ cup superfine sugar
1 teaspoon vanilla
⅓ cup brewed coffee
¼ cup coffee-flavored liqueur
2 tablespoons softened unsalted butter

In a food processor blend the chocolate, the sugar, the vanilla, and a pinch of salt until the chocolate is chopped coarse. In a small saucepan combine the coffee and the liqueur, bring the liquid to a boil, and with the motor running add it to the processor in a stream. Add the butter and blend the sauce until it is smooth. Serve the sauce over ice cream. Makes about 1¼ cups.

Raspberry Sauce

a 10-ounce package frozen raspberries in
    syrup, thawed, reserving the syrup
fresh lemon juice to taste

In a food processor or blender purée the berries with the syrup and force the purée through a fine sieve into a bowl, pressing hard on the solids. Stir in the lemon juice and transfer the sauce to a serving bowl or pitcher. *The sauce may be made up to 3 days in advance and kept covered and chilled.* Stir the sauce before serving. Makes about 1 cup.

Raspberry Chocolate Sauce

a 10-ounce package frozen raspberries in
    syrup, thawed
4 ounces sweet chocolate, cut into pieces
3 tablespoons unsweetened cocoa powder
¼ cup superfine sugar
2 tablespoons softened unsalted butter

In a small saucepan bring the raspberries to a boil in their syrup. In a food processor chop the chocolate coarse and with the motor running add the raspberry mixture, blending the mixture until it is smooth. Add the cocoa powder, the sugar, and the butter and blend the sauce until it is combined well. Serve the sauce as a topping for ice cream. Makes about 1⅓ cups.

DESSERTS

CAKES

Apricot Coffeecake

1 stick (½ cup) plus 2 tablespoons unsalted
   butter, softened
1 cup granulated sugar
3 large eggs, beaten lightly
2 cups plus 2 tablespoons all-purpose flour
1 teaspoon double-acting baking powder
1 teaspoon baking soda
1 teaspoon cinnamon
¼ teaspoon freshly grated nutmeg
¼ teaspoon salt
1 cup sour cream
a 17-ounce can apricot halves, drained, patted
   dry, and chopped
½ cup firmly packed dark brown sugar

In a bowl cream together 1 stick of the butter and the granulated sugar and beat the mixture until it is light and fluffy. Add the eggs and beat the mixture until it is combined well. Sift together 2 cups of the flour, the baking powder, the baking soda, the cinnamon, the nutmeg, and the salt and beat the mixture into the egg mixture alternately with the sour cream. Spread the batter evenly in a buttered and floured 10-inch-square cake pan and scatter the apricots over it. In a small bowl blend together the remaining 2 tablespoons butter, the remaining 2 tablespoons flour, and the brown sugar, sprinkle the mixture over the batter, and bake the cake in a preheated

350° F. oven for 1 hour, or until a tester comes out clean. *The coffeecake keeps, covered and chilled, for up to 3 days.* Serve the cake warm.

Blueberry Cupcakes

1 cup all-purpose flour
⅔ cup granulated sugar
1 teaspoon double-acting baking powder
1 teaspoon cinnamon
¼ teaspoon salt
1 large egg, beaten lightly
½ stick (¼ cup) unsalted butter, melted
½ cup sour cream
1 cup blueberries, picked over
½ cup confectioners' sugar
1 tablespoon fresh lemon juice
1 teaspoon grated lemon rind

In a bowl sift together the flour, the granulated sugar, the baking powder, the cinnamon, and the salt. Add the egg, the butter, and the sour cream, stir the mixture until it is just combined, and fold in the blueberries gently. Pour the batter into twelve ⅓-cup muffin tins lined with paper cupcake liners and bake the cupcakes in a preheated 375° F. oven for 30 to 40 minutes, or until a tester comes out clean. Transfer the cupcakes to a rack and let them cool.

In a bowl whisk together the confectioners' sugar, the lemon juice, and the lemon rind and spread 1 teaspoon of the glaze over each cupcake. Let the cupcakes stand until the glaze is hardened and transfer them to a portable container. Makes 12 cupcakes.

Chocolate Raspberry Dobostorte

For the cake layers

6 large eggs, separated, the whites at room
   temperature
¾ cup plus 1 tablespoon sugar
1 teaspoon vanilla
1 cup cake flour (not self-rising)
¼ teaspoon salt
a pinch of cream of tartar

For the raspberry filling

½ cup seedless raspberry jam
1 tablespoon framboise
1 tablespoon fresh lemon juice, or to taste

For the chocolate buttercream

3 ounces semisweet chocolate, chopped
2 ounces unsweetened chocolate, chopped
½ cup sugar
¼ teaspoon cream of tartar
5 large egg yolks
2 sticks (1 cup) unsalted butter, cut into ¼-
   inch slices
2 tablespoons framboise

½ cup toasted and skinned hazelnuts
   (procedure on page 275), chopped fine

For the caramel

1 cup sugar
¼ teaspoon cream of tartar

13 hazelnuts, toasted and skinned for garnish

Make the cake layers: In a large bowl with an electric mixer beat the egg yolks until they are thick and pale, beat in ½ cup of the sugar, and beat the mixture for 5 minutes. Beat in the vanilla. Sift the flour and the salt together over the yolk mixture and fold them in gently but thoroughly. In another bowl beat the whites with a pinch of salt until they are frothy, add the cream of tartar, and beat the whites until they hold soft peaks. Add the remaining 5 tablespoons sugar, a little at a time, beating, and beat the whites until they just hold stiff peaks. Stir one third of the whites into the batter and fold in the remaining whites gently but thoroughly. Invert three 8-inch-round cake pans and butter and flour the undersides. Spread a generous ½ cup of the batter with an icing spatula or a knife on each underside in an even layer and bake the cake layers on the same rack in the middle of a preheated 350° F. oven for 7 to 9 minutes, or until they are pale golden. Let the cake layers cool for 2 minutes and loosen the edges with a thin-bladed knife. Transfer the layers to racks and let them cool. Wipe the pans clean with paper towels and make 6 more layers in the same manner. *When the layers have cooled completely they may be stacked between sheets of waxed paper, wrapped in plastic wrap, and chilled for 1 day. Remove the wax paper very carefully.*

Make the raspberry filling: In a small saucepan combine the jam, the framboise, and the lemon juice, heat the mixture over moderately low heat, whisking, until it is smooth, and let it cool to room temperature.

Make the chocolate buttercream: In the top of a double boiler set over barely simmering water melt the semisweet and unsweetened chocolate, stirring constantly, until the mixture is smooth and let it cool to room temperature. In a small saucepan combine the sugar, the cream of tartar, and ¼ cup water, cook the mixture over moderate heat, stirring and washing down the sugar crystals clinging to the sides of the pan with a brush dipped in cold water until the sugar is dissolved, and bring the syrup to a boil. Boil the syrup, undisturbed, until it registers 238° F. on a candy thermometer. While the syrup is boiling, in a heatproof bowl with an electric mixer beat the egg yolks for 3 to 4 minutes, or until they are thick and pale. As soon as the syrup reaches 238° F., add it to the yolks in a thin stream, beating constantly, and beat the mixture for 10 minutes, or until the bowl is no longer hot. Beat in the butter, 1 slice at a time, beat in the chocolate, and beat the buttercream until it is smooth. Add the framboise drop by drop, beating constantly, and chill the buttercream until it is just firm enough to spread.

With a sharp knife trim the edges of the cake layers so that the layers are all the same size and shape, reserving the best layer, wrapped in plastic wrap, for the caramel top. Arrange one layer on a cake stand, using a small dab of the chocolate buttercream to anchor it to the stand, and spread it with 3 heaping tablespoons of the buttercream. Spread a second cake layer with 2 tablespoons of the raspberry filling, invert the layer, raspberry side down, onto the buttercream-spread layer, and spread the layer with 3 heaping tablespoons of buttercream. Continue to layer the remaining cake in the same manner. After spreading the eighth layer with the buttercream, spread the remaining buttercream around the sides of the cake. Chill the cake for 5 minutes to firm the buttercream slightly and press the chopped hazelnuts around the sides. *The cake may be prepared up to this point 2 days in advance and kept covered with an inverted bowl and chilled.*

Make the caramel: In a small saucepan combine the sugar, the cream of tartar, and ½ cup water, cook the mixture over moderate heat, stirring and washing down the sugar crystals clinging to the sides of the pan with a brush dipped in cold water until the sugar is dissolved, and bring the syrup to a boil. Boil the syrup, undisturbed, until it begins to turn a pale golden and swirl the pan gently until it is a golden brown caramel. While the syrup is boiling put the reserved cake layer on a rack set over a few sheets of foil to protect the work surface and have ready a buttered knife. Pour enough of the caramel immediately over the cake layer to coat it with a thin layer, reserving the remaining caramel in the pan, and, working very quickly, draw the knife through the caramel glaze down to the cake, marking off 12 slices. (These lines decorate the cake and make it easier to slice without shattering the hardened caramel.) When the caramel has cooled completely, trim any caramel that has dripped around the edge with scissors.

Make the garnish: Set a few sheets of foil over the work surface to protect it, invert a large sieve over the foil, and insert a wooden pick into the bottom of each whole hazelnut. Heat the reserved caramel over moder-

ately low heat, swirling the pan, until it is melted. Dip the hazelnuts carefully into the caramel and insert the other end of the wooden picks into the sieve to allow the caramel to cool and harden. (Be very careful not to drip any caramel onto your hands or wear 2 pairs of rubber gloves to protect them from burns.) When the caramel-coated hazelnuts have cooled completely, "glue" them onto the caramel-coated top cake layer, using some additional caramel, reheated, if necessary. Let the cake come to room temperature, arrange the caramel layer on top, and with a knife smooth the buttercream and chopped hazelnuts up around the edge of the top layer. Serves 12.

Chocolate Shell Cakes

1 stick (½ cup) unsalted butter, cut into bits
3 ounces bittersweet chocolate, cut into bits
⅓ cup Dutch process cocoa powder plus
    additional for dusting the cakes
⅔ cup all-purpose flour
3 large eggs at room temperature
½ cup granulated sugar
confectioners' sugar for dusting the cakes

Butter well and flour five 4-inch-wide scallop shells.

In a double boiler set over barely simmering water melt the butter and the chocolate, remove the mixture from the heat, and let it cool to room temperature.

In a small bowl sift together the cocoa and the flour. In a bowl with an electric mixer beat the eggs with the granulated sugar for 8 to 10 minutes, or until the mixture is thick and pale. Sift one fourth of the flour mixture over the egg mixture and fold it in gently. Pour in one fourth of the chocolate mixture, fold it in gently, and continue adding the remaining flour mixture and the remaining chocolate mixture alternately in the same manner, folding the batter gently after each addition until it is just combined. Divide the batter evenly among the prepared scallop shells and smooth the top with a metal spatula, leaving a ¼-inch rim around the shell and mounding the batter slightly at the hinged end. Arrange the shells on the top of a muffin tin (this keeps them level so that the batter doesn't spill while the cakes are baking) and bake them in a preheated 375° F. oven for 25 to 30 minutes, or until a tester comes out clean. Invert the cakes carefully onto a rack and let them cool. *The cakes may be made 1 day in advance and kept in an airtight container.* Sprinkle some of the cakes with the additional cocoa and the confectioners' sugar and rub the mixture in to give the shells a textured appearance. Makes 5 cakes.

Cranberry Pecan Shortcakes

½ cup sifted all-purpose flour
¾ teaspoon double-acting baking powder
5 tablespoons sugar
⅛ teaspoon salt
2 tablespoons chopped pecans, toasted lightly,
    cooled, and ground
2 tablespoons chilled unsalted butter, cut into bits
3 tablespoons heavy cream
½ cup cranberries, picked over
sweetened whipped cream as an accompaniment

Into a bowl sift together the flour, the baking powder, 1 tablespoon of the sugar, and the salt, stir in the pecans, and blend in the butter until the mixture resembles coarse meal. Add the heavy cream and stir the mixture with a fork until it just forms a dough. Knead the dough gently on a floured surface for 30 seconds, roll or pat it out into a ½-inch-thick round, and with a floured 3-inch round cutter cut out 2 rounds, gathering and rolling out the scraps if necessary. Bake the rounds on a buttered baking sheet set on another baking sheet in a preheated 425° F. oven for 10 to 12 minutes, or until they are pale golden. (The double sheet method prevents the rounds from browning too much.) Transfer the shortcakes to a rack, let them cool until they can be handled, and split them in half horizontally.

While the shortcakes are baking, in a heavy saucepan combine ¼ cup water, the remaining 4 tablespoons sugar, and the cranberries, bring the water to a boil, stirring, and simmer the mixture, stirring occasionally, for 5 minutes, or until it is thickened slightly. Transfer the sauce to a metal bowl set in a larger bowl of ice and cold water and stir it until it is cooled to lukewarm. Arrange the bottom halves of the shortcakes cut sides up on 2 serving dishes, spoon half the sauce over them, and cover the sauce with the top halves. Top the shortcakes with the remaining sauce and a dollop of the whipped cream. Serves 2.

Independence Day Ice-Cream Cake

For the cake
1 stick (½ cup) unsalted butter, softened
1 cup sugar
2 large eggs at room temperature
½ cup sour cream
1¼ cups all-purpose flour
½ teaspoon double-acting baking powder
¼ teaspoon baking soda
¼ teaspoon salt
For the ice creams
6 large egg yolks
2 cups sugar
3 cups milk
1½ teaspoons vanilla
1½ cups well chilled heavy cream
1¾ cups sliced strawberries
3 cups blueberries, picked over
½ teaspoon cinnamon

fresh whole strawberries for garnish

Make the cake: In a large bowl with an electric mixer cream the butter, add the sugar, and beat the mixture until it is light and fluffy. Add the eggs, 1 at a time, beating well after each addition, add the sour cream, and beat the mixture until it is just combined. Into a bowl sift together the flour, the baking powder, the baking soda, and the salt, add the mixture to the butter mixture, and

stir the batter until it is just combined. Pour the batter into a buttered and floured 9-inch springform pan, smoothing the top, and bake it in the middle of a preheated 350° F. oven for 45 to 55 minutes, or until a tester comes out clean. Let the cake cool in the pan on a rack for 10 minutes, remove the bottom and sides of the pan, and let the cake cool completely.

Make the ice creams: In a bowl with an electric mixer beat the egg yolks and the sugar for 5 minutes and add the milk, scalded, in a stream, beating at low speed. Transfer the custard to a heavy saucepan and cook it over moderately low heat, stirring, until it thickens and coats the spoon lightly, but do not let it boil. Remove the pan from the heat and stir in the vanilla. Strain the custard through a fine sieve into a large metal bowl set over a bowl of ice and cold water, chill it, stirring occasionally, until it is very cold, and stir in the cream. In a food processor purée the sliced strawberries, in a bowl combine the purée with 2 cups of the custard mixture, and freeze the mixture in an ice-cream freezer according to the manufacturer's instructions. In the rinsed-out food processor purée the blueberries with the cinnamon, add the remaining custard mixture, and freeze the mixture in an ice-cream freezer according to the manufacturer's instructions. Keep both ice creams frozen until it is time to assemble the cake.

Slice the cake horizontally into 4 layers and put the top layer, cut side up, in the bottom of the springform pan. Soften the ice creams, if necessary, by beating them with an electric mixer (they should be just soft enough to spread). Spread half the blueberry ice cream with a large spoon on the cake layer and top it with the second cake layer, pressing the cake down gently to even out the ice cream. Spread all of the strawberry ice cream on top of the cake and top it with the third cake layer, pressing the cake down gently. Spread the remaining blueberry ice cream on top of the cake and top it with the last cake layer, cut side down, pressing the cake down gently. Freeze the cake, covered, for at least 3 hours or overnight. Cut the cake with a serrated knife, arrange the slices on a platter, and garnish them with the whole strawberries. *Any remaining slices may be frozen, wrapped well in plastic and foil.* Serves 8 to 10.

Lime Cheesecake

For the crust
¾ cup gingersnap crumbs or graham cracker crumbs
2 tablespoons sugar
3 tablespoons melted unsalted butter

For the filling
12 ounces cream cheese, softened
⅓ cup sugar
3 large eggs at room temperature
2 teaspoons grated lime rind
3 tablespoons fresh lime juice
For the topping
¾ cup sour cream
1 teaspoon sugar
1 teaspoon fresh lime juice
For the garnish
the rind from 1 large lime, cut into fine
    julienne strips
⅓ cup sugar

raspberry sauce (page 240) as an
    accompaniment

Make the crust: In a bowl combine the gingersnap crumbs, the sugar, and the butter, press the mixture evenly onto the bottom and halfway up the sides of a buttered 6½- to 7-inch springform pan, and chill the pan.

Make the filling: In a large bowl with an electric mixer cream the cream cheese, add the sugar, and beat the mixture well. Add the eggs, 1 at a time, beating well after each addition, and beat in the lime rind and the lime juice. Spoon the filling into the springform pan, smoothing the top, and bake the cheesecake in the middle of a preheated 325° F. oven for 45 minutes. (The filling will not appear to be set.) Remove the pan from the oven.

Make the topping: In a small bowl stir together the sour cream, the sugar, and the lime juice, spread the topping evenly over the cheesecake, and bake the cheesecake in the 325° F. oven for 8 minutes more, or until the topping is just set. Transfer the cheesecake to a rack, let it cool completely, and chill it, covered, for at least 2 hours or overnight. Let the cheesecake stand at room temperature for 15 minutes before serving.

Make the garnish 1 hour before serving: In a small saucepan of boiling water blanch the lime rind for 1 minute and drain it. In the same small pan combine the rind, the sugar, and ¼ cup water, bring the liquid to a boil over moderate heat, stirring until the sugar is dissolved, and boil it for 4 minutes, or until the rind is translucent and the liquid is reduced. Add ¼ cup cold water, bring the liquid to a boil, and strain the mixture through a fine sieve, discarding the liquid. Let the rind cool and arrange it decoratively around the edge of the cheesecake. Serve the cheesecake with the raspberry sauce. Serves 4 to 6.

Prune Cakes with Rum-Flavored Syrup

½ cup pitted prunes
6 tablespoons sugar
2 teaspoons dark rum
½ cup all-purpose flour
⅛ teaspoon salt
½ teaspoon double-acting baking powder
5 tablespoons unsalted butter, softened
1 large egg
1½ teaspoons vanilla
vanilla ice cream as an accompaniment

In a small saucepan combine the prunes, ½ cup water, and 2 tablespoons of the sugar, bring the water to a boil, and simmer the prunes for 2 minutes. Stir in the rum and let the mixture cool for 5 minutes. Drain the prunes, reserving the cooking liquid, and quarter them.

Into a bowl sift together the flour, the salt, and the baking powder. In another bowl with an electric mixer beat the butter and the remaining 4 tablespoons sugar until the mixture is light and fluffy, add the egg and the vanilla, and beat the mixture well. Add the flour mixture and blend the mixture at low speed until it is just combined. Stir in the prunes, divide the batter among six buttered ⅓-cup muffin tins, and bake the cakes in a preheated 350° F. oven for 15 to 18 minutes, or until a tester comes out clean. While the cakes are baking, boil the reserved cooking liquid in a saucepan until it is reduced to about 3 tablespoons. Invert the cakes onto a rack, brush the bottoms with the syrup, and let the cakes cool for 5 minutes. Serve the cakes warm with the ice cream. *The cakes can be kept wrapped tightly and chilled for 3 days.* Makes 6 cakes.

Apple-Filled Rolled Spice Cake

For the filling
¾ pound Golden Delicious apples, peeled, cored, and chopped
¼ cup sugar
¼ cup cranberries, picked over
a 3-inch cinnamon stick
For the cake
5 large egg whites at room temperature
a pinch of cream of tartar
1 cup sugar
5 large egg yolks
¾ cup sifted cake flour (not self-rising)
2 teaspoons cinnamon
¼ teaspoon ground allspice

confectioners' sugar for dusting the cake
¼ cup strained apricot jam, heated
whipped cream as an accompaniment

Make the filling: In a saucepan combine the apples, the sugar, the cranberries, the cinnamon stick, and ¼ cup water, bring the mixture to a simmer, stirring, and simmer it, stirring occasionally, for 20 to 30 minutes, or until the apples are very soft and the liquid is evaporated. Remove the cinnamon stick, purée the filling in a blender, and let it cool to room temperature. *The filling may be prepared up to 4 days in advance and kept covered and chilled.*

Make the cake: In a large bowl beat the egg whites with a pinch of salt until they are frothy, add the cream of tartar, and beat the whites until they hold soft peaks. Add ½ cup of the sugar, a little at a time, beating, and

beat the whites until they hold stiff glossy peaks. In another large bowl beat the yolks with the remaining ½ cup sugar until the mixture is thick and pale, fold in the whites, and sift the flour, the cinnamon, and the allspice over the mixture. Fold the dry ingredients into the mixture and spread the batter evenly in a 15½- by 10½-inch jelly-roll pan lined with buttered foil. Rap the pan on a hard surface to eliminate any air bubbles and bake the cake in a preheated 350° F. oven for 12 to 15 minutes, or until it is colored lightly and just firm to the touch. Let the cake cool in the pan on a rack, remove it from the pan by lifting it out with the foil, and spread it with the filling. Roll up the cake, starting with a long side and removing the foil carefully, transfer it to a serving board seam side down, and trim the ends on the diagonal with a serrated knife. *At this point the cake may be chilled, covered, overnight.*

Cut strips of wax paper, arrange them at intervals diagonally across the cake, and sift the confectioners' sugar over the cake lightly. Remove the strips and with a pastry brush glaze the unsugared strips with the jam. Serve the cake with the whipped cream. Serves 6 to 8.

Tangerine Buttermilk Pound Cake

the peel from 3 tangerines, chopped
2 cups sugar
2 sticks (1 cup) unsalted butter, softened
4 large eggs at room temperature
2½ cups all-purpose flour
1 teaspoon double-acting baking powder
½ teaspoon baking soda
½ teaspoon salt
¾ cup buttermilk or substitute 3 tablespoons
    dried buttermilk powder combined with ¾
    cup water
thin wedges of tangerine for garnish if desired

In a food processor grind fine the peel, with the motor running add the sugar, and blend the mixture well. In a large bowl with an electric mixer cream the butter, add the sugar mixture, a little at a time, and beat the mixture until it is light and fluffy. Add the eggs, 1 at a time, beating well after each addition. Into a bowl sift together the flour, the baking powder, the baking soda, and the salt and add the mixture to the butter mixture alternately with the buttermilk, beginning and ending with the flour mixture and blending the batter after each addition. Divide the batter between 2 buttered and floured loaf pans, 8½ by 4½ by 2½ inches, and bake it in the middle of a preheated 350° F. oven for 50 to 60 minutes,

or until a tester comes out clean. Let the cakes cool in the pans on racks for 10 minutes, turn them out onto the racks, and let them cool completely. *The cakes keep, wrapped tightly in plastic wrap and chilled, for up to 4 days.* Serve the cakes at room temperature. Cut the cakes crosswise into ¼-inch slices, arrange the slices decoratively on a platter, and garnish the platter with the tangerine wedges if desired. Makes 2 cakes.

COOKIES

Apricot Jam Hearts

2 sticks (1 cup) unsalted butter
1 cup granulated sugar
2 teaspoons grated lemon rind
1 large egg
2¼ cups all-purpose flour
¼ teaspoon salt
a 12-ounce jar apricot jam
confectioners' sugar for decorating

In a large bowl cream the butter, add the sugar, and beat the mixture until it is light and fluffy. Add the rind and the egg and beat the mixture until it is just combined well. Into a bowl sift together the flour and the salt and add the mixture to the butter mixture, stirring until the dough is just combined. Divide the dough among 4 sheets of wax paper and chill it, wrapped in the paper, for at least 2 hours or overnight. Roll out 1 piece of the dough a little less than ¼ inch thick between sheets of wax paper and freeze it on a flat surface for 10 minutes, or until it is very firm. Remove the top sheet of wax paper carefully, with a 2¾-inch-wide heart-shaped cutter cut out hearts, and with a 1⅛-inch-wide heart-shaped cutter cut out the centers from half the hearts. Transfer the whole hearts and hollowed hearts to a baking sheet and bake them in the middle of a preheated 350° F. oven for 10 to 12 minutes, or until the edges are golden. Let the cookies cool on the baking sheet for 1 minute, transfer them with a spatula to racks, and let them cool completely. Make cookies with the scraps and the remaining dough in the same manner. *The cookies may be made up to this point 1 day in advance and kept covered and chilled.* Spread the tops of the solid hearts with a thin layer of the apricot jam and put a hollowed heart on top of each solid heart. Sift a little confectioners' sugar over the edges of the cookies and fill the hearts with the remaining apricot jam. Makes about 24 cookies.

Brandy Snaps with Strawberries

For the brandy snaps
½ stick (¼ cup) unsalted butter
¼ cup sugar
¼ cup unsulphured light molasses
1 teaspoon ground ginger
⅛ teaspoon salt
½ cup all-purpose flour
2 teaspoons brandy

1½ pints strawberries, hulled and sliced
2½ tablespoons light rum, or to taste
2½ tablespoons sugar, or to taste
whipped cream or ice cream as an
 accompaniment if desired

Make the brandy snaps: In a saucepan combine the butter, the sugar, the molasses, the ginger, and the salt and cook the mixture over moderately low heat, stirring, until the sugar is dissolved. Remove the pan from the heat and stir in the flour and the brandy. Spoon tablespoons of the batter 6 inches apart onto a buttered baking sheet and bake the brandy snaps in the middle of a preheated 325° F. oven for 12 to 15 minutes, or until they begin to darken. Let the brandy snaps stand on the baking sheet on a rack for 3 minutes, or until they are firm enough to roll. Wrap the brandy snaps around *cannoli* molds or 1-inch-thick wooden dowels, let them stand until they have hardened completely, and slide them off the molds carefully. Make brandy snaps in batches with the remaining batter in the same manner, heating the batter each time if it has thickened. *The brandy snaps may be made 1 day in advance and kept in an airtight container.*

In a bowl toss the strawberries with the rum and the sugar, fill each brandy snap with about ¼ cup of the mixture, and serve the brandy snaps with the whipped cream or ice cream if desired. Makes about 10 brandy snaps.

Carrot Macaroons

1 cup blanched almonds
½ cup sugar
3 large egg whites at room temperature
¼ pound carrots, grated coarse, preferably in a
 food processor
a pinch of cream of tartar

In a food processor pulverize the almonds with ¼ cup of the sugar. In a bowl combine the almond mixture with 1 of the egg whites and the carrots. In another bowl beat the remaining 2 egg whites with a pinch of salt until they are frothy, add the cream of tartar, and beat the whites until they hold soft peaks. Beat in the remaining ¼ cup sugar, a little at a time, and beat the whites until they hold stiff peaks. Stir one fourth of the whites into the carrot mixture and fold in the remaining whites. Drop the batter by rounded tablespoons 2 inches apart onto baking sheets lined with buttered foil and bake the macaroons in the middle of a preheated 350° F. oven for 15 minutes, or until they are golden brown. Transfer the macaroons to racks and let them cool. *The macaroons can be stored in airtight containers layered with wax paper for up to 2 days.* Makes about 24 cookies.

Chocolate Hazelnut Macaroons

1 cup hazelnuts, toasted and skinned (procedure
 on page 275) and cooled completely
¾ cup sugar
2 ounces (2 squares) unsweetened chocolate,
 melted
5 large egg whites at room temperature
¼ teaspoon salt
a pinch of cream of tartar
sliced blanched almonds for decoration

In an electric coffee or spice grinder or in a blender grind fine in small batches the hazelnuts, transferring them as they are ground to a bowl. Stir in ½ cup of the sugar, the chocolate, and 2 of the egg whites and stir the mixture until it is blended well. (The mixture will be stiff.) In a large bowl with an electric mixer beat the remaining 3 whites with the salt until they are frothy, add the cream of tartar, and beat the whites until they hold soft peaks. Beat in gradually the remaining ¼ cup sugar, a little at a time, and beat the whites until they hold stiff peaks. Stir one fourth of the whites into the nut mixture to lighten it and fold in the remaining whites gently but thoroughly. Transfer the mixture to a pastry bag fitted with a ½-inch plain tip and pipe 1-inch-wide mounds 2 inches apart onto baking sheets lined with foil shiny side down. Set an almond slice on the center of each mound and bake the macaroons in the middle of a preheated 350° F. oven for 10 minutes. Let the macaroons cool on the baking sheet and peel them from the foil. *The macaroons will keep for up to 3 days in an airtight container in dry weather.* Makes about 75 macaroons.

Coconut Almond Wafers

½ cup vegetable shortening
¾ cup sugar
1 large egg
¾ cup sifted cake flour (not self-rising)
¼ teaspoon salt
¾ cup lightly packed sweetened shredded
    coconut
¼ teaspoon almond extract
sliced unskinned almonds for topping

In a bowl with an electric mixer cream the shortening, add the sugar, and beat the mixture until it is light and fluffy. Beat in the egg, add the flour and the salt, and blend the mixture well. Stir in the coconut and the almond extract. *The dough may be prepared up to 2 days in advance and kept covered and chilled.* Spoon level teaspoons of the dough 1 inch apart onto greased baking sheets, flatten each mound slightly with a finger dipped in cold water, and press an almond slice gently into the center of each one. Bake the wafers in the middle of a preheated 375° F. oven for 7 to 8 minutes, or until the edges are golden, transfer them with a spatula to racks, and let them cool. *The coconut almond wafers may be made up to 2 days in advance and kept sealed in an airtight container in a cool, dry place.* Makes about 75 wafers.

Orange Pecan Thins

1 navel orange
½ cup pecans
1 cup sugar
1 stick (½ cup) unsalted butter, softened
1 tablespoon orange-flavored liqueur
1 large egg
1½ cups all-purpose flour
¼ teaspoon salt

With a swivel-bladed vegetable peeler remove the rind from half the orange, reserve the orange for another use, and in a food processor blend the rind with the pecans and the sugar until the rind and the pecans are chopped fine. Add the butter and blend the mixture until it is combined well. Add the liqueur and the egg and blend the mixture until it is combined well. Add the flour and the salt and combine the dough by pulsing the motor until the dough just forms a ball. On a sheet of wax paper form the dough into a 10-inch log. Chill the dough, wrapped in the wax paper, for at least 5 hours or up to 24 hours. Slice the dough into ¼-inch rounds, bake the cookies 1 inch apart on baking sheets in a preheated 350° F. oven for 10 minutes, or until the edges are golden, and let them cool on a rack. *The cookies may be stored in an airtight container for up to 4 days.* Makes about 40 cookies.

249

PIES AND PASTRIES

Chocolate Mousse Tart

For the shell
1 recipe *pâte brisée* (page 274)
dried beans or raw rice for weighting the shell
1 ounce bittersweet chocolate, melted
For the mousse
2 ounces bittersweet chocolate
2 tablespoons strong brewed coffee
2 large egg yolks
1 teaspoon vanilla
3 large egg whites at room temperature
a pinch of cream of tartar
2 tablespoons sugar
For the garnish
1 ounce bittersweet chocolate

raspberry sauce (page 240) as an
   accompaniment

Make the shell: Roll out the dough into a ⅛-inch-thick rectangle on a floured surface, fit it into a 14- by 4½-inch rectangular flan form set on a baking sheet, and crimp the edge decoratively. Prick the bottom lightly with a fork and chill the shell for 30 minutes. Line the shell with wax paper, fill the paper with the beans, pushing the beans against the sides to support the sides, and bake the shell in the lower third of a preheated 425° F. oven for 15 minutes. Remove the beans and the paper carefully and bake the shell for 3 to 5 minutes more, or until it is pale golden. Let the shell cool in the flan form on the baking sheet for 10 minutes. Remove the shell from the flan form carefully, transfer it to a rack, and let it cool completely. Slide the shell onto a platter and drizzle the melted chocolate over the bottom, spreading the chocolate with a rubber spatula gently to cover the bottom completely. Chill the shell for 15 minutes.

Make the mousse: In the top of a double boiler set over barely simmering water melt the chocolate with the coffee, stirring until the mixture is smooth. Remove the pan from the heat and whisk in the egg yolks, 1 at a time, whisking well after each addition and the vanilla. Transfer the mixture to a large bowl. In a bowl beat the egg whites with a pinch of salt until they are frothy, add the cream of tartar, and beat the whites until they hold soft peaks. Beat in the sugar and beat the mixture until it holds stiff peaks. Stir one fourth of the whites into the

chocolate mixture, fold in the remaining whites, and spoon the mousse into the shell, spreading it evenly. Chill the tart.

Prepare the garnish while the tart is chilling: In the top of a double boiler set over barely simmering water melt the chocolate and transfer it to a paper cone made from wax paper or parchment paper. (The hole at the point should be as small as possible.) Pipe the chocolate decoratively over the mousse and chill the tart for 1 hour. *The tart may be made up to 6 hours in advance and kept chilled.* Let the tart stand at room temperature for 15 minutes before serving. Serve the tart with raspberry sauce. Serves 4 to 6.

Cranberry Maple Pear Pie

3 cups (a 12-ounce bag) fresh or frozen
   cranberries, picked over
1 cup maple syrup
1 pound pears, peeled, cored, and cut into
   ¼-inch pieces
4½ teaspoons cornstarch dissolved in
   2 tablespoons cold water
flaky pie pastry (recipe follows)

In a saucepan combine the cranberries, the syrup, and the pears, bring the mixture to a boil, and simmer it, stirring occasionally, for 3 to 4 minutes, or until the cranberries have popped. Stir the cornstarch mixture, add it to the cranberry mixture, stirring, and simmer the mixture, stirring, for 1 minute, or until it is thickened. Transfer the mixture to a bowl and let it cool. *The cranberry mixture may be made up to 1 day in advance and kept covered and chilled.*

Roll out the larger ball of dough ⅛ inch thick on a lightly floured surface, fit it into a 9-inch (4-cup) pie plate, and trim the edge, leaving a ½-inch overhang.

Reserve the scraps, wrapped in plastic and chilled, and chill the shell while cutting the dough for the lattice crust. Roll out the other ball of dough ⅛ inch thick and with a fluted pastry wheel or a knife cut out ½-inch strips of the dough. Transfer the strips to a baking sheet and chill them for 10 minutes, or until they are just firm enough to work with. (If the strips get too cold they will be brittle and break.)

Cut out a template from cardboard in the shape of a maple leaf about 3 inches long and 2½ inches wide. Roll out the reserved scraps ⅛ inch thick on the lightly floured surface and freeze the dough on a small baking sheet for 5 minutes, or until it is firm. Using the template as a tracer, cut out 2 maple leaves from the dough with scissors or a sharp knife and chill them on a flat surface.

Spoon the filling into the shell, spreading it evenly, and arrange the lattice strips on top, twisting each strip corkscrew fashion. Trim the ends of the strips flush with the overhang of the shell, pressing them onto the shell, turn up the overhanging dough, and crimp the edge decoratively. Score the pastry maple leaves decoratively with a knife, arrange them on the lattice, and bake the pie in the upper third of a preheated 425° F. oven for 40 to 45 minutes, or until the pastry is golden and the filling is bubbling. Let the pie cool on a rack. *The pie may be made up to 1 day in advance and kept, covered loosely, in a cool, dry place. If making the pie 1 day in advance reheat it in a preheated 350° F. oven for 10 to 15 minutes to crisp the crust.* Serve the pie warm or at room temperature.

Flaky Pie Pastry

2¼ cups all-purpose flour
½ teaspoon salt
½ stick (¼ cup) cold unsalted butter, cut into bits
½ cup cold vegetable shortening, cut into
   pieces

In a bowl combine the flour and the salt, add the butter, and blend the mixture until it resembles coarse meal. Add the shortening and blend the mixture until it resembles meal. Add 4 tablespoons ice water, tossing the mixture with a fork, or enough to form the mixture into a soft but not sticky dough, and form the dough into a ball. If making a double-crust pie, or one with a lattice crust, divide the dough into 2 balls, one slightly larger than the other. If making 2 single-crust pies halve the dough. The dough may be rolled out immediately or *it may be kept, wrapped in wax paper and chilled, for up to 2 days.* Makes enough dough for 1 double 9-inch crust or 2 single 9-inch crusts.

Cream Puffs with Vanilla Ice Cream and Cherry Sauce
  For the puffs
  1 recipe *pâte à chou* (page 271)
  For the sauce
  ¼ cup fresh lemon juice
  five 2-inch-long strips of lemon rind
  five 2-inch-long strips of orange rind
  a 4-inch cinnamon stick
  2½ cups dry red wine
  1¼ cups sugar
  1 pound sweet cherries, stemmed and pitted

  8 small scoops (about 1 quart) of vanilla ice
    cream, arranged in a jelly-roll pan and
    frozen until hard
  whipped cream if desired
  confectioners' sugar for sifting

Make the puffs: In a large pastry bag fitted with a ¾-inch star tip (number 8) pipe the *pâte à chou* onto a buttered baking sheet, forming 8 mounds, each 3 inches in diameter, and leaving 2 to 3 inches between the puffs. Bake the puffs in the upper third of a preheated 425° F. oven for 10 minutes, reduce the heat to 400° F., and bake the puffs for 20 minutes more, or until they are puffed and golden. Pierce the side of each puff with the tip of a sharp knife and let the puffs stand in the turned-off oven with the door ajar for 30 minutes. Transfer the puffs to a rack and let them cool completely.

Make the sauce: In a heavy saucepan combine the lemon juice, the lemon rind, the orange rind, the cinnamon stick, the wine, and the sugar, bring the mixture to a boil, stirring, and simmer it for 5 minutes. Add the cherries, simmer the mixture for 15 minutes, and transfer the cherries with a slotted spoon to a bowl. Discard the lemon rind, the orange rind, and the cinnamon stick and reduce the sauce over high heat to about 1¼ cups. Pour the sauce over the cherries and let it cool.

Slice the top off each puff with a serrated knife, discard any uncooked dough in the centers, and fill each puff with a scoop of the ice cream. If desired, with a pastry bag fitted with a decorative tip pipe the whipped cream around the rim of each puff. Replace the tops of the puffs and sift the confectioners' sugar over them. Transfer the cream puffs to a platter, transfer the sauce to a serving bowl, and serve the dessert immediately. Serves 8.

Lattice-Crust Peach Pie

For the dough

3 cups all-purpose flour

¾ teaspoon salt

1 cup cold lard, cut into bits

about 1 tablespoon fresh lemon juice

For the filling

3 pounds peaches, peeled and sliced

¼ cup fresh lemon juice, or to taste

5 tablespoons all-purpose flour

¾ cup sugar

¼ teaspoon salt

a pinch of mace

2 tablespoons cold unsalted butter, cut into bits

an egg wash made by beating 1 large egg yolk
   with 1 tablespoon water

¼ cup apricot preserves

Make the dough: In a bowl combine the flour and the salt, add the lard, and blend the mixture until it resembles coarse meal. Stir in the lemon juice and ½ cup cold water, or enough to just form a dough, and knead the dough lightly to distribute the lard. Divide the dough into 2 balls, one slightly larger than the other, and chill it, wrapped in wax paper, for 30 minutes.

Make the filling: In a large bowl toss the peaches with the lemon juice. In a small bowl combine well the flour, the sugar, the salt, and the mace, add the mixture to the peaches, and toss the mixture until it is combined well.

Roll out the larger ball of dough ⅛ inch thick on a lightly floured surface, fit it into a 10-inch pie pan, and trim the edge, leaving a ½-inch overhang. Chill the shell while cutting the dough for the lattice crust. Roll out the other ball of dough ⅛ inch thick and with a knife or a fluted pastry wheel cut out ¾-inch strips of the dough. Transfer the strips to a baking sheet and chill them for 5 minutes, or until they are just firm enough to work with. (If the strips get too cold they will be brittle and break.)

Spoon the filling into the shell, mounding it slightly in the center, dot it with the butter, and arrange the lattice strips on top. Trim the ends of the strips flush with the overhang of the shell and brush some of the egg wash between the ends of the strips and the overhang, pressing the dough together. Turn the edges of the dough under, pressing them against the inside of the pan, and brush the dough with some of the remaining egg wash. Bake the pie on a baking sheet lined with foil to catch any drips in the lower third of a preheated 400° F. oven for 25 minutes, reduce the heat to 350° F., and bake the pie for 25 to 30 minutes more, or until the crust is golden brown and the juices are bubbling. Let the pie

cool on a rack for 30 minutes and brush the filling with the preserves, heated and strained. Serve the pie at room temperature.

Pecan Pumpkin Pie

½ recipe flaky pie pastry (page 251)
For the pumpkin layer
¾ cup canned pumpkin purée
2 tablespoons firmly packed light brown sugar
1 large egg, beaten lightly
2 tablespoons sour cream
⅛ teaspoon cinnamon
⅛ teaspoon freshly grated nutmeg
For the pecan layer
¾ cup light-corn syrup
½ cup firmly packed light brown sugar
3 large eggs, beaten lightly
3 tablespoons unsalted butter, melted and cooled
2 teaspoons vanilla
¼ teaspoon freshly grated lemon rind
1½ teaspoons fresh lemon juice
¼ teaspoon salt
1⅓ cups pecans

Roll out the dough ⅛ inch thick on a lightly floured surface, fit it into a 9-inch (4-cup) pie plate, and crimp the edge decoratively. Chill the shell while making the filling layers.

Make the pumpkin layer: In a small bowl whisk together the pumpkin purée, the brown sugar, the egg, the sour cream, the cinnamon, and the nutmeg until the mixture is smooth.

Make the pecan layer: In a small bowl combine well the corn syrup, the brown sugar, the eggs, the butter, the vanilla, the rind, the lemon juice, and the salt and stir in the pecans.

Spread the pumpkin mixture evenly in the chilled pie shell and spoon the pecan mixture over it carefully. Bake the pie in the upper third of a preheated 425° F. oven for 20 minutes, reduce the heat to 350° F., and bake the pie for 20 to 30 minutes more, or until the filling is puffed slightly. (The center will appear to be not quite set.) Let the pie cool on a rack. *The pie may either be made up to 4 hours in advance and kept in a cool, dry place or it may be made as much as 1 day in advance and kept covered loosely and chilled. If making the pie 1 day in advance reheat it in a preheated 350° F. oven for 10 to 15 minutes, or until the crust is crisp.* Serve the pie warm or at room temperature.

Strawberry Rhubarb Pie

For the shell
1⅓ cups all-purpose flour
½ teaspoon salt
½ cup cold lard, cut into bits
1 large egg, beaten lightly
2 teaspoons fresh lemon juice
For the filling
2 cups 1-inch fresh rhubarb pieces or a 1-pound bag frozen rhubarb, thawed and drained well
1 pint strawberries, hulled and halved
3 tablespoons cornstarch
3 tablespoons fresh lemon juice, or to taste
½ teaspoon cinnamon
a pinch of ground cloves
1 cup granulated sugar

¼ cup strawberry preserves
1 tablespoon confectioners' sugar for sprinkling
whipped cream or ice cream as an accompaniment if desired

Make the shell: In a bowl combine the flour and the salt, add the lard, and blend the mixture until it resembles coarse meal. Stir in the egg, the lemon juice, and 1½ to 2 tablespoons ice water, or enough to form a soft dough. Knead the dough lightly with the heel of the hand to combine it, form it into a ball, and chill it, wrapped in wax paper, for 30 minutes.

Make the filling: In a bowl combine the rhubarb and the strawberries. In a small bowl whisk together the cornstarch, the lemon juice, the cinnamon, and the cloves, add the mixture and the granulated sugar to the fruit, tossing the filling to combine it well, and let the filling stand for 15 minutes.

Roll out the dough ⅛ inch thick on a lightly floured surface, drape it over a 9-inch ceramic or glass pie plate, and trim the edge, leaving a 2-inch overhang. Spoon the filling into the shell and fold the overhang of the dough over the filling, ruffling it decoratively. Bake the pie in a preheated 450° F. oven for 10 minutes, reduce the heat to 350° F., and bake the pie for 35 to 40 minutes, or until the crust is golden and the filling is bubbling. Let the pie cool on a rack for at least 30 minutes, brush the filling with the preserves, heated, and sift the confectioners' sugar over the crust. Serve the pie with the whipped cream or ice cream if desired.

CUSTARDS, PUDDINGS, AND MOUSSES

Chocolate Butterscotch Pudding Parfaits

For the chocolate pudding
2 cups milk
⅓ cup unsweetened cocoa powder
⅓ cup sugar
3 tablespoons cornstarch
¼ teaspoon cinnamon
1 teaspoon vanilla
For the butterscotch pudding
2 tablespoons unsalted butter
½ cup firmly packed dark brown sugar
2 cups milk
3 tablespoons cornstarch
1 teaspoon vanilla

Make the chocolate pudding: In a heavy saucepan scald 1½ cups of the milk. In a bowl stir together the cocoa powder, the sugar, the cornstarch, the cinnamon, and a pinch of salt, add the remaining ½ cup milk, and whisk the mixture until the cocoa is dissolved. Add the scalded milk in a stream, whisking, and transfer the mixture to the pan. Bring the mixture to a boil over moderate heat, whisking, and simmer it, whisking, for 2 minutes. Remove the pan from the heat, stir in the vanilla, and transfer the pudding to a heatproof bowl. Cover the bowl immediately with plastic wrap to prevent a skin from forming and let the pudding cool, covered, stirring occasionally.

Make the butterscotch pudding: In a heavy saucepan melt the butter over moderately low heat, stir in the brown sugar, and cook the mixture, stirring, until it is bubbly. Remove the pan from the heat and stir in 1½ cups of the milk. In a small bowl dissolve the cornstarch in the remaining ½ cup milk and add the mixture in a stream to the sugar mixture, whisking. Bring the mixture to a boil over moderate heat, whisking, and simmer it, whisking, for 2 minutes. Remove the pan from the heat, stir in the vanilla and a pinch of salt, and transfer the pudding to a heatproof bowl. Cover the bowl immediately with plastic wrap to prevent a skin from forming and let the pudding cool, covered, stirring occasionally.

Stir the puddings well, spoon them in layers into 4 parfait glasses, beginning with chocolate and ending with butterscotch and a dollop of the chocolate pudding. Chill the parfaits, covered, for at least 1 hour or up to 5 hours. Serves 4.

Coconut Cream Pudding with Ginger Crumb Crust

1½ tablespoons unsalted butter
½ teaspoon ground ginger
⅓ cup crushed vanilla wafers (about 10)
2 tablespoons cornstarch
3 tablespoons sugar
1⅓ cups half-and-half
½ teaspoon vanilla
½ cup sweetened flaked coconut

In a small saucepan melt the butter over low heat and stir in the ginger and the vanilla wafers. Reserve 1 teaspoon of the crumb mixture, divide the remaining mixture between two 1-cup dessert dishes, pressing it down lightly on the bottoms of the dishes, and chill the dishes while the pudding is being made. In a heavy saucepan combine the cornstarch and the sugar, add ½ cup of the half-and-half, and whisk the mixture until the cornstarch is dissolved. Stir in the remaining half-and-half, bring the mixture to a boil over moderate heat, whisking, and simmer it, whisking, for 2 minutes. Remove the pan from the heat and stir in the vanilla and the coconut. Transfer the pudding to a metal bowl set in a bowl of ice and cold water, stir it until it is cold, and divide it between the 2 chilled dishes. Sprinkle the reserved crumb mixture over the puddings and chill the puddings for 15 minutes. Serves 2.

Kahlúa Mocha Mousse with Chocolate Leaves

2½ ounces imported bittersweet chocolate
  (available at specialty foods shops), cut into bits
1½ ounces unsweetened chocolate, cut into bits
2 tablespoons very strong coffee
2 tablespoons Kahlúa
2 large eggs at room temperature, separated
¼ cup sugar
a pinch of cream of tartar
½ cup well chilled heavy cream
chocolate leaves (recipe follows) for garnish

In the top of a double boiler set over barely simmering water melt the chocolates with the coffee and the Kahlúa, stirring occasionally. In a bowl with an electric mixer beat the egg yolks with 3 tablespoons of the sugar until the mixture is thick and pale and stir in the chocolate mixture. In another bowl beat the egg whites with a pinch of salt until they are frothy, add the cream of tartar, and beat the whites until they hold soft peaks. Beat in the remaining 1 tablespoon sugar gradually and beat the whites until they just hold stiff peaks. In a chilled bowl beat the cream until it holds soft peaks. Stir one fourth of the whites into the chocolate mixture and fold in the remaining whites and the whipped cream gently but thoroughly. Pour the mousse into a 1-quart shallow dish and chill it, covered, for at least 2 hours, or until it is set. *The mousse may be made 1 day in advance and kept covered and chilled.* Arrange some of the chocolate leaves decoratively on top of the mousse and serve the remaining leaves separately. Serves 4 to 6.

Chocolate Leaves

3 ounces imported bittersweet chocolate
    (available at specialty foods shops), cut into bits
twenty-four 2-inch lemon leaves or other
    decorative nonpoisonous leaves (available
    at florists)

In the top of a double boiler set over barely simmering water melt the chocolate. With a spoon coat the back (non-shiny) side of each leaf with the chocolate, being careful not to let the chocolate drip onto the shiny side. Put the leaves, chocolate side up, on a jelly-roll pan lined with wax paper and prop the edges of the leaves with pieces of foil or paper towel to allow the edges to curl. Chill the leaves for 20 minutes, or until the chocolate has hardened, and, working quickly, peel off the lemon leaves. (If the chocolate gets too soft chill the leaves for 5 minutes more, or until the chocolate has hardened.) Keep the chocolate leaves chilled until just before serving. Makes 24 chocolate leaves.

Mocha Meringues in Cappuccino Custard

For the meringues
2 large egg whites at room temperature
a pinch of cream of tartar
¼ cup sugar
1 teaspoon instant espresso powder
1 teaspoon Dutch-process cocoa powder
For the custard
2 large egg yolks
2 tablespoons sugar
3 tablespoons heavy cream
3 tablespoons milk
¼ cup strong brewed coffee
½ teaspoon instant espresso powder

1 ounce semisweet chocolate, grated coarse,
    for garnish

Make the meringues: In a bowl with an electric mixer or a whisk beat the egg whites with a pinch of salt until they are frothy, add the cream of tartar, and beat the whites until they hold soft peaks. Beat in the sugar, a little at a time, and beat the whites until they hold stiff peaks. Beat in the espresso powder and the cocoa powder and beat the mixture until the espresso powder is dissolved. With a ¼-cup ice-cream scoop or a small ladle dipped into warm water form the meringue into 4 balls and slip them into a saucepan of 3 inches barely simmering water. Poach the meringues for 8 minutes, flip them over, and poach them for 8 minutes more, or until they are barely firm (do not let the water come to a boil). Transfer the meringues with a slotted spoon to paper towels to drain and chill them, covered loosely, on a plate. *The meringues may be made 1 day in advance and kept covered and chilled.*

Make the custard: In a bowl with the electric mixer beat together the egg yolks and the sugar until the mixture is thick and pale. In a heavy saucepan combine the cream, the milk, the coffee, and the espresso powder and heat the liquid over moderate heat, stirring, until it is hot. Add the cream mixture to the yolk mixture in a stream, stirring, transfer the mixture to the pan, and cook it over moderately low heat, stirring with a wooden spoon, until it is thickened, but do not let it boil. Strain the custard through a fine sieve into a metal bowl set in a bowl of ice, let it cool, stirring occasionally, and chill it, covered, for at least 30 minutes or up to 2 days. Makes about ¾ cup.

Spoon some of the custard onto each of 2 chilled plates, arrange 2 meringues in the center of each plate, and garnish them with the chocolate. Serves 2.

Creamy Rice Pudding

¾ cup heavy cream
1¼ cups milk
⅓ cup long-grain rice
1 large whole egg, beaten lightly
1 large egg yolk, beaten lightly
¼ cup firmly packed dark brown sugar
¼ teaspoon vanilla

In a saucepan combine the cream and the milk and bring the liquid to a boil. Add the rice and simmer the mixture, covered, stirring occasionally, for 20 minutes, or until the rice is tender. In a bowl whisk together the whole egg, the egg yolk, and the brown sugar, add ½ cup of the rice mixture, 1 tablespoon at a time, beating, and add the egg mixture to the remaining rice mixture, stirring. Cook the pudding over moderate heat, stirring, until it is thickened, but do not let it boil, and stir in the vanilla. Serves 2.

Snow Pudding "Eggs" with Raspberry Sauce (Lemon Mousse with Raspberry Sauce)

For the mousse
2½ teaspoons unflavored gelatin
¾ cup sugar
¼ cup fresh lemon juice
1 teaspoon grated lemon rind
3 large egg whites at room temperature
a pinch of cream of tartar
For the sauce
three 10-ounce packages frozen raspberries,
    thawed and drained
1½ tablespoons sugar
3 tablespoons heavy cream

6 tablespoons toasted sliced almonds for
    garnish

Make the mousse: In a large bowl sprinkle the gelatin over ¼ cup cold water and let it soften for 10 minutes. Add 1 cup boiling water and ½ cup of the sugar and stir the mixture until the sugar is dissolved. Stir in the lemon juice and rind and chill the mixture for 1 hour, or until it just begins to set. With an electric mixer beat the mixture until it is light and frothy. In another large bowl beat the egg whites with a pinch of salt until they are frothy, add the cream of tartar, and beat the whites until they hold soft peaks. Beat in the remaining ¼ cup sugar, a little at a time, and beat the meringue until it holds stiff glossy peaks. Stir the meringue gently into the lemon

mixture and chill the mousse, covered, for 1 hour, or until it is set. *The mousse may be made 1 day in advance and kept covered and chilled.*

Make the sauce: In a food processor purée the raspberries with the sugar and the cream and force the mixture through a sieve into a bowl. *The sauce may be made 1 day in advance and kept covered and chilled.*

Divide the sauce among 6 chilled plates, with a soup spoon or an oval ice-cream scoop dipped in water spoon out the mousse in egg shapes, arranging 3 scoops on each plate, and sprinkle each dessert with 1 tablespoon of the almonds. Serves 6.

Steamed Nut Puddings

2 large egg yolks
1 tablespoon firmly packed dark brown sugar
1 tablespoon sweetened flaked coconut
2 tablespoons fine fresh bread crumbs
¼ cup pecans, toasted lightly, cooled, and
    ground fine
2 large egg whites at room temperature
¼ cup honey
1½ teaspoons fresh lemon juice
For the topping
¼ cup pecans, toasted lightly and chopped
¼ cup sweetened flaked coconut, toasted until
    golden

In a bowl with an electric mixer beat the egg yolks and the brown sugar until the mixture is thick and pale and fold in the coconut, the bread crumbs, and the pecans. In another bowl beat the egg whites until they just hold stiff peaks, stir one fourth of the whites into the yolk mixture, and fold in the remaining whites. Spoon the batter into 2 oiled ¾-cup custard cups, put the cups in a steamer set over boiling water, and steam the puddings, covered, for 5 to 7 minutes, or until a tester comes out clean. Transfer the puddings to a rack and let them cool.

In a small heavy saucepan combine the honey and the lemon juice and cook the mixture over moderately high heat, undisturbed, until the glaze is thickened slightly.

Make the topping: In a small bowl toss together the pecans and the coconut. Brush the puddings with the glaze and sprinkle them with the topping. Serves 2.

Rum Zabaglione with Strawberries and Amaretti

For the strawberries
1 pint strawberries, hulled and cut into sixths lengthwise
1 tablespoon sugar
1 tablespoon dark rum
⅓ cup crushed *amaretti* (Italian almond macaroons, available at specialty foods shops and some supermarkets)
For the zabaglione
6 large egg yolks
¼ cup sugar
⅓ cup dry white wine
¼ cup dark rum

Prepare the strawberries: In a bowl toss the strawberries with the sugar and the rum and let them macerate for 20 minutes. Divide the berries among four 12-ounce goblets and sprinkle each serving with 1 tablespoon of the *amaretti*.

Make the zabaglione: In a large heatproof bowl beat the egg yolks with an electric mixer, beat in the sugar, a little at a time, and beat the mixture until it is pale and thick. Set the bowl over a pan of simmering water and beat the mixture for 1 minute. Add the wine and the rum in a slow stream, beating constantly, and beat the mixture at high speed for 6 to 10 minutes, or until it is very light and thickened and the beater leaves a pattern in its wake. Remove the bowl from the pan and beat the mixture for 1 minute more. Spoon the zabaglione into the goblets and sprinkle each serving with some of the remaining *amaretti*. Serve the desserts immediately. Serves 4.

FROZEN DESSERTS

Ginger Granita

2 ounces fresh gingerroot, chopped (a scant ½ cup)
½ cup sugar
4 teaspoons fresh lemon juice, or to taste

In a blender or food processor grind the gingerroot, add 1 cup water, and purée the mixture. In a saucepan combine the purée, 3 cups water, and the sugar, bring the mixture to a boil, stirring until the sugar is dissolved, and simmer the syrup for 5 minutes. Strain the syrup through a fine sieve into a bowl, pressing hard on the solids, and let it cool. Stir in the lemon juice and chill the mixture, covered, for 1 to 2 hours, or until it is cold. *The mixture may be made up to this point 1 day in advance and kept covered and chilled.* Stir the mixture, transfer it to 2 metal ice cube trays without the dividers or a shallow metal bowl, and freeze it, stirring it with a fork every 20 to 30 minutes depending on the temperature of the freezer and crushing the large frozen clumps, for 2 to 3 hours, or until it is firm but not frozen hard. Scrape the granita with a fork to lighten the texture and serve it in chilled bowls. Makes about 1 quart.

Gunpowder Green Tea Granita

⅔ cup sugar
⅓ cup gunpowder green tea leaves (available at Oriental markets, specialty foods shops, and some supermarkets)
2 tablespoons fresh lemon juice, or to taste

In a saucepan combine the sugar and 3½ cups water, bring the mixture to a boil, stirring until the sugar is dissolved, and stir in the tea leaves. Remove the pan from the heat and let the tea leaves steep, covered, for 5 minutes. Strain the mixture through a fine sieve into a bowl, let it cool, and chill it, covered, for 1 to 2 hours, or until it is cold. Stir in the lemon juice, transfer the mixture to 2 metal ice cube trays without the dividers or a shallow metal bowl, and freeze it, stirring it with a fork every 20 to 30 minutes depending on the temperature of the freezer, and crushing the large frozen clumps, for 2 to 3 hours, or until it is firm but not frozen hard. Scrape the granita with a fork to lighten the texture and serve it in chilled bowls. Makes about 1 quart.

Plum Granita

1 pound red or purple plums, pitted and
   chopped
⅔ cup sugar
1 tablespoon fresh lemon juice, or to taste
½ teaspoon vanilla

In a saucepan combine the plums, the sugar, and 2½ cups water and bring the mixture to a boil, stirring until the sugar is dissolved. Simmer the mixture, covered, for 5 minutes and let it cool for 5 minutes. In a blender or food processor purée the mixture, strain the purée through a fine sieve into a bowl, pressing hard on the solids, and let it cool. Stir in the lemon juice and the vanilla and chill the mixture, covered, for 1 to 2 hours, or until it is cold. *The mixture may be made up to this point 1 day in advance and kept covered and chilled.* Stir the mixture, transfer it to 2 metal ice cube trays without the dividers or a shallow metal bowl, and freeze it, stirring it with a fork every 20 to 30 minutes depending on the temperature of the freezer, and crushing the large frozen clumps, for 2 to 3 hours, or until it is firm but not frozen hard. Scrape the granita with a fork to lighten the texture and serve it in chilled bowls. Makes about 1 quart.

Sour Cherry Granita

½ cup dry white wine
¼ cup honey
¼ cup sugar
1 pound fresh sour cherries, pitted, or a
   1-pound can sour cherries packed in water,
   reserving the liquid

In a saucepan combine 1 cup water, the wine, the honey, and the sugar and bring the mixture to a boil,
stirring until the sugar is dissolved. Simmer the syrup for 4 minutes and let it cool. In a blender or food processor purée the fresh cherries with ½ cup water or the canned cherries with the reserved liquid and force the purée through a fine sieve into a bowl. Stir in the syrup and chill the mixture, covered, for 1 to 2 hours, or until it is cold. *The mixture may be made up to this point 1 day in advance and kept covered and chilled.* Stir the mixture, transfer it to 2 metal ice cube trays without the dividers or a shallow metal bowl, and freeze it, stirring it with a fork every 20 to 30 minutes depending on the temperature of the freezer, and crushing the large frozen clumps, for 2 to 3 hours, or until it is firm but not frozen hard. Scrape the granita with a fork to lighten the texture and serve it in chilled bowls. Makes about 1 quart.

Ice Cream in Chocolate Cups with Caramel Cages

4 ounces semisweet chocolate, broken into bits
1 cup sugar
a pinch of cream of tartar
½ pint vanilla ice cream
Strawberries for garnish if desired

Melt the chocolate in a double boiler set over barely simmering water and with a small spoon spread it evenly on the inside bottom and sides of 2 double layers of fluted cupcake papers, spreading the papers open so that the sides are slanting outward. Put the chocolate cups in small bowls and chill them for 30 minutes. Peel the papers carefully from the chocolate and chill the chocolate cups until they are needed. *The cups may be made 1 day in advance and kept chilled.*

Cover the outsides of two 6-ounce ladles with foil, smooth down the foil completely, and oil it lightly. (One ladle will suffice if you work quickly.) In a heavy

saucepan combine the sugar with ½ cup water and the cream of tartar and cook the mixture, covered, over moderately low heat, swirling the pan occasionally, until the sugar is dissolved. Remove the lid and cook the syrup over moderately high heat until it begins to turn pale golden, about 340° F. on a candy thermometer. (The syrup will get much darker as it sits.) Remove the pan from the heat, prop it up on one side so that the syrup accumulates on the other, and let the syrup sit for 8 minutes. Dip a small spoon into the caramel, hold the ladle inverted over the pan, and drizzle the caramel over it, working quickly, to form a web. Prop up the ladle, allowing the caramel to cool completely, and repeat the procedure with the second ladle. Pry the foil-lined cages gently from the ladles, trim with scissors any stray caramel strands, and peel off the foil carefully. (If using only 1 ladle, let the first application of caramel cool for 3 minutes, pry it with the foil from the ladle, and let it stand to finish cooling, setting it down carefully to maintain its round shape.) *The caramel cages may be made 4 hours in advance and kept in a cool, dry place.*

Fill each chocolate cup with a scoop of the ice cream and set a caramel cage over each scoop. Arrange the desserts on a serving tray and garnish them with the strawberries if desired. To break the cages tap them with the back of a spoon. Serves 2.

Fruitcake Parfaits

2 cups finely chopped fruitcake
3 tablespoons dark rum, or to taste
1 quart vanilla ice cream, softened slightly
½ cup well chilled heavy cream
slices of red and green candied fruit if desired
   for garnish

In a bowl toss the fruitcake with the rum and let it stand for 10 minutes. In each of six 6-ounce parfait glasses make layers of the ice cream and the fruitcake mixture, beginning with a layer of ice cream and ending with a layer of fruitcake, and freeze the filled parfait glasses, covered loosely, for at least 30 minutes or up to 24 hours. *If freezing for longer than 2 hours, let the parfaits stand at room temperature for 5 to 10 minutes to soften slightly before serving.* Just before serving, in a chilled bowl beat the cream until it just holds stiff peaks, transfer it to a pastry bag fitted with a decorative tip, and pipe it decoratively onto the parfaits, covering the tops. Garnish the parfaits with the candied fruit if desired. Serves 6.

Frozen Strawberry Cream Parfaits

a 10-ounce package frozen sliced strawberries
   in syrup, unthawed
¼ cup heavy cream
5 pecan shortbread cookies, ground coarse
   (about ½ cup)
2 tablespoons finely chopped pecans, toasted
   lightly, if desired

Working quickly cut the block of frozen strawberries into 1½-inch pieces. In a food processor purée the strawberry pieces, with the motor running add the cream, and blend the mixture just until it is smooth. Spoon one fourth of the strawberry cream into each of two 1-cup goblets, sprinkle each layer with ¼ cup of the shortbread crumbs, and top the crumbs with another layer of the strawberry cream. Sprinkle the parfaits with the pecans if desired and serve them immediately. Serves 2.

Lemon Sherbet with Starfruit

1¾ cups sugar
the rind of 3 lemons, removed with a
   vegetable peeler
1 cup strained fresh lemon juice
1 large egg white
slices of starfruit (carambola, available at
   specialty produce markets and some
   supermarkets)
mint sprigs for garnish if desired

In a saucepan combine the sugar, the lemon rind, and 2 cups water, bring the mixture to a boil, stirring until the sugar is dissolved, and simmer the syrup for 5 minutes. Let the syrup cool, strain it through a sieve into a bowl, and stir in the lemon juice. Chill the syrup, covered, for 2 hours, or until it is cold. *The syrup may be made 1 day in advance and kept covered and chilled.* Freeze the syrup in an ice-cream freezer according to the manufacturer's instructions until it is almost frozen but still mushy. In a bowl beat the egg white until it holds soft peaks, add it to the sherbet, and continue to freeze the sherbet in the ice-cream freezer until it is frozen. Remove the dasher and continue to freeze the sherbet, covered, until it is firm. *The sherbet may be made up to this point 3 days in advance and kept covered tightly and frozen.* Serve scoops of the sherbet with the starfruit slices on dessert dishes and garnish each serving with a mint sprig if desired. Makes about 1 quart, serving 8.

Apple Rosemary Sorbet

1 cup sugar
4 cups apple juice
1 tablespoon dried rosemary
⅓ cup fresh lemon juice
For the garnish
8 small fresh rosemary sprigs
1 small red apple
1 small Granny Smith apple

In a saucepan combine the sugar, the apple juice, the dried rosemary, and the lemon juice, bring the mixture to a boil, stirring until the sugar is dissolved, and let it steep off the heat for 15 minutes. Strain the mixture through a very fine sieve lined with a double thickness of rinsed and squeezed cheesecloth into a metal bowl, set the bowl in a larger bowl of ice and cold water, and stir the mixture until it is cold. Freeze the mixture in an ice-cream freezer according to the manufacturer's instructions until it is firm enough to scoop. *The sorbet may be made 1 day in advance and kept frozen.* Serve the sorbet garnished with the rosemary sprigs and thin slices of the apples. Makes about 1 quart.

Cold Raspberry Soufflé with Hazelnut Praline

flavorless vegetable oil for oiling the collar
four 10-ounce packages frozen raspberries in syrup, thawed and drained, reserving the syrup
3 envelopes unflavored gelatin
12 large eggs, separated and the whites at room temperature
½ teaspoon salt
¾ teaspoon cream of tartar
½ cup sugar
3 cups well chilled heavy cream
3 cups hazelnut praline (recipe follows)
whipped cream and fresh raspberries for garnish
Frangelico chocolate sauce (page 239) as an accompaniment

Fit each of two 1¼-quart soufflé dishes with a 6-inch-wide band of wax paper, doubled and brushed with the oil, to form a collar extending 3 inches above the rim. In a food processor or blender purée the raspberries with 1 cup of the reserved syrup and force the purée through a fine sieve into a bowl. In a small saucepan sprinkle the gelatin over 1 cup of the remaining syrup and let it soften for 10 minutes.

In a heatproof bowl beat the egg yolks with a portable electric mixer until they are pale and thick and beat in the remaining raspberry syrup and 1 cup of the raspberry purée. Set the bowl over a pan of simmering water and beat the mixture for 5 to 7 minutes, or until it is thickened. Remove the bowl from the pan and beat the mixture for 1 minute. Heat the gelatin mixture over moderately low heat, stirring, until the gelatin is melted and beat the mixture into the yolk mixture with the remaining raspberry purée. Set the bowl in a larger bowl of ice and cold water and let the mixture cool, stirring often, until it is cooled completely and is the consistency of raw egg white.

In a large bowl with an electric mixer beat the egg whites with the salt until they are frothy, beat in the cream of tartar and the sugar, a little at a time, and beat the whites until they hold soft peaks. In a chilled large bowl with chilled beaters beat the cream until it holds soft peaks. Transfer the raspberry mixture to a large bowl, stir one fourth of the whites into it, and fold in the remaining whites with 2 cups of the praline. Fold in the cream gently but thoroughly, spoon the mousse into the soufflé dishes, smoothing the tops, and chill the soufflés, covered, for at least 3 hours, or until they are set. *The soufflés may be made up to this point 1 day in advance and kept covered and chilled.* Just before serving remove the collars carefully, garnish the outer edges of the soufflés with some of the remaining praline, and garnish the tops with the whipped cream and the raspberries. Serve the soufflés with the sauce. Serves 20.

Hazelnut Praline

2 cups sugar
1½ cups hazelnuts, toasted and skinned (procedure on page 275)

In a heavy saucepan combine the sugar and ⅓ cup water, bring the mixture to a boil over moderate heat, stirring and washing down any sugar crystals clinging to the sides with a brush dipped in cold water until the sugar is dissolved, and boil the syrup, swirling the pan, until it turns a light caramel. Stir in the hazelnuts, return the syrup to a boil, and boil it until it is a slightly darker caramel. Pour the praline immediately onto a well oiled marble slab or baking sheet and let it cool completely. Break the praline into pieces and in a food processor or blender grind it fine in batches. The praline keeps, covered and chilled, in a glass jar indefinitely. Makes about 3 cups.

FRUIT FINALES

Almond Crisps with Apple Filling

3½ tablespoons softened unsalted butter
6 tablespoons granulated sugar
¼ teaspoon vanilla
1 tablespoon lightly beaten egg
½ cup all-purpose flour
¼ cup plus 1 tablespoon finely chopped
    blanched almonds
1 McIntosh apple (about 5 ounces)
1 tablespoon fresh lemon juice, or to taste
For the glaze
2 tablespoons confectioners' sugar
1 teaspoon fresh lemon juice

In a bowl with an electric mixer cream the butter, beat in ¼ cup of the granulated sugar, and beat the mixture until it is light and fluffy. Beat in the vanilla and the egg until the mixture is just combined. Into a bowl sift together the flour and a pinch of salt and stir in ¼ cup of the almonds. Stir the flour mixture into the butter mixture, a little at a time, until the dough is just combined and roll out the dough ⅛ inch thick between sheets of wax paper. Peel off the top sheet of paper carefully and cut out 4 rounds 1 inch apart with a floured 3-inch cutter. Invert the dough onto a buttered baking sheet, peel away the wax paper carefully, and remove the excess dough from the baking sheet. Bake the rounds in the middle of a preheated 350° F. oven for 10 to 12 minutes, or until the edges are golden, transfer them to a rack, and let them cool. (The excess dough can be rolled out once more, cut into rounds, and baked in the same manner and reserved for another use.)

While the rounds are baking, in a small saucepan bring the remaining 2 tablespoons granulated sugar and ½ cup water to a boil. Add the apple, peeled and

chopped fine, and the 1 tablespoon lemon juice and cook the mixture for 6 to 8 minutes, or until the apple is softened and the mixture is thickened. Add the remaining 1 teaspoon almonds, toasted lightly, and let the mixture cool for 2 minutes. Spread the apple filling on 2 of the rounds and top them with the remaining 2 rounds.

Make the glaze: In a small bowl combine the confectioners' sugar with the 1 teaspoon lemon juice, stir the mixture until it is smooth, and brush the glaze on the crisps. Serves 2.

Cinnamon Apple Rings

4 Granny Smith apples, peeled, cored whole,
    and cut into ¼-inch rings
2 teaspoons cinnamon
a pinch of freshly grated nutmeg, or to taste
½ cup confectioners' sugar
3 tablespoons cold unsalted butter, cut into bits
vanilla ice cream as an accompaniment

Arrange the apple rings in one layer in a buttered jelly-roll pan. In a small bowl combine the cinnamon, the nutmeg, and the sugar, sift the mixture over the apples, and dot the apples with the butter. Broil the apples under a preheated broiler about 2 inches from the heat for 3 to 5 minutes, or until they are tender and caramelized. Transfer the apple rings with a metal spatula to dessert plates, drizzle them with the pan juices, and serve them with the ice cream. Serves 4.

Apricot Clafouti

½ cup plus 1 tablespoon milk
1 large egg
1½ tablespoons Cognac or other brandy
3 tablespoons granulated sugar
3½ tablespoons all-purpose flour
½ pound fresh apricots, sliced ¼ inch thick
sifted confectioners' sugar for dusting

In a blender blend the milk, the egg, the Cognac, and the granulated sugar until the mixture is combined, add the flour, and blend the mixture until it is just smooth. Arrange the apricot slices in a buttered 3-cup shallow baking dish, pour the milk mixture over them, and bake the mixture in a preheated 350° F. oven for 30 to 35 minutes, or until the *clafouti* is golden and puffed. Let the *clafouti* cool for 5 minutes, dust it with the confectioners' sugar, and serve it warm. Serves 2.

Cantaloupe Melon Molds

1½ cups cubed cantaloupe
1 tablespoon fresh lemon juice, or to taste
1 tablespoon sugar
1 package unflavored gelatin
4 decoratively cut slices of cantaloupe and 4
   mint sprigs for garnish

In a food processor or blender purée the cubed cantaloupe with the lemon juice and the sugar until it is very smooth and force the purée through a fine sieve into a bowl. In a small bowl sprinkle the gelatin over 2 tablespoons cold water and let it soften for 5 minutes. Stir in 2 tablespoons boiling water and stir the mixture until the gelatin is dissolved completely. Stir the gelatin mixture into the cantaloupe purée, combining the mixture well, and divide the mixture among four ¼-cup melon molds or other decorative molds that have been rinsed with cold water but not dried. Arrange the molds in a cake pan filled with ice and ½ inch cold water and chill them for 45 to 50 minutes, or until they are set. Hold the molds briefly under warm water, run a thin knife around the edge of the molds, and invert the molds onto chilled plates. Any molds that are not served immediately may be kept, covered and chilled, overnight. Garnish the molds with the cantaloupe slices and the mint sprigs.

Fresh Fruit with Raspberry Sauce

a 10-ounce package frozen raspberries,
   thawed, including the juice
1 tablespoon fresh lemon juice, or to taste
6 cups bite-size pieces seasonal fresh fruit

In a blender blend the raspberries including the juice with the lemon juice until the sauce is smooth. Divide the fruit among bowls and serve it with the sauce, strained if desired. Serves 6.

Pink Grapefruit and Orange Sections

1 pink grapefruit
1 large navel orange
about 2 tablespoons fresh orange juice
1 tablespoon honey

With a long serrated knife cut away the peel, including the pith, from the grapefruit and the orange and working over a bowl cut the sections free from the membranes, squeezing any remaining juice from the membranes and reserving the juice. Divide the sections among 2 bowls. Measure the reserved juice, adding enough additional orange juice, if necessary, to measure a total of ¼ cup, blend in the honey, and drizzle the mixture over the fruit. Serves 2.

Rum-Marinated Mango Crêpes

2 ripe mangoes, peeled and cut into ¾-inch
   pieces
2 tablespoons fresh lemon juice
1 tablespoon granulated sugar
⅓ cup dark rum
12 crêpes (recipe follows)
1 tablespoon melted unsalted butter
confectioners' sugar for dusting

In a bowl toss together the mangoes, the lemon juice, the granulated sugar, and the rum. Fold the crêpes into quarters and put them on a baking sheet. Brush the tops of the crêpes with the butter and bake the crêpes in a preheated 400° F. oven for 10 minutes, or until they are browned lightly and slightly crisp.
   Stuff each crêpe with about ¼ cup of the mango mixture, transfer the crêpes to a platter, and dust them with the confectioners' sugar. Serves 6.

Crêpes

½ cup all-purpose flour
¼ cup milk
2 large eggs
1½ tablespoons unsalted butter, melted and
   cooled
½ teaspoon sugar
vegetable oil or clarified butter (procedure on
   page 278) for cooking the crêpes

In a food processor or blender blend the flour, ½ cup water, the milk, the eggs, the butter, the sugar, and a pinch of salt for 5 seconds. Turn off the motor and with a rubber spatula scrape down the sides of the container.

Blend the batter for 20 seconds more, transfer it to a bowl, and let it stand, covered with plastic wrap, for 1 hour.

Heat a 6- to 7-inch crêpe pan or non-stick pan over moderately high heat until it is hot. Brush the pan lightly with the oil, heat the oil until it is hot but not smoking, and remove the pan from the heat. Stir the batter, half-fill a ¼-cup measure with it, and off the heat pour the batter into the pan. Tilt and rotate the pan quickly to cover the bottom with a thin layer of the batter and return any excess batter to the bowl. Return the pan to the heat, loosen the edge of the crêpe with a metal spatula, and cook the crêpe until the underside is browned lightly. Turn the crêpe, brown the other side, and transfer the crêpe to a plate or kitchen towel. Make crêpes with the remaining batter in the same manner, brushing the pan lightly with oil as necessary.

The crêpes may be prepared in advance, stacked, wrapped in plastic wrap, and refrigerated or frozen for up to 3 days. Makes about 12 crêpes.

Oranges in Caramel Syrup

4 navel oranges, peel and pith discarded,
    sliced crosswise
2 teaspoons grated orange rind
⅔ cup sugar
2 tablespoons orange-flavored liqueur

Arrange the orange slices in a shallow serving dish and sprinkle them with the rind. In a small heavy saucepan combine the sugar and 3 tablespoons water, cook the mixture over moderate heat, stirring and washing down the sides of the pan with a brush dipped in cold water, until the sugar is dissolved, and boil it, undisturbed, until it is a golden caramel. Put the pan in the sink and add very carefully 2 tablespoons water and the liqueur. (The syrup will spatter slightly.) Cook the syrup over moderate heat, stirring, until the caramel is dissolved and drizzle it over the oranges. Serve the oranges at room temperature or chilled. Serves 4.

Sliced Oranges with Almond Custard Sauce

6 navel oranges, chilled
2 cups almond custard sauce (recipe follows),
    chilled
¼ cup sliced blanched almonds, toasted lightly

With a serrated knife cut the rind and pith from the oranges and cut the oranges crosswise into ¼-inch

slices. Cover the bottom of a large rimmed platter with some of the sauce, arrange the oranges on the sauce, and sprinkle them with the almonds. Serve the remaining sauce separately. Serves 6.

Almond Custard Sauce

2 large whole eggs
2 large egg yolks
3 tablespoons sugar
1½ cups milk
2 tablespoons almond-flavored liqueur

In a heatproof bowl whisk together well the whole eggs, the egg yolks, and the sugar. Add the milk, scalded, in a slow stream, whisking constantly, transfer the mixture to a heavy saucepan, and cook it over moderately low heat, stirring constantly with a wooden spoon, until it is thickened slightly (175° F. to 180° F. on a candy thermometer), being careful not to let it boil. Remove the pan from the heat and stir in the liqueur. Strain the sauce through a fine sieve into a metal bowl set in a larger bowl of ice and cold water, let it cool, stirring occasionally, and chill it, covered, for 1 hour. *The sauce keeps, covered and chilled, for up to 2 days.* Makes about 2 cups.

Spiced Plum Compote

1¼ pounds plums, halved and pitted
½ cup sugar
1 vanilla bean
a 3½-inch cinnamon stick
five ½-inch-wide strips of orange rind
¼ cup dried currants
1 tablespoon apricot brandy
¼ cup heavy cream as an accompaniment

In a saucepan combine the plums, the sugar, 1 cup water, the vanilla bean, the cinnamon stick, the orange rind, and the currants, bring the liquid to a boil, stirring until the sugar is dissolved, and simmer the mixture, stirring occasionally, for 10 to 15 minutes, or unil the plums are tender. Transfer the plums with a slotted spoon to a bowl, add the brandy to the syrup mixture, and boil the mixture until it is reduced to about ⅔ cup. Pour the syrup mixture over the plums, removing the vanilla bean, the cinnamon stick, and the orange rind, and serve the compote warm or chilled drizzled with the cream. Serves 2.

Brandied Pear Crisp

1½ cups old-fashioned rolled oats
¼ cup all-purpose flour
1 cup firmly packed dark brown sugar
1 teaspoon cinnamon
½ teaspoon ground ginger
¼ teaspoon freshly grated nutmeg
¼ teaspoon salt
1 stick (½ cup) cold unsalted butter, cut into bits
¼ cup brandy
2 pounds firm-ripe pears, peeled, cored, and
   sliced thin
1 tablespoon fresh lemon juice
2 tablespoons granulated sugar
vanilla ice cream as an accompaniment if
   desired

In a bowl blend together the oats, the flour, the brown sugar, the cinnamon, the ginger, the nutmeg, the salt, the butter, and 2 tablespoons of the brandy. In another bowl toss the pears with the remaining 2 tablespoons brandy, the lemon juice, and the granulated sugar and turn the mixture into a well buttered shallow 14- by 12-inch gratin dish. Spread the oat mixture evenly over the pears and bake the crisp in a preheated 350° F. oven for 45 minutes, or until the pears are tender and the topping is crisp. Serve the dessert with the ice cream if desired. Serves 6.

Ginger Poached Pears

½ cup sugar
2 tablespoons honey
a 2-inch piece of gingerroot, peeled and cut
   into about 30 paper-thin slices with a
   vegetable peeler
3 cups dry white wine
4 firm ripe pears, peeled and cored, keeping
   the pears whole
1 pint vanilla ice cream
¼ cup chopped candied ginger

In a saucepan combine the sugar, the honey, the gingerroot, the wine, and 2 cups water, bring the mixture to a boil, stirring, and simmer the syrup, covered, for 15 minutes. Add the pears stem end up, poach them, covered with a buttered round of wax paper and the lid, over moderately low heat for 15 minutes, or until they are

tender, and transfer them to a bowl. Boil the syrup until it is reduced by half and strain it over the pears. Divide the ice cream among 4 chilled bowls, top each mound with 1 pear, halved lengthwise, and some of the hot syrup, and garnish each serving with 1 tablespoon of the candied ginger. Serves 4.

Sautéed Pears with Walnuts

6 firm Anjou pears, peeled and sliced
½ stick (¼ cup) unsalted butter
¼ cup fresh lemon juice
¼ cup sugar, or to taste
1 cup chopped walnuts
⅓ cup dark rum, or to taste
whipped cream

In a large skillet sauté half the pears in 2 tablespoons of the butter over high heat, shaking the skillet, for 3 to 5 minutes, or until they are just tender, and transfer them to a platter. Sauté the remaining pears in the remaining 2 tablespoons butter in the same manner and transfer them to the platter. Add to the skillet the lemon juice, the sugar, the walnuts, and the rum and cook the mixure over moderately high heat, swirling the skillet, until it is reduced to a thick glaze. Drizzle the glaze over the pears and serve the pears with the whipped cream. Serves 6.

Poached Pineapple and Banana with Rum Chantilly

½ cup granulated sugar
¼ teaspoon vanilla
1 cup fresh pineapple chunks
1 large banana
⅓ cup well chilled heavy cream
1 teaspoon confectioners' sugar
½ teaspoon dark rum, or to taste

In a saucepan combine the granulated sugar, the vanilla, and 1½ cups water, bring the mixture to a boil, and simmer the syrup, covered, for 5 minutes. Add the pineapple and simmer it, stirring occasionally, for 6 minutes. Cut the banana crosswise into ½-inch slices, add it to the syrup, and simmer the mixture for 1 minute, or until the banana is just tender. Transfer the fruit with a slotted spoon to a metal bowl set in a bowl of ice and cold water, stir it carefully until it is cool, and divide it between 2 serving dishes. Bring the syrup to a boil and boil it until it is reduced to about ½ cup. Transfer the syrup to the metal bowl set in the bowl of ice and cold water, stir it until it is cool, and pour the desired amount over the fruit. In a bowl with an electric mixer beat the cream until it holds soft peaks, add the confectioners' sugar and the rum, and beat the cream until it just holds stiff peaks. Spoon the whipped cream over the fruit and serve the desserts immediately. Serves 2.

BEVERAGES

ALCOHOLIC BEVERAGES

Chambord Spritzer

1 ounce (1 pony) Chambord (black raspberry-
    flavored liqueur)
1½ ounces (1 jigger) white wine
1 tablespoon fresh lemon juice
chilled seltzer or club soda
a twist of lemon peel for garnish

In a tall glass combine the Chambord, the wine, the
lemon juice, and 4 ice cubes. Fill the glass with the seltzer, stir the drink, and garnish it with the peel. Makes 1
drink.

Mandarin Champagne

2 teaspoons Mandarin Napoleon liqueur
about ¾ cup chilled Champagne
1 bottled mandarin orange section for garnish

Into a 6-ounce stemmed glass pour the liqueur, fill
the glass with the Champagne, and garnish the drink
with the orange section. Makes 1 drink.

Mimosas
(Champagne and Orange Juice)

3 cups chilled strained fresh orange juice
1 bottle chilled Champagne

Into a large pitcher pour the orange juice, add the
Champagne, and stir the mixture gently. Serves 6.

Double Orange Spritzer

1½ ounces (1 jigger) Cointreau
3 ounces (2 jiggers) strained fresh orange juice
1 tablespoon strained fresh lemon juice
chilled seltzer or club soda
1 orange slice for garnish

In a tall glass combine the Cointreau, the orange and
lemon juices, and 4 ice cubes. Fill the glass with the
seltzer, stir the drink, and garnish it with the orange
slice. Makes 1 drink.

Margarita Spritzer

1½ ounces (1 jigger) tequila
1 ounce (1 pony) fresh lime juice
1 ounce (1 pony) triple sec
chilled seltzer or club soda
1 lime slice for garnish

In a tall glass combine the tequila, the lime juice, the
triple sec, and 4 ice cubes. Fill the glass with the seltzer,
stir the drink, and garnish it with the lime slice. Makes 1
drink.

Pineapple Daiquiris

1 pineapple, peeled, cored, and sliced (about
   2 cups), reserving 6 thin slices for garnish
9 ounces (6 jiggers) light rum
¼ cup sugar
6 small fresh mint sprigs for garnish

In a blender in 2 batches blend half the pineapple, half
the rum, half the sugar, and about 2 cups ice cubes per
batch for 1 minute, or until the mixture is smooth, divide the mixture among chilled stemmed glasses, and
garnish each glass with a reserved pineapple slice and a
mint sprig. Makes 6 drinks.

Pineapple Rum Spritzer

1½ ounces (1 jigger) white rum
3 ounces (2 jiggers) unsweetened pineapple
   juice
1 tablespoon fresh lime juice
chilled seltzer or club soda
1 lime slice for garnish

In a tall glass combine the rum, the pineapple and
lime juices, and 4 ice cubes. Fill the glass with the seltzer, stir the drink, and garnish it with the lime slice.
Makes 1 drink.

Pink Gin Spritzer

1½ ounces (1 jigger) gin
3 ounces (2 jiggers) cranberry juice
1 teaspoon grenadine
chilled seltzer or club soda
1 orange slice for garnish

In a tall glass combine the gin, the cranberry juice,
the grenadine, and 4 ice cubes. Fill the glass with the
seltzer, stir the drink, and garnish it with the orange
slice. Makes 1 drink.

Watermelon Screwdrivers

3 pounds watermelon, rind and seeds
   discarded, cut into chunks
2 tablespoons fresh lemon juice
4 jiggers (¾ cup) of vodka
4 cups fresh orange juice, strained
4 mint sprigs for garnish

In a food processor or blender purée the watermelon
with the lemon juice in batches, transfer the mixture to
ice cube trays with the dividers in, and freeze it. Divide
the watermelon cubes among 4 glasses and into each
glass pour 1 jigger of the vodka and 1 cup of the orange
juice. Stir the drinks and garnish each one with a mint
sprig. Makes 4 drinks.

Wild Turkey Spritzer

1½ ounces (1 jigger) Wild Turkey
1½ ounces (1 jigger) strained fresh orange
   juice
1½ ounces (1 jigger) strained fresh lime juice
1 tablespoon sugar syrup (page 279)
chilled seltzer or club soda
1 orange slice for garnish

In a tall glass combine the Wild Turkey, the orange
and lime juices, the sugar syrup, and 4 ice cubes. Fill the
glass with the seltzer, stir the drink, and garnish it with
the orange slice. Makes 1 drink.

NONALCOHOLIC BEVERAGES

Lemonade

2¼ cups strained fresh lemon juice
1½ to 2 cups sugar
For the garnish
2 lemons, cut into paper-thin slices
mint sprigs
whole strawberries, hulled

In a pitcher combine the lemon juice, 1½ cups of the
sugar, and 5 cups cold water, stir the mixture until the
sugar is dissolved, and add more sugar if desired. *The
lemonade may be made up to 1 day in advance and kept
covered and chilled.* To serve stir in about 2 cups ice
cubes and garnish the lemonade with the lemon slices,
the mint sprigs, and the whole hulled strawberries.
Makes about 8 cups.

Limeade

2 cups strained fresh lime juice
¾ to 1 cup sugar
For the garnish
2 limes, cut into paper-thin slices
mint sprigs
whole strawberries, hulled

In a pitcher combine the lime juice, ¾ cup of the sugar, and 5 cups cold water, stir the mixture until the sugar is dissolved, and add more sugar if desired. *The limeade may be made up to 1 day in advance and kept covered and chilled.* To serve stir in about 2 cups ice cubes and garnish the limeade with the lime slices, the mint sprigs, and the whole hulled strawberries. Makes about 8 cups.

Rich Hot Chocolate

¼ cup unsweetened cocoa powder
¼ cup firmly packed dark brown sugar
2 cups milk
1 teaspoon vanilla

In a heavy saucepan combine the cocoa, the brown sugar, a pinch of salt, and ¼ cup cold water and heat the mixture over low heat, whisking, until the cocoa is dissolved and the mixture is a paste. Add gradually the milk, scalded, whisking constantly, and heat the mixture over moderately low heat, whisking, until it is hot, but do not let it boil. Stir in the vanilla and pour the hot chocolate into a heated coffee pot or 2 very large coffee cups. Serves 2.

A GOURMET ADDENDUM: PROVISIONS AND PROVISOS

The Gourmet Addendum is a variation on the Gourmet's Pantry column in the magazine, which contains basic recipes—for stocks, sauces, and the like—called for in each issue. Similarly, the following basic recipes are called for in other recipes in this book. Then, as a bonus, we have used these basic recipes to create a surprising variety of brand-new recipes, some savory, some sweet. For example, once you have made a basic *pâte à chou*, we've suggested a number of ways to use it: for hors d'oeuvre puffs to serve with cocktails; mixed into mashed potatoes for a superb vegetable accompaniment; or for a cream puff dessert. Five other master, basic, recipes are included, all with their own variations.

The provisions for these combinations are easily available; we have limited the master recipes in this chapter to those employing very basic ingredients—butter, flour, eggs, sugar. Nut preparations are perhaps an exception to this, but we assume most good cooks are also bakers, and are aware of the delights to be derived from prepared pistachios and hazelnuts stashed in the freezer.

The provisos are equally simple: Provided you make the master recipe, it is easy to enjoy the variations.

PÂTE À CHOU

Pâte à chou, cream puff pastry, is made from a simple dough of water, butter, flour, and eggs. You can use the basic dough to make elegant miniature cocktail puffs.

With the addition of a little sugar, you can prepare cream puffs (or éclairs, or profiteroles) for dessert. And when you have leftover mashed potatoes on hand, you can whip up a classic French potato combination, *pommes Dauphine*. These delightful variations follow the basic master recipe.

Pâte à Chou

1 stick (½ cup) unsalted butter, cut into pieces
¼ teaspoon salt
1 cup all-purpose flour
3 to 5 large eggs

In heavy saucepan bring to a boil 1 cup water with the butter and the salt over high heat. Reduce the heat to moderate, add the flour all at once, and beat the mixture with a wooden paddle until it leaves the sides of the pan and forms a ball. Transfer the mixture to a bowl and with an electric mixer at high speed beat in 3 of the eggs, 1 at a time, beating well after each addition. The batter should be stiff enough to just hold soft peaks. If it is too stiff break 1 or 2 more of the eggs into a bowl, beat the egg lightly, and add enough of it to the batter to thin it to the proper consistency.

To store, rub the surface of the warm *pâte à chou* with butter, let the dough cool, and chill it, wrapped in plastic wrap, for up to 3 days. To use, warm the dough over very low heat, stirring constantly, until it is tepid. Makes 2½ cups.

Miniature Hors d'Oeuvre Puffs

1 cup *pâte à chou,* warmed to tepid
a pinch of cayenne
an egg wash made by beating together 1 large
    egg with 1 teaspoon water and a pinch of
    salt
smoked gouda and ham filling, black olive
    filling, or smoked salmon and dill filling
    (all recipes follow)

In a bowl combine the *pâte à chou* with the cayenne, transfer it to a pastry bag fitted with a ¼-inch tip, and pipe it onto a buttered and floured baking sheet, forming mounds, each 1-inch in diameter, and leaving 1½ to 2 inches between the puffs. Brush the puffs with the egg wash, pressing down lightly with the pastry brush to make uniformly sized puffs, and bake them in the upper third of a preheated 425° F. oven for 10 minutes. Reduce the heat to 400° F. and bake the puffs for 6 to 8 minutes more, or until they are puffed and golden. Pierce the side of each puff with the tip of a small sharp knife and let the puffs stand in the turned-off oven with the door ajar for 30 minutes. Transfer the puffs to a rack, let them cool completely, and fill them with a suggested filling. *Unfilled puffs may be frozen, stored in plastic bags, and reheated in a 400° F. oven for 7 to 10 minutes, or until heated through before filling.* Makes about 25 to 28 puffs.

Smoked Gouda and Ham Filling

1 recipe (25 to 28) miniature hors d'oeuvre
    puffs
¼ pound smoked Gouda or similar cheese
6 tablespoons heavy cream
3 tablespoons softened unsalted butter
3 tablespoons minced Westphalian ham,
    prosciutto, or similar ham
1 teaspoon Dijon-style mustard
½ teaspoon drained bottled horseradish,
    or to taste

In a food processor purée the cheese, add the heavy cream and butter, and purée the mixture until it is smooth. Add the ham, the mustard, the horseradish, and salt and pepper to taste and process the mixture until it is just combined. Transfer the filling to a pastry bag fitted with a ¼-inch tip and pipe it into the puffs. Serve the puffs within 30 minutes after filling. *The filling may be prepared ahead and kept chilled, covered, overnight.* Makes about 1 cup.

Black Olive Filling

1 recipe (25 to 28) miniature hors d'oeuvre
    puffs
15 Kalamata olives, pitted
1½ slices homemade-type white bread, cubed
1 small garlic clove, chopped
1 large egg
1 tablespoon fresh lemon juice
½ cup olive oil

In a food processor purée the olives, the bread, and the garlic and add the egg, the lemon juice, and salt and pepper to taste. With the motor running add the oil in a stream and process the mixture until it is thick and the consistency of mayonnaise. Transfer the filling to a pastry bag fitted with a ¼-inch tip and pipe it into the puffs. Serve the puffs within 30 minutes after filling. *The filling may be prepared ahead and kept chilled, covered, overnight.* Makes about 1 cup.

Smoked Salmon and Dill Filling

1 recipe (25 to 28) miniature hors d'oeuvre
    puffs
¼ pound smoked salmon, chopped
3 ounces cream cheese, softened
3 tablespoons sour cream
1 tablespoon minced scallion or grated onion,
    drained
1 tablespoon snipped fresh dill
1 teaspoon fresh lemon juice

In a food processor process the salmon, the cream cheese, the sour cream, the scallion, the dill, the lemon

HECHTLINGER

juice, and salt and pepper to taste until the mixture is smooth. Transfer the filling to a pastry bag fitted with a ¼-inch tip and pipe it into the puffs. Serve the puffs within 30 minutes after filling. *The filling may be prepared ahead and kept chilled, covered, overnight.* Makes about 1 cup.

Old-Fashioned Cream Puffs

For the puffs
1 recipe (2½ cups) *pâte à chou,* warmed to
    tepid
2 teaspoons sugar
For the pastry cream
3 large egg yolks
½ cup sugar
2 tablespoons cornstarch, sifted
2 tablespoons all-purpose flour, sifted
1 cup milk, scalded
2 tablespoons unsalted butter
2 teaspoons vanilla
1½ to 2 tablespoons rum, Cognac, or similar
    flavoring
¾ cup well chilled heavy cream, whipped to
    soft peaks
½ cup ground nuts, such as toasted and
    skinned hazelnuts (page 275) or blanched
    and oven-dried pistachios (page 277), if
    desired
For the glaze
6 ounces unsweetened chocolate, chopped
    into bits
2 ounces semisweet chocolate, chopped into
    bits
¾ stick (6 tablespoons) unsalted butter
confectioners' sugar for garnish

Make the puffs: With a wooden spoon beat the sugar into the dough. With a large pastry bag fitted with a ¾-inch tip pipe the *pâte à chou* onto a buttered and floured baking sheet, forming 6 mounds, each 3½ inches in diameter, and leaving 2 to 3 inches between the puffs. Bake the puffs in the upper third of a preheated 425° F. oven for 15 minutes, reduce the heat to 400° F., and bake the puffs for 20 minutes more, or until they are puffed and golden. Pierce the side of each puff with the tip of a sharp knife and let the puffs stand in the turned-off oven with the door ajar for 30 minutes. Transfer the puffs to a rack and let them cool completely.

Make the pastry cream: In a bowl with an electric mixer beat the egg yolks, add the sugar, a little at a time,

beating, and beat the mixture until it ribbons when the beater is lifted. Add the cornstarch and the flour, beating, and add the milk in a stream, whisking. Transfer the mixture to a heavy saucepan, bring it to a boil over moderately low heat, stirring constantly, and simmer it, stirring constantly, for 2 minutes. Beat in the butter. Strain the pastry cream through a fine sieve into a bowl and stir in the vanilla and the rum. Let the pastry cream cool, covered with a sheet of buttered wax paper directly on the surface, and chill it for at least 1 hour, or until it is firm.

Before filling the puffs, whisk the pastry cream until it is smooth and fold in the whipped cream and, if desired, the nuts.

Make the glaze: In a double boiler set over simmering water melt the chocolate with the butter, stirring, until the mixture is smooth.

With a small spoon or cocktail fork scrape out any uncooked dough in the centers of the puffs through the side opening or slice the top off each puff with a serrated knife and discard any uncooked dough in the centers. Fill each puff with some of the pastry cream, replace the tops, and spoon the glaze over the puffs. Let the glaze stand for 5 minutes and sift the confectioners' sugar over the puffs. Serves 6.

Pommes Dauphine

1 cup *pâte à chou*
1 cup mashed potatoes
4 tablespoons freshly grated Parmesan
2 tablespoons snipped fresh chives or thinly
    sliced scallion greens
freshly grated nutmeg to taste
vegetable oil for deep-frying

In a large bowl stir together the *pâte à chou,* the potatoes, the Parmesan, the chives, the nutmeg, and salt and pepper to taste until the mixture is smooth.

In a deep fryer or heavy deep saucepan add enough oil to measure 3 inches and heat it over moderate heat to 350° F. Dip 2 teaspoons in the oil, scoop a rounded teaspoon of the potato mixture onto one spoon, and with the other teaspoon push the potato puff into the oil. Form potato puffs with the remaining dough in the same manner. Cook the puffs, in batches, turning them, for 4 to 6 minutes, or until they are golden brown. Transfer the puffs with a slotted spoon to an ovenproof plate lined with paper towels and keep them warm in a 200° F. oven while preparing the remaining puffs. Sprinkle the potato puffs with salt to taste. Makes about 24 puffs.

PÂTE BRISÉE

Pâte brisée is the basic French pastry dough. As a crust it has innumerable uses: for open-faced tarts and sweet custard flans; for quiches and meat pies, including turnovers; for meat and poultry pâtés; and for savory tarts, tartlets or barquettes.

Leftover *pâte brisée* dough can be used to make excellent appetizers, such as the cheese straws and hazelnut coins included below. When rolled in sugar, leftover *pâte brisée* also makes lovely crisp cookies—the perfect accompaniment for fresh fruit or ice cream. See the recipe for vanilla sugar wafers.

Pâte Brisée

1¼ cups all-purpose flour
¾ stick (6 tablespoons) cold unsalted butter, cut into bits
2 tablespoons cold vegetable shortening
¼ teaspoon salt

In a large bowl blend the flour, the butter, the vegetable shortening, and the salt until the mixture resembles meal. Add 3 tablespoons ice water, toss the mixture until the water is incorporated, and form the dough into a ball. Knead the dough lightly with the heel of the hand against a smooth surface for a few seconds to distribute the fat evenly and re-form it into a ball. Dust the dough with flour and chill it, wrapped in wax paper, for 1 hour.

Fruit-Filled Turnovers

1 recipe *pâte brisée*
an egg wash made by beating together 1 large egg with 1 teaspoon water and a pinch of salt
about 1 cup fruit preserves, such as cherry, plum, or raspberry
ice cream or lightly whipped cream as an accompaniment if desired

Roll the *pâte brisée* into a round ⅛ inch thick on a lightly floured surface and with a 4-inch cutter cut out rounds. Brush the rounds with the egg wash and spoon 2 teaspoons of the preserves into the center of each round. Fold the dough over the preserves and crimp the edges. Arrange the turnovers on a greased baking sheet and chill them for 30 minutes. Brush the turnovers with the egg wash once more and score the top of each in a cross-hatch design. Bake the turnovers in a preheated 375° F. oven for 20 to 25 minutes, or until they are golden. Let the turnovers cool for 5 minutes and transfer them to racks to cool to warm. Serve the turnovers with the ice cream or lightly whipped cream if desired. Makes 12 turnovers.

Vanilla Sugar Wafers

1 recipe *pâte brisée*
¾ cup vanilla sugar (available at specialty foods shops) or granulated sugar
1 teaspoon grated lemon rind
1 teaspoon grated orange rind
an egg wash made by beating together 1 large egg with 1 teaspoon water and a pinch of salt
1 teaspoon vanilla

Roll the *pâte brisée* into a round ⅛ inch thick, sprinkling both sides of the dough with ½ cup of the vanilla sugar or granulated sugar, using the sugar as you would flour, and distribute the lemon and orange rinds evenly over the dough, patting them in. Cut the dough into 1½-inch shapes with a cookie cutter, arrange the cutouts ½ inch apart on greased baking sheets, and chill them for 30 minutes. If you are using vanilla sugar, brush the cookies with the egg wash with a pastry brush, omitting the vanilla entirely, sprinkle them with the remaining ¼ cup sugar, and bake them in a preheated 350° F. oven for 15 to 18 minutes, or until they are golden. If you are using granulated sugar, combine the egg wash with the vanilla, brush the cookies with the glaze, and proceed with the recipe. Let the cookies cool for 5 minutes on the baking sheets and transfer them to racks to cool completely. Makes about 48 wafers.

Hazelnut Coins

1 recipe *pâte brisée*
an egg wash made by beating together 1 large egg with 1 teaspoon water and a pinch of salt
1 cup ground skinned and toasted hazelnuts (page 275)
½ teaspoon coarse salt, or to taste
¼ teaspoon ground cinnamon, or to taste

Roll the *pâte brisée* into a round ¼ inch thick on a lightly floured surface and cut it into 1½-inch rounds with a cookie cutter. Arrange the rounds ½ inch apart on greased baking sheets and brush them with the egg wash. In a small bowl combine the hazelnuts, the salt, and the cinnamon. Sprinkle the rounds liberally with the hazelnut mixture, patting it into the dough, and chill them for 30 minutes. Bake the rounds in a preheated 350° F. oven for 18 to 20 minutes, or until they are firm. Let the coins cool on the sheets for 5 minutes and transfer them to racks to cool completely. Makes about 48 rounds.

Cheese Straws

1 recipe *pâte brisée*
¼ pound finely grated sharp Cheddar
an egg wash made by beating together 1 large
    egg with 1 teaspoon water and a pinch of salt
paprika to taste
poppy seeds to taste

Roll the *pâte brisée* into a rectangle ⅛ inch thick on a lightly floured surface. Sprinkle the dough with the cheese and with the fingertips pat the cheese into the dough. Beginning with a long side fold over the dough about 3½ inches onto itself. Continue to fold the dough onto itself, letter-fashion, forming a rectangular block, and fold under the ends, sealing them well. Chill the dough, wrapped in plastic wrap, for at least 30 minutes. Roll the dough into a rectangle ¼ inch thick on a lightly floured surface and trim the edges. Brush the dough with the egg wash, sprinkle it with the paprika and the poppy seeds, and cut it into straws about 5 inches long and ½ inch wide. Arrange the straws ½ inch apart on a lightly greased baking sheet and chill them for 30 minutes. Bake the straws in a preheated 400° F. oven for 15 to 20 minutes, or until they are golden. Let the straws cool for 5 minutes and transfer them to racks to cool completely. Makes about 36 cheese straws.

HAZELNUTS

Ground hazelnuts make a sublime base for pastries and cakes. They can also be used in meringues; a hazelnut *dacquoise* or praline being just as delicious as one made with almonds. And they are wonderful in herb butters, as a coating for both poultry and fish, or in stuffing. Whole hazelnuts, not surprisingly, make lovely decorations.

For flavor and freshness, grind nuts just before using. Nuts with high oil content, such as hazelnuts and almonds, must be ground carefully, or the oil will separate out and render the mixture dense. A food processor, which does the job quickly, is recommended. Store leftover ground nuts in the freezer, for they spoil easily. For notes on storing nuts, see page 277.

To Toast and Skin Hazelnuts

Spread the hazelnuts in one layer in a baking pan and toast them in a preheated 350° F. oven for 10 to 15 minutes, or until they are colored lightly and the skins blister. Wrap the nuts in a dish towel and let them steam for 1 minute. Rub the nuts in the towel to remove the skins and let them cool.

Roasted Hazelnut Mix

½ pound each of toasted and skinned
  hazelnuts, raw cashews, blanched whole
  almonds, and macadamia nuts
3 tablespoons clarified butter (page 278)
coarse salt to taste

In a large shallow baking pan melt the butter, add the nuts, and toss them to coat them with the butter. Roast the nuts in a preheated 300° F. oven, stirring occasionally, for 1 hour to 1 hour and 15 minutes, or until they are golden. Season the nuts with the salt. Various seasonings can be added to the roasted nuts depending upon personal taste—chili powder, angostura bitters, Worcestershire sauce, curry powder, cayenne, cinnamon, allspice, nutmeg, even sugar. Makes 2 pounds.

Hazelnut-Coated Chicken Scallops

4 boneless chicken scallops (about ¼ pound
  each), cut ¼-inch-thick from the breast
flour for dredging
1 large egg beaten with 2 teaspoons vegetable
  oil
½ cup ground toasted and skinned hazelnuts
  combined with ½ cup dry, stale bread
  crumbs
6 tablespoons clarified butter (page 278)
sauce Choron (page 279) as an
  accompaniment if desired

Dredge the chicken scallops in the flour, shaking off the excess, dip them in the egg, and coat them in the hazelnut mixture. Season the scallops with salt and pepper and chill them for 15 minutes. In a non-stick skillet cook the scallops in batches in the butter over moderate heat for 3 minutes on each side, or until they are firm but still springy to the touch. Serve the scallops with the sauce Choron if desired. Serves 4.

Hazelnut Butter

1 stick (½ cup) unsalted butter, softened
¾ cup ground toasted and skinned hazelnuts
1 tablespoon snipped fresh chives
1 tablespoon minced fresh parsley
1 teaspoon fresh lemon juice
½ teaspoon Dijon-style mustard
Worcestershire sauce to taste

In a bowl combine well the butter, the hazelnuts, the chives, the parsley, the lemon juice, the mustard, the Worcestershire sauce, and salt and pepper to taste. Rinse a piece of wax paper in cold water, spoon the butter in log-like fashion onto the lower third of the wax paper, and roll the butter into a log, twisting the ends to compact its shape. Chill the butter for a least 2 hours, or until it is firm. Serve the butter on broiled fish and poultry or over steamed vegetables. Makes about ¾ cup.

Hazelnut Snow Balls

2 sticks (1 cup) unsalted butter, softened
⅔ cup granulated sugar
1 teaspoon vanilla
2¼ cups sifted all-purpose flour
1 cup finely ground toasted and skinned
  hazelnuts
sifted confectioners' sugar for garnish

In a bowl with an electric mixer cream the butter, add the sugar, a little at a time, and beat the mixture until it is light and fluffy. Stir in the vanilla, the flour, and the hazelnuts, form the mixture into a ball, and chill the dough, covered, for at least 1 hour, or until it is firm. Break off 1-inch pieces of the dough, roll them into balls, and arrange the balls 1 inch apart on greased baking sheets. Bake the cookies in a preheated 350° F. oven for 15 to 18 minutes, or until they are pale golden. Let the cookies cool on the sheets for 5 minutes and transfer them to racks to cool completely. Sprinkle the cookies with the confectioners' sugar. Makes about 48 cookies.

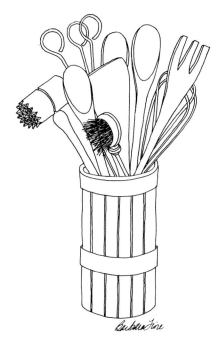

PISTACHIO NUTS

In Middle Eastern and East Indian cuisines, pistachio nuts are used in savory sauces, rices, and stews and as the basis of a number of aromatic desserts. In western cookery the versatile pistachio is used in ice cream and other dessert creams, to decorate pastries and cakes, and for savory terrines, pâtés, mousses, and stuffings.

Because of their high fat content, nuts can easily turn rancid. They should be stored in airtight containers in a cool, dark place.

To Blanch and Oven-Dry Pistachio Nuts

In a heatproof bowl pour boiling water to cover over the desired amount of pistachio nuts, shelled, let the nuts stand for 1 minute, and drain them. Turn the nuts out onto a dish towel and rub off the skins. Dry the nuts on a baking sheet in a preheated 300° F. oven for 15 minutes.

Chicken Liver Mousseline with Pistachios

1 onion, minced
3 shallots, sliced
¾ stick (6 tablespoons) unsalted butter
1 pound chicken livers, trimmed, rinsed, and
    patted dry
¼ teaspoon dried thyme
½ bay leaf, crumbled
⅛ teaspoon ground cloves
⅛ teaspoon ground cinnamon
⅛ teaspoon freshly grated nutmeg
2 tablespoons Tawny Port
½ cup chopped blanched and oven-dried
    pistachios
¼ cup minced fresh parsley leaves
½ cup well chilled heavy cream, whipped to
    soft peaks
toast points as an accompaniment if desired

In a skillet cook the onion and the shallots in the butter over moderate heat, stirring, for 5 minutes, or until the onion is softened. Add the chicken livers, the thyme, the bay leaf, the cloves, the cinnamon, the nutmeg, and salt and pepper to taste and cook the mixture, stirring occasionally, for 5 minutes, or until the livers are just cooked through. Add the Port and simmer the mixture for 1 minute. Let the mixture cool for 5 min-

utes, transfer it to a food processor, and purée it until it is smooth. Transfer the mixture to a bowl, let it cool to warm, and stir in the pistachios and parsley. Fold the whipped cream into the mixture, season the *mousseline* with salt and pepper, and transfer it to a serving dish or terrine. Chill the *mousseline,* covered, for at least 2 hours or overnight. Serve the *mousseline* with the toast points if desired. Makes about 3 cups.

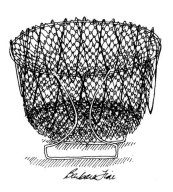

Pistachio Rice Stuffing

3 tablespoons unsalted butter
2 whole cloves
1 small bay leaf
a 1-inch cinnamon stick, cracked
1 onion, minced
1 cup long-grain rice
⅛ teaspoon ground turmeric, for color, if
    desired
2 cups chicken stock (page 119) or canned
    chicken broth
½ cup chopped blanched and oven-dried
    pistachios
¼ cup raisins

In a saucepan melt the butter over moderate heat, add the cloves, the bay leaf, and the cinnamon, and cook the spices, stirring, for 1 minute. Add the onion and cook it, stirring occasionally, for 5 minutes, or until it is softened. Add the rice, toss it to coat it with the butter, and add the turmeric, the stock, the pistachios, the raisins, and salt and pepper to taste. Bring the stock to a boil, cover the rice with a buttered round of wax paper and the lid, and cook it in a preheated 350° F. oven for 15 to 18 minutes, or until it is just tender. Transfer the rice to a bowl and let it cool completely before using it as a stuffing. Remove the cloves, bay leaf, and cinnamon stick. If using the stuffing as a pilaf to accompany poultry or meats, cook it about 5 minutes longer, or until the rice is tender. Makes about 5 cups.

Pistachio Ice Cream

1 cup sugar
a 4-inch vanilla bean, chopped into small pieces
3 cups milk
6 large egg yolks
1 cup blanched and oven-dried pistachios,
   ground to a paste in a food processor
½ teaspoon almond extract
1 cup well chilled heavy cream, whipped to
   soft peaks

In a food processor or blender blend the sugar with the vanilla bean until the bean is pulverized. In a heavy saucepan combine the sugar mixture with the milk and scald the mixture over moderate heat, stirring. In a large bowl with an electric mixer beat the egg yolks until they are pale and thick and pour the milk mixture through a fine sieve into the bowl in a stream, stirring. Transfer the mixture to another heavy saucepan and cook it over moderately low heat, stirring, until it thickens and coats the spoon. Stir in the pistachios and the almond extract. Transfer the custard to a metal bowl set in a bowl of cracked ice, let it cool, covered with a round of wax paper, and chill it in the refrigerator for 2 hours. Freeze the custard in an ice-cream freezer according to the manufacturer's instructions. When the ice cream is almost frozen add the whipped cream to the ice-cream freezer and continue to freeze the ice cream until it is frozen. Makes about 1 quart.

Pistachio Apple Tart

1 recipe *pâte brisée* (page 274)
2 pounds McIntosh or Granny Smith apples,
   peeled, cored, and cut into slices
1 tablespoon fresh lemon juice
2 teaspoons grated lemon rind
For the pistachio cream
1 stick (½ cup) unsalted butter, softened
½ cup sugar
2 large eggs
½ cup finely ground blanched and oven-dried
   pistachios
½ cup finely ground blanched almonds
1 tablespoon all-purpose flour
1 teaspoon vanilla
½ teaspoon almond extract

½ cup apricot jam, sieved
2 tablespoons Cognac
1 tablespoon whole blanched and oven-dried
   pistachios for garnish

Roll the *pâte brisée* into a round ⅛ inch thick on a lightly floured surface, fit it into a 10-inch tart pan with a removable bottom, and crimp the edge decoratively. Prick the shell lightly with a fork and chill it for 30 minutes, or until it is firm.

In a bowl toss the apples with the lemon juice and rind.

Make the pistachio cream: In a bowl with an electric mixer cream the butter, add the sugar, a little at a time, and beat the mixture until it is light and fluffy. Add the eggs and beat the mixture until it is combined. Stir in the pistachios, the almonds, the flour, the vanilla, and the almond extract. Pour the cream into the shell and arrange the apple slices in concentric circles over the cream, gently pressing them into it. Bake the tart on a baking sheet in the lower third of a preheated 375° F. oven for 45 to 50 minutes, or until the apples are tender and the top is golden brown. Let the tart cool slightly on a rack.

In a small saucepan heat the apricot jam with the Cognac over moderate heat, stirring, until it is syrupy and spoon it over the tart. Garnish the top of the tart with the whole pistachios.

CLARIFIED BUTTER

Once clarified (skimmed of its milky solids), butter will not burn or change color in cooking; when refrigerated, covered, it will keep indefinitely. Clarified butter can thus be combined with cream or eggs for elegant sauces and can be used for sautéing delicate foods with subtle flavors, such as fish fillets and chicken breasts.

To Clarify Butter

unsalted butter, cut into 1-inch pieces

In a heavy saucepan melt the butter over low heat. Remove the pan from the heat, let the butter stand for 3 minutes, and skim the froth. Strain the butter through a sieve lined with a double thickness of rinsed and squeezed cheesecloth into a bowl, leaving the milky solids in the bottom of the pan. Pour the clarified butter into a jar or crock and store it, covered, in the refrigerator. *The butter keeps indefinitely, covered and chilled.* When clarified, butter loses about one fourth of its original volume.

Béarnaise Sauce

3 tablespoons tarragon vinegar
3 tablespoons dry white vermouth
2 tablespoons minced shallot
4 tablespoons minced fresh tarragon or
   2 teaspoons dried
¼ teaspoon salt, or to taste
10 peppercorns, crushed
2 tablespoons heavy cream
3 large egg yolks
1 cup plus 2 tablespoons clarified butter
fresh lemon juice to taste

In a small heavy saucepan combine the vinegar, the vermouth, the shallot, 3 tablespoons fresh tarragon or all the dried, the salt, and the peppercorns and reduce the liquid over moderately high heat to about 2 tablespoons. Remove the pan from the heat and add the cream. Add the egg yolks, 1 at a time, and whisk the mixture over very low heat until it is thick. Whisk in the butter, 1 tablespoon at a time, over low heat, lifting the pan occasionally to cool the mixture so that the sauce does not separate. Strain the sauce through a fine sieve into another heavy saucepan and stir in the remaining 1 tablespoon tarragon (or parsley) and the lemon juice. Keep the sauce warm, covered with buttered wax paper, in a pan of warm water. Serve the sauce with broiled meat, poultry, or fish and vegetables. Makes about 1⅓ cups.

Sauce Choron
(Tomato-Flavored Béarnaise Sauce)

1 recipe (1⅓ cups) béarnaise sauce, heated
1½ tablespoons tomato paste

In a bowl whisk together the béarnaise sauce and the tomato paste until the sauce is combined well. Serve the sauce with meat, poultry, fish or vegetables. Makes about 1½ cups.

Sauce Noisette
(Hollandaise Sauce with Brown Butter)

1 cup plus 2 tablespoons clarified butter
2 tablespoons white-wine vinegar
¼ teaspoon salt
a few grinds of white pepper
3 large egg yolks, beaten lightly
fresh lemon juice to taste

In a small heavy saucepan simmer the clarified butter over low heat, stirring, until it is nut brown.

In another small heavy saucepan combine the vinegar, 2 tablespoons water, the salt, and the white pepper and reduce the liquid over moderately high heat to about 2 tablespoons. Remove the pan from the heat and add 1 tablespoon cold water. Add the egg yolks and whisk the mixture over very low heat until it is thick. Whisk in the butter, 1 tablespoon at a time, over low heat, lifting the pan occasionally to cool the mixture and making certain that the sauce does not separate. Add the lemon juice and salt to taste. Keep the sauce warm, covered with buttered wax paper, in a pan of warm water. Serve the sauce with broiled fish or vegetables. Makes about 1½ cups.

SUGAR SYRUP

Sugar syrup, a simple preparation of one part sugar to two parts water, can be used to soak *babas* and *savarins* and to moisten *génoise* layers and other sponge cakes. It can also be employed as a poaching liquid for fruits; as a base for fruit coolers, iced tea drinks, shrubs, and fruit syrups; and for sherbets, *sorbets,* and *granite.* And when that simple is boiled down, it becomes an essential ingredient in Italian meringue, with which you can create meringue shells, *vacherins,* or the outside covering for baked Alaska.

Sugar Syrup

1 cup sugar

In a saucepan combine the sugar and 2 cups water and bring the mixture to a boil, stirring and washing down any sugar crystals clinging to the sides with a brushed dipped in cold water until the sugar is dissolved. Cook the syrup over moderate heat, undisturbed, for 5 minutes and let it cool. *The syrup keeps indefinitely, chilled, in a sealed jar.* Makes about 2½ cups.

Lime Sherbet

1 recipe (2½ cups) sugar syrup
1 cup fresh lime juice
1 tablespoon grated lime rind
1 large egg white beaten until stiff with 1
　　tablespoon sugar

In a heavy saucepan simmer the syrup for 5 minutes. Transfer the syrup to a bowl, stir in the lime juice and the rind, and chill the mixture until it is cold. Freeze the mixture in an ice-cream freezer according to the manufacturer's instructions. When the sherbet is almost frozen, add the egg white and continue to freeze the mixture in the ice-cream freezer until it is of sherbet consistency. Makes about 3 cups.

Note: Fresh lemon juice may be substituted for the lime juice, but in the case of lemon sherbet increase the amount of rind to 1½ tablespoons.

Peaches Cardinal

2 recipes (5 cups) sugar syrup
the peel and juice of 1 lemon plus 1
　　tablespoon fresh lemon juice
a 4-inch vanilla bean, split lengthwise
4 ripe but firm peaches
a 10-ounce package frozen raspberries in
　　syrup, thawed
1 tablespoon kirsch
confectioners' sugar to taste
fresh raspberries and softly whipped cream for
　　garnish if desired

In a saucepan combine the sugar syrup with the lemon peel, the juice of 1 lemon, and the vanilla bean, bring the liquid to a boil, and simmer it for 5 minutes. Add the peaches and poach them at a bare simmer for 8 minutes, or until they are just tender. Let the peaches cool in the syrup, slip off their skins and halve them, discarding the pits. Transfer the peaches to a bowl, strain the cooking liquid over them, and chill the peaches, covered, for at least 2 hours, or until they are cold.

In a food processor purée the frozen raspberries with the syrup, the remaining 1 tablespoon lemon juice, the kirsch, and sugar to taste. Strain the sauce through a fine sieve into a bowl.

Divide the peaches, drained, among stemmed dessert glasses, spoon the raspberry sauce over them, and garnish each glass with some of the fresh raspberries and whipped cream if desired. Serves 4.

Italian Meringue

1 recipe (2½ cups) sugar syrup
4 large egg whites at room temperature
a pinch of cream of tartar
1 tablespoon sugar
1 teaspoon vanilla
1 to 2 tablespoons Cognac or other flavoring

In a small heavy saucepan bring the sugar syrup to a boil and boil it over moderate heat, shaking the pan and washing down any sugar crystals clinging to the sides with a brush dipped in cold water, until it reaches the hard-ball stage, or a candy thermometer registers 248° F.

In a large bowl with an electric mixer beat the egg whites with a pinch of salt until they are frothy, add the cream of tartar, and beat the whites until they form soft peaks. Add the sugar and beat the whites until they hold

stiff peaks. With the electric mixer running add the hot syrup to the whites in a stream, beating, and beat the meringue until it is cool. Beat in the vanilla and the Cognac Makes about 4 cups.

Hazelnut Mocha Rochers

½ recipe (2 cups) Italian meringue
2 teaspoons espresso coffee granules dissolved in 1 tablespoon hot water
2 teaspoons Frangelico or dark rum, or to taste
½ cup ground toasted and skinned hazelnuts (page 275)

3 tablespoons chocolate bits
confectioners' sugar for garnish

In a large bowl beat the Italian meringue with the espresso coffee and the Frangelico until the mixture is just combined and fold in the hazelnuts and the chocolate bits. Spoon teaspoons of the mixture 1 inch apart onto baking sheets lined with parchment paper and sift the confectioners' sugar lightly over them. Bake the meringues in a preheated 275° F. oven for 40 to 45 minutes, or until they are firm to the touch. Let the meringues cool on racks and store them in airtight containers. Makes about 48 meringues.

GUIDES TO THE TEXT

GUIDE TO RECIPES
IN THE MENU COLLECTION

Recipes for dishes featured in the Menu Collection appear on the pages indicated below

Tea
Potato Biscuits, 107
Sardine Anchovy Butter, 107
Cream Cheese and Olive Ribbon Sandwiches, 176
Radish Hearts, 209
Tangerine Buttermilk Pound Cake, 247
Chocolate Hazelnut Macaroons, 248

Coffee and Dessert
Chocolate Mousse Tart, 250
Lime Cheesecake, 245
Raspberry Sauce, 240

A FIRESIDE DINNER

Artichokes Gribiche, 192
Eggplant Rollatini with Three Cheeses, 201
Rugola Salad, 222
Prosciutto Bread, 101
Ginger Poached Pears, 264

EASTER BRUNCHES

Asparagus Custards with Canadian Bacon and
  Maltaise Sauce, 193
Scallion Drop Biscuits, 108
Rum-Marinated Mango Crêpes, 262

Brioches Stuffed with Brandied Chicken Livers, 168
Minted Peas and Onions, 205
Snow Pudding ''Eggs'' with Raspberry Sauce, 256

A SPRING DINNER

Salmon Steaks au Poivre with Lime Butter, 126
Lacy Potato Pancakes, 206
Buttered Peas in Tomato Cups, 205
Strawberry Rhubarb Pie, 253

AN INFORMAL BUFFET

Sausage in Pastry with Honey Mustard, 152
Herb-Marinated Mozzarella, 178
Braised Veal Roast with Vegetables Provençale, 146
Steamed Rice, 190
French Bread (Quick-Rise and Slow-Rise), 100
Boston Lettuce and Radicchio Salad with Orange
  Vinaigrette, 220
Cream Puffs with Vanilla Ice Cream and Cherry
  Sauce, 251

ELEGANT BUT EASY

Jalapeño Scallop Mousses with Shrimp, 133
Deviled Roast Rock Cornish Game Hens, 168
French Fried Sweet Potatoes, 208

Green Beans Vinaigrette with Red Onion and
  Coriander, 194
Rum Zabaglione with Strawberries and Amaretti, 257

A REHEARSAL DINNER

Avocado Mousse with Salmon Roe, 194
Melba Toast Hearts, 109
Summer Squash Soup with Coriander Swirl, 117
Pistachioed Turkey Ballottine with Madeira Sauce, 171
Buttered Sugar Snap Peas and Carrots, 205
Bulgur and Wild Rice Pilaf, 187
Cold Raspberry Soufflé with Hazelnut Praline, 260
Frangelico Chocolate Sauce, 239
Apricot Jam Hearts, 247

AN EARLY SUMMER COCKTAIL PARTY

Mandarin Champagne, 267
Pineapple Daiquiris, 268
Rugola Horseradish Dipping Sauce with Crudités, 95
Tuna Escabeche, 97
Miniature Corn Muffins with Deviled Corn, 89
Anchovy and Mozzarella Pastry Fish, 85
Indonesian Crab-Meat Canapés, 90
Gazpacho-Stuffed Cherry Tomatoes, 87

JULY FOURTH ALFRESCO

Roasted Potato Skins with Scallion Dip, 206
Beer-Batter Fried Chicken, 160
Fireworks Coleslaw, 224
Bacon and Potato Salad, 225
Corn on the Cob with Basil Butter, 198
Bread-and-Butter Pickles, 200
Butter Fan Rolls, 99
Lattice-Crust Peach Pie, 252
Limeade, 269
Lemonade, 268

A SUMMER COOKOUT

Rosemary Shrimp, 136
Lamb Chops Stuffed with Feta, 154
Mint-Marinated Grilled Red Onions, 204
Lemon Rice Salad, 229
Independence Day Ice-Cream Cake, 244

PICNICS

At the Beach
Watermelon Screwdrivers, 268
Fresh Tortilla Chips, 97
Tropical Chicken Salad, 216
Korean Beef Salad, 215
Lobster Horseradish Salad, 218
Chocolate Shell Cakes, 243

MENU RECIPE GUIDE

On a Fishing Trip
Cold Confetti Vegetable Soup, 117
Pan-Fried Brook Trout with Bacon, 131
Rosemary New Potato Salad with Roquefort, 225
Spicy Okra Ratatouille, 204
Blueberry Cupcakes, 241

DINNER FROM A COOL KITCHEN

Sashimi, 128
Oriental Noodles with Peanut Sauce, 185
Spicy Carrot, Daikon, and Napa Cabbage Salad, 223
Cantaloupe Melon Molds, 262

AUTUMN CHICKEN DINNERS

Sorrel Soup with Salmon Quenelles, 116
Rolled Stuffed Chicken Breast with Hot Pepper
    Sauce, 158
Saffron Rice Timbales, 190
Warm Lima Bean Salad, 224
Kahlúa Mocha Mousse with Chocolate Leaves, 254

Vegetable ''Pasta'' with Tomato Concassé, 211
Stuffed Chicken Normandy, 158
Sweet Potatoes Duchesse, 208
Sweet-and-Sour Braised Red Cabbage, 197
Brandy Snaps with Strawberries, 248

A TAPAS PARTY

Toasted Hazelnuts, 90
Marinated Black and Green Olives, 93
Toasted Blanched Almonds, 85
Chick-Pea and Chorizo Salad, 88
Pork and Ham Meatballs in Sherry Pepper Sauce, 94
Squid and Celery Salad, 96
Garlic Shrimp, 96
Mussels with Ham, Peppers, and Tomatoes, 92
Octopus Salad, 92
Chorizo-Stuffed Mushrooms, 92
Steamed Clams with Peppers and Ham, 89

A CHINESE DINNER

Garlic Peanuts, 94
Braised Black Mushrooms, 203
Szechwan Pickled Cucumbers, 200
Bean Curd Noodles with Celery and Carrot, 195
Steamed Stuffed Fish Rolls, 124
Stir-Fried Shrimp and Snow Peas in Bird's Nest, 136
Spicy Pork and Peppers, 150
Steamed Lotus Buns, 150
Stir-Fried Watercress, 212
Clear Chicken Soup with Chicken Balls, Watercress,
    and Mushrooms, 113
Lemon Sherbet with Starfruit, 259
Coconut Almond Wafers, 249

SIMPLY STYLISH

Seafood Sausage with Lemon Herb Sauce, 128
Filets Mignons Persillés, 142
Oven-Fried Potatoes, 207
Turnip and Carrot Julienne, 210
Oranges in Caramel Syrup, 263

A COUNTRY THANKSGIVING

Pickled Carrot Sticks, 198
Pickled Cauliflower, 198
Fried Oysters with Tartar Sauce, 132
Roast Turkey with Smoked Sausage and Rosemary
    Stuffing, 170
Corn Sticks, 103
Onion Raisin Cranberry Confit, 237
Riced Sweet Potatoes, 208
Riced Mashed Potatoes, 207
Caraway Cabbage, 196
Cranberry Maple Pear Pie, 250
Pecan Pumpkin Pie, 253

THANKSGIVING FOR A SMALL
GATHERING

Purée of Fennel Soup, 115
Turkey Scaloppine with Cassis Cranberry Sauce, 172
Savory Bread Pudding, 173
Crisp-Baked Acorn Squash Rings, 210
Sautéed Brussels Sprouts with Bacon, 196
Brandied Pear Crisp, 264

CHRISTMAS DINNER

Mushroom Charlottes with Port and Currant Sauce, 202
Roast Prime Ribs of Beef with Cracked Pepper
    Crust, 142
Potato Brioches, 206
Green Beans and Lima Beans with Herb Butter, 194
Endive, Watercress, and Beet Salad with Orange
    Caraway Vinaigrette, 221
Apple Rosemary Sorbet, 260
Chocolate Raspberry Dobostorte, 242

POST-CHRISTMAS BRUNCH

Two-Bean and Bacon Soup, 111
Parmesan Toasts, 109
Shepherd's Pie Crêpes, 143
Winter Tomato Sauce, 239
Honey-Glazed Carrots, 198
Spinach Romaine Salad with Creamy Horseradish
    Dressing, 222
Fruitcake Parfaits, 259

GENERAL INDEX

INDEX OF
45-MINUTE RECIPES

*Starred entries can be prepared in 45 minutes or less but require additional unattended time

INDEX OF RECIPE TITLES

Page numbers in *italics* indicate color photographs